HEATH MATHEMATICS
CONNECTIONS

Edward Manfre
James M. Moser
Joanne E. Lobato
Lorna Morrow

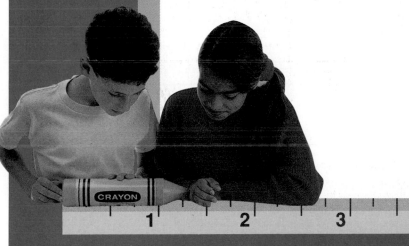

HEATH

D.C. Heath and Company
Lexington, Massachusetts / Toronto, Ontario

HEATH MATHEMATICS CONNECTIONS

Authors

Edward Manfre is a former elementary, intermediate, and secondary schoolteacher who has for over twenty years created classroom materials that encourage thinking. He has also conducted workshops on instructional methods and problem solving.

James Moser has been a teacher of mathematics at several levels, a teacher educator, a researcher, and a curriculum developer. He is the author of mathematics textbooks for elementary, secondary, and college students. Currently he is a mathematics consultant for the Wisconsin Department of Public Instruction.

Joanne Lobato has taught at the secondary level and has worked as a designer of mathematics software for grades K-8. She conducts research on elementary schoolchildren and frequently presents teacher workshops.

Lorna Morrow has taught at the elementary, secondary, and college levels, and has written numerous books, articles, and curriculum materials on topics in mathematics.

Contributing Authors

B. Joan Goodman, Los Lunas Elementary School, Los Lunas, New Mexico
Lee V. Stiff, North Carolina State University, Raleigh, North Carolina
William F. Tate, University of Wisconsin, Madison, Wisconsin

ACKNOWLEDGMENTS
Editorial: Rita Campanella, Savitri Kaur Khalsa, Lorraine O'Donnell, Susan D. Rogalski
Design: Robert H. Botsford, Ingrid Cooper, Carmen Johnson
Production: Pamela Tricca
Marketing: Jean Banks, Mary I. Connolly
Permissions: Dorothy Burns McLeod

ABOUT THE COVER
Cover Design: Linda Fishborne

Cover Photography: Bruno Joachim Studio
Theme: Fractions of a region, of length, and of sets provide students with visual models of fractions at work. The Fraction Bars illustrated and used in this book were created by Professor Albert B. Bennett, Jr. of the University of New Hampshire and Dr. Patricia S. Davidson of the University of Massachusetts, Boston. Decimal Squares were created by Professor Bennett.

Published simultaneously in Canada

Printed in the United States of America

International Standard Book Number: 0-669-30914-1

2 3 4 5 6 7 8 9 10 -VHP- 99 98 97 96 95 94 93 ☐

CONTENTS

1 Place Value

Chapter Opener • Connections to Money Sense **1**

1.1 **Estimation** • Estimating How Many **2**
1.2 **Estimation** • Using Tens to Estimate **4**
1.3 **Mental Math** • Using Facts **6**
● 1.4 **Problem Solving** • Problem Solver's Guide **8**
1.5 Place Value—Hundreds and Thousands **10**
1.6 Fives and Tens **12**
1.7 Rounding to the Nearest 10 and 100 **14**
1.8 Rounding Sensibly **16**

Section Review **17**

1.9 Place Value to One Million **18**
● 1.10 How Much Is a Million? **20**
1.11 Rounding Larger Numbers **22**
✳ 1.12 Comparing and Ordering **24**
1.13 Identifying Money **26**
✳ 1.14 **Problem Solving Strategy Review** • Make a Table **28**
1.15 Making Change **30**
1.16 Money Sense **32**
1.17 **Problem Solving** • Not Enough Information **34**

Section Review **35**
Chapter Test **36**
Cumulative Review **37**
Excursion • **Numeration:** Writing Roman Numerals **38**

● Cooperative Learning   ✳ Algebra

2 Addition and Subtraction

Chapter Opener • Connections to Art **40**

✻ 2.1 Properties and Rules **42**
✻ 2.2 **Mental Math** • Addition and Subtraction **44**
  2.3 **Mental Math** • Using 5, 50, and 500 **46**
● 2.4 **Problem Solving Strategy Review** • Make a Diagram **48**
  2.5 **Estimation** • Estimating Sums **50**
  2.6 **Adding 2- and 3-Digit Numbers** **52**
  2.7 Three or More Addends **54**
  2.8 **Estimation** • Estimating Sums by Rounding **56**

Section Review **57**

  2.9 **Estimation** • Estimating Differences **58**
 2.10 Subtracting Greater Numbers **60**
 2.11 **Problem Solving** • Using Math Sense **62**
 2.12 Zeros in Subtraction **64**
 2.13 Using Addition and Subtraction **66**
 2.14 **Problem Solving Strategy Application** • Using Strategies **68**

Section Review **69**
Chapter Test **70**
Cumulative Review **71**
Excursion • **Cultural Diversity:** Consumer Math **72**

● Cooperative Learning   ✻ Algebra

3 Collecting, Organizing, and Using Data

Chapter Opener • Connections to Statistics   **74**

3.1   Collecting and Recording Data   **76**
3.2   Organizing Data in a Bar Graph   **78**
● 3.3   **Problem Solving Strategy Review** • Make a List   **80**
3.4   Pictographs   **82**
3.5   Line Graphs   **84**
3.6   Circle Graphs   **86**
3.7   Using Data   **88**
● 3.8   **Problem Solving** • Does the Answer Fit the Problem?   **90**

Section Review   **91**

● 3.9   Making Predictions   **92**
3.10   Comparing Probabilities   **94**
● 3.11   Listing What Can Happen   **96**
● 3.12   Making Better Predictions   **98**
3.13   **Mental Math** • Addition and Subtraction   **100**

Section Review   101
Chapter Test   102
Cumulative Review   103
Excursion • **Probability:** Changing the Chances   **104**

4 Multiplication and Division Facts

Chapter Opener • Connections to Estimation   **106**

4.1   Understanding Multiplication   **108**
4.2   Multiplying by 5 and 10   **110**
4.3   Understanding Division   **112**
4.4   Dividing by 5 and 10   **114**
∗ 4.5   Properties and Rules   **116**
● 4.6   Making a Facts Table   **118**
4.7   **Choose a Computation Method** •
Mental Math or Paper and Pencil   **120**

● Cooperative Learning   ∗ Algebra

Section Review 121

∗ 4.8 Multiplying by 2, 4, and 8 **122**
∗ 4.9 Dividing by 2, 4, and 8 **124**
● 4.10 **Problem Solving Strategy Review** • Make a Plan **126**
∗ 4.11 Multiplying and Dividing by 3 and 6 **128**
∗ 4.12 Multiplying and Dividing by 7 and 9 **130**
● 4.13 Multiples **132**
● 4.14 Factors **134**
∗ 4.15 **Mental Math** • Multiplication Patterns **136**
4.16 **Problem Solving Strategy Application** • Using Strategies **138**
∗ 4.17 **Mental Math** • Division Patterns **140**
4.18 **Special Topic** • Line Plots **142**

Section Review 143
Chapter Test 144
Cumulative Review 145
Excursion • **Number Theory:** Factor Trees **146**

5 Geometry

Chapter Opener • Connections to Science **148**

5.1 Flips **150**
● 5.2 Turns **152**
5.3 Angles **154**
5.4 Symmetry **156**
● 5.5 **Problem Solving Strategy Review** • Make a Model **158**
5.6 Slides **160**
∗ 5.7 Ordered Pairs **162**
5.8 Quadrilaterals and Other Polygons **164**
5.9 **Problem Solving Strategy Application** • Using Strategies **166**

Section Review 167

5.10 Counting Squares **168**
5.11 Area **170**
5.12 Congruence and Similarity **172**
● 5.13 Solids **174**

● Cooperative Learning ∗ Algebra

● 5.14 Visualization **176**

● 5.15 Volume **178**

5.16 **Problem Solving Strategy Application** • Using Strategies **180**

Section Review 181
Chapter Test 182
Cumulative Review 183
Excursion • **Number Theory:** Modeling Square Numbers **184**

6 Multiplying by 1-Digit Numbers

Chapter Opener • Connections to Social Studies **186**

6.1 **Estimation** • Estimating Products **188**

✳ 6.2 Multiplying with Array Diagrams **190**

6.3 Multiplying 2-Digit Numbers **192**

6.4 Multiplying 3-Digit Numbers **194**

● 6.5 **Problem Solving Strategy Review** • Guess and Check **196**

6.6 **Choose a Computation Method** • Exact or Estimate **198**

Section Review 199

6.7 Multiplying 4-Digit Numbers **200**

6.8 **Problem Solving Strategy Application** • Using Strategies **202**

6.9 Multiplying Money **204**

6.10 **Problem Solving Strategy Application** • Using Strategies **206**

Section Review 207
Chapter Test 208
Cumulative Review 209
Excursion • **Using Technology:** Logo **210**

● Cooperative Learning ✳ Algebra

7 Dividing by 1-Digit Numbers

Chapter Opener • Connections to Science   **212**

7.1   Division with Remainders   **214**
7.2   Understanding Remainders   **216**
7.3   **Estimation** • Estimating Quotients   **218**
7.4   Two-Digit Quotients   **220**
● 7.5   **Problem Solving Strategy Introduction** • Make Notes   **222**
7.6   Three-Digit Quotients   **224**
7.7   **Problem Solving Strategy Application** • Using Strategies   **226**

Section Review   **227**

7.8   Zeros in the Quotient   **228**
● 7.9   Divisibility   **230**
● 7.10   **Problem Solving Strategy Development** • Make Notes   **232**
7.11   Dividing Money   **234**
7.12   Using Division Sense   **236**
7.13   Finding Averages   **238**
7.14   **Problem Solving** • Using Math Sense   **240**

Section Review   **241**
Chapter Test   **242**
Cumulative Review   **243**
Excursion • **Using Technology:** Logo   **244**

8 Fractions

Chapter Opener • Connections to Language Arts   **246**

8.1   Fractions   **248**
● 8.2   Fractions and Equivalence   **250**
8.3   Equivalence and Simplest Form   **252**
● 8.4   Exploring Order of Fractions   **254**
8.5   Comparing and Ordering Fractions   **256**
8.6   **Problem Solving** • Using Math Sense   **258**

● Cooperative Learning   ＊ Algebra

Section Review 259

● 8.7 Exploring Fractional Parts of a Number **260**
  8.8 Fractional Parts of a Number **262**
● 8.9 **Problem Solving Strategy Application** • Using Strategies **264**
  8.10 Mixed Numbers **266**
  8.11 **Problem Solving Strategy Application** • Using Strategies **268**

Section Review 269
Chapter Test 270
Cumulative Review 271
Excursion • **Using Technology:** Logo **272**

9 Addition and Subtraction of Fractions

Chapter Opener • Connections to Critical Thinking **274**

  9.1 Adding and Subtracting Like Fractions **276**
● 9.2 Using Fractions **278**
● 9.3 Adding and Subtracting Fractions **280**
  9.4 Choose a Computation Method **282**

Section Review 283

  9.5 Adding Unlike Fractions **284**
  9.6 Subtracting Unlike Fractions **286**
  9.7 Adding and Subtracting Mixed Numbers **288**
● 9.8 **Problem Solving Strategy Introduction** •
       Use Simpler Numbers **290**
● 9.9 **Problem Solving Strategy Development** •
       Use Simpler Numbers **292**
  9.10 **Special Topic** • Time Zones **294**

Section Review 295
Chapter Test 296
Cumulative Review 297
Excursion • **Cultural Diversity:**
Mean, Mode, and Median **298**

● Cooperative Learning   * Algebra

10 Measurement and Time

Chapter Opener • Connections to Science **300**

10.1 Inch, Half Inch, and Quarter Inch **302**
10.2 Foot, Yard, and Mile **304**
10.3 Perimeter **306**
● 10.4 Measurement Lab **308**
● 10.5 **Problem Solving Strategy Application** • Using Strategies **310**
10.6 Customary Units of Capacity **312**
10.7 Ounce, Pound, and Ton **314**

Section Review 315

10.8 Centimeter and Millimeter **316**
10.9 Decimeter, Meter, and Kilometer **318**
10.10 Metric Units of Capacity **320**
10.11 Gram and Kilogram **322**
10.12 **Problem Solving Strategy Application** • Using Strategies **323**
10.13 Temperature **324**
10.14 Elapsed Time **326**
● 10.15 Using a Calendar **328**
10.16 **Problem Solving Strategy Application** • Using Strategies **330**

Section Review 331
Chapter Test 332
Cumulative Review 333
Excursion • **Cultural Diversity:** Decision Making **334**

11 Decimals

Chapter Opener • Connections to Estimation **336**

● 11.1 Exploring Tenths **338**
● 11.2 Exploring Tenths and Hundredths **340**
11.3 Place Value and Decimals **342**
11.4 Comparing Decimals **344**
* 11.5 Ordering Decimals **346**

● Cooperative Learning   * Algebra

x

● 11.6 **Problem Solving Strategy Application** • Using Strategies **348**
11.7 **Choose a Computation Method** • Calculator or Mental Math **350**

Section Review **351**

11.8 **Estimation** • Using Rounding to Estimate **352**
11.9 Adding Decimals **354**
11.10 Subtracting Decimals **356**
11.11 Using Decimals **358**
● 11.12 **Problem Solving** • Using Math Sense **360**
11.13 **Estimation** • Estimating with Money **362**

Section Review **363**
Chapter Test **364**
Cumulative Review **365**
✳ **Excursion** • **Cultural Diversity:** Algebra **366**

12 Multiplying by 2-Digit Numbers

Chapter Opener • Connections to Science **368**

✳ 12.1 **Mental Math** • Using Patterns **370**
12.2 **Estimation** • Estimating Products **372**
12.3 Multiplying by Multiples of Ten **374**
12.4 **Problem Solving Strategy Application** • Using Strategies **376**
✳ 12.5 Multiplying with Array Diagrams **378**
✳ 12.6 Multiplying 2-Digit Numbers **380**
12.7 Logical Reasoning **382**

Section Review **383**

✳ 12.8 Multiplying 3-Digit Numbers **384**
12.9 Multiplying Money **386**
12.10 Multiplying Three Factors **388**
12.11 **Problem Solving** • Using Math Sense **390**

Section Review **391**
Chapter Test **392**
Cumulative Review **393**
Excursion • **Cultural Diversity:** Area **394**

● Cooperative Learning ✳ Algebra

xi

13 Dividing by 2-Digit Numbers

Chapter Opener • Connections to Social Studies   **396**

＊13.1   **Mental Math** • Using Patterns   **398**

  13.2   **Estimation** • Estimating Quotients   **400**

●13.3   **Problem Solving Strategy Application** • Using Strategies   **402**

  13.4   One-Digit Quotients   **404**

  13.5   Two-Digit Quotients   **406**

  13.6   **Problem Solving Strategy Application** • Using Strategies   **408**

Section Review   **409**

  13.7   Using Division   **410**

  13.8   Using Division for Averages   **412**

  13.9   **Problem Solving Strategy Application** • Using Strategies   **414**

Section Review   **415**

Chapter Test   **416**

Cumulative Review   **417**

Excursion • **Cultural Diversity:** Better Buy   **418**

● Cooperative Learning   ＊ Algebra

MORE PRACTICE   420

HANDBOOK   463

DATA BOOK   464

Almanac   464
Highest Waterfalls in the World
Rainfall
Animals' Fastest Speeds
Tall Trees in the U.S.A.
NBA Lifetime Scoring Leaders

Atlas   467
Average Temperatures of Florida Cities
Mileage Map in Southeast U.S.A.
Flight Distances in U.S.A.

General Information   470
Airport Flight Guide
Floor Plan
Lunch Room Take-Out Menu
Pumpkin Muffin Recipe
Bean Stem Growth
Variety Video Sale
Garden Center Price List
Table of Measures

INDEPENDENT STUDY   474
Tips for Problem Solving
Tips for Doing Mental Math
Tips for Estimating
Study Tips
Using Your Textbook
Tips for Working Together
Learning to Use a Calculator

REFERENCE SECTION   488
Glossary   488
Index   499

CHAPTER 1

PLACE VALUE

Connections

Money Sense

Counting Your Pennies Each member of the Krieger family has a penny bank. Every few months, they get together to count their pennies.

They put stacks of 50 pennies into paper wrappers. A full wrapper is called a *roll* of pennies. When they finish, the family cash in their pennies at the bank. They use the money to buy something for the whole family.

It takes time to wrap a large pile of pennies. Each person has to count out 50 pennies at a time. Often they lose count and have to start over. Sylvia discovered an easier way to count to 50. She counts her pennies into stacks of 10. Then she uses 5 stacks to make a full roll of pennies.

Today the Kriegers wrapped a large pile of pennies. How many rolls of pennies did they wrap? How much money is that?

ESTIMATING HOW MANY

Mrs. David likes to have a weekly estimating contest in her fourth-grade class. Below are the children's estimates. Since this is the first week of school, the children have not had much practice in estimating.

195	388	725	515	900	475
500	246	450	600	550	666
765	542	395	642	828	505
999	711	248	500	747	369

Mrs. David uses a table to record the estimates.

Estimating Contest		
Range of Estimates	Tally	Number of Students
0-99		0
100-199	/	1
200-299	//	2
300-399	///	3
400-499	//	2
500-599	//// /	6
600-699	///	3
700-799	////	4
800-899	/	1
900-999	//	2
TOTAL		24

Mrs. David counted the beans in the jar beforehand. She wrote that number inside the lid of the jar. When the contest was over, the jar was opened to show the actual amount on the lid.

547

1. Which estimate is closest to the actual amount?

2. How do you think the students made their estimates?

A bar graph is another way to show the results.

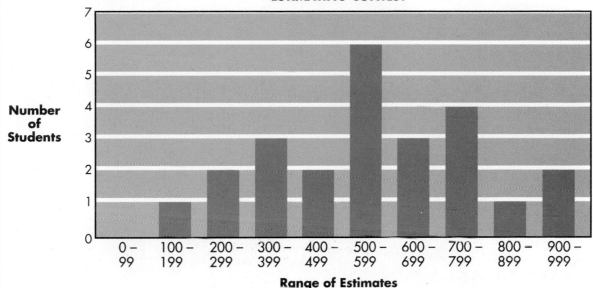

ESTIMATING CONTEST

Number of Students

Range of Estimates

Use the bar graph to answer each question.

3. How many students estimated between 500 and 599?

4. In which range did no students estimate?

5. Which ranges of estimates had the same number of students?

6. How many students are in Mrs. David's class?

7. How many students are in half of the class?

8. Did less than half of the students make estimates below 500?

9. Did more than half the students estimate above 600?

Critical Thinking

10. Do you think Mrs. David's students will get better at estimating after a month of contests? Explain your answer.

PROJECT • Estimation

Plan an estimating contest. Fill up a jar with some item. Have each student give an estimate. Make a table of the results.

USING TENS TO ESTIMATE

Mrs. David's class enjoyed the estimating contest. She decided to do some more estimation activities.

Mrs. David places on her desk a tall, thin jar filled with marbles.

She asks a student to take 10 marbles out of the jar. This picture shows how the jar looks after 10 marbles are removed.

1. About how many more times could 10 marbles be removed before the jar is empty? Explain.

2. About how many marbles do you think were in the full jar? Explain.

a.

b.

c.

Next, Mrs. David places on her desk a wider, shorter jar filled with marbles.

The picture above shows the jar after a student has removed 10 marbles.

The picture above shows the jar after 10 students each removed 10 marbles.

Look at the jars at the bottom of page 4.

3. About how many times could 10 marbles be removed before the jar in photo c would be empty?

4. About how many marbles do you think were in the full jar?

▶ The jar to the right was full. Now, 100 marbles have been removed.

5. About how many marbles do you think were in the full jar?

SUMMING IT UP

6. If you start at 0, what number will you get counting by 10's ten times?

7. If you start at 0, what number will you get counting by 100's ten times?

8. In exercise 1, suppose each child had taken 13 marbles instead of 10. Would that be easier or harder to estimate? Why?

COOPERATIVE • LEARNING

PROJECT • Estimation

Work with a small group. Get a large jar and a bag of marbles. Put 50 marbles in the jar. Then estimate how many marbles will fill the jar. Continue to fill the jar to check your estimate.

USING FACTS

You can use what you know about place value
and basic facts to add mentally.

8	8 tens	80
+ 4	+ 4 tens	+ 40
12	12 tens	120

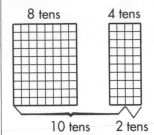

8 tens   4 tens

10 tens   2 tens

**12 tens is the same
as 10 tens + 2 tens
which is 100 + 20 = 120**

You can also subtract mentally.

15	15 hundreds	1500
− 6	− 6 hundreds	− 600
9	9 hundreds	900

Think

• How can the basic fact 9 − 5
help you subtract 5000
from 9000?

Other Examples

6	6 thousands	6000
+ 7	+ 7 thousands	+ 7000
13	13 thousands	13,000

GUIDED PRACTICE

Write the answer.

1. a. 9 + 3   b. 90 + 30   c. 900 + 300

2. a. 7 + 7   b. 700 + 700   c. 7000 + 7000

3. a. 11 − 3   b. 110 − 30   c. 1100 − 300

*Critical
Thinking* 4. What basic fact can help you subtract 9000
from 17,000?

INDEPENDENT PRACTICE

Write the answer.

5. 6 + 9　　　**6.** 14 − 5　　　**7.** 9 + 4　　　**8.** 13 − 7　　　**9.** 7 + 6

10. 8000 + 5000　　　**11.** 9000 + 6000　　　**12.** 600 − 300　　　**13.** 130 − 70

14. 50 + 20 + 10　　　　**15.** 70 + 30 + 40　　　　**16.** 1400 − 500

17. 150 − 80　　　　**18.** 600 + 500　　　　**19.** 900 − 600

20. 13,000 − 7000　　　　**21.** 8000 + 8000　　　　**22.** 500 + 800

23. Write each pair of numbers whose sum is 100.

10	60	30	80
40	20	70	90

24. Write each pair of numbers whose sum is 1000.

500	800	700	600
200	500	300	400

••

PROJECT • Game

COOPERATIVE • LEARNING

Work with a partner. You will need 10 number cards (1–10), 8 red counters, and 8 yellow counters. Copy the game board below on a piece of paper.

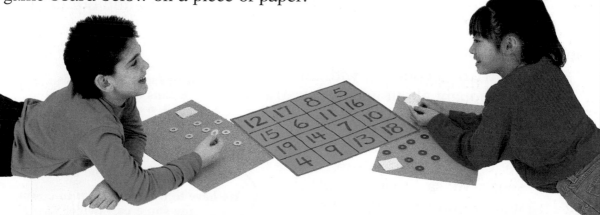

a. Put the 1–5 cards face down in one deck. Put the 6–10 cards face down in another deck.

b. Pick 2 cards from the same deck or different decks. Add or subtract. Put a counter on the square with the answer.

c. The first player with 4 counters in a row wins.

PROBLEM SOLVER'S GUIDE

There are no magic rules to make solving problems easy. But the Problem Solver's Guide can help.

One time, we used the Guide to help plan our booth at the carnival.

COOPERATIVE • LEARNING

OUR PROBLEM

We planned to make a stack of cans in the shape of a triangle. We wanted to know how many cans we needed to make the stack 6 rows high.

OUR SOLUTION

UNDERSTAND

What is going on in the problem? ⟶ We are making a stack of cans.

What do we know? ⟶ We know its shape and the number of rows.

What do we need to find out? ⟶ We need to find out the total number of cans.

TRY

We tried to come up with an idea. We thought about adding because we needed a total.

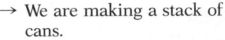

A triangle has 3 sides.
6 cans on each side
6 + 6 + 6 = 18 ⟵ Total

LOOK BACK

We checked if our answer made sense. We saw that we had added without understanding the problem completely.

We need to include all the cans, not just the cans along the outside.

We have to be careful not to count the same can twice.

We **tried** again. This time we drew a picture. We saw a pattern. The total would be 21 cans.

We **looked back** again. Our answer made sense.

```
    x         1
   x x        2
  x x x       3
 x x x x     4
x x x x x    5
x x x x x x   6
```

Work in groups to solve each problem. The Problem Solver's Guide may help.

1. Nicky's mother is taking Nicky and 4 of his friends to the carnival. In what order should Nicky's mother pick up his four friends to take the shortest route?

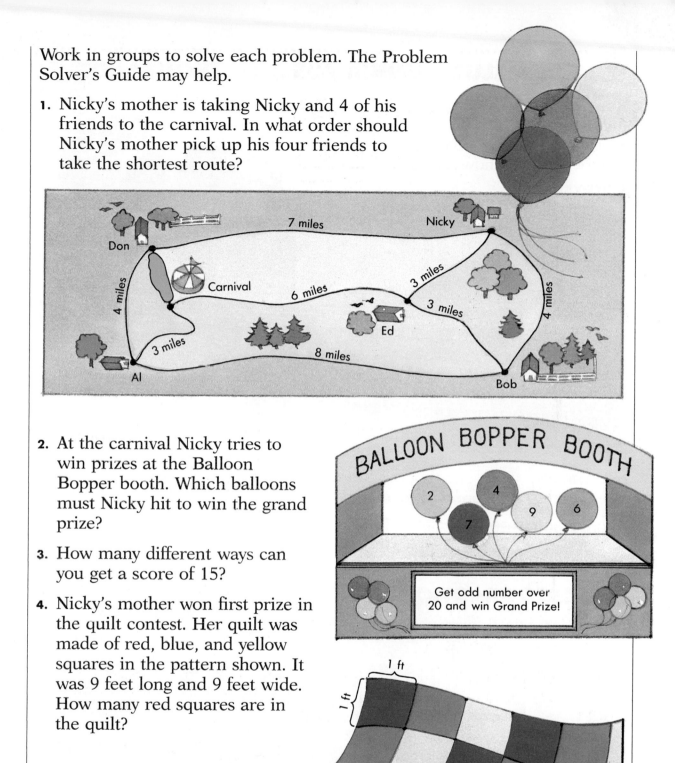

2. At the carnival Nicky tries to win prizes at the Balloon Bopper booth. Which balloons must Nicky hit to win the grand prize?

3. How many different ways can you get a score of 15?

4. Nicky's mother won first prize in the quilt contest. Her quilt was made of red, blue, and yellow squares in the pattern shown. It was 9 feet long and 9 feet wide. How many red squares are in the quilt?

BALLOON BOPPER BOOTH

Get odd number over 20 and win Grand Prize!

1 ft

PLACE VALUE—HUNDREDS AND THOUSANDS

Mrs. David's class recycles aluminum cans. After the first four weeks, the class had collected one thousand three hundred twenty-seven cans. This number can be shown in several ways.

PLACE-VALUE BLOCKS

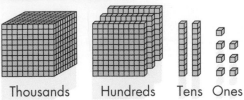

Thousands   Hundreds   Tens Ones

STANDARD FORM 1327

PLACE-VALUE CHART

Thousands	Hundreds	Tens	Ones
1	3	2	7

 Think

- How many hundreds squares are in each thousands cube?

- What digit is in the greatest place? What is its value?

You can also write one thousand three hundred twenty-seven in **expanded form.**

1000 + 300 + 20 + 7   or   1 thousand + 3 hundreds + 2 tens + 7 ones

GUIDED PRACTICE

Write in standard form.

1.
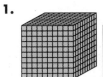

2.

Thousands	Hundreds	Tens	Ones
8	9	0	8

3. six thousand one hundred seven

4. 1000 + 700 + 30 + 6

Write in words.

5. 343   **6.** 181   **7.** 4309   **8.** 9720

Critical Thinking **9.** In exercise 8, what is the value of the digit in the tens place?

INDEPENDENT PRACTICE

Write in standard form.

10. five hundred thirty   **11.** 6000 + 40 + 2   **12.** 1000 + 200 + 20

13. 3000 + 700 + 9   **14.** eight hundred sixteen   **15.** 5000 + 400 + 6

Write in words.

16. 635   **17.** 203   **18.** 9999   **19.** 5730   **20.** 261   **21.** 1077

22. In the number 4076, what is the value of the digit in the hundreds place?

23. In the number 7349, what is the value of the digit in the thousands place?

PROJECT • Game

Play this game with a partner.

a. Fold each of eight index cards into 4 sections.

b. For each number below, write the number in 4 different ways as shown.

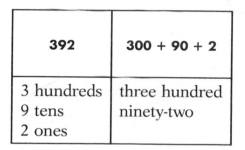

392	300 + 90 + 2
3 hundreds 9 tens 2 ones	three hundred ninety-two

392	538
611	290
876	399
408	155

c. Cut each card into 4 smaller cards to make a deck of 32 cards.

d. Play Fish. You need all 4 cards for the same number to make a "book." The player with more books wins.

FIVES AND TENS

The number 10 is very useful. We use it to think about place value. The number 5 is also important.

$$5 + 5 = 10$$

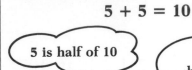

5 is half of 10

5 is halfway between 0 and 10

10 is very useful.

These number lines show other halfway points.

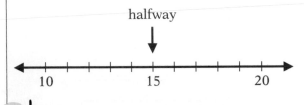

halfway

10   15   20

halfway

0   50   100

Think

- What number is halfway between 200 and 300? Between 50 and 100?

Halfway points can help you estimate distance. This is a map of North Dakota. Fargo is about 200 miles from Bismarck. About how far is Valley City from Bismarck?

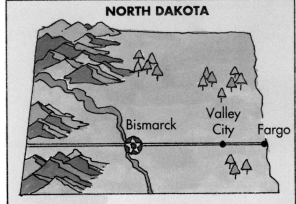

NORTH DAKOTA

Bismarck   Valley City   Fargo

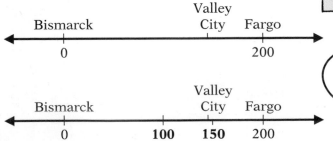

Bismarck   Valley City Fargo
0   200

Bismarck   Valley City Fargo
0   100   150   200

Halfway between 0 and 200 is *100*.
Halfway between 100 and 200 is *150*.

So, Valley City is about 150 miles from Bismarck.

GUIDED PRACTICE

Draw a number line to show the halfway point between each pair of numbers.

1. 70, 80 **2.** 120, 130 **3.** 300, 400 **4.** 0, 1000

Write about what number the arrow is pointing to.

5.

6.

Critical Thinking 7. For exercises 5 and 6, is there only one correct answer for each? Why or why not?

INDEPENDENT PRACTICE

Write the number that is halfway between each pair of numbers.

8. 60, 70 **9.** 90, 100 **10.** 120, 130 **11.** 350, 360
12. 100, 200 **13.** 700, 800 **14.** 1000, 2000 **15.** 8000, 9000

Write about what number the arrow is pointing to.

16. 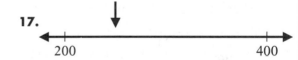 **17.**

Problem Solving

18. Is Riverton more than or less than 50 miles from Hill City?

19. About how far is Cedar Falls from Hill City?

20. Which city is about 260 miles from Hill City?

21. About how far is Casper from Soda Springs?

ROUNDING TO THE NEAREST 10 AND 100

A **rounded** number tells *about* how many.

Joe and his family drove 687 miles to the Grand Canyon. When they returned home, Joe told his friends they had driven about 700 miles. Joe rounded 687 to 700.

Look at the folded number line.

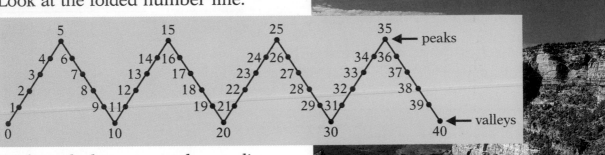

Each peak shows a number ending in 5. These numbers are halfway between two tens. The tens are at the bottom of each fold, in the valleys.

1. What number is halfway between 30 and 40?

2. What number is halfway between 10 and 20?

3. How are all the halfway numbers alike?

Suppose you placed a counter on the number 37 and let go. The counter would slide to 40 because 40 is the ten that is nearest to 37.

4. Would a counter placed at 28 slide to 20 or to 30?

5. Is 28 closer to 20 or to 30?

Instead of saying that 23 is closer to 20, you can say that 23 rounded to the nearest ten is 20.

6. On which numbers can you place the counter so that it slides to 20?

7. Is 35 closer to 30 or to 40? Why?

You round halfway numbers, such as 5 and 15, to the higher ten. You would round 25 to 30.

8. Would you round 17 to 10 or to 20?

9. Would you round 35 to 30 or to 40?

10. Would you round 8 to 0 or to 10?

11. Would you round 23¢ to 20¢ or to 30¢? How do you know?

This number line shows numbers in the hundreds.

12. How are the halfway numbers on the hundreds line like the halfway numbers on the tens line?

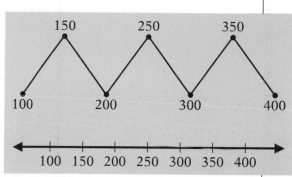

13. Suppose you put a counter at 230. To which number would it slide?

14. Would you round 350 to 300 or to 400?

15. Would you round $1.75 to $1.00 or to $2.00? How do you know?

Critical Thinking

SUMMING IT UP

16. How are the halfway numbers on all of the number lines alike? How are they different?

17. What does it mean to round a number to the nearest 10?

PROJECT • Number Sense

The numbers in these examples have been rounded. Discuss with your group why exact numbers were not needed in these examples. Think of other ways to use rounded numbers. Look in newspapers and magazines. Bring in 3 examples of rounded numbers. Compare your ideas with another group.

ROUNDING SENSIBLY

Sometimes it makes sense to round numbers. Other times it does not make sense.

A student talked to the principal about plans for a school fair. At the right are his notes, and below is the article he wrote from the notes.

> **Notes**
> school fair, September 19, begin 9:30 A.M. end 3:45 P.M., 12 booths, 483 tickets sold so far, school wants to raise enough to buy a computer costing $1498.95, 102 pies and cakes

> **SCHOOL TO RAISE MONEY TO BUY COMPUTER**
> On about September 20, the Devon School Fair will be held. Almost 500 tickets have been sold already.
> There will be 12 booths with games and activities. The fair is to begin at 10:00 A.M. and end at 4:00 P.M. A hundred pies and cakes will be on sale.
> The school hopes to raise $1498.95 to buy a new computer for the school.

Critical Thinking

INDEPENDENT PRACTICE

Use the article and the notes above to answer each question.

1. Which numbers did the student round? Which of these numbers would you not have rounded? Explain.

> Olympic field day, 89 students to compete, 7 contests, 4th grade class, 21 ribbons to be awarded, 9:15 A.M. to 12:30 P.M., October 17

2. Which numbers did the student not round? Which of those numbers would you have rounded? Explain.

3. Use the notes at the right to write a short article. Round numbers when it makes sense.

MATH LOG

What are some reasons for rounding numbers? What are some times it does not make sense to round numbers?

SECTION REVIEW

for pages 2–16

Write the letter of the correct answer.

1. The distance between New York and Los Angeles is two thousand four hundred fifty-nine miles. This number in standard form is:
   a. 2495
   b. 2459
   c. 2000 + 400 + 59
   d. 20,000 + 459

2. To fly round trip from New York City to Chicago is about 1680 miles. The value of the digit in the greatest place is:
   a. 10, or ten
   b. 100, or one hundred
   c. 1000, or one thousand
   d. 10,000, or ten thousand

Write in standard form.

3. seven thousand four hundred

4. 7 hundred thirty

5. 4000 + 100 + 3

6. 300 + 16

Write the value of 2 in each number.

7. 5234   8. 2610   9. 1702   10. 123

For each number, write the digit in the tens place. Then write the digit in the hundreds place.

11. 7834   12. 4791   13. 3943

Write each number in words.

14. 4792   15. 2494   16. 9249

The height of the Sears Tower, the tallest skyscraper, is 1559 feet.

17. Write the height in words.

Round each number to the nearest hundred.

18. 192   19. 345   20. 768   21. 839

PLACE VALUE TO ONE MILLION

The moon looks as if it is close to the earth. But the closest it ever gets is three hundred fifty-six thousand, four hundred kilometers.

Expanded form:
300,000 + 50,000 + 6000 + 400

Standard form:
356,400

In numbers larger than 9999, write a comma between the thousands place and the hundreds place.

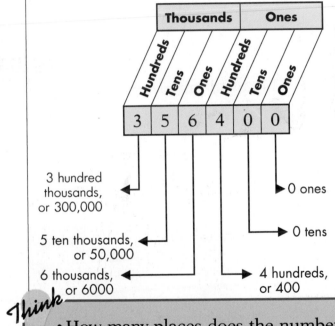

PLACE VALUE CHART

Thousands			Ones		
Hundreds	Tens	Ones	Hundreds	Tens	Ones
3	5	6	4	0	0

3 hundred thousands, or 300,000

5 ten thousands, or 50,000

6 thousands, or 6000

4 hundreds, or 400

0 tens

0 ones

Think

- How many places does the number above have?

- What is the value of the digit in the greatest place?

Other Examples

one hundred seven thousand, two

100,000 + 7000 + 2
107,002

twenty-three thousand, four hundred three

20,000 + 3000 + 400 + 3
23,403

GUIDED PRACTICE

Write the number in standard form.

1. 200,000 + 60,000 + 700 + 4
2. five hundred six thousand
3. 60,000 + 5000 + 800 + 20 + 3
4. one hundred twelve thousand, fifty

Write in words.

5. 790,018
6. 11,475
7. 840,317

Critical Thinking 8. In exercise 5, what is the value of the 9?

INDEPENDENT PRACTICE

Write the number in standard form.

9. seventeen thousand, five hundred
10. eight hundred thousand, twenty
11. three hundred seven thousand, five hundred sixty-one
12. 200,000 + 40,000 + 800 + 10 + 9
13. 90,000 + 700 + 4
14. 100,000 + 70,000 + 3000 + 20 + 2

Write in words.

15. 467,824
16. 500,020
17. 71,432

Write the value of the 8.

18. 601,877
19. 578,219
20. 35,080
21. 786,393

PROJECT • Numeration

Work with a partner.

Use sheets of small-squared paper as shown to the right. Make a model of 10,000 and 100,000. Use tape to attach the separate parts together to make a single large square or large rectangle.

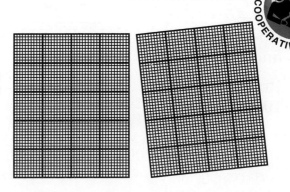

More Practice Set 1.9, p. 421

HOW MUCH IS A MILLION?

Groups:
- small groups

You will need:
- squared paper
- scissors
- 10 books

You already know the number 999,999. What number is 1 more than 999,999? The number after 999,999 is one **million.**

▶ Here are some facts about one million.

- Suppose one million students your age stand side by side in a straight line. The line would stretch about 190 miles. This is more than the distance between Chicago, Illinois, and Indianapolis, Indiana.

- Suppose one million people stand on each other's shoulders to make a human tower. That tower would be about 758 miles high. The world's tallest mountain is less than 6 miles high.

▶ Here are some more facts about one million.

- One million is written like this: 1,000,000.

- It is 1000 thousands, or 10 hundred thousands.

▶ Work with your group to find out how much one million is. On squared paper, mark off and cut out a block 10 squares long and 10 squares wide.

1. How many squares is this in all? How did you find out?

2. How many blocks would you need to show 1000 squares?

3. How many blocks would you need to show 10,000 squares? 100,000 squares? 1,000,000 squares?

Now stack 10 books that are the same thickness. Measure the pile. Record the measurement.

4. Would a stack of 100 books be as tall as you? Would it be as high as the ceiling of your classroom?

5. Would a stack of 1000 books be as tall as your school?

6. Would a stack of 1 million books be as tall as a flagpole? As tall as a skyscraper?

Now have one group member count to 100 by ones. Have another person use a watch to time how long it takes.

7. How long did it take to count to 100 by ones?

8. Which would take longer to count? Why?
   a. from 1 to 100
   b. from 932,401 to 932,500

9. Do you think someone could count to 1 million by 1's in an hour? Why or why not?

Critical Thinking •••••••••••••••••••

SUMMING IT UP

10. How did knowing the height of a stack of 10 books help you figure out the height of a stack of 100 books?

PROJECT • Number Sense

Work with a small group. Share your results with other groups.

a. Think of items you use every day. Could you fit 1 million of any item in your classroom at one time?

b. Find out the number of letters in a newspaper. Is it more than or less than a million?

c. How high would a stack of a million pennies be?

d. How long would 1 million paper clips end to end be?

ROUNDING LARGER NUMBERS

▶ Ms. Bitts is a reporter for the *Daily Reporter*. She is writing about a video game contest that 2837 children entered. Below are two possible ways she could round the headline. How should she round 2837 in the headline?

Ms. Bitts could round 2837 to the nearest **hundred**.

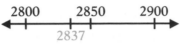

Ms. Bitts could round 2837 to the nearest **thousand**.

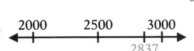

Think

≋ • Which number would you use in the headline? Why?

▶ You can use number lines like the ones above to help you round.

Here's another way you can round any number.

Find the place value you are rounding to.	→	Look at the digit to the right of that place.	→	Round up if it is 5 or greater. Round down if it is less than 5.

Round	240	240		240 rounds to 200
to the	1256	1256		1256 rounds to 1300
nearest	6470	6470		6470 rounds to 6500
hundred.	_82	_82		82 rounds to 100

Other Examples

Round 715 to the nearest ten.

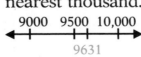

715 → 720

Round 9631 to the nearest thousand.

9631 → 10,000

Round the numbers to the nearest hundred. Then round to the nearest thousand. Use number lines when they are helpful.

1. 1234
2. 4720
3. 610
4. 1594

5. 5923
6. 2460
7. 1572
8. 4567

9. 984
10. 2719
11. 2008
12. 6135

Critical Thinking 13. Write a 4-digit number where rounding to the nearest thousand is just as close as rounding to the nearest hundred.

INDEPENDENT PRACTICE

Round the numbers to the nearest hundred. Then round to the nearest thousand. Use number lines when they are helpful.

14. 1679
15. 5670
16. 845
17. 7503

18. 7492
19. 7575
20. 1454
21. 2455

22. 6666
23. 3003
24. 3401
25. 8765

26. 999
27. 2952
28. 9745
29. 3051

PROJECT • Number Sense

Look through a newspaper or magazine to find large numbers. Find examples of the following:

• a rounded number
• a rounded money amount
• an exact number

Critical Thinking Explain how you decided whether or not the number was rounded.

COMPARING AND ORDERING

The chart shows some of the highest waterfalls in the world. Which waterfall is higher, Angel or Sutherland?

Line up the digits by place value:

3281

1904

Compare the digits. Start with the greatest place value.

3000 > 1000

Angel is higher than Sutherland.

Waterfalls	
Name of Waterfall	Height (in feet)
Angel (Venezuela)	3281
Gavarnie (France)	1384
Ribbon (U.S.A.)	1612
Sutherland (New Zealand)	1904
Takkakaw (Canada)	1650

 Think

- Do you think that Angel is *exactly* 3281 feet high? Explain.

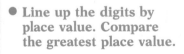

The other 3 waterfall heights can be ordered by comparing digits.

Compare 1384, 1650, and 1612. Then order the numbers from greatest to least.

- Line up the digits by place value. Compare the greatest place value.

1384
1650
1612
↓
1000 = 1000 = 1000

The thousands places are equal in value.

- Compare the next greatest place value.

1384
1650
1612
↓
600 > 300

So, 1612 and 1650 are greater than 1384.

- Continue to compare if you need to.

1650
1612
↓
50 > 10

So, 1650 is greater than 1612.

From greatest to least, the heights are ordered 1650 feet; 1612 feet; 1384 feet.

GUIDED PRACTICE

Write > or <.

1. 632 ● 689   **2.** 2938 ● 293   **3.** 1482 ● 1464   **4.** 4892 ● 4634

Write the numbers in order from greatest to least.

5. 473; 234; 589   **6.** 579; 831; 597   **7.** 689; 5432; 475; 5987

Critical Thinking **8.** Without comparing digits, how could you find the answer to exercise 2?

INDEPENDENT PRACTICE

Write > or <.

9. 276 ● 274   **10.** 345 ● 3459   **11.** 5438 ● 6437   **12.** 7458 ● 7432

Write the numbers in order from greatest to least.

13. 643; 642; 661   **14.** 794; 714; 764   **15.** 498; 567; 143

16. 1674; 1699; 9048; 2648   **17.** 874; 9463; 8346; 3459

18. 5007; 389; 507; 962   **19.** 2410; 658; 241; 47

Problem Solving Use the chart on page 24.

20. Niagara Falls has a height of 167 feet. Which is higher, Takkakaw or Niagara Falls?

21. Upper Yosemite has a height of 1430 feet. Of the waterfalls listed on page 24, which are lower than Upper Yosemite?

22. **Data Book** Go to page 464 in the almanac section. Use the chart on waterfalls. Order the top five from greatest to least.

Maintain • Addition and Subtraction Facts

Write the answer.

1. 18 − 9   **2.** 6 + 7   **3.** 13 − 5   **4.** 8 + 7   **5.** 14 − 9

6. 15 − 6   **7.** 16 − 8   **8.** 12 − 9   **9.** 6 + 5   **10.** 3 + 8

IDENTIFYING MONEY

Denise wants to buy a lighted globe from the map store. The globe costs eighty-five dollars and seventy cents. Denise has these coins and bills. Can she buy the globe?

When you count money, organize the bills and coins in groups from greatest to least. Then count.

$20 → $40 → $60 → $70 → $80 → $85

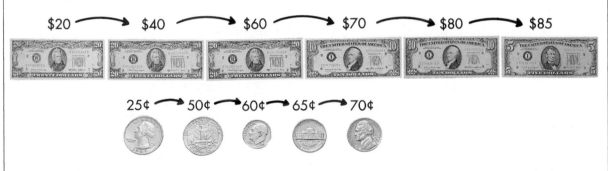

25¢ → 50¢ → 60¢ → 65¢ → 70¢

Denise can buy the globe.

Write eighty-five dollars and seventy cents as:

$85.70

> Write a dollar sign. Use a decimal point to separate dollars and cents.

Think

- How does organizing money in groups from greatest to least help you to count?

Other Examples

one hundred dollars and six cents ⟶ $100.06
forty-two cents ⟶ $0.42, or 42¢
six cents ⟶ $0.06, or 6¢

GUIDED PRACTICE

Write the amount of money.

1. eighteen dollars, 2 quarters

2. 3 dimes, 2 pennies

3. ninety-eight dollars and five pennies

4. 3 quarters, 1 dime, 1 nickel

Find the pattern. Write the next three numbers.

5. 20¢, 30¢, 40¢, ▧, ▧, ▧

6. $2.25, $2.50, $2.75, ▧, ▧, ▧

7. 10¢, 15¢, 20¢, ▧, ▧, ▧

8. $10, $12, $14, ▧, ▧, ▧

Critical Thinking
9. What bills and coins could you use to get the amount in exercise 3?

....

INDEPENDENT PRACTICE

Write the amount of money.

10. ninety-eight cents

11. twelve dollars and one cent

12. 1 fifty-dollar bill, 2 five-dollar bills

13. 3 dimes, 5 nickels

Find the pattern. Write the next three numbers.

14. $35.00, $45.00, $55.00, ▧, ▧, ▧

15. $15.25, $15.30, $15.35, ▧, ▧, ▧

16. $10.25, $10.50, $10.75, ▧, ▧, ▧

Write the amount, using the dollar sign and decimal point.

17. one penny more than seventeen dollars

18. ten dollars less than sixty dollars and fifty cents

19. one hundred dollars less than three hundred dollars

20. one thousand dollars more than 500 dollars

MAKE A TABLE

> You may remember that making a table can help you solve some problems.
>
> I made a table to help save up to buy a collie.

MY PROBLEM

The collie cost $77 and I had only $45. I planned to save $5 every week. I needed to know how many weeks it would be until I could buy the collie.

MY SOLUTION

I made a table and began to fill it in. I started by writing in the $45 I already had.

Weeks	now
Money	$45

At the end of 1 week, I would have $5 more. That would make $50 in all.

Weeks	now	1
Money	$45	$50

I kept filling in my table. After 6 weeks I would have $75. That still would not be enough.

Weeks	now	1	2	3	4	5	6
Money	$45	$50	$55	$60	$65	$70	$75

Can you figure out when I would be able to buy the collie?

Would I have enough money left over to buy a dog dish for $2.50?

GUIDED PRACTICE

Read the problem. Copy and finish the table to solve.

1. Barbara is making pillows for dollhouse furniture to sell at the dollhouse show. She can make 3 pillows in an hour. Barbara wants to make 12 pillows. If she begins work at 9 A.M., at what time will she be finished?

Time	Pillows
9 A.M.	0
10 A.M.	3
11 A.M.	

....

APPLICATION

Work in groups to solve each problem. Make a table when it helps.

2. Amy has $28. She plans to save $3 each week. In how many weeks will she have enough money to buy a telescope that costs $49?

3. Ryan has $40 and Sara has $25. Each week, Ryan saves $2 and Sara saves $5. In how many weeks will they have the same amount of money?

4. Doug has 18 dinosaur stamps and Beth has 8. As a birthday present, Doug promises to give Beth one of his stamps each day until they both have the same number of stamps. How many days will that take?

5. Brenda needs nickels to play Nickel Toss at the Charity Fair. She has 3 quarters and 1 dime. How many nickels can she get for these coins?

6. Sergio is making a triangle pattern by pasting stars in rows. He needs 1 star to make 1 row, 3 stars to make 2 rows, 6 stars to make 3 rows, and 10 stars to make 4 rows. How many stars does he need to make 8 rows? HINT: Look for a pattern in your table.

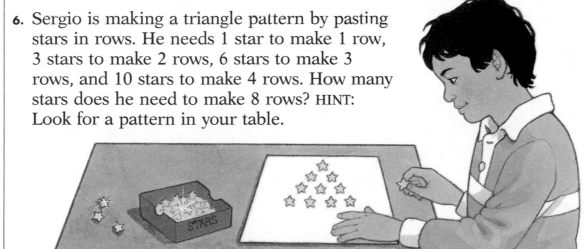

COOPERATIVE · LEARNING

MAKING CHANGE

Many stores have cash registers that tell the amount of change if the salesclerk enters the amount of money the customer gives.

Quick-Print Copy	
Mdse	$4.26
Tax	$0.21
Total	$4.47
Cash	$5.00
Change	$0.53

PENCILS

NOTE PADS

Think

- What are the fewest coins that could be used to give the customer the correct change for this sale? (Do not use half-dollars.)

Even though modern cash registers figure the change, many salesclerks still use the "old fashioned" way of giving the change to the customer. They count up from the amount of the sale to the amount given.

"four forty-seven"	"forty-eight"	"forty-nine"	"fifty"	"seventy-five"	"five dollars"
$4.47	$0.48	$0.49	$0.50	$0.75	$5.00

GUIDED PRACTICE

Write the fewest bills and coins you could receive as change. Use play money when it helps. Do not use half-dollars.

1. Cost: $0.39

   Cash given: $1.00

2. Cost: $6.58

   Cash given: $10.00

3. Cost: $12.01

   Cash given: $15.01

Critical Thinking 4. Why do you think $15.01 was given in cash in exercise 3?

Write the coins and bills you could receive as change.

5. Cost: 31¢

Amount given:
51¢

6. Cost: $0.27

Amount given:
$1.00

7. Cost: $1.44

Amount given:
$10.00

8. Copy and complete the table. Use a calculator if you wish.

	Total Cost	Cash Given	Change
a.	$15.38	$20.00	?
b.	$1.89	$2.00	?
c.	$4.55	$5.05	?
d.	$5.01	$6.00	?
e.	$11.20	?	$3.80
f.	$9.98	?	$10.02

9. For each example in exercise 8, write what bills and coins to use to make the change.

Problem Solving Use play money or draw pictures when it helps.

10. Elizabeth bought a coloring book that cost $0.29. She gave the clerk two quarters. How could the clerk give her the correct change with 5 coins?

11. Julio buys a baseball bat and ball for $14.99. He gives the cashier $20.00. How much change should he get back?

12. Michael bought a birthday card for 59¢. He gave the salesclerk three coins and got 16¢ change. What coins did he give to the clerk?

13. Julio buys a baseball hat for $17.23. What cash could he give to get 3 one-dollar bills in change?

MONEY SENSE

Barbara and Samantha shop for tapes at Music Land. With their ten-dollar bills they each purchase a tape that costs $9.49. The cashier gives Barbara 2 quarters and a penny. Samantha receives different coins for change.

Think

- What are two combinations of coins Samantha could have received in change?

- What combinations of silver coins have the same money value as one quarter?

GUIDED PRACTICE

For each amount, write the least number of pennies you could have.

1. $0.38 **2.** $0.95 **3.** $15.16 **4.** $1.67

Exchange each amount to get as many quarters as you can. Write the number of quarters.

5. $0.38 **6.** $0.95 **7.** $5.16 **8.** $1.67

Critical Thinking **9.** For exercises 1–4, which amounts could be made with no nickels? Do not use more than four pennies.

INDEPENDENT PRACTICE

Exchange each amount to get as many quarters
as you can. Write the number of quarters.

10.

11.

12.

13. 50 pennies   **14.** 10 dimes   **15.** 25 nickels

16. $4.00   **17.** $2.50   **18.** $1.75

Problem Solving Use counters or draw the money to help you.

19. Rick has three coins in his pockct. He has 45¢. What are the three coins?

20. Suzanne owed her dad 63¢. She paid him with six coins. What coins did she give him?

21. Chris exchanged his two quarters with Sally for seven coins worth the same amount. What coins did Sally give him?

22. Carmen had five coins. Only two of them were the samc. They were worth $0.46. What coins were they?

23. George has 4 coins. Altogether thcy are worth more than 50¢. His total amount is an even number. Only two of the coins are the same. He has one penny. How much money does he have?

Critical Thinking

24. Write a puzzle about the number of coins needed to make a certain amount. Give it to a friend to solve.

CHALLENGE • Rounding

....

Round each of these money amounts to the nearest $5
($5, $10, $15, $20, $25, and so on).

1. $18.39   **2.** $23.95   **3.** $51.60   **4.** $22.75   **5.** $32.15

NOT ENOUGH INFORMATION

I have one dollar. Can I buy a book cover?

We cannot tell. We need to know how much a book cover costs.

If you get stuck, remember....
Tips for Problem Solving
on pages 474–475

Solve each problem. If there is not enough information, tell what you need to know.

1. A box of markers is marked "On Sale—$2 off the regular price." How much will Andrew save by buying the box of markers on sale?

2. Two book covers cost $2.20. Shen has 2 one-dollar bills and some dimes. Does she have enough to buy the two book covers?

3. A ruler costs $2.20. Jody has 2 one-dollar bills and some nickels. Does she have enough to buy the ruler?

4. The sale price for a box of pens is $2. Denise has $3. How much can she save buying the pens on sale?

5. Diana is buying a notebook for $2. Will she have enough money left to buy a pen for 50¢?

6. Elton gets out of school at 3:30. His piano lesson starts at 4:00. Will he get there on time?

SECTION REVIEW

for pages 18–34

Write each number in standard form.

1. sixty-four thousand, twenty-four

2. fifty thousand, seven

3. two hundred thirteen thousand, five

4. 500,000 + 30,000 + 6000 + 5

Write each number in words.

5. 83,206

6. 690,111

Write > or <.

7. 3216 ● 3460

8. 4527 ● 4517

9. 231 ● 2310

10. 3986 ● 491

Round each number to the nearest thousand.

11. 7278

12. 3982

13. 4590

14. 1242

Write the amount of money.

15. 1 ten-dollar bill, 1 five-dollar bill, 3 quarters, 2 pennies

16. 1 twenty-dollar bill, 4 one-dollar bills, 3 dimes, one nickel

Write the least number of bills and coins you would receive as change. Do not use half-dollars.

17. Cost of item: $0.45

Amount given: $1.00

18. Cost of item: $6.98

Amount given: $10.00

Write the number of quarters you could have.

19. $0.50

20. $3.00

21. $2.75

22. $4.25

Solve each problem.

23. Rico buys a bag of pretzels for $0.75. He gives the clerk $1.00 How much change does he receive?

24. Kathy had 30 cents. Then she gave Tom a nickel. She has five coins left. What coins could she have?

CHAPTER TEST

Write the value of the 6.

1. 260,900   **2.** 89,672   **3.** 506,298   **4.** 682,125

Write the number in standard form.

5. Four hundred twenty thousand   **6.** Two thousand nine hundred four

Write the numbers in order from greatest to least.

7. 771; 1702; 936; 710   **8.** 603; 60; 3160; 630

9. 424; 4013; 480   **10.** 970; 1050; 907; 960

Write the number rounded to the nearest hundred.

11. 623   **12.** 2349   **13.** 471   **14.** 6,872

Write the number rounded to the nearest thousand.

15. 8727   **16.** 5198   **17.** 1522   **18.** 5488

Write the number in standard form.

19. 300,000 + 18,000 + 91   **20.** 12,000 + 600 + 87

21. 500,000 + 3000 + 200 + 3   **22.** 79,000 + 800 + 20 + 9

Write the bills and coins you would receive as change.

23. Cost: $14.48
Amount given: $20.00

24. Cost: 82¢
Amount given: 90¢

PROBLEM SOLVING

Solve each problem.

Rachel   Bixford   Tandy   Fayville Beacon Springwell   Milford   Faxton

0   100   200   300   400   500 miles

25. About how far is Fayville from Rachel?

26. Is Springwell greater or less than 50 miles from Beacon?

CUMULATIVE REVIEW

Write the number in standard form.

1. 4000 + 600 + 7

2. 8000 + 400 + 90

3. three thousand twelve

4. five thousand seven hundred six

What does the blue digit in the number stand for?

5. 954

6. 50

7. 396

8. 668

Round to the nearest ten.

9. 79

10. 248

11. 3604

12. 7986

Round to the nearest hundred.

13. 768

14. 229

15. 4568

16. 8209

Write the numbers in order from least to greatest.

17. 470; 69; 496; 4096

18. 3842; 8432; 843; 3824

19. 2202; 220; 2020

Copy and complete the table. Then write what bills and coins you need to make the change.

	Total Cost	Cash Given	Change
20.	$13.98	$20.00	?
21.	$ 7.31	$10.00	?
22.	$ 8.14	$ 9.00	?
23.	$17.02	$20.02	?

Solve each problem.

24. Barry gave the clerk $20.00 for a $17.25 shirt. How much change will he get back? Explain how you got your answer.

25. Cindy bought wrapping paper for $7.30. She has a $10 bill and some change. How much should she pay if she wants to get back three $1 bills?

EXCURSION

NUMERATION

WRITING ROMAN NUMERALS

The ancient Romans used letters to name numbers.

$I = 1$ $V = 5$ $X = 10$ $L = 50$ $C = 100$ $D = 500$ $M = 1000$

You can find what some numbers are by adding the value of the letters. The letters are arranged from greatest to least value, starting at the left. For example, XXXVIII:

X	X	X	V	I	I	I
↓	↓	↓	↓	↓	↓	↓
10	10	10	5	1	1	1

$10 + 10 + 10 + 5 + 1 + 1 + 1 = 38$

So, XXXVIII = 38.

You can find what other numbers are by subtracting the value of the letters. You subtract when a numeral for a smaller number is to the left of a numeral for a larger number. For example, XL or CM:

X   L
↓   ↓
10 50 $50 - 10 = 40$

C   M
↓   ↓
100 1000 $1000 - 100 = 900$

So, XL = 40.

So, CM = 900.

For some others, you need to add *and* to subtract.

For example, XLVII:

```
 Subtract        Add
X       L      V   I   I
10      50     5   1   1
    \   /       \  |  /
     40     +     7     = 47
```

So, XLVII = 47.

Write the number each Roman numeral stands for.

1. XXV
2. IX
3. XXXIV
4. XXIX
5. XVI
6. XLIV
7. L
8. XXXI
9. XIII
10. XLVII
11. XXXVI
12. XIX

Write each number in Roman numerals.

13. 26
14. 37
15. 15
16. 7
17. 42
18. 9
19. 18
20. 49
21. 25
22. 17

Use Roman numerals to complete the clock face.

23.

Write the number each Roman numeral stands for.

24.

MDCCIV

25.

XXIV

26.

MCMLX

27.

THE END
©MCMLXXIX

ADDITION AND SUBTRACTION

Art

Buying Art Supplies This year Matt plans to take oil painting lessons after school. He has been saving some of his allowance in order to buy art supplies. So far he has saved $14.50.

His art teacher sent Matt a list of supplies he would need to start the class. So Matt stopped by the art supply store to check on the prices of the items on his list.

Look at the price list. What is the total cost of these supplies? Which items can Matt afford to buy? How much more money will he need to save, to buy the rest of his supplies? Compare answers with your classmates.

1 large Canvas	$2.75
2 small canvases	3.50
1 large brush	3.50
1 medium brush	4.00
2 small brushes	3.75
1 table easel	1.00
thinner	2.75
TOTAL	?

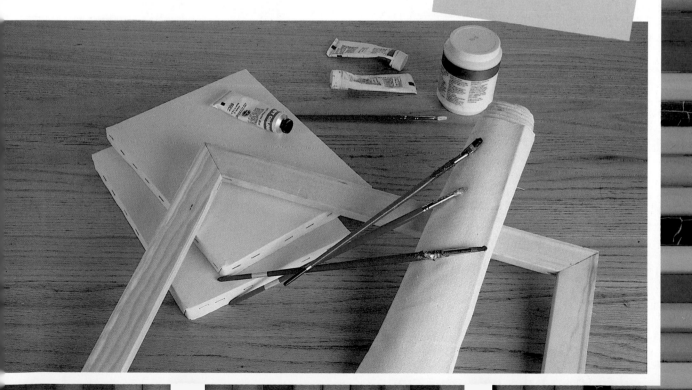

PROPERTIES AND RULES

Properties of addition and rules for subtraction
can help you find sums and differences.

Addition Properties	Subtraction Rules
Order Property: When the order of two addends is changed, the sum stays the same. Example 1: $4 + 1 = 1 + 4$ Example 2: $62 + 34 = 34 + 62$	Subtracting zero from a number equals that number. Example 1: $3 - 0 = 3$ Example 2: $42 - 0 = 42$
Zero Property: The sum of zero and one other addend is the other addend. Example 1: $9 + 0 = 9$ Example 2: $0 + 25 = 25$	Subtracting a number from itself equals zero. Example 1: $8 - 8 = 0$ Example 2: $51 - 51 = 0$

Grouping Property: When the
grouping of addends is changed,
the sum stays the same.

Example 1:
$$(23 + 31) + 5 = 23 + (31 + 5)$$
$$54 + 5 = 23 + 36$$
$$59 = 59$$

Think
• Is there an order property for subtraction?

GUIDED PRACTICE

Copy and complete. Use the properties and rules.

1. $458 - \blacksquare = 0$
2. $72 - \blacksquare = 72$
3. $632 + 0 = \blacksquare$
4. $682 + 158 = 158 + \blacksquare$
5. $(21 + \blacksquare) + 16 = 21 + (14 + 16)$
6. $6 + 0 + 6 = (\blacksquare + 6) + 0$
7. $4 + 5 + 6 + 5 = (4 + 6) + (5 + \blacksquare)$

Critical Thinking 8. How do the addition properties and
subtraction rules help you compute?

42

Copy and complete. Use the properties and rules.

9. $7 + 3 = 3 + \blacksquare$

10. $19 - \blacksquare = 19$

11. $\blacksquare + 0 = 161$

12. $715 - 715 = \blacksquare$

13. $(5 + 5) + 3 = 5 + (\blacksquare + 3)$

Write the answer.

14. $5 + 3 + 7 + 5$

15. $9 + 9 + 0 + 2$

16. $7 + 6 + 7 + 6$

17. $4 + 1 + 6 + 9$

18. $29 - 0$

19. $2 + 0 + 8 + 5$

Match the exercises that have the same answer.

20. $68,430 + 42,637$

21. $(12 + 34) + 86$

22. $10 - 10$

23. $12 + 0 + 164$

24. $378 + 0$

25. $5 + 2 + 8 + 2$

a. $(5 + 8) + 4$

b. $0 + 378$

c. $42,637 + 68,430$

d. $12 + (86 + 34)$

e. $84 - 84$

f. $164 + 12$

Problem Solving

26. How much will 2 sport jerseys cost?

27. Carl bought 3 things for exactly $25. What did he buy?

28. Jerrod buys a sport jersey and a pair of shin guards. If he pays with a twenty-dollar bill, how much change will he get?

— SALE —
BUY **1** SPORT JERSEY AND GET **$5** OFF A SECOND JERSEY.

$12

22

$9

$8 — A PAIR

CHALLENGE • Patterns

Continue each pattern.

1. △ □ ○ ○ □ △ □ ○ ○ □ △ □ ○ ○ □ △ _ _ _ _

2. $1, 2, 4, 5, 7, 8, 10, \_\, , \_\, , \_\, , \_$

ADDITION AND SUBTRACTION

An important mental math strategy is to break up numbers into other numbers that are easier to work with.

▶ Add 37 to 8 mentally.

Break the 37 into 30 and 7.
Then, use the basic fact:
7 + 8 = 15

Break the 8 into 3 and 5.
Adding 3 to 37 gives you 40.
Then, add 5 more.

$$30 + 7 + 8 \qquad \text{OR} \qquad 37 + 3 + 5$$

$$30 + \underset{\diagdown\diagup}{15} = 45 \qquad\qquad \underset{\diagdown\diagup}{40} + 5 = 45$$

So, 37 + 8 = 45.

Think

• How would you mentally add 57 to 8? Explain.

▶ You can also break apart numbers to subtract mentally.

Subtract: 52 − 3

Break up 3 into 2 and 1.
First, subtract 2 to get down to 50.

52 − 2 = 50

Then, subtract 1 more.

50 − 1 = 49

So, 52 − 3 = 49.

Subtract: 35 − 7

Break up 7 into 5 and 2.
First, subtract 5 to get down to 30.

35 − 5 = 30

Then, subtract 2 more.

30 − 2 = 28

So, 35 − 7 = 28.

Think

• How would you mentally subtract 8 from 64? Explain.

GUIDED PRACTICE

Write the answer. Use mental math.

1. 38 + 4   2. 3 + 59   3. 67 + 7   4. 28 + 5

5. 22 − 3   6. 54 − 6   7. 85 − 7   8. 33 − 6

Critical Thinking 9. What is another way to solve exercise 1 using mental math?

INDEPENDENT PRACTICE

Write the answer. Use mental math.

10. 17 + 7   11. 55 + 6   12. 49 + 3   13. 23 + 5

14. 5 + 38   15. 61 + 9   16. 78 + 3   17. 27 + 4

18. 24 − 5   19. 48 − 7   20. 52 − 4   21. 36 − 6

22. 51 − 3   23. 55 − 8   24. 37 − 9   25. 87 − 5

26. 30 − 6   27. 21 − 5   28. 12 − 3   29. 25 − 7

PROJECT • Game

Play this game with a partner.

a. Copy the box and the triangle of numbers on a piece of paper.

b. Cross out a number in the triangle and subtract it from the last circled number. (Begin with 40.) Circle the difference in the row of numbers in the box.

c. Take turns with your partner. Player 2 repeats step *b*.

d. The first player to circle the difference of 10, wins the game. (If you are unable to reach 10 exactly, the next-to-last player wins.)

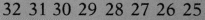

```
(40) 39 38 37 36 35 34 33
 32 31 30 29 28 27 26 25
 24 23 22 21 20 19 18 17
 16 15 14 13 12 11 10
```

```
        9
      1   3
    2   7   4
  5   6   10   8
```

USING 5, 50, AND 500

Tony wants to know how much it will cost to buy an apple and a package of peanuts. He does not have paper and pencil with him to do the addition. So, Tony uses mental math to add 25¢ + 45¢.

Tony breaks apart both numbers so he can use the fact that 5¢ + 5¢ = 10¢.

20¢ + 5¢ + 40¢ + 5¢

5¢ and 5¢ equals 10¢
20¢ + 40¢ = 60¢
10¢ + 60¢ = 70¢

So, an apple and a bag of peanuts cost 70¢.

Think

• How can you mentally find the double of 35? (That is 35 + 35.) Explain.

▶ You can also break apart numbers to make use of the facts:
50 + 50 = 100 and 500 + 500 = 1000.

Add: 3500 + 2500

3000 + 500 + 2000 + 500

5000 + 1000 = 6000

So, 3500 + 2500 = 6000.

Add: 4050 + 2050

4000 + 50 + 2000 + 50

6000 + 100 = 6100

So, 4050 + 2050 = 6100.

GUIDED PRACTICE

Write the sum. Use mental math.

1. 55 + 15
2. 75 + 45
3. 250 + 350
4. 600 + 650
5. 305 + 405
6. 825 + 105
7. 1500 + 3500
8. 1050 + 6050
9. 25 + 45 + 25

Critical Thinking 10. Show two ways to solve exercise 9.

....

INDEPENDENT PRACTICE

Write the sum. Use mental math.

11. 35 + 25
12. 65 + 15
13. 75 + 75
14. 250 + 450
15. 600 + 350
16. 605 + 205
17. 425 + 305
18. 2500 + 2500
19. 6500 + 1500
20. 4050 + 2050
21. 6000 + 5500
22. 850 + 850
23. 25 + 15 + 35
24. 60 + 45 + 25
25. 75 + 20 + 35

26. List each pair of numbers in the box with a sum of 100.

60	35	85	70	65
55	40	15	30	45

27. List each pair of numbers in the box with a sum of 1000.

450	800	650	250	295
750	200	350	705	550

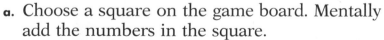

PROJECT • Game

Play this game with a partner. Each player needs five counters.

a. Choose a square on the game board. Mentally add the numbers in the square.
b. Your partner decides if your answer is correct or not. If the answer is correct, put one of the counters on the square.
c. Take turns with your partner. Player 2 repeats steps *a* and *b*.
d. The player with three counters in a line in any direction wins the game.

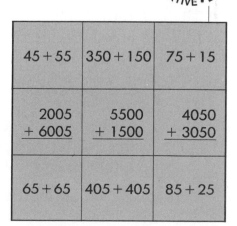

45 + 55	350 + 150	75 + 15
2005 + 6005	5500 + 1500	4050 + 3050
65 + 65	405 + 405	85 + 25

MAKE A DIAGRAM

Making a diagram can often help you solve a problem. I remember the time a diagram helped me plan a fence around a swimming pool . . .

MY PROBLEM

The pool was a square, 20 feet long and 20 feet wide. I wanted to build a fence around the pool 10 feet from the edge. I needed to know how much fencing to buy.

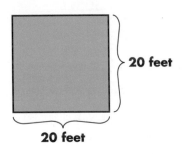

20 feet

20 feet

MY SOLUTION

I made a *diagram*. First I drew a square for the pool.

Then I drew the fence. I labeled the diagram to show that the fence would be 10 feet from the pool.

The diagram helped me see how to find the length of one side of the fence. Length of one side: 10 + 20 + 10 = 40 feet.

The diagram also helped me see that all 4 sides of the fence would be the same length. Now I could find the total amount of fencing.

Can you figure out how much fencing I needed?

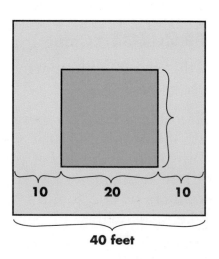

10   20   10

40 feet

GUIDED PRACTICE

Read the problem. Copy and finish the diagram to help you solve.

1. Mary made 3 model boats. It took her 2 hours to make each boat. She started at 9 A.M. At what time did Mary finish all 3 boats if she worked without stopping?

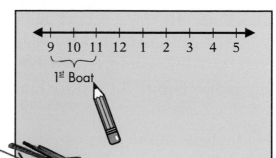

APPLICATION

Work with a small group to solve each problem. Make a diagram when it helps.

2. There are 4 square tables, each 6 feet long. Dawn plans to put them in a row with 2 feet of space between each table. How long will the row be?

3. Ms. DeBold plans to build a fence all around her pool. The pool is a rectangle 30 feet long and 20 feet wide. The fence will be 15 feet from the pool. How many feet of fencing does Ms. DeBold need?

4. Dave walks 4 blocks from home. He turns left and walks 3 blocks. He turns left again and walks 2 blocks. How many blocks is the shortest way home?

5. Connie's work crew has to paint a line down the middle of a straight road. The road connects the towns of Dayton, Antly, and Cerritos. How many miles of road must be painted?

Distances

Dayton to Antly—3 miles
Antly to Cerritos—7 miles
Cerritos to Dayton—4 miles

49

ESTIMATING SUMS

Sail-Away Tours is offering a cruise. If altogether the travel agents sell at least 800 tickets, then they get to go along. Have they sold 800 tickets yet?

Travel Agent	Number of Tickets Sold
Rick	247
Suzanne	168
Juan	125
Rolando	373

You can use **front-end estimation** to get a rough estimate.

Add the digits in the greatest place.

$$
\begin{array}{rll}
247 & \longrightarrow & 2 \text{ hundred} \\
168 & \longrightarrow & 1 \text{ hundred} \\
125 & \longrightarrow & 1 \text{ hundred} \\
+\,373 & \longrightarrow & +\,3 \text{ hundred} \\
\hline
& & 7 \text{ hundred}
\end{array}
$$

Rough estimate: 700

Think

- Is the exact sum greater than or less than 700? How can you tell?

To see if at least 800 tickets have been sold, you need to adjust your rough estimate. Look for groups of about 100 in the other digits.

$$
\left.\begin{array}{r} 2\ 47 \\ 1\ 68 \end{array}\right\} \text{ about 100}
$$

4 tens + 6 tens = 10 tens, or 100
So, 47 + 68 is about 100.

$$
\left.\begin{array}{r} 1\ 25 \\ +\ 3\ 73 \end{array}\right\} \text{ about 100}
$$

25 + 73 is about 100.

Rough estimate: 700   **Adjusted estimate:** 700 + 100 + 100 = 900

Because 900 > 800, at least 800 tickets have been sold.

Other Example

$$
\begin{array}{rll}
6486 & \longrightarrow & 6 \text{ thousand} \\
+\,2550 & \longrightarrow & +\,2 \text{ thousand} \\
\hline
& & 8 \text{ thousand}
\end{array}
$$

$$
\left.\begin{array}{r} 6486 \\ +\,2550 \end{array}\right\} \text{ about 1000}
$$

Rough estimate: 8000   Adjusted estimate: 8000 + 1000 = 9000

1. List three number pairs in the box with sums of about 100.

2. List three number pairs in the box with sums of about 1000.

34		17	
	56		52
95		78	

219		485	
	847		530
158		853	

Critical Thinking

3. Explain your method for finding the pairs in exercise 1.

INDEPENDENT PRACTICE

Make a front-end estimate. Then adjust. Write your adjusted estimate.

4. 634
   + 178

5. 3529
   + 4486

6. 2846
   + 2159

7. 1618
    3335
  + 2547

8. 292
    126
    211
  + 281

9. 2487 + 3521

10. 6528 + 2339

11. 532 + 179 + 220

12. 3428 + 1526 + 1537

13. 145 + 121 + 261 + 195

14. 1462 + 2039

15. 2673 + 4970

16. 320 + 410 + 153

Problem Solving Estimate to solve each problem.

The chart on the right shows how many pounds of fruit the ship's chef ordered for the meals on the cruise.

17. Did the chef order at least 400 pounds of pineapples and strawberries?

18. Did the chef order at least 1000 pounds of fruit?

19. Which did the chef order more of— melons or strawberries and pineapples together?

20. The chef ordered about 800 pounds of two types of fruit. Which types did he order?

Type of Fruit	Number of Pounds
Pineapples	365
Strawberries	147
Oranges	125
Melons	482

ADDING 2- AND 3-DIGIT NUMBERS

Jim Cody has 278 bales of hay in one barn and 139 bales in another. Altogether, how many bales of hay does Jim have?

Think

- What numbers can you use to estimate how many bales of hay Jim has?

- What does your estimate tell you about your exact answer?

Add 139 to 278 to find how many bales Jim has.

Line up the places. You can write:

$$278$$
$$+ 139$$

- **Add the ones. Regroup?**

$$\begin{array}{r} 1 \\ 278 \\ + 139 \\ \hline 7 \end{array}$$

- **Add the tens. Regroup?**

$$\begin{array}{r} 1\,1 \\ 278 \\ + 139 \\ \hline 17 \end{array}$$

- **Add the hundreds. Regroup?**

$$\begin{array}{r} 1\,1 \\ 278 \\ + 139 \\ \hline 417 \end{array}$$

Jim has 417 bales of hay.

Other Examples

$$\begin{array}{r} 1 \\ \$1.63 \\ + 0.75 \\ \hline \$2.38 \end{array} \qquad \begin{array}{r} 1 \\ 408 \\ + 77 \\ \hline 485 \end{array} \qquad \begin{array}{r} 1 \\ 88 \\ + 76 \\ \hline 164 \end{array} \qquad \begin{array}{r} 135 \\ + 63 \\ \hline 198 \end{array}$$

GUIDED PRACTICE

Write the sum.

1. 38 ft + 73 ft

2. 681 + 19

3. $3.75 + $2.16

Critical Thinking

4. When you add two numbers, what is the greatest number of ones you can have before regrouping? Explain your answer.

Write the sum.

5. 93
   + 69

6. 47
   + 84

7. 250
   + 250

8. 623
   + 293

9. 238
   + 709

10. $2.85
    + .75

11. 309 mi
    + 15 mi

12. 455
    + 66

13. 850
    + 100

14. 980
    + 980

15. 725 + 25

16. 324 + 324

17. 183 + 17

Problem Solving Estimate to solve when you can.

Field A
238 sheep

Field B
344 sheep

Field C
396 sheep

Field D
158 sheep

18. Which two fields have a total of 740 sheep?

19. Which two fields have a difference of 80 sheep?

20. In which two fields is the total number of sheep equal to that of a third field?

21. Name two fields together that have more than 600 sheep. How do you know?

22. Five workers can shear 700 sheep in three days. Can they shear all the sheep in fields A, B, and C in three days?

23. Are there more than or fewer than 1000 sheep in all the fields?

MATH LOG

When would you estimate to solve a problem? When would you need to find an exact answer?

THREE OR MORE ADDENDS

Sally works at Cycle World. If her total sales are more than $1100 in one month, she will receive a bonus. Will Sally receive a bonus this month?

Think

• Which numbers would you use to estimate the sum?

• Is an estimate enough to solve the problem? Why or why not?

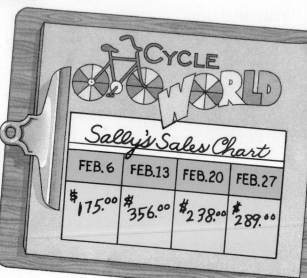

Sally's Sales Chart

FEB. 6	FEB. 13	FEB. 20	FEB. 27
$175.00	$356.00	$238.00	$289.00

You can add $189 to $238 to $356 to $275, to find Sally's total sales for the month.

● Add the ones. Regroup?

$$
\begin{array}{r}
2 \\
\$175 \\
356 \\
238 \\
+ \ 289 \\
\hline
8
\end{array}
$$

● Add the tens. Regroup?

$$
\begin{array}{r}
2\,2 \\
\$175 \\
356 \\
238 \\
+ \ 289 \\
\hline
58
\end{array}
$$

● Add the hundreds. Regroup?

$$
\begin{array}{r}
2\,2 \\
\$175 \\
356 \\
238 \\
+ \ 289 \\
\hline
\$1058
\end{array}
$$

Sally's sales for the month totaled $1058. She will not receive a bonus this month.

GUIDED PRACTICE

The chart shows how many people signed up for the Bikers USA races.

1. How many people signed up for the 5-mile race?

2. How many people signed up for the 20-mile race?

 Critical Thinking 3. Write two different ways you can add to find the sums in exercises 1 and 2.

	AGE GROUPS			
RACE	UNDER 20	20–30	30–40	40+
5-mile	175	148	85	72
20-mile	63	52	47	40

Write the sum.

4.	5.	6.	7.	8.
12 ft	135	$14.50	1695	$14.60
23 ft	206	2.11	2056	12.85
+ 34 ft	+ 154	+ 0.15	191	1.92
			+ 74	+ 0.91

9. $0.21 + $0.11 + $0.35 + $0.32

10. 15 + 14 + 13 + 12 + 19

11. 2356 + 1568 + 3299 + 2671

12. $23.50 + $3.50 + $0.42

13. 658 + 76 + 10

14. 4550 + 196 + 584

Problem Solving Estimate when you can.

15. At Cycle World, Inez buys two reflectors and a horn. She has a ten-dollar bill and a five-dollar bill. Is that enough?

16. John spent $15 on a reflector, a mirror, and a bell. How much was the bell?

17. Karen buys a horn, a reflector, a bell, and a basket. Does she get a free cap?

18. Mr. Shaw wants to buy a helmet for $47.22, a bike rack for $34.78, and a tool kit for $26.25. Will this be more than or less than $100? How did you decide?

CYCLE WORLD
·S·A·L·E·
BIKE EXTRAS FOR LESS

HORNS $9.50   REFLECTORS $1.75
MIRRORS $8.25   BASKETS $10.95

ALSO REDUCED !!!
BELLS, HELMETS, SEATS AND MORE!
SPEND $20.00 AND GET A FREE BICYCLE CAP

Maintain • Place Value

What is the value of the underlined digit?

1. 1<u>2</u>7

2. <u>7</u>92

3. <u>4</u>739

4. 545<u>8</u>

5. 3<u>2</u>,624

6. 1<u>6</u>,348

7. <u>3</u>28,136

8. 971,2<u>9</u>3

ESTIMATING SUMS BY ROUNDING

You have already learned to estimate using front-end estimation. Another way to estimate sums is by rounding. Both methods are useful.

Estimate: 396 + 268 + 524

Round each number to the greatest place. Then add.

$$
\begin{array}{rcr}
396 & \longrightarrow & 400 \\
268 & \longrightarrow & 300 \\
+\,524 & \longrightarrow & +\,500 \\
\hline
& & 1200
\end{array}
$$

Think

- How is a front-end estimate different from a rounded estimate?

Other Examples

$$
\begin{array}{rcr}
\$0.79 & \longrightarrow & \$0.80 \\
0.16 & \longrightarrow & 0.20 \\
+\,0.62 & \longrightarrow & +\,0.60 \\
\hline
& & \$1.60
\end{array}
$$

$$\$2.97 + \$3.29$$
$$\downarrow \qquad \downarrow$$
$$\$3.00 + \$3.00 = \$6.00$$

INDEPENDENT PRACTICE

Estimate by rounding to the greatest place.

1. 187 + 231
2. 3986 + 2827
3. $0.29 + $0.43
4. $3.28 + $2.95
5. $1.87 + $1.32 + $4.16
6. 1782 + 2511 + 1302

Estimate by making a front-end estimate or by rounding.

7. 524 + 388
8. $0.23 + $0.81 + $0.97
9. 409 + 263 + 142 + 185

Problem Solving Estimate to solve each problem.

10. It costs $5.00 for a ticket to the school fair. Lee has $2.42 that she earned, $1.29 saved, and $2.78 from her allowance. Can she buy a ticket?

11. The fair will display 1000 origami birds. So far, Sue has made 148 birds, Ali has made 412, and Lin has made almost 300. Are more birds needed?

More Practice Set 2.8, p. 426

SECTION REVIEW

for pages 42–56

Write the answer.

1. 702 + 93

2. 644 − 644

3. 445 + 500

4. 75 + 0

5. 769 + 901

6. 179 − 179

7. 87 + 92 = ■ + 87

8. (19 + 12) + 17 = 19 + (■ + 17)

Write the letter of the correct answer.

9. 457 + 288
   a. 635
   b. 6316
   c. 745
   d. 735

10. 577 + 346
    a. 913
    b. 8114
    c. 813
    d. 923

11. 5451 + 5498
    a. 11,849
    b. 10,949
    c. 1949
    d. 11,049

12. 581 + 7179
    a. 7760
    b. 8660
    c. 776
    d. 8760

13. 8176 + 2363
    a. 11,439
    b. 1539
    c. 11,539
    d. 10,539

14. 7234 + 2968
    a. 1202
    b. 12,192
    c. 10,202
    d. 11,202

15. 6709 + 7314
    a. 14,023
    b. 15,013
    c. 1423
    d. 14,123

16. 8845 + 1374
    a. 10,219
    b. 11,119
    c. 9119
    d. 91,210

17. 835 + 787 + 890
    a. 2215
    b. 2512
    c. 2302
    d. 2502

Solve.

18. Which three items can you buy
    for exactly $52?

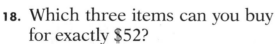

$22.00 $10.00 $32.00 $20.00

ESTIMATING DIFFERENCES

▶ Harry and Hannah are two hippos at
the zoo. Harry weighs 5480 pounds.
Hannah weighs 3975 pounds.
Estimate the difference
between their weights.

You could make a *front-end*
estimate.

**Subtract the digits in
the greatest place.**

$$
\begin{array}{r}
5480 \text{ lb} \longrightarrow 5000 \text{ lb} \\
- 3975 \text{ lb} \longrightarrow -3000 \text{ lb} \\
\hline
2000 \text{ lb}
\end{array}
$$

You could use *rounding* instead.

**Round each number to the greatest
place. Then subtract.**

$$
\begin{array}{r}
5480 \text{ lb} \longrightarrow 5000 \text{ lb} \\
- 3975 \text{ lb} \longrightarrow -4000 \text{ lb} \\
\hline
1000 \text{ lb}
\end{array}
$$

Both 2000 pounds and 1000 pounds are
reasonable estimates.

▶ Estimate the difference between 5463 pounds
and 5128 pounds.

● Your front-end estimate will be zero.
Your rounded estimate will also be zero.

$$
\begin{array}{r}
5463 \text{ lb} \longrightarrow 5000 \text{ lb} \\
- 5128 \text{ lb} \longrightarrow -5000 \text{ lb} \\
\hline
0 \text{ lb}
\end{array}
$$

● You know the difference is greater than
zero. Subtracting in the next greatest
place will give you a more reasonable
estimate.

$$
\begin{array}{r}
5463 \text{ lb} \longrightarrow 5400 \text{ lb} \\
- 5128 \text{ lb} \longrightarrow -5100 \text{ lb} \\
\hline
\text{Estimate:} \qquad 300 \text{ lb}
\end{array}
$$

A reasonable estimate is 300 pounds.

Think
● Is the actual difference greater
than or less than 300 pounds?
How do you know?

GUIDED PRACTICE

Estimate. Use the method you like best.

1. 927
    − 543

2. 6899
    − 2463

3. $7.22
    − 2.78

4. 746
    − 718

5. 6743 − 6489   6. 847 − 691   7. $32.48 − $22.96

8. Explain how you estimated the difference in exercise 5.

INDEPENDENT PRACTICE

Estimate. Use the method you like best.

9. 3884
    − 3295

10. 94,378
     − 52,481

11. 5432
     − 2876

12. 8643
     − 7348

13. $12.41
     − 10.82

14. 26,834
     − 21,432

15. 987 − 619   16. 6226 − 1523   17. $6.95 − $4.27

18. 2928 − 2021   19. 625 − 415   20. $8.75 − $2.95

Problem Solving

Estimate to solve each problem.

21. About how much more does the bear weigh than the tiger?

22. Which animal weighs about 400 pounds more than the ostrich?

23. Which two animals have a difference of about 700 pounds?

24. Does the horse weigh at least 500 pounds more than the tiger?

Animal	Weight
Polar Bear	732 pounds
Horse	968 pounds
Tiger	415 pounds
Ostrich	287 pounds

More Practice Set 2.9, p. 426

SUBTRACTING GREATER NUMBERS

Tony takes a 353-mile train ride from Baytown to Sunville. The train stops in Port Johnson, 178 miles from Baytown. How much farther must he travel to reach Sunville?

• When Tony stops in Port Johnson, is he about halfway between Baytown and Sunville? Explain.

You can subtract 178 miles from 353 miles.

First, write: 353 mi
             − 178 mi

• Are there enough ones? Regroup? Subtract the ones.	• Enough tens? Regroup? Subtract the tens.	• Subtract the hundreds.
$\begin{array}{r} {}^{4}\ {}^{13} \\ 3\ \cancel{5}\ \cancel{3}\ \text{mi} \\ -\ 1\ 7\ 8\ \text{mi} \\ \hline 5 \end{array}$	$\begin{array}{r} {}^{2}\ {}^{14}\ {}^{13} \\ \cancel{3}\ \cancel{5}\ \cancel{3}\ \text{mi} \\ -\ 1\ 7\ 8\ \text{mi} \\ \hline 7\ 5 \end{array}$	$\begin{array}{r} {}^{2}\ {}^{14}\ {}^{13} \\ \cancel{3}\ \cancel{5}\ \cancel{3}\ \text{mi} \\ -\ 1\ 7\ 8\ \text{mi} \\ \hline 1\ 7\ 5\ \text{mi} \end{array}$

Check by adding.
$\begin{array}{r} 175 \\ +\ 178 \\ \hline 353 \end{array}$

Tony must travel 175 miles farther.

Other Examples

$\begin{array}{r} {}^{2}\ {}^{14} \\ \cancel{3}\ \cancel{4} \\ -\ 1\ 7 \\ \hline 1\ 7 \end{array}$
$\begin{array}{r} \quad{}^{8}\ {}^{15} \\ 6\ 8\ \cancel{9}\ \cancel{5} \\ -\quad 1\ 6\ 7 \\ \hline 6\ 7\ 2\ 8 \end{array}$
$\begin{array}{r} 893\ \text{ft} \\ -\ 412\ \text{ft} \\ \hline 481\ \text{ft} \end{array}$
$\begin{array}{r} {}^{4}\ {}^{11}\ \ {}^{13} \\ \$\ \cancel{5}\ \cancel{2}\ .\ \cancel{3}\ 7 \\ -\quad 1\ 8\ .\ 5\ 6 \\ \hline \$\ 3\ 3\ .\ 8\ 1 \end{array}$

GUIDED PRACTICE

Write the difference.

1. 69	2. 88	3. 774	4. 532	5. 332
− 58	− 39	− 17	− 166	− 148

60

Estimate to solve. Write > or <.

6. 268 − 168 ● 200   **7.** 100 ● 428 − 150   **8.** 7452 − 2549 ● 5000

9. How did you decide which symbol to use?

INDEPENDENT PRACTICE

Write the difference.

10.	53 ft	**11.**	$5.96	**12.**	621	**13.**	496 mi	**14.**	$3.32
	− 41 ft		− 1.98		− 11		− 255 mi		− 0.67

15.	$0.98	**16.**	473	**17.**	1596	**18.**	$16.53	**19.**	2332
	− 0.98		− 92		− 898		− 4.69		− 79

Estimate to solve. Write > or <.

20. 95 − 49 ● 20   **21.** 876 − 491 ● 600   **22.** 3000 ● 4321 − 2856

Problem Solving

23. Tony has $43.27 in all. His train ticket home costs $11.75. What is the greatest amount he can spend and still pay for his train ticket?

24. Tony and his grandparents arrive at the zoo at 2:00 P.M. The sign shows the ticket prices. Tony has $6.00. Does he have enough money to buy two adult tickets and one child's ticket?

25. Tony is amazed by the size of the grizzly bear. Tony weighs 84 pounds. The bear weighs 853 pounds. How much heavier than Tony is the bear?

SUNVILLE ZOO TICKETS

Adult $2.50
Child $1.75

After 1:00 P.M., the price for each ticket is $0.50 less.

CHALLENGE • Number Sense

Use the numbers in the box to fill in the circles. The sum on each side of the triangle equals 38.

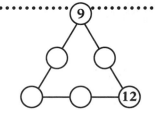

17	12	12
15	14	9

PROBLEM SOLVING
USING MATH SENSE

"I can reach 6 feet high."

"This bean bag is 2 feet high. If I stand on it, I can reach 8 feet, because 6 feet + 2 feet = 8 feet."

"That does not make sense. The bean bag does not stay 2 feet high when you stand on it!"

Think
- Why does it not make sense to add 6 feet and 2 feet?

Read each story. Does the underlined sentence make sense? Tell why or why not.

1. José finished his chores at 3 P.M. Teri worked 2 hours longer than José did. So, Teri finished in 5 hours.

2. Jessica is 3 years older than Karen. So, in 2 years Jessica will be 5 years older than Karen.

3. John turned on his calculator. He wanted to enter 8, but pressed 6 by mistake. He said, "Since I have entered 6 already, I'll just press 2 to get 8."

4. The button for Channel 11 on Misha's television is not working. He says, "I'll just press the buttons for Channel 7 and Channel 4."

5. Tanya has three more pencils than Mark. "I will give Mark 3 of my pencils," says Tanya. "Then we will have the same amount."

6. George lives at 25 Elm Street. Gina lives at 85 Elm Street. The address of their school is 215 Elm Street. So, Gina lives closer to the school.

7. "When I stand on a scale with one leg in the air, I weigh 80 pounds," says Andy. "If I have both legs on the scale, then I will weigh 160 pounds."

8. Judy weighs 50 pounds and Linda weighs 60 pounds. If they stand on a scale together, the scale will show 110 pounds.

9. Pete says, "If I add to something, it gets bigger." His friend says, "OK, let us add some dirt to this hole and watch it get bigger."

10. Make up your own story. Ask a friend if it makes sense.

ZEROS IN SUBTRACTION

One hundred years ago, the people of Millburn planted a Douglas fir tree. It is now 153 feet tall. The tallest fir tree is 302 feet tall. What is the difference in height between the Douglas fir and the tallest fir tree?

You can subtract 153 feet from 302 feet.

● Enough ones? No; regroup. No tens; regroup hundreds.	● Regroup tens.	● Subtract.	
2 10 3̸ Ø 2̸ ft − 1 5 3 ft	9 2 1̸0̸ 12 3̸ Ø 2̸ ft − 1 5 3 ft	9 2 1̸0̸ 12 3̸ Ø 2̸ ft − 1 5 3 ft 1 4 9 ft	**Check by adding.** 149 + 153 302

The tallest fir tree is 149 feet taller than the Douglas fir.

Think

• Why must you regroup twice in the tens place?

Other Examples

| 9
5 1̸0̸ 10
6̸ Ø Ø m
−   2 3 m
5 7 7 m | 2 10 5 10
3̸ Ø 6̸ Ø
−   7 1 6
2 3 4 4 | 7   10
$ 8̸ . Ø 6
−   6 . 5 1
$ 1 . 5 5 | 9   9
2 1̸0̸   1̸0̸ 12
$ 3̸ Ø . Ø 2̸
−   1 6 . 6 8
$ 1 3 . 3 4 |

GUIDED PRACTICE

Write the difference.

1.   300 mi
    − 146 mi

2.   6004
    − 689

3.   5007
    − 3846

4.   9060
    − 8573

5. $4.01
    − 2.46

Critical Thinking 6. How can you check the answer to exercise 4?

INDEPENDENT PRACTICE

Write the difference.

7.   907
  − 532
	8. 470
	  − 45
		9. $9.07
		  − 1.29
			10. 206
			  − 89
				11. $3.87
				  − 0.96

12.   26,004
  − 14,832
	13. 5089
	  − 498
		14. $56.24
		  − 9.54
			15. 301
			  − 67	

16. 4702 − 1792

17. $14.06 − $0.90

18. 600 − 478

19. 698 − 403

20. 5691 − 3218

21. 7010 − 4121

Problem Solving Data Book Go to the Almanac section on page 465. Use the chart on trees to answer each question.

22. How much taller is the white oak than the mountain ash?

23. Are more of the trees shorter than or taller than 150 feet?

24. The height of the Chrysler Building in New York City is 1046 feet. How much taller is it than the tallest tree on the chart?

25. Do all beech trees grow to be exactly 124 feet tall? Explain.

26. Write your own problem about the data from the chart. Give it to a friend to solve.

Maintain • **Comparing Numbers**

Copy and complete. Write > or <.

1. 4583 ● 483

2. 7610 ● 7819

3. 8491 ● 8486

4. 63 ● 6218

USING ADDITION AND SUBTRACTION

Students at the Stratton School are collecting cans for their annual recycling drive. At the end of each week of the drive, the students record the number of cans they have collected. During week 2, they collected 1187 cans. How many more cans must they collect to tie last year's record?

Think

- Have the students collected more than half of last year's total? How can you tell?

One way to solve the problem is to add first and then subtract.

1025 first week	2911 total collected last year
+ 1187 second week	− 2212 cans collected so far
2212 cans collected so far	699 cans left to collect

The students need to collect 699 more cans to tie last year's record.

INDEPENDENT PRACTICE

Write the answer.

1. 42,341 mi
    + 24,457 mi

2. 94,025
    − 94,024

3. $333.47
    −   9.99

4. $625.95
    +   80.21

Problem Solving The chart shows the number of cans collected by each school in Lendon this year. Use this chart, the picture on page 66, and a calculator to solve each problem.

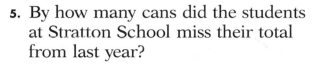

5. By how many cans did the students at Stratton School miss their total from last year?

6. How many more cans did Stratton School need to collect to reach a total of 3000 cans this year?

7. Did the five schools collect a total of more than 15,000 cans? How did you decide?

8. Which school's total is closest to 3000 cans?

9. Upton School had collected fewer than 2000 cans before the final week. Did Upton School collect more than a thousand cans in the final week? How did you decide?

10. Look at the newspaper headline. There are almost 10,000 households in Lendon. Which is greater, the number of households that took part in the Spring Drive or the number that did not take part?

RECYCLING DRIVE	
School	**Number of Cans**
Reed	3905
Stratton	2614
Tindall	2978
Upton	3246
Valley	3580

More Practice Set 2.13, p. 428

PROBLEM SOLVING
USING STRATEGIES

If you get stuck, remember....
Tips for Problem Solving
on pages 474–475

Captain Spear owns a very small island. He tells tourists that there is buried treasure on the island, but no one has found it yet.

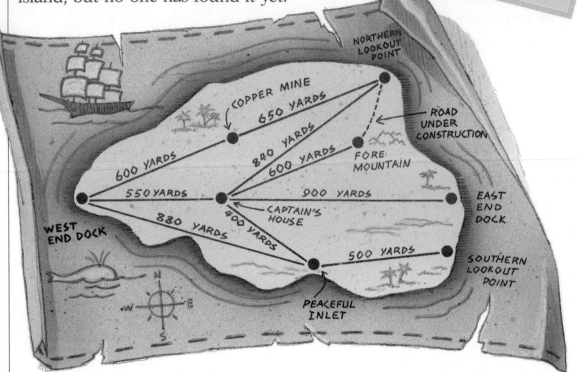

Use the map to solve each problem. Estimate when it helps.

1. You just landed at West End Dock and want to see the view from one of the lookout points. Which one is closer? How did you decide?

2. Which is the best estimate for the length of the road under construction?
   a. 150 yards   b. 300 yards   c. 900 yards

3. Find the treasure. Captain Spear says it is buried at one of the locations on the map. He says the shortest distance from Peaceful Inlet to the treasure is 1480 yards. If the Captain is right, where is the treasure buried?

SECTION REVIEW

for pages 58–68

Write the letter of the correct answer.

1. 4057 − 288
   a. 3822
   b. 4345
   c. 3769
   d. 4879

2. 500 − 346
   a. 154
   b. 846
   c. 54
   d. 254

3. 9501 − 5398
   a. 4013
   b. 4103
   c. 5297
   d. 4003

4. 6901 − 979
   a. 5922
   b. 5832
   c. 6078
   d. 5902

5. 8106 − 3263
   a. 3943
   b. 5163
   c. 4903
   d. 4843

6. 9034 − 2668
   a. 7638
   b. 11,702
   c. 6366
   d. 6066

7. 6713 − 2814
   a. 3899
   b. 9527
   c. 4909
   d. 3296

8. 7225 − 1687
   a. 5358
   b. 5538
   c. 5423
   d. 6648

9. 3459 − 608
   a. 4067
   b. 4051
   c. 2851
   d. 3067

10. The Taylor family drove 386 miles on Wednesday, 428 miles on Thursday, and 162 miles on Friday. They saw 87 signs for places to eat. How far did they drive on those three days?

11. Mr. Taylor spent $22.20 for gasoline on Wednesday. He spent $2.60 more than that on Thursday. How much did he spend on gas in those two days?

CHAPTER TEST

Write the answer.

1. 28 + 73

2. 642 + 58

3. 121 + 195 + 404 + 137

4. 1165 − 246

5. $35.76 − $9.57

6. 290 + 61 + 183

7. 2900 − 831

8. 46 + 55

9. 3042 − 447

10.
$1.67
+ 0.71

11.
8439
− 7893

12.
55
+ 15

13.
$17.60
− 10.89

14.
369
− 276

15.
4238
− 658

16.
3030
− 320

17.
708
− 54

Copy and complete. Use the properties and rules.

18. ■ + 0 = 258

19. 9 + 6 = 6 + ■

20. (3 + 7) + 4 = 3 + (■ + 4)

21. 12 − ■ = 12

22. ■ − 594 = 0

23. (44 + ■) + 8 = 44 + (31 + 8)

PROBLEM SOLVING

Solve each problem.

24. Last year, the owner of Black Cow Farms spent $4450 to purchase some milking cows. This year, the owner spent $1000 more than that. How much did the owner spend on cows in the two years?

25. In one season, one cow produces enough milk to make 1080 pounds of butter. Another cow produces enough milk to make 940 pounds of butter. How much butter can be made from the milk of the two cows in one season?

26. The largest cow on Black Cow Farms weighs 1660 pounds. The smallest cow weighs 1335 pounds. What is the difference in weight between the largest cow and the smallest cow?

27. In one year, two cows produced 12,000 gallons of milk each, while a third cow produced 13,300 gallons of milk. How many gallons of milk did the three cows produce that year?

CUMULATIVE REVIEW

Write the number in standard form.

1. 100,000 + 50,000 + 300 + 9

2. eight hundred nine thousand

3. 400,000 + 10,000 + 7000 + 50

4. six hundred thirty thousand, twenty

Write the value of the seven.

5. 2748

6. 472,605

7. 32,876

8. 789,654

9. 27,839

10. 72,841

Round to the nearest hundred.

11. 462

12. 924

13. 2370

14. 5088

Round to the nearest thousand.

15. 5725

16. 6198

17. 4681

18. 8709

Copy and complete. Use the properties and rules.

19. $17 + 54 = 54 + \blacksquare$

20. $72 - 0 = \blacksquare$

21. $0 + \blacksquare = 150$

22. $651 - 651 = \blacksquare$

23. $4020 - \blacksquare = 4020$

24. $(7 + 9) + 6 = 7 + (\blacksquare + 6)$

Write the sum.

25. 85 + 25

26. 350 + 250

27. 525 + 166

28. 435 + 36

29. 45 + 716

30. 678 + 291

Solve each problem.

31. Wilmington Middle School has 325 sixth graders, 350 seventh graders, and 375 eighth graders. How many students are enrolled in the middle school? Explain how you got your answer.

32. The electric bill for Wilmington Middle School was $2045 this year, $2207 last year, and $1934 two years ago. Is the bill for this year higher or lower than the bill two years ago? How do you know?

EXCURSION

CULTURAL DIVERSITY

CONSUMER MATH

Businesses and individual people use checking accounts to keep track of the money they spend. A check register like the one shown below is a record of money spent on goods and services. It is also a record of the balance or money left in the account.

You will need a calculator.

No.	Date	Description	Withdrawal (−) *Amount taken out*	Deposit (+) *Amount put in*	Balance *Amount in account at that time*
					$1730.80
510	Oct. 12	Espinola Electric Company	96.00		96.00
					1634.80
511	Oct. 13	Santa Clara Silver Company	285.20		285.20
	Oct. 14	Deposit		66.14	

To find the balance in the account after the deposit on October 14, follow these steps:

a. Look at the balance at the top of the right-hand column.
b. Use your calculator to subtract the amount of check number 510.

$$1730.80 - 96.00 = $$
1634.8

c. Now, subtract the amount of check number 511.

$$1634.80 - 285.20 = $$
1349.6

d. Notice that on October 14, a deposit of $66.14 was made. Add this deposit to the balance to find the new balance.

$$1349.60 + 66.14 = $$
1415.74

The new balance is $1,415.74.

Many Native American artists in the Southwest and in other parts of the United States sell their artwork. These artworks include pottery, baskets, and jewelry.

Suppose that the check register below is for the business of one of these artists. Use a calculator to solve each problem.

No.	Date	Description	Withdrawal (−)	Deposit (+)	Balance
					$9125.18
27	Dec. 9	Clarke Box Co.	1980.67		1980.67
					7144.51
28	Dec. 9	The Earring Tree	340.00		340.00
					6804.51
	Dec. 10	Deposit		3500.00	
29	Dec. 11	Postmaster	76.00		
30	Dec. 12	Sombrillo Art Supplies	25.75		
31	Dec. 12	Joe Montoya	495.93		

1. What is the beginning balance on December 9?

2. What is the balance at the end of the day on December 9?

3. What is the new balance after the deposit on December 10?

4. What is the new balance after check number 29?

5. What is the new balance after check number 30?

6. What is the new balance after check number 31?

7. The artist makes a deposit of $204.00 on December 13. What is the new balance?

8. How did you find the answer to exercise 7?

Statistics

Baseball Cards Collecting baseball cards is a popular hobby. The front of a card shows a player's picture. It also names the player's position and team. The back of the card has many facts. It lists all of the player's statistics. It may even name the player's hometown and date of birth.

If the player is a pitcher, the card lists wins and losses. For hitters, the cards list batting averages and the number of homeruns. Many numbers are printed on each card.

Pass around a stack of baseball cards. Everyone should choose one card. Ask each person to make up questions using information from the card. The questions do not have to be about baseball. You may think of history or geography questions. Try to stump each other with your questions.

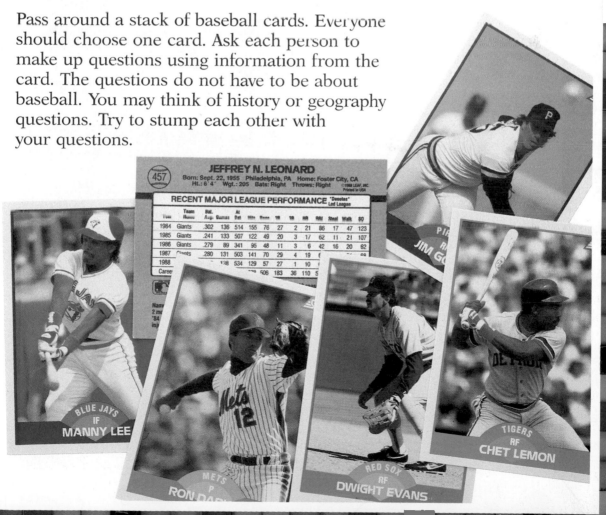

JEFFREY N. LEONARD
457 Born: Sept. 22, 1955 Philadelphia, PA Home: Foster City, CA
Ht.: 6' 4" Wgt.: 205 Bats: Right Throws: Right ©1988 LEAF, INC.
Printed in USA

RECENT MAJOR LEAGUE PERFORMANCE "Denotes" Led League

Year	Team Name	Bat. Avg.	Games	At Bat	Hits	Runs	2B	3B	HR	RBI	Steal	Walk	SO
1984	Giants	.302	136	514	155	76	27	2	21	86	17	47	123
1985	Giants	.241	133	507	122	49	20	3	17	62	11	21	107
1986	Giants	.279	89	341	95	48	11	3	6	42	16	20	62
1987	Giants	.280	131	503	141	70	29	4	19	6			
1988			138	534	129	57	27	1	10				
Caree				506	183	36	110	5					

BLUE JAYS
IF
MANNY LEE

METS
P
RON DARL

RED SOX
RF
DWIGHT EVANS

PIR
R
JIM GO

TIGERS
RF
CHET LEMON

COLLECTING AND RECORDING DATA

Diane needs to collect facts, or **data,** for a report about how long animals live. One way to collect data is to look in an encyclopedia or a book about the subject.

fox lives 7 years
elephant lives 40 years
tiger lives 16 years
guinea pig lives 4 years
chimpanzee lives 22 years

Diane makes a table to record the data she finds.

Title: tells what table is about

Heading: tells about each column

Data: the facts

LIFE SPANS OF ANIMALS

ANIMAL	LIFE SPAN
Guinea Pig	4 years
Fox	7 years
Tiger	16 years
Chimpanzee	22 years
Elephant	40 years

Think
- In what order is the data in Diane's table?

Another way to collect data is to take a **survey.** Glenn takes a survey of his classmates. He asks each student, "Of the following zoo animals, which is your favorite?" He makes a table like the one at the right to record each student's choice with one tally mark.

Think
- Why were tally marks useful for Glenn?

FAVORITE ZOO ANIMALS

ANIMAL	TALLY	TOTAL
Polar Bear	|||	3
Lion	||||| ||	7
Chimpanzee	||||| |||||		11
Kangaroo	||	2

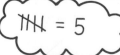

||||| = 5

GUIDED PRACTICE

1. Glenn surveyed the class about their pets.

Copy and complete the table using Glenn's data.

Data: Jean—dog, Erin—goldfish, Bill—cat, Hank—bird, Allen—cat, Phil—dog, Lin—cat, Barry—goldfish, Lita—cat, Curtis—dog

KINDS OF PETS STUDENTS OWN		
Pet	Tally	Total
Dog	///	3
	//	
	////	
	/	

2. What is the least popular pet among the students?

3. How many students own pets?

4. How many students own goldfish?

Critical Thinking **5.** Can you tell from this table how many students are in the class? Explain.

INDEPENDENT PRACTICE

Data Book Go to the Almanac section on page 465. Use the data there to make a table about how fast animals can run.

6. Which animals can run at the same speed?

7. What animal can run the fastest?

8. Which data below would you record in the table you made?
  a. A pig can live 10 years.
  b. A coyote can run 43 miles per hour.
  c. A chimpanzee can weigh 150 pounds.
  d. A wart hog can run 30 miles per hour.

CHALLENGE   Logical Reasoning

Critical Thinking Sam, Luiz, Tim, and Matt are the first four batters on the Redbirds baseball team. Luiz bats just before Sam. Tim bats just after Matt. Matt is not the first batter. In what order do the players come to bat?

ORGANIZING DATA IN A BAR GRAPH

BREAKFAST CHOICES OF FOURTH-GRADERS

Food	Tally	Total
Eggs	卌 卌 卌	15
Hot Cereal	卌 卌 卌 |||	18
Pancakes	卌 |||	8
Cold Cereal	卌 卌 卌 ||	17
Toast	卌 ||	7

Meg took a survey of 65 fourth-graders. She asked, "Of the five breakfast foods listed, which one do you have for breakfast most often?"

Meg wrote tally marks next to the list of five choices. The table at the left shows the results of her survey.

Then Meg showed the data in a bar graph. First, she titled the bar graph. Along the side of the graph are the number of students. Meg started her graph at zero and marked off by 5's to 20. Along the bottom of the graph are the names of each breakfast food.

When making the bar graph, Meg could have put the numbers along the bottom and listed the breakfast foods along the side.

Think

- Which makes it easier to see the results of the survey— the table or the graph? Why?

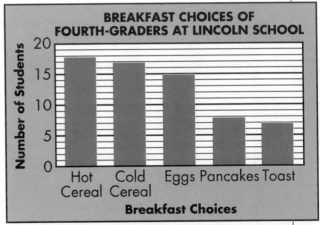

BREAKFAST CHOICES OF FOURTH-GRADERS AT LINCOLN SCHOOL

Number of Students / Breakfast Choices

BREAKFAST CHOICES OF FOURTH-GRADERS AT LINCOLN SCHOOL

Breakfast Choices / Number of Students

GUIDED PRACTICE

1. Use the data in the table. Copy and complete the bar graph below on squared paper.

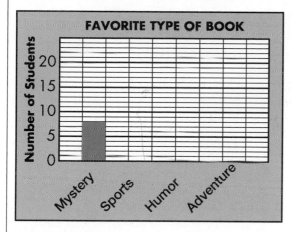

FAVORITE TYPE OF BOOK

Book Type	Tally	Total
Mystery	ЖЖ |||	8
Sports	ЖЖ ЖЖ ||||	14
Humor	ЖЖ ЖЖ		11
Adventure	ЖЖ ЖЖ ЖЖ ||	17

2. How many students voted in the survey?

3. Did more than half the students vote for sports and adventure books?

Critical Thinking 4. How did you find the number of students who voted in the survey?

INDEPENDENT PRACTICE

5. Use squared paper to make a bar graph of this chart.
   a. Give your graph a title.
   b. Label the bottom and side of the graph.
   c. Decide what numbers you will use to mark along the graph.

FOURTH-GRADE SURVEY		
Favorite Book	Tally	Total
Henry and Ribsy	ЖЖ ||	7
Harriet the Spy	ЖЖ	5
Bridge to Terabithia	ЖЖ ЖЖ ЖЖ		16
The BFG	|||	3
Charlotte's Web	ЖЖ ЖЖ	10
Freddy Plays Football	ЖЖ ||||	9

Problem Solving Use the chart or graph to answer each question.

6. How many votes did the most popular book get?

7. If each student voted only once, how many students were in the survey?

Critical Thinking 8. Did more than half the class vote for *Bridge to Terabithia*?

9. Write a word problem about your bar graph. Give it to a friend to solve.

More Practice Set 3.2, p. 429

MAKE A LIST

> Making a list can help you solve some problems. It helps even more if your list has a pattern. I remember when I made a list to help sell a model airplane kit.

MY PROBLEM

With this kit, people can make different model airplanes by using different bodies and wings. They can use a red, blue, or green body. They can use red, blue, yellow, or green wings. I needed to know how many different planes could be built.

MY SOLUTION

First, I listed the different planes that I could build with the red body. I used *R* for red, *B* for blue, and so on.

Then, I listed the planes I could build with the blue body.

Finally, I listed the planes I could build with the green body.

Do you see how I found out that 12 different planes could be built with the kit?

Can you see the pattern I used to make my list?

Body	Wings
R	R
R	B
R	Y
R	G
B	
B	R
B	B
B	Y
G	G
G	R
G	B

GUIDED PRACTICE

Read the problem. Copy and finish the list to help you.
Describe the pattern in the list.

1. Storytime is a computer game with 3 parts: Castles, Knights, and Beasts. You can play the 3 parts in any order. How many ways can you play the game?

APPLICATION

Work with a small group to solve each problem. Make a list when it helps.

2. Amy and her parents are driving from Bern to Wilton. What are all the different routes they can take that are less than 200 miles?

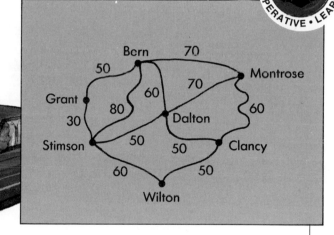

3. Tony has a dog named Spot. He notices that he can use the letters in SPOT to make the word *pots*. How many other ways can the letters be arranged? What are some of the words that can be made with those letters?

4. The members of the Treetop Club decide to make a color code for the alphabet. They will put the colors red, purple, yellow, and orange in different orders. Each order will stand for one letter. Are there enough possible orders for all 26 letters?

A: R   P   Y   O
B: R   P   O   Y
C:

PICTOGRAPHS

Sneakers for Less sells five different types of sneakers. This pictograph shows the number of sneakers sold in one week.

A **pictograph** is a graph that uses pictures to stand for data. Each picture stands for more than 1 item. The key tells you how many each picture stands for.

SNEAKERS SOLD IN ONE WEEK		
Basketball	👟👟👟👟👟👟👟👟👟👟 ◗	
Running	👟👟👟👟👟👟👟👟👟👟👟👟👟👟	
Tennis	👟👟👟👟👟👟👟👟👟👟 ◗	
Aerobic	👟👟👟👟👟👟👟👟👟👟	
Walking	👟👟👟👟👟👟👟👟👟👟	

Key: 👟 = 10 pairs of sneakers   ◗ = 5 pairs of sneakers

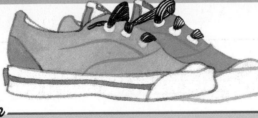 

 Think
- Why is it helpful to have pictures stand for more than 1 item?

Use the pictograph to decide how many pairs of tennis sneakers were sold in one week. Count by 10's and then by 5's to find the number of sneakers sold.

That week 105 pairs of tennis sneakers were sold.

 Think
- Could this graph show 107 pairs of sneakers exactly? Explain.

Use the pictograph on page 82 to solve each problem.

1. What two types of sneakers did the store sell the same amount of?

2. What type of sneakers did the store sell the least number of?

3. How many fewer pairs of basketball sneakers were sold than running sneakers?

4. **Critical Thinking** Were more than 500 pairs of sneakers sold in the week? How did you get your answer?

INDEPENDENT PRACTICE

Use the pictograph to solve each problem.

COMPACT DISCS SOLD AT MUSICLAND THE WEEK OF MARCH 8–MARCH 14
Monday ⊙ ⊙ ⊙ ⊙ ⊙ ⊙ ⊙ ◖
Tuesday ⊙ ⊙ ⊙ ⊙ ⊙ ⊙
Wednesday ⊙ ⊙ ⊙ ⊙ ⊙ ⊙ ⊙ ⊙ ◖
Thursday ⊙ ⊙ ⊙ ⊙ ⊙ ⊙ ⊙ ⊙ ⊙ ⊙
Friday ⊙ ⊙ ⊙ ⊙ ⊙ ◖
Saturday ⊙ ⊙ ⊙ ⊙ ⊙ ⊙ ⊙ ⊙ ⊙ ⊙ ⊙ ⊙ ◖
Sunday ⊙ ⊙ ⊙ ⊙ ⊙ ⊙ ⊙ ◖
Key: ⊙ = 100 CDs   ◖ = 50 CDs

5. How many compact discs were sold on Monday?

6. How many more compact discs were sold on Wednesday than on Tuesday?

7. Were more than 5000 compact discs sold during the week? How did you get your answer?

8. Write a summary of the data in two sentences. Include the data you think is important.

PROJECT • Statistics

Work with a small group to make a pictograph. Survey how many cars, trucks, and buses go by the main entrance of your school.

LINE GRAPHS

For a science project, Roland keeps this record of the temperature at 1:00 P.M. each day for two weeks in October.

To display his information, Roland decides to show his data on a **line graph.** A line graph shows the change over a period of time.

Temperature 1:00 P.M.	
Date	Degrees
Oct. 1	60
Oct. 2	62
Oct. 3	64
Oct. 4	61
Oct. 5	58
Oct. 6	79
Oct. 7	80
Oct. 8	80
Oct. 9	78
Oct. 10	70
Oct. 11	62
Oct. 12	60
Oct. 13	58
Oct. 14	59

OCTOBER 1:00 P.M. TEMPERATURES

Roland writes the number of degrees at the left of the graph. He writes the dates at the bottom of the graph. Each point on the graph stands for the temperature at 1:00 P.M. that day.

Think

- What does it mean when the line slopes downward?

- Why are the numbers between 0 and 50 not shown?

GUIDED PRACTICE

Copy and complete the line graph on page 84. Use the graph to answer each question.

1. How many degrees did the temperature rise from October 5 to October 6?

2. When was the temperature the highest?

3. How many times did the temperature go above 60 degrees?

4. Between what two dates did the greatest change in temperature occur?

Critical Thinking 5. Write a sentence about what the data on the graph tell you.

....

INDEPENDENT PRACTICE

Data Book Go to the Atlas section on page 467.

6. Use the data to make a line graph of the average monthly temperature in Fort Myers, Florida.

Use the chart or line graph to answer each question.

7. Between what two months is the greatest rise in temperature?

8. What month has the lowest temperature?

9. How many months was the average temperature in the 80's?

10. Write two sentences about the data.

Critical Thinking 11. Write your own question about the graph. Give it to a friend to solve.

....

Maintain • Mixed Practice

Write the answer.

1.	2.	3.	4.	5.
398 + 777	479 − 52	51 + 269	962 − 86	32,460 + 9,999

CIRCLE GRAPHS

The table below shows how the members of Tricia's class travel to school.

HOW STUDENTS IN OUR CLASS TRAVEL TO SCHOOL	
Way of Traveling	Number of Students
Bus	11
Car	6
Walk	4
Bicycle	3

You can show the same information in a **circle graph**.

HOW STUDENTS IN OUR CLASS TRAVEL TO SCHOOL

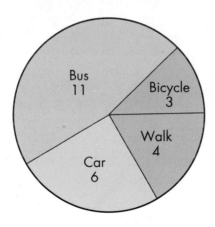

A circle graph shows the parts that make up the whole group.

- How many students are in the whole class? How do you know?

- Is the fraction of the class that travels by bus more than or less than half?

GUIDED PRACTICE

Use the circle graph on page 86 to answer
each question.

1. Do more students travel to
   school by car or by bicycle?

2. What fraction of the students
   come to school by car?

3. Is the fraction of students not
   taking the bus more than or less
   than half?

   Critical Thinking

4. Which would make it easier to
   answer exercise 3—the circle
   graph or the table?

....

INDEPENDENT PRACTICE

The circle graph shows the rubbish
the town of Lendon recycled last year.

RECYCLED RUBBISH

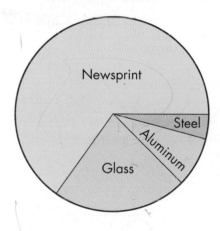

Use the circle graph to solve each problem.

5. Was more newsprint or glass
   collected? How can you tell?

6. Did glass make up more than or
   less than half of the rubbish?

7. Order from least to greatest the
   items recycled.

8. Can you tell how much rubbish
   was collected? Explain.

Critical Thinking

9. Write two sentences about the
   data on the circle graph.

 MATH LOG

What kinds of data can be shown on a circle graph?

USING DATA

The fourth grade is having a bake sale to raise money for a field trip. The top bar graph shows the results of last year's bake sale.

Students took surveys of family members. The bottom bar graph shows the results of the survey. The data will help to plan this year's bake sale.

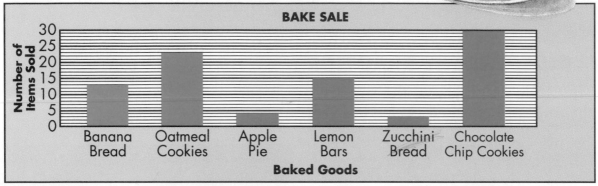

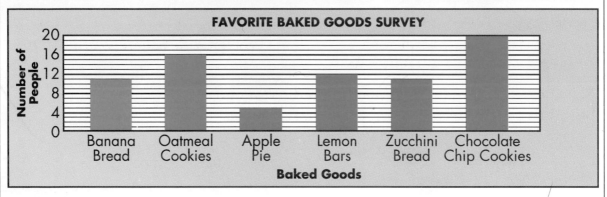

INDEPENDENT PRACTICE

Use the graphs above to answer each question.

1. Which item was most popular in the sale? Why do you think so?

2. Which items had sales of more than 15?

3. How are the graphs the same? How are they different?

4. How many people were in the survey this year?

Critical Thinking 5. Can you tell from last year's sales how many people bought baked goods? Explain.

Critical Thinking 6. Based on the data from the two graphs, is there any item you would not sell this year? Explain.

These line graphs show the average monthly temperatures in two cities.

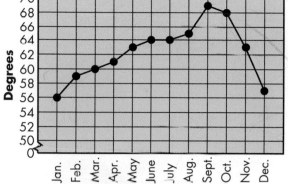

AVERAGE MONTHLY TEMPERATURES SAN FRANCISCO

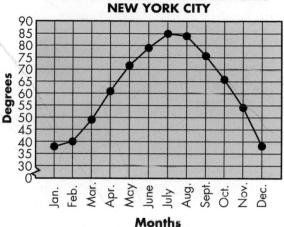

AVERAGE MONTHLY TEMPERATURES NEW YORK CITY

Critical Thinking

7. Can you tell from the graphs what the highest one-day temperature reading was in these cities? Explain.

8. How are the degree labels different in the graphs? Why is the difference important to notice?

9. How are the temperature patterns in the two graphs alike? How are they different?

10. How would these graphs help you plan a winter visit to these cities?

These circle graphs show the instruments played by students in two fourth-grade classes.

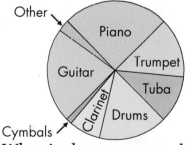

INSTRUMENTS PLAYED BY MRS. WHITE'S CLASS

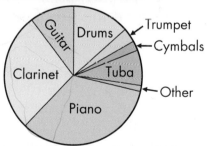

INSTRUMENTS PLAYED BY MR. ROMANO'S CLASS

11. What is the most popular instrument in both classes?

12. Can you tell from the graphs in which class more students play instruments? Explain.

13. About what fraction of the students play the two most popular instruments in Mrs. White's class?

14. Suppose there are 24 students in each class. Do more than 12 students play the piano in each class? How did you decide?

PROBLEM SOLVING
DOES THE ANSWER FIT THE PROBLEM?

If you get stuck, remember....

Tips for Problem Solving

on pages 474–475

When you solve a problem, look back to make sure your answer fits what the problem is asking for.

1. Ellen wants to buy 2 compact discs that cost $7.49 each and a poster for $2.75. Is $20.00 enough for those 3 items?
   a. She needs more than $10.00.
   b. She will get $2.27 change.
   c. For her items, $20.00 is enough.
   d. The 3 items will cost $17.73.

Think

- Which choice answers what the problem asks for?

- Without solving the problem, how could you tell that the other choices do not answer the question?

Work with a partner. Write the letter of the choice that answers what the problem is asking for.

2. Ellen bought a 20-foot roll of material to make 2 guitar straps. She needs 8 feet of material for each strap. How much material will be left over?
   a. Yes, there is enough material for 2 straps.
   b. She uses 4 feet for the left strap and 4 feet for the right strap.
   c. She will have 4 feet left.
   d. She will use 16 feet of material.

3. One of the compact discs Ellen bought was made in 1987. The other was made in 1991. Which disc is older?
   a. 4 years
   b. Ellen bought 2 discs in all.
   c. The disc is 4 years old.
   d. the disc made in 1987

SECTION REVIEW

for pages 76–90

Use the graphs below to answer each question.

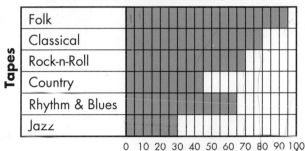

TAPES SOLD BY S&S MUSIC IN MAY

Tapes	
Folk	
Classical	
Rock-n-Roll	
Country	
Rhythm & Blues	
Jazz	

0 10 20 30 40 50 60 70 80 90 100
Number of Tapes Sold

NUMBER OF CAPS SOLD PER DAY

Monday	
Tuesday	
Wednesday	
Thursday	
Friday	

Key ⬤ = 10 caps

1. a. How many more folk tapes were sold than rhythm and blues?

b. What was the total number of jazz and classical tapes sold?

c. How many tapes were sold in May?

2. a. How many caps were sold on Monday?

b. How many caps were sold in five days?

c. Were more than half the caps sold during the first 3 days of the week?

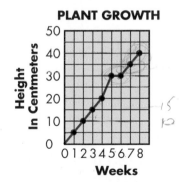

PLANT GROWTH

Height In Centimeters
50 40 30 20 10 0
0 1 2 3 4 5 6 7 8
Weeks

OUR FAVORITE BOOKS

Sports
Adventure Stories
Animal Stories
Mysteries

3. a. Between what two weeks did the plant grow the most?

b. How many centimeters did the plant grow from the second to the third week?

c. After eight weeks, how tall was the plant?

4. a. What fraction of the class prefer adventure stories?

b. There are 24 students in the class. How many students prefer adventure stories?

c. Altogether, how many students prefer sports, animal stories, and mysteries?

MAKING PREDICTIONS

In this lesson, you will learn to make predictions.

Groups:

• small groups

You will need:

• 1 yellow, 2 red, 2 green, and 5 blue connecting cubes

• a paper bag

• recording sheet

▶ Put 10 connecting cubes in a bag. Use the same colors and numbers as in the picture above.

1. Without looking, pick a connecting cube. Record the color and then put the connecting cube back. Repeat this process four more times. Tally the results on your recording sheet in a table like the one at the right.

	Tally	Total
Blue		
Red		
Green		
Yellow		

2. What color connecting cube did you pick most often?

▶ A **prediction** is making a guess about something that hasn't yet happened. You can use information about what's already happened to make better predictions about what will happen.

Discuss with your class.

3. In the first five tries, what color was picked most often by the other groups?

4. Suppose you were to pick again. What color connecting cube do you think is most likely to be picked? Explain.

Continue working with your group.

5. Pick a sixth connecting cube. Tally the color picked in your table. Is it the color you predicted?

6. Continue picking and tallying your picks in your chart until you have picked a total of ten times. Which color was picked most often in ten tries?

7. Repeat the process of picking ten times and tallying your results until you have completed the remaining three tables on your recording sheet.

Critical Thinking

SUMMING IT UP

8. Look at the three tables. What color was picked most often? Why do you think this is so?

9. Can you be sure before you pick a connecting cube what color will be picked?

10. Would you be likely to get the same results if you made the same number of picks again? Why or why not?

11. Supose there were 1 yellow, 2 blue, 2 green, and 5 red connecting cubes in a bag. Which color would you predict would be picked most often? Why?

12. From one of your tables, make a bar graph that shows your results. Compare and discuss with another group.

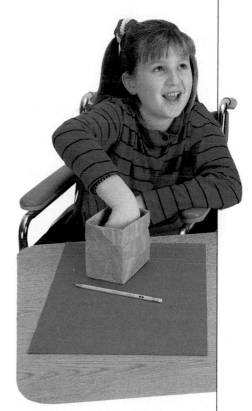

MATH LOG

A jar contains 5 blue marbles, 3 red marbles, and 1 yellow marble. If you made 50 tries, do you think that blue would be picked most often? That yellow would be picked least often? Explain.

COMPARING PROBABILITIES

If José does not look, is he more likely to pick a blue connecting cube or a yellow connecting cube from the jar?

Of the 6 cubes in the jar, 1 is blue. So, there is 1 chance out of 6 that he will pick blue.

Of the 6 cubes in the jar, 2 are yellow. So, there are 2 chances out of 6 that he will pick yellow.

Think

- Why is José more likely to pick a yellow connecting cube than a blue connecting cube?

- Can you be sure which connecting cube José will pick? Explain.

There are 3 chances out of 6 that José will pick red. There are 2 chances out of 6 that he will pick yellow. There is 1 chance out of 6 that he will pick blue.

So, red is most likely to be picked. Blue is least likely to be picked.

GUIDED PRACTICE

Use the spinners to answer each question. Copy and complete exercise 1.

A

1. What are the chances of spinner A stopping on
   a. red? ■ out of ■
   b. green? ■ out of ■

2. There are 4 sections on spinner B. Is the chance of spinning green 1 out of 4? Explain.

B
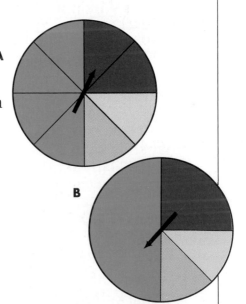

Critical Thinking 3. Which color is spinner B most likely to stop on? Which colors are least likely to be stopped on? Why?

4. Which is more likely:
   a. spinner A stopping on red?
   b. spinner B stopping on green?

94

INDEPENDENT PRACTICE

For each result below, tell which spinner—C, D, or E—you would choose. Tell why.

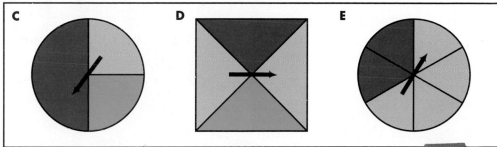

5. You need to spin red to win.

6. If you spin red, you lose.

7. You need to spin blue to win.

Use the spinners above and the connecting cubes to the right. Tell which is more likely to happen. Write *a*, *b*, or *same*.

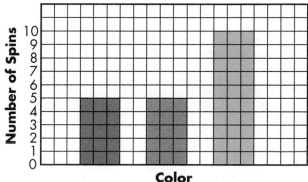

8. **a.** Spinner C stops on red.
   b. Spinner E stops on red.

9. **a.** picking a red cube
   b. picking a blue cube

10. **a.** picking a green cube
    b. picking a yellow cube

11. **a.** Spinner C stops on green.
    b. Spinner D stops on green.

12. **a.** Spinner D stops on blue.
    b. Spinner E stops on blue.

13. **a.** Spinner C stops on red.
    b. picking a yellow cube

CHALLENGE • Probability

Critical Thinking

This graph shows the results of 20 spins on a spinner.

Make a spinner that would have results like those shown on the graph. Then, use your spinner to make 20 spins. Make a bar graph of the results. Discuss how your graph compares with the graph on the right.

SPINNER RESULTS

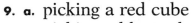

LISTING WHAT CAN HAPPEN

The digits in the number 248 are arranged in order from least to greatest.

Groups:

• pairs

You will need:

• paper

• scissors

• a recording sheet

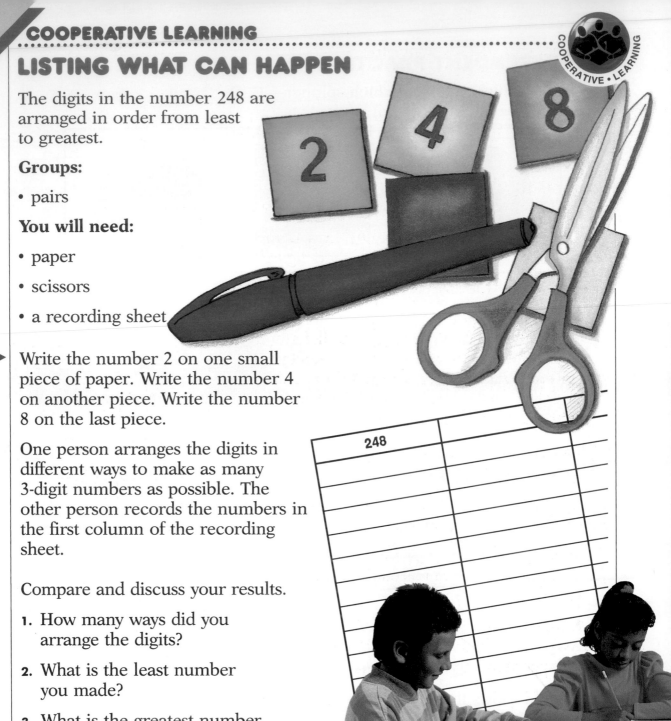

▶ Write the number 2 on one small piece of paper. Write the number 4 on another piece. Write the number 8 on the last piece.

One person arranges the digits in different ways to make as many 3-digit numbers as possible. The other person records the numbers in the first column of the recording sheet.

Compare and discuss your results.

1. How many ways did you arrange the digits?

2. What is the least number you made?

3. What is the greatest number you made?

▶ Repeat with three other digits. Be sure they are all different. Arrange the digits to make as many different 3-digit numbers as you can. Record the numbers in the second column of the recording sheet.

4. What can you say about the number of ways that any three different digits can be arranged?

Copy each digit below on a small piece of paper.

5 9 3 6

5. If the number 5 is always first, how many different ways can you arrange the digits?

6. If the number 6 is always last, how many different ways can you arrange the digits?

7. Predict how many ways you can arrange the four digits.

8. With your partner, arrange the digits in as many different ways as you can. Record the different arrangements in the third column of the recording sheet. Compare your results with your predictions.

 Critical Thinking

SUMMING IT UP

Compare the number of different arrangements that you can make for three and four items.

9. What do you notice about the number of different arrangements as the number of items increases?

10. Suppose you have four items. How can you make sure that you don't use the same arrangements twice, or skip a possible arrangement?

MAKING BETTER PREDICTIONS

In this lesson, you will try to use what you have learned to make better predictions.

Groups: small group

You will need:

• 1 red, 1 blue, and 1 green connecting cube
• a bag
• a recording sheet

Place the connecting cubes in a bag or other container so you cannot see them.

1. Suppose you pick the 3 connecting cubes one by one. Leave each cube out after each pick.
   a. In what order do you think you will pick them?
   b. How sure are you that you will be right?
   c. Try it.
   d. How many in your group got the result they predicted?

2. Suppose you pick the 3 connecting cubes one by one, a total of 30 times.
   a. About how many times do you think you will pick them in this order: red first, then green, then blue? Write your prediction. HINT: Think about the different orders that are possible. Keep track of the different orders.

Order	Tally	Total
Red - Green - Blue		
Red - Blue - Green		

   b. Try it. Make sure you put the connecting cubes back each time and mix them up before you pick again. Keep track of your results on the recording sheet.

3. Look at your results and the prediction you made.
  a. How close was your prediction?
  b. If you were to pick the 3 connecting cubes another 30 times, would you change your prediction? Why or why not?

4. Answer each question.
  a. How many groups did the experiment in exercise 2?
  b. How many times did each group pick 3 connecting cubes?
  c. In the whole class, how many times were the 3 connecting cubes picked?
  d. About how many times do you think the 3 connecting cubes were picked in the order red-green-blue?

5. Now combine the results of all the groups. Check your prediction. Write the results for each group on the recording sheet.

Order	Group					Total
	A	B	C	D	E	
Red-Green-Blue						
Red-Blue-Green						

● ●

SUMMING IT UP

6. How did you make your predictions?

7. Which predictions were you the most sure of? The least sure of? Explain.

8. Without looking at the chart of results for the whole class, predict about how many times the red connecting cube was picked first. Check your prediction.

● ●

Maintain ● **Place Value**
Round to the greatest place.

1. 38   **2.** 426   **3.** 595   **4.** 4619   **5.** 35,682

ADDITION AND SUBTRACTION

The fourth-graders at Greenwood School sell dried fruit to raise money for a class trip. How many boxes do Ms. O'Keefe's class and Mr. Truong's class sell together?

Dried Fruit Sale	
Classes	Number of Boxes Sold
Mrs. Smith's class	90
Mr. Lobato's class	49
Ms. O'Keefe's class	65
Mr. Truong's class	29

► You want to find a total.

Add 65 to 29.

You can use mental math.

$65 + 29 = \blacksquare$
$65 + 30 = 95$ Notice that 29 is 1 less than 30. It is easier to add 30 than 29.

$95 - 1 = 94$ Since you added 1 too many, subtract 1.

So, $65 + 29 = 94$.

► You can use mental math to subtract 49 from 65.

$65 - 49 = \blacksquare$
$65 - 50 = 15$ Notice that 49 is 1 less than 50. It is easier to subtract 50 than 49.

$15 + 1 = 16$ Since you subtracted 1 too many, add 1 back.

So, $65 - 49 = 16$.

INDEPENDENT PRACTICE

Write the answer. Use mental math.

1. $44 + 29$ 2. $32 + 49$ 3. $66 + 19$ 4. $78 + 19$

5. $85 - 49$ 6. $37 - 19$ 7. $54 - 29$ 8. $62 - 19$

Problem Solving Use the table above.

9. How many more boxes of dried fruit did Mrs. Smith's class sell than Mr. Truong's class?

10. Mr. Lobato's class had 14 boxes of dried fruit left after the sale. How many boxes did the class start with?

More Practice Set 3.13, p. 431

SECTION REVIEW

for pages 92–100

Write the letter of the correct answer.

1. There are 6 blue buttons, 2 red buttons, and 1 yellow button in a bag. If you pick one button without looking, what color are you most likely to pick?

    a. Blue, because there are more blue.

    b. Yellow, because they are the brightest.

    c. Red, because there are 2.

    d. You have the same chance of picking each color.

2. A spinner has 4 equal sections. There are 2 red sections, 1 blue section, and 1 green section. Which color will you land on when you spin the spinner?

    a. You will land on red.

    b. You will land on blue.

    c. You will land on green.

    d. You cannot tell for sure.

Use the spinner to answer each question. What are the chances of the spinner landing on:

3. red? ▦ out of ▦

4. yellow? ▦ out of ▦

5. green? ▦ out of ▦

6. blue? ▦ out of ▦

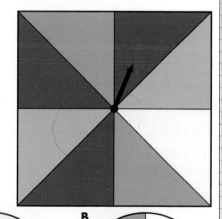

Use the spinners. Tell which is more likely to happen. Write *a, b,* or *same.*

7. **a.** Spinner A stops on blue.
    b. Spinner B stops on green.

8. **a.** Spinner A stops on yellow.
    b. Spinner B stops on white.

CHAPTER TEST

AVERAGE MONTHLY TEMPERATURE—CHICAGO

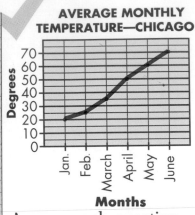

SURVEY: STUDENTS' FAVORITE COLORS

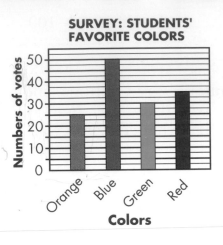

SURVEY: STUDENTS' FUTURE CAREER CHOICES

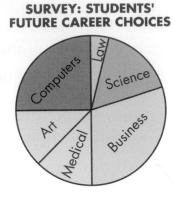

Answer each question.

1. By how many degrees did the average temperature rise from January to June?

2. When was the average temperature the highest?

3. How many students voted in the survey on favorite colors?

4. Did more than half the students choose law as a career?

SPORTS MAGAZINES SOLD IN ONE WEEK

Skiing	▬	▬	▬	▬	▭				
Tennis	▬	▬	▬	▬	▬	▬	▭		
Hockey	▬	▬	▬	▬					
Basketball	▬	▬	▬	▬	▬	▬	▭		
Running	▬	▬	▬	▬	▬				

Key:
▬ = 10 magazines
▭ = 5 magazines

5. How many magazines were sold during the week?

6. What type of magazine did the store sell the fewest of?

7. What two types of magazines did the store sell the same number of?

8. How many fewer skiing than tennis magazines were sold?

PROBLEM SOLVING

Use the spinners to answer each question.

9. What are the chances of Spinner A stopping on green?

10. What are the chances of Spinner B stopping on green?

SPINNER A   **SPINNER B**

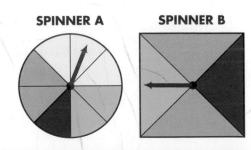

CUMULATIVE REVIEW

Write the numbers in order from greatest to least.

1. 475; 4577; 5470; 5468

2. 1001; 1100; 111; 101

3. 9865; 5569; 9658; 9568

4. 3812; 3821; 4831; 3281

Write the answer.

5.
```
  $13.50
    2.78
+   0.61
```

6.
```
   492
   101
 + 238
```

7.
```
   11
   14
   35
 + 10
```

8.
```
  1280
  5755
  2361
+ 4002
```

9.
```
  27
- 19
```

10.
```
  548
 - 88
```

11.
```
  $66.72
 - 15.78
```

12.
```
  9751
 - 189
```

13.
```
  7095
 - 814
```

14.
```
  4506
 - 1285
```

15.
```
  6005
 - 1579
```

16.
```
  $40.09
 -  5.76
```

Use the pictograph and circle graph to answer the questions.

17. What was the total attentance for all three games? How did you find your answer?

18. Would it be a good idea for the Home Run Heroes to play in a stadium that had a total of 200 seats? Why or why not?

19. What is the most popular amusement park ride?

20. Suppose 100 children had voted for their favorite ride. How many children voted for the roller coaster? How did you get your answer?

**Home Run Heroes
Baseball Game Attendance**

Game 1	⊖ ⊖
Game 2	⊖ ⊖ ⊖ ⊖
Game 3	⊖ ⊖ ⊖

Key: ⊖ = 100 People   ⊖ = 50 People

Favorite Amusement Park Rides

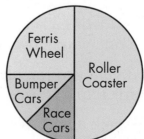

EXCURSION

PROBABILITY

CHANGING THE CHANCES

Molly and Sue spin a spinner like the one at the right. They keep a tally of their spins in a table.

After 5 spins, Molly notices that white still has not come up. Molly thinks that white will have to come up next.

Color	Tally	Total
White		
Red		
Blue		

Sue explains: "Each time you spin, the chance of landing on a color is the same as it was before the spin. It doesn't matter which color the spinner has landed on before."

1. Do you think Sue is right? Does the spinner remember what happened on the last spin?

Sometimes one result will change the chances for another result. For instance, suppose you choose a card from a set of 10 digit cards. Then you put the one you chose in your desk.

Critical Thinking

2. Have you changed the chances of picking any other card? Explain.

3. Now you pick again. What are the chances of picking the card that is in your desk?

Answer each question. Explain your answer.

4. You are spinning a spinner like the one at the right. In three spins, the spinner has landed once on red, once on white, and once on blue. Will the spinner land on yellow on the next spin? Does it matter what the three spins before were?

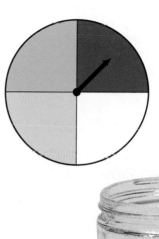

5. You are picking connecting cubes out of a jar like the one on the right. After each pick, you put the connecting cube in your pocket. So far, you have picked red, yellow, and white. Do the three connecting cubes you have already picked make any difference to the next pick?

Do this experiment. Copy the table at the right. You will need a number cube. Roll the number cube and record the results in your table.

Roll the number cube 30 times. Record the results.

6. Did some numbers not come up?

7. Make a bar graph of the results.

Critical Thinking

8. Do you think that the chances of all numbers coming up are the same? Explain.

Digit	Tally	Total
1		
2		
3		
4		
5		
6		

CHAPTER 4

MULTIPLICATION AND DIVISION FACTS

Connections

Estimation

Practicing Estimation How many fish are in the picture? You may not be able to count them all. It is easier to estimate. Have everyone in class make an estimate and write it down. Collect the estimates and list them on the chalkboard. Now make another estimate. Follow these steps.

- On a piece of unlined paper draw a rectangle the same size as the fish picture.

- Then use a ruler to measure and divide the rectangle into 16 equal parts as shown here.

- Use a pair of scissors to cut out 1 of the 16 blocks.

- Place the paper over the picture. Count the number of fish you can see through the open block.

- Using a calculator, multiply the number by 16.

This answer is your new estimate. Make a list of new estimates on the chalkboard. How does this list compare to your first estimates?

UNDERSTANDING MULTIPLICATION

You can recognize poison ivy by the 3 leaflets that grow on each stem. If a poison ivy plant has 6 stems, how many leaflets does it have?

Here are some ways to solve the problem.

DRAW AN ARRAY
You can draw an array and count.
An **array** is an arrangement of objects in rows.
The number of objects in each row is the same.

XXX
XXX
XXX } 6 groups with
XXX } 3 in each group
XXX
XXX

ADD
You can add.   } 6 groups
$3 + 3 + 3 + 3 + 3 + 3 = 18$ } 3 in each group

MULTIPLY
You can multiply. } 6 groups
$6 \times 3 = 18$ } 3 in each group

The poison ivy plant has 18 leaflets.

Think
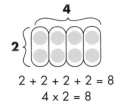

• If a plant has 3 stems with 9 leaflets on each stem, which method would you use to find how many leaflets are on the plant? Why?

Other Examples

4

2 {

$2 + 2 + 2 + 2 = 8$
$4 \times 2 = 8$

$6 + 6 + 6 = 18$
$3 \times 6 = 18$

$3 + 3 + 3 + 3 + 2 = 14$

GUIDED PRACTICE

Write an addition sentence. Then write a multiplication sentence for the picture if you can.

1.

2.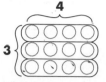

3.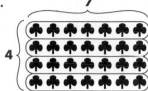

4.

5.

6.

Critical Thinking 7. Is it possible to write a multiplication sentence for every addition sentence? Why or why not?

INDEPENDENT PRACTICE

Write an addition sentence and a multiplication sentence for each picture.

8.

9.

10.

Write the letter of the exercise that has the same answer.

11. 4×7 a. 2×9

12. $8 + 8 + 8 + 8$ b. 4×8

13. $9 + 9$ c. $7 + 7 + 7 + 7$

14. 3×5 d. $5 + 5 + 5$

Problem Solving Make a diagram when it helps.

15. Virginia creeper looks like poison ivy but has 5 leaflets on each stem instead of 3. How many leaflets would be on 6 stems of Virginia creeper?

16. Toby sees a Virginia creeper plant and a poison ivy plant. They have a total of 16 leaflets. How many leaflets does each have? How many stems?

More Practice Set 4.1, p. 432

109

MULTIPLYING BY 5 AND 10

Karlena reads the ad on the right and thinks, "Wow! I could build a whole island full of volcanoes."

How many volcanoes can Karlena build if she buys 5 kits? If she buys 10 kits?

EARTH TOYS SPECIAL!

VOLCANO KITS FOR SALE

Each kit contains:
☐ DIRECTIONS
☐ WORK TRAY

(ENOUGH MATERIAL FOR 3 VOLCANOES)

EACH KIT COSTS: $9.

To find the answers, you can multiply. Use the table.

	0	1	2	3	4	5	6	7	8	9	10
5 ×	0	5	10	15	20	25	30	35	40	45	50
10 ×	0	10	20	30	40	50	60	70	80	90	100

Multiply 3 by 5.

$5 \times 3 = 15$

↑   ↑   ↑
factor factor product

$$\begin{array}{r} 3 \\ \times\ 5 \\ \hline 15 \end{array}$$

Multiply 3 by 10.

$10 \times 3 = 30$

$$\begin{array}{r} 3 \\ \times\ 10 \\ \hline 30 \end{array}$$ ← factor
← factor
← product

If she buys 5 kits, Karlena can build 15 volcanoes. If she buys 10 kits, Karlena can build 30 volcanoes.

Think

- Compare the products of 5 × 3 and 10 × 3. What do you notice? Why do you think this is so?

- What patterns do you see in the products when you multiply by 5? By 10?

GUIDED PRACTICE

Write the product.

1. 10
    × 0

2. 5
    × 9

3. 6
    × 5

4. 3
    × 10

5. 5
    × 1

6. 10
    × 4

7. 10
    × 10

8. a. 2 × 5
   b. 2 × 10

9. a. 7 × 5
   b. 7 × 10

10. a. 5 × 5
    b. 5 × 10

11. a. 8 × 5
    b. 8 × 10

Critical Thinking 12. If you know that 5 × 12 = 60, how can you find 10 × 12?

....

INDEPENDENT PRACTICE

Write the product.

13. 5
    × 4

14. 4
    × 5

15. 10
    × 1

16. 10
    × 5

17. 5
    × 0

18. 10
    × 9

19. 10
    × 6

20. 10
    × 2

21. 5
    × 7

22. 10
    × 8

23. 3
    × 5

24. 5
    × 8

25. 1
    × 5

26. 5
    × 2

Problem Solving Use the ad on page 110 for exercise 27.

27. Karlena's mother says she can buy 3 volcano kits. How much will 3 volcano kits cost?

28. To paint the volcanoes, Karlena buys 4 packages of paint. Each package should have 3 jars. When she opens all the packages, there are only 10 jars. How many jars are missing?

MATH LOG

Explain about the digit in the ones place of the product when you multiply by 10. Explain about the digit in the ones place of the product when you multiply by 5.

UNDERSTANDING DIVISION

▶ Workers at the museum workshop are building models of 3-masted sailing ships. They have 27 masts. How many model ships can they build?

You need to find how many groups of 3 there are in 27. Below are some ways to do this.

You can draw an array to find how many groups of 3 there are in 27. XXX XXX XXX XXX XXX XXX XXX XXX XXX	There are 9 groups of 3 in 27.

You can subtract 3 until you reach 0.

27	24	21	18	15	12	9	6	3		Beginning with 27, subtract 3 nine times.
− 3	− 3	− 3	− 3	− 3	− 3	− 3	− 3	− 3		
24	21	18	15	12	9	6	3	0		

You can use a multiplication fact to help you. $9 \times 3 = 27$ So, $27 \div 3 = 9$.	If you know $9 \times 3 = 27$, then you know that $27 \div 3 = 9$.

The workers can build 9 model ships.

▶ There are 24 workers who build model ships. They work in 4 equal teams. How many workers are on each team?

To find the number of workers on each team, you can use counters or a multiplication fact to help you.

$4 \times 6 = 24$

So, $24 \div 4 = 6$.

There are 6 workers on each team.

Think

- Suppose the workers worked in 3 equal teams. How would you find the number of workers on each team?

112

GUIDED PRACTICE

Write a division sentence for each multiplication sentence.

1. $4 \times 3 = 12$ **2.** $6 \times 5 = 30$ **3.** $2 \times 5 = 10$ **4.** $9 \times 10 = 90$

Divide. Use a related multiplication fact to help you.

5. $21 \div 3$ **6.** $25 \div 5$ **7.** $30 \div 6$ **8.** $42 \div 7$ **9.** $24 \div 4$

Critical Thinking **10.** Write a different division sentence for exercise 2.

INDEPENDENT PRACTICE

Write a division sentence for each array.

11.   **12.**    **13.**

Divide. Use a related multiplication fact or counters to help you.

14. $45 \div 5$ **15.** $56 \div 7$ **16.** $64 \div 8$ **17.** $36 \div 9$ **18.** $63 \div 7$

19. $20 \div 5$ **20.** $36 \div 4$ **21.** $49 \div 7$ **22.** $32 \div 8$ **23.** $40 \div 8$

24. $48 \div 6$ **25.** $18 \div 9$ **26.** $24 \div 3$ **27.** $16 \div 4$ **28.** $36 \div 6$

29. $27 \div 3$ **30.** $50 \div 5$ **31.** $40 \div 10$ **32.** $28 \div 7$ **33.** $54 \div 9$

Problem Solving Draw a diagram when it helps.

34. A worker is making model coaches. Each model coach is pulled by 4 model horses. The worker has 34 model horses. Are there enough horses to make 8 coaches?

35. On tours of the workshop, visitors are taken through in groups of 9. The tour lasts 15 minutes. How long will it take for 36 people to tour the workshop?

Critical Thinking **36.** Make up a division word problem of your own. Give your problem to a friend to solve.

More Practice Set 4.3, p. 432

DIVIDING BY 5 AND 10

► Amy needs to buy 30 muffins for a party. If she chooses 5 kinds of muffins, how many of each kind will she buy?

Muffin Special!
We have 10 kinds of muffins:

- Blueberry
- Corn
- Raisin
- Oat
- Cinnamon

- Apple
- Cranberry
- Pumpkin
- Carrot
- Banana

You can divide to find the answer.

Divide 30 by 5. Use a multiplication fact.

$5 \times \blacksquare = 30$
$5 \times 6 = 30$
So, $30 \div 5 = 6.$

↑   ↑   ↑
dividend divisor quotient

If Amy chooses 5 kinds of muffins, she will buy 6 of each kind.

► If she chooses 10 kinds of muffins, how many of each kind will she buy?

You can divide to find the answer.

Divide 30 by 10. Use a multiplication fact.

$10 \times \blacksquare = 30$
$10 \times 3 = 30$
So, $30 \div 10 = 3.$

divisor ⟶ $10\overline{)30}$ 3 ← **quotient**
↑
dividend

If Amy chooses 10 kinds of muffins, she will buy 3 of each kind.

Think

- Suppose you wanted to find $60 \div 5$ and $60 \div 10$. Without dividing, how can you tell which quotient will be greater?

GUIDED PRACTICE

Write the quotient. Think of a multiplication fact to help you.

1. $5\overline{)25}$ 2. $10\overline{)30}$ 3. $5\overline{)30}$ 4. $10\overline{)80}$ 5. $5\overline{)20}$

Critical Thinking 6. What multiplication fact would help you solve exercise 5?

INDEPENDENT PRACTICE

Write the quotient.

7. $5\overline{)15}$ 8. $10\overline{)40}$ 9. $10\overline{)20}$ 10. $5\overline{)40}$ 11. $5\overline{)45}$

12. $5\overline{)50}$ 13. $5\overline{)25}$ 14. $10\overline{)100}$ 15. $5\overline{)35}$ 16. $10\overline{)90}$

17. $35 \div 5$ 18. $70 \div 10$ 19. $80 \div 10$ 20. $10 \div 5$ 21. $50 \div 10$

Problem Solving Amy's cooking class made a pictograph to show what they baked in class. Use the graph to answer each question.

22. How many more corn muffins than blueberry muffins did Amy's class bake?

23. Ten students shared the corn muffins equally. How many did each student get?

24. Amy packed the blueberry muffins. If each box holds 5 muffins, how many boxes did she use?

Critical Thinking 25. Write a word problem that can be answered using the pictograph. Give your word problem to a friend to solve.

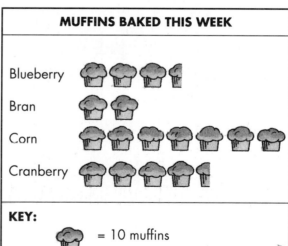

MUFFINS BAKED THIS WEEK

Blueberry

Bran

Corn

Cranberry

KEY:

 = 10 muffins

 = 5 muffins

PROPERTIES AND RULES

The properties of multiplication and the rules for division can help you find products and quotients.

Multiplication Properties	Division Rules
Order Property: If you change the order of the factors, then the product stays the same. **Example 1:** $3 \times 5 = 5 \times 3$ **Example 2:** $2 \times 117 = 117 \times 2$	If you divide a number other than 0 by itself, the quotient is always 1. **Example 1:** $9 \div 9 = 1$ **Example 2:** $27 \div 27 = 1$
Property of Zero: If you multiply any factor and 0, the product is 0. **Example 1:** $7 \times 0 = 0$ **Example 2:** $0 \times 238 = 0$	If you divide 0 by any other number, the quotient is always 0. **Example 1:** $0 \div 2 = 0$ **Example 2:** $0 \div 31 = 0$
Property of One: If you multiply any factor by 1, the product will be the same as that factor. **Example 1:** $4 \times 1 = 4$ **Example 2:** $1 \times 51 = 51$	If you divide any number by 1, the quotient is always that number. **Example 1:** $9 \div 1 = 9$ **Example 2:** $132 \div 1 = 132$
Grouping Property: If you change the grouping of the factors, the product remains the same. **Example 1:** $(1 \times 2) \times 5 = 1 \times (2 \times 5)$ $10 = 10$	A number cannot be divided by 0. **Example 1:** $6 \div 0$ is not possible **Example 2:** $47 \div 0$ is not possible

Think

- What are two different ways you can group $5 \times 7 \times 2$?

- How can the order property make it easier to multiply?

GUIDED PRACTICE

Copy and complete the number sentence.

1. $175 \times \blacksquare = 175$　　2. $\blacksquare \times 43 = 0$　　3. $129 \div \blacksquare = 129$　　4. $\blacksquare \div 87 = 0$

5. $(2 \times 3) \times 5 = \blacksquare \times (3 \times 5)$　　6. $\blacksquare \times 99 = 99 \times 36$　　7. $\blacksquare \times 1 = 32$

Critical Thinking 8. What property helped you complete exercise 6?

INDEPENDENT PRACTICE

Copy and complete the number sentence.

9. ■ ÷ 1 = 145 **10.** 16 × ■ = 5 × 16 **11.** 1384 × ■ = 0 **12.** ■ × 246 = 246

13. (4 × 17) × 3 = 4 × (■ × 3)　　　　**14.** 42 × 36 = ■ × 42

15. 7 × (■ × 5) = (7 × 3) × 5　　　　**16.** ■ ÷ 500 = 0

Write the letter of the exercise with the same answer.

17. 324 × 0　　　　　　　**a.** 42 ÷ 42

18. (39 × 4) × 25　　　　**b.** 175 ÷ 1

19. 175 × 1　　　　　　　**c.** 39 × (4 × 25)

20. 27 ÷ 27　　　　　　　**d.** 7 × 62

21. 62 × 7　　　　　　　**e.** 0 ÷ 324

Problem Solving

Critical Thinking

22. Use any of the numbers in the box to show 3 multiplication properties and 3 division rules. You can use any number more than once. Label each property or rule.

1　2　0　7　8　5　10　35
428　　50　　80　　100
3126　　48,957　　654,281

Maintain • Using Graphs

Use the graph to answer each question.

1. Which fruit received twice as many votes as the pear?

2. How many students voted?

3. Did more than or less than half the students vote for the apple?

4. What is the difference between the number of votes for the top two favorites?

Which is Your Favorite Fruit?

Number of Students — Fruit: Pear, Banana, Peach, Orange, Apple

MAKING A FACTS TABLE

In this lesson, you and a partner will complete a facts table to help you see number patterns.

Groups:

• partners

You will need:

• a recording sheet

In the facts table, the blue numbers are factors. Find the box where the red row starting with 5 crosses the yellow column starting with 3. The number in that box, 15, is the product of the factors 5 and 3. So, 5 × 3 = 15.

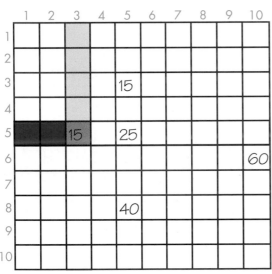

Read the table to answer each question.

1. Which other row and column cross to give a product of 15?

2. Find 25 in the table. What are the factors of 25?

3. What is the product of 8 × 5?

4. What are two multiplication facts for 60?

Work with your partner to fill in as much of the facts table as you can. The questions that follow can help you. Discuss them with your partner.

5. How can you use the patterns that you found with 5's and 10's in multiplying by 5 and by 10?

6. What is the product of 1 and any other number?

7. How does knowing $8 \times 5 = 40$ help you to find 5×8?

8. After you find the product of 2 and another number, how can you find the product of 4 and that number?

9. How can you use repeated addition to find products?

10. What patterns can you find in the rows across or columns down? How can you use these patterns to find missing products?

 Critical Thinking

SUMMING IT UP

Compare tables with other groups. Discuss how you found the facts to complete your tables.

11. Which row or column did you fill in first? Why?

12. How did one row or column help you fill in another one?

13. What are two patterns that you found?

14. How can you use the facts table to find division facts?

CHOOSE A COMPUTATION METHOD

MENTAL MATH OR PAPER AND PENCIL

Sometimes you can use mental math to compute. Other times you will need paper and pencil. Whether you compute using mental math or using pencil and paper is up to you.

Question to consider:

- Are the numbers too difficult to compute in your head?

INDEPENDENT PRACTICE

Write the answer. Write whether or not you used mental math to find the answer.

1. $\begin{array}{r} 600 \\ - 400 \end{array}$
2. $\begin{array}{r} 816 \\ + 437 \end{array}$
3. $\begin{array}{r} 37 \\ + 4 \end{array}$
4. $\begin{array}{r} 122 \\ - 3 \end{array}$
5. $\begin{array}{r} 35 \\ + 29 \end{array}$
6. $\begin{array}{r} 46 \\ 298 \\ + 37 \end{array}$

7. $50 + 20 + 50$
8. $\$14.56 - \$3.29$
9. $50 - 29$
10. $58 - 40$

Problem Solving

11. Lisa babysits for 4 hours. She makes $3 an hour. How much money does Lisa make?

12. Ron works for his father for 5 days. He works 8 hours each day. How many hours does Ron work?

13. Toby has $38.75. She wants to buy a video game for $18.95 and a book for $25.65. Does she have enough money?

14. John saves $14. Rick saves $2 more than John. Lou saves $4 less than Rick. How much do the boys save altogether?

Critical Thinking 15. For which problems did you choose to use mental math? Why?

More Practice Set 4.7, p. 434

SECTION REVIEW

for pages 108–120

Write the product.

1. 3×10
2. 4×10
3. 5×7
4. 9×5
5. 2×5
6. 2×10
7. 10×10
8. 8×5
9. 7×10
10. 6×5
11. 4×5
12. 0×10

Write the quotient.

13. $10 \div 10$
14. $25 \div 5$
15. $40 \div 5$
16. $30 \div 5$
17. $15 \div 5$
18. $50 \div 5$
19. $100 \div 10$
20. $35 \div 5$

Write the letter of the exercise with the same answer.

21. $1 + 1 + 1 + 1$
22. $5 + 5 + 5 + 5 + 5 + 5 + 5 + 5$
23. 7×5
24. 3×0
25. $9 + 9 + 9 + 9 + 9 + 9$
26. 7×2
27. 6×7
28. 4×4

a. 8×5
b. $4 + 4 + 4 + 4$
c. $5 + 5 + 5 + 5 + 5 + 5 + 5$
d. $7 + 7 + 7 + 7 + 7 + 7$
e. $2 + 2 + 2 + 2 + 2 + 2 + 2$
f. $0 + 0 + 0$
g. 6×9
h. 4×1

Solve each problem.

29. There are 5 rows in the classroom. There are 5 chairs in each row. How many chairs are in the room?

30. Sharon has 30 extra baseball cards. She divides the cards exactly among 5 friends. How many cards will each friend receive?

MULTIPLYING BY 2, 4, AND 8

Since 2 doubled is 4, and 4 doubled is 8, you can see patterns when you multiply by 2, 4, and 8.

	0	1	2	3	4	5	6	7	8	9	10
× 2	0	2	4	6	8	10	12	14	16	18	20
× 4	0	4	8	12	16	20	24	28	32	36	40
× 8	0	8	16	24	32	40	48	56	64	72	80

Think

• What patterns do you notice in the products of 2, 4, and 8?

If you forget a multiplication fact with 4 or 8, you can use the doubles pattern to figure it out. For example, to multiply 7 by 8:

Start with 2.　　2 × 7 = 14
Double 2 is 4.　　4 × 7 = 28　Double 14 is 28.　　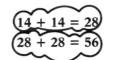 14 + 14 = 28
Double 4 is 8.　　8 × 7 = 56　Double 28 is 56.　　28 + 28 = 56

GUIDED PRACTICE

Write the product. Use the doubles pattern when it helps.

1. **a.** 2 × 3　　**2.** **a.** 8 × 2　　**3.** **a.** 2 × 9　　**4.** **a.** 7 × 2
　　b. 4 × 3　　　　**b.** 8 × 4　　　　**b.** 4 × 9　　　　**b.** 7 × 4
　　c. 8 × 3　　　　**c.** 8 × 8　　　　**c.** 8 × 9　　　　**c.** 7 × 8

Copy and complete. Write >, <, or =.

5. 4 × 4 ● 8 × 6　　　　**6.** 2 × 9 ● 4 × 8　　　　**7.** 3 × 8 ● 5 × 4

8. Explain how the doubles pattern helped you find the products in exercise 3.

INDEPENDENT PRACTICE

Write the product. Use the doubles pattern when it helps.

9. a. 2×5
  b. 4×5
  c. 8×5

10. a. 6×2
  b. 6×4
  c. 6×8

11. a. 2×4
  b. 4×4
  c. 8×4

12. a. 2×10
  b. 4×10
  c. 8×10

13. 8×7

14. 7×4

15. 8×8

16. 9×2

Copy and complete. Write >, <, or =.

17. $2 \times 4 \bullet 3 \times 4$

18. $6 \times 4 \bullet 6 \times 8$

19. $6 \times 4 \bullet 3 \times 8$

20. $8 \times 9 \bullet 4 \times 9$

21. $10 \times 2 \bullet 5 \times 4$

22. $9 \times 2 \bullet 8 \times 1$

Write a multiplication fact that doubles the product.

23. 4×8

24. 6×4

25. 8×5

26. 3×4

Problem Solving Remember, some problems may not have enough information.

27. At Saturday's game, Jan and 8 friends will be cheering. At halftime, they will each wave a flag for 2 minutes at the same time. How long will the flags be waved at halftime?

28. Jan wants to get more people to help cheer at halftime. Will she need twice as many flags?

CHALLENGE • Patterns

Critical Thinking

Copy and complete the table below to continue the pattern from page 122.

	11	12	13	14	15	16	17	18	19	20
× 2										
× 4										
× 8										

What method did you use?

DIVIDING BY 2, 4, AND 8

Bob has 12 model cars. Below are two ways he can store them.

2 boxes
6 cars in each box

4 boxes
3 cars in each box

The quotient table below shows division by 2 and by 4.

Divisors	Dividends										
	0	2	4	6	8	10	12	14	16	18	20
÷ 2	0	1	2	3	4	5	6	7	8	9	10
÷ 4	0		1		2		3		4		5

Notice that when you divide by 2, the quotient is twice as large as when you divide by 4.

$12 \div 2 = 6$
$12 \div 4 = 3$

The quotient table below shows division by 4 and by 8.

Divisors	Dividends										
	0	4	8	12	16	20	24	28	32	36	40
÷ 4	0	1	2	3	4	5	6	7	8	9	10
÷ 8	0		1		2		3		4		5

Think

- What pattern do you see when you divide the same number by 4 and by 8?

- How is this pattern similar to dividing by 2 and by 4?

GUIDED PRACTICE

Write the quotient. Use a pattern to help you.

1. a. $8 \div 2$
   b. $8 \div 4$

2. a. $16 \div 2$
   b. $16 \div 4$

3. a. $32 \div 4$
   b. $32 \div 8$

4. a. $24 \div 4$
   b. $24 \div 8$

5. $40 \div 4$

6. $12 \div 4$

7. $20 \div 4$

8. $16 \div 8$

Critical Thinking 9. If you know that $64 \div 4 = 16$, how can that help you find the quotient of $64 \div 8$?

INDEPENDENT PRACTICE

Write the quotient. Usc a pattern to help you.

10. a. $24 \div 4$
    b. $24 \div 2$

11. a. $16 \div 8$
    b. $16 \div 4$

12. a. $28 \div 4$
    b. $28 \div 2$

13. a. $40 \div 8$
    b. $40 \div 4$

14. $72 \div 8$

15. $36 \div 4$

16. $80 \div 8$

17. $20 \div 2$

18. $64 \div 8$

19. $4 \div 4$

20. $6 \div 2$

21. $8 \div 8$

22. $16 \div 8$

23. $48 \div 8$

24. $18 \div 2$

25. $56 \div 8$

Problem Solving Draw diagrams, make tables, or use other strategies.

26. Gilbert has 16 model cars. How many model cars will Gilbert have left if he gives half of thcm to Roger?

27. Mateo has 5 model cars. For his birthday, he gets 3 model car kits. He can build 4 cars with each kit. How many cars will Mateo have?

28. Brett buys 56 baseball cards. The cards come in packages of 8. How many packages does he buy?

29. A package of baseball cards costs $3. Each package contains 8 cards. How much will 40 cards cost?

MAKE A PLAN

It often takes more than one step to solve a problem. Making a plan can help you keep track of the steps. One time, I made a plan to help save for a team jacket.

MY PROBLEM

A team jacket costs $50. It costs $2 for each letter sewn on the jacket. I needed to know how much a jacket with the word TIGERS would cost.

MY SOLUTION

I thought of a plan. It had 3 steps.

STEP 1   Find how many letters in TIGERS.

STEP 2   Find how much the letters would cost.

STEP 3   Find the total cost of the jacket and the letters.

Then I carried out my plan.

STEP 1   I counted 6 letters in TIGERS.

STEP 2   I multiplied to find the cost for the 6 letters.
$6 \times \$2 = \$12$

STEP 3   I added $12 to the cost of a jacket to find the total cost.

Figure out how much the jacket cost.

126

GUIDED PRACTICE

Copy and complete the plan. Solve the problem.

1. John will help paint a fence that has 32 sections. John can paint 4 sections in an hour. How many sections can he paint from 11:00 A.M. to 2:00 P.M.?

STEP 1 Find the number of hours from 11:00 A.M. to 2:00 P.M.	STEP 2

APPLICATION

Work with a small group. Make a plan when it helps. ⋯⋯⋯⋯⋯⋯

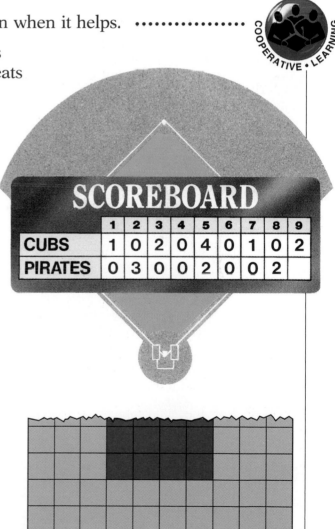

2. At the class play, there are 10 rows with 8 seats in each row. Only 4 seats are empty. How many people are watching the play?

3. How many runs do the Pirates need in the ninth inning to win the game?

4. Angelo has 3 quarters and 2 dimes to spend at the school fair. If he buys 4 finger puppets that cost 10¢ each, how much will he have left?

5. Jack and 3 of his friends are going fishing. Jack finds 7 worms, Jamal finds 8, Sue finds 10, and Marcy finds 11. If they share the worms equally, how many should each child get?

6. Joan is making a square design with red and blue tiles. The red part will also be square. How many blue tiles are in the design? How many red tiles are in the design?

SCOREBOARD

	1	2	3	4	5	6	7	8	9
CUBS	1	0	2	0	4	0	1	0	2
PIRATES	0	3	0	0	2	0	0	2	

MULTIPLYING AND DIVIDING BY 3 AND 6

The multiplication table below shows the
products when you multiply by 3 and by 6.

Factors											
Factors	0	1	2	3	4	5	6	7	8	9	10
× 3	0	3	6	9	12	15	18	21	24	27	30
× 6	0	6	12	18	24	30	36	42	48	54	60

You know that 6 is the double of 3.
So, 6 times any number is double
3 times that same number.

$3 \times 4 = 12$
$6 \times 4 = 24$

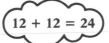

Use the doubles pattern to help you multiply by 6.
For example, to multiply 6 by 7:

Start with 3. $3 \times 7 = 21$ $21 + 21 = 42$
The double of 3 is 6. $6 \times 7 = 42$

Think

- If you know that $3 \times 21 = 63$, how can
  that help you find 6×21?

What you have noticed about 3 and 6 can also help you
to divide. Look at the quotient table.

Dividends											
Divisors	0	3	6	9	12	15	18	21	24	27	30
÷ 3	0	1	2	3	4	5	6	7	8	9	10
÷ 6	0		1		2		3		4		5

Think

- What pattern do you notice in the
  quotients when you divide the same
  number by 3 and by 6?

GUIDED PRACTICE

Write the answer. Use a pattern to help you.

1. a. 3×3
    b. 6×3

2. a. 3×9
    b. 6×9

3. a. $18 \div 3$
    b. $18 \div 6$

4. a. $24 \div 3$
    b. $24 \div 6$

5. $54 \div 6$

6. 8×3

7. 10×6

8. $48 \div 6$

Critical Thinking 9. Explain how you solved exercise 2.

INDEPENDENT PRACTICE

Write the answer. Use a pattern to help you.

10. a. 3×8
    b. 6×8

11. a. 5×3
    b. 5×6

12. a. $36 \div 6$
    b. $36 \div 3$

13. a. $24 \div 6$
    b. $24 \div 3$

14. $42 \div 6$

15. 6×6

16. 3×5

17. $30 \div 3$

18. 10×3

19. 7×3

20. $36 \div 6$

21. 6×0

22. $60 \div 6$

23. $21 \div 3$

24. $27 \div 3$

25. 2×6

26. $15 \div 3$

27. $9 \div 3$

28. $6 \div 1$

Problem Solving

29. Kirk, Joan, and Phil plan a field day. They each invite 5 friends. If everyone comes, how many people will attend the field day?

30. Phil and 14 other people sign up for the 4-legged race. If they race in teams of 3, how many teams will be in the race?

Maintain • Mixed Practice

Write the answer.

1.
$$984 - 390$$

2.
$$603 - 58$$

3.
$$6479 + 42$$

4.
$$1555 + 394$$

5.
$$43,456 - 3,948$$

MULTIPLYING AND DIVIDING BY 7 AND 9

Look at the multiplication table below. It shows the products when you multiply by 7 and by 9.

Factors											
Factors	0	1	2	3	4	5	6	7	8	9	10
× 7	0	7	14	21	28	35	42	49	56	63	70
× 9	0	9	18	27	36	45	54	63	72	81	90

Think

- Which facts do you already know?

- Add the digits in each of the products for the 9's. What do you notice about each sum?

What you know about multiplying 7 and 9 can help you to divide by 7 and by 9. Look at the quotient tables below.

Divisor	Dividends										
Divisor	0	7	14	21	28	35	42	49	56	63	70
÷ 7	0	1	2	3	4	5	6	7	8	9	10

Divisor	Dividends										
Divisor	0	9	18	27	36	45	54	63	72	81	90
÷ 9	0	1	2	3	4	5	6	7	8	9	10

Related facts can help you multiply and divide by 7 and by 9.

Since $7 \times 9 = 63$,
then $9 \times 7 = 63$,
        $63 \div 7 = 9$,
        $63 \div 9 = 7$.

Since $9 \times 10 = 90$,
then $10 \times 9 = 90$,
        $90 \div 9 = 10$,
        $90 \div 10 = 9$.

GUIDED PRACTICE

Write the product.

1. 7×3 **2.** 7×6 **3.** 9×8 **4.** 9×5 **5.** 3×9

Copy and complete the related number sentences.

6. $7 \times \blacksquare = 42$
  $6 \times 7 = \blacksquare$
  $\blacksquare \div 6 = 7$
  $42 \div \blacksquare = 6$

7. $\blacksquare \times 4 = 36$
  $\blacksquare \times 9 = 36$
  $36 \div \blacksquare = 9$
  $\blacksquare \div 9 = 4$

8. $\blacksquare \times 9 = 81$
  $81 \div \blacksquare = 9$

Critical Thinking **9.** How can the answer to exercise 1 help you to answer exercise 2?

INDEPENDENT PRACTICE

Write the product.

10. 7×5 **11.** 9×6 **12.** 4×9 **13.** 9×10 **14.** 0×9

15. 9×9 **16.** 0×7 **17.** 1×9 **18.** 7×10 **19.** 7×7

Write the quotient. Then write a related multiplication sentence.

20. $21 \div 7$ **21.** $81 \div 9$ **22.** $63 \div 7$ **23.** $70 \div 7$ **24.** $35 \div 7$

25. $90 \div 9$ **26.** $45 \div 9$ **27.** $49 \div 7$ **28.** $56 \div 7$ **29.** $54 \div 9$

Problem Solving Use the chart to answer each question.

FREDERICK DOUGLASS LIBRARY
Daily Fine for Overdue Items

Item	Fine
Children's Book	5¢
Adult Book	10¢
Audio Tape	10¢

30. Nancy has 2 children's books and 1 audio tape that are 7 days overdue. What will her fine be?

31. Mrs. Walsh paid 90¢ for an overdue adult book. How many days overdue was the book?

32. On October 17, Rick returned an overdue audio tape. The fine was 70¢. When was the tape due?

33. Gina paid 35¢ for 7 overdue children's books that were taken out together. How many days late were they?

More Practice Set 4.12, p. 435

MULTIPLES

You can use a hundreds chart and counting to find the multiples of a number. A **multiple** is the product of a number and any other number. For example: $4 \times 2 = 8$, so 8 is a multiple of 4 and a multiple of 2.

Groups:

- partners

You will need:

- a recording sheet
- a yellow and a blue crayon
- 10×10 squared paper

1	2	3	4	5	6	7	8	9	10
11	12	13	14	15	16	17	18	19	20
21	22	23	24	25	26	27	28	29	30
31	32	33	34	35	36	37	38	39	40
41	42	43	44	45	46	47	48	49	50
51	52	53	54	55	56	57	58	59	60
61	62	63	64	65	66	67	68	69	70
71	72	73	74	75	76	77	78	79	80
81	82	83	84	85	86	87	88	89	90
91	92	93	94	95	96	97	98	99	100

1	2	3	4	5	6	7	8	9	10
11	12	13	14	15	16	17	18	19	20
21	22	23	24	25	26	27	28	29	30
31	32	33	34	35	36	37	38	39	40
41	42	43	44	45	46	47	48	49	50
51	52	53	54	55	56	57	58	59	60
61	62	63	64	65	66	67	68	69	70
71	72	73	74	75	76	77	78	79	80
81	82	83	84	85	86	87	88	89	90
91	92	93	94	95	96	97	98	99	100

1	2	3	4	5	6	7	8	9	10
11	12	13	14	15	16	17	18	19	20
21	22	23	24	25	26	27	28	29	30
31	32	33	34	35	36	37	38	39	40
41	42	43	44	45	46	47	48	49	50
51	52	53	54	55	56	57	58	59	60
61	62	63	64	65	66	67	68	69	70
71	72	73	74	75	76	77	78	79	80
81	82	83	84	85	86	87	88	89	90
91	92	93	94	95	96	97	98	99	100

1	2	3	4	5	6	7	8	9	10
11	12	13	14	15	16	17	18	19	20
21	22	23	24	25	26	27	28	29	30
31	32	33	34	35	36	37	38	39	40
41	42	43	44	45	46	47	48	49	50
51	52	53	54	55	56	57	58	59	60
61	62	63	64	65	66	67	68	69	70
71	72	73	74	75	76	77	78	79	80
81	82	83	84	85	86	87	88	89	90
91	92	93	94	95	96	97	98	99	100

1	2	3	4	5	6	7	8	9	10
11	12	13	14	15	16	17	18	19	20
21	22	23	24	25	26	27	28	29	30
31	32	33	34	35	36	37	38	39	40
41	42	43	44	45	46	47	48	49	50
51	52	53	54	55	56	57	58	59	60
61	62	63	64	65	66	67	68	69	70
71	72	73	74	75	76	77	78	79	80
81	82	83	84	85	86	87	88	89	90
91	92	93	94	95	96	97	98	99	100

1	2	3	4	5	6	7	8	9	10
11	12	13	14	15	16	17	18	19	20
21	22	23	24	25	26	27	28	29	30
31	32	33	34	35	36	37	38	39	40
41	42	43	44	45	46	47	48	49	50
51	52	53	54	55	56	57	58	59	60
61	62	63	64	65	66	67	68	69	70
71	72	73	74	75	76	77	78	79	80
81	82	83	84	85	86	87	88	89	90
91	92	93	94	95	96	97	98	99	100

One person counts by 2's from 20 to 50. The other person uses the yellow crayon to shade the counted numbers on the chart. These numbers are all multiples of 2.

1. What pattern do you see?

Use your pattern to complete the rest of the chart.

Now one person counts by 3's from 3 to 51. The other person uses a blue crayon to shade the counted numbers on a second chart. These numbers are all multiples of 3.

2. What pattern do you see?

Use your pattern to complete the rest of the chart. List the first 15 multiples of 2 and the first 15 multiples of 3.

3. Which numbers appear on both lists?

When a number is a multiple of two or more numbers, it is called a **common multiple.** The first six common multiples of 2 and 3 are 6, 12, 18, 24, 30, and 36.

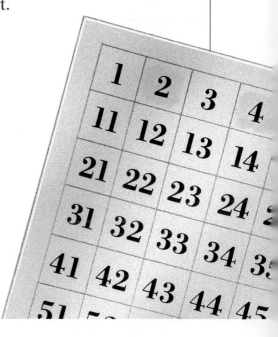

For each exercise below, use a hundred chart, shading and counting to find the multiples.

4. by 2's and 5's   5. by 3's and 5's   6. by 4's and 8's   7. by 3's and 9's

8. List the first ten multiples of each number in exercises 4–7.

9. Write the common multiples of each pair of numbers in exercises 4–7.

Critical Thinking •••••••••••••••••••••••••

SUMMING IT UP

10. Look at the chart you shaded for exercise 7. What do you notice? Why do you think that is?

11. Is every number a multiple of itself? How do you know?

12. What number has no multiple other than itself?

•••

PROJECT • Multiples

Design a pattern using 10 x 10 squared paper and crayons. Use the multiples of at least three different numbers. Use the same color to shade all the multiples of one number. Use a different color to shade all the multiples of another number. Show your pattern to a friend. Ask your friend to name the multiples you used to make your pattern.

COOPERATIVE • LEARNING

FACTORS

You know that some products can have more than one pair of factors. In this lesson you will explore some numbers with several factors.

Groups: • partners

You will need: • squared paper

• a blue, a yellow, and a red crayon

• a recording sheet

The rectangular arrays at the right show 4 × 6 = 24 and 3 × 8 = 24.

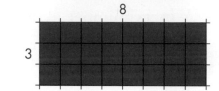

1. How many squares are in each array?

Use squared paper and a red crayon. Draw all the rectangular arrays that have 24 squares. Label the sides.

2. Is 5 a factor of 24? How do you know?

3. How many factors of 24 are there? List them on the recording sheet.

NUMBER	FACTORS	COMMON FACTORS
24		
18		
18 and 24		

Use squared paper and a blue crayon. Draw all the rectangular arrays that have 18 squares. Label the sides.

4. List all the factors of 18 on the recording sheet.

Cut out all the arrays of 18 squares. Compare each one with the arrays of 24 squares. Try to find the arrays with matching sides. For example:

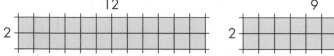

5. Name all the matching sides that are common to 18 and 24. List them on the recording sheet.

A number that is a factor of two or more numbers is called a **common factor.**

Use squared paper and a yellow crayon. Draw all the rectangular arrays that have 16 squares.

6. List all the factors of 16.

Compare each one with the arrays of 24 squares. Find all the matching sides that are common to 16 and 24.

7. List the common factors of 16 and 24.

8. You have already listed the common factors of 18 and 24. Now list the common factors of 16, 18, and 24.

Critical Thinking

SUMMING IT UP

9. Why is every number a factor of itself?

10. What two numbers are common factors of all even numbers?

11. Do you think a number that has 8 as a factor will have 4 as a factor? Explain.

12. How would you use multiplication to find the factors of a number?

PROJECT • Problem Solving

Work with a small group.

Winston's Fruit Store is making special fruit baskets. The list at the right shows how much fruit is left. They have to make 4 more baskets. Each one must have 7 kinds of fruit in it. All 4 baskets should be the same.

- How many of each fruit will you put in each basket?

- How many pieces of fruit will be left over?

- Compare the fruit in your baskets with another group.

pineapples	8	bananas	16
strawberries	48	peaches	28
cantaloupes	4	plums	32
apples	20	nectarines	40
oranges	24	pears	12

MULTIPLICATION PATTERNS

Seeing a pattern can help you to multiply tens, hundreds, and thousands mentally.

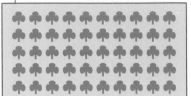

 Use a calculator to complete each multiplication sentence. Write the completed number sentence.

1. 5 × 1 = 5
5 × 10 = 50
5 × 100 = 500
5 × 1000 = 5000

2. 3 × 1 = ■
3 × 10 = ■
3 × 100 = ■
3 × 1000 = ■

3. 9 × 1 = ■
9 × 10 = ■
9 × 100 = ■
9 × 1000 = ■

4. 4 × 6 = ■
4 × 60 = ■
4 × 600 = ■
4 × 6000 = ■

5. 8 × 4 = ■
8 × 40 = ■
8 × 400 = ■
8 × 4000 = ■

6. 5 × 7 = ■
5 × 70 = ■
5 × 700 = ■
5 × 7000 = ■

7. What patterns do you see in the multiplication sentences in exercises 1–6?

Copy and complete each number sentence. Use a pattern to help you.

8. 3 × 2 = ■
3 × 20 = ■
3 × 200 = ■
3 × 2000 = ■

9. 6 × 3 = ■
6 × 30 = ■
6 × 300 = ■
6 × 3000 = ■

10. 5 × 4 = ■
5 × 40 = ■
5 × 400 = ■
5 × 4000 = ■

 Use a calculator to check your products.

11. Which patterns helped you the most?

Use a pattern to find each product.

12. 6 × 80   **13.** 4 × 500   **14.** 9 × 5000   **15.** 7 × 100   **16.** 8 × 50

SUMMING IT UP

17. Discuss with a friend how to solve the problems at the right without using a calculator or paper and pencil. Make up a mental math rule that you and your friend can depend on.

7×800

8×4000

5×80

A

5		8
	4	
6		2

18. Test your mental math rule. Choose one factor from box A. Use it to multiply each of the factors in box B. Write each sentence. Use a calculator to check. Discuss your rule with the class.

B

300	80	2000
4000	30	500
6000		700

PROJECT • Mental Math

Your group is going to plan a model city. The diagram below shows how many blocks are needed to build different kinds of buildings. You have 100,000 blocks to work with. Use as many of the blocks as you can. Do not include more than 9 buildings of one kind in your plan.

5000 blocks	4000 blocks	3000 blocks	2000 blocks	700 blocks	90 blocks	15 blocks
OFFICE BUILDING	APARTMENT	SCHOOL	STORE	HOUSE	GARAGE	DOG HOUSE

Use a recording sheet like the one below to show your plan.

Kind of Building	Number of Buildings of This Kind	Number of Blocks Per Building	Total Blocks Used

Share your plan with the class.

PROBLEM SOLVING
USING STRATEGIES

If you get stuck, remember....
Tips for Problem Solving
on pages 474–475

Mr. Phillips is the gym teacher at the new Norwood School. He is going to order supplies from two catalogs as shown below. There will be no more than 60 students in each gym class.

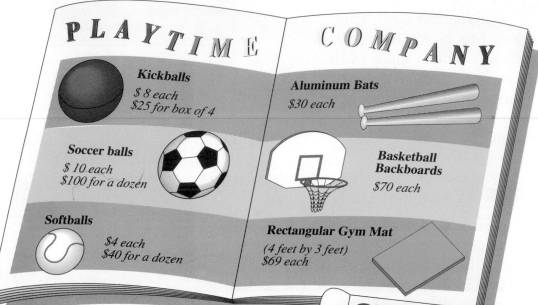

PLAYTIME   COMPANY

Kickballs
$ 8 each
$25 for box of 4

Aluminum Bats
$30 each

Soccer balls
$ 10 each
$100 for a dozen

Basketball Backboards
$70 each

Softballs
$4 each
$40 for a dozen

Rectangular Gym Mat
(4 feet by 3 feet)
$69 each

Work with a small group. Make a diagram, a table, or use other strategies.

1. Mr. Phillips needs to order 1 soccer ball for every 8 students in a class.
   a. How many soccer balls should he order?
   b. Which company charges less? How do you know?

2. Mr. Phillips needs to order 1 kickball for every 6 students.
   a. How many kickballs should he order?
   b. Which company charges less? How do you know?

SPORTS ✚ PLUS

KICKBALLS
$7 each

SOCCER BALLS
$9 each

SOFTBALLS
$6 each
Buy 2, get 1 free

ALUMINUM BATS
$27 each

BASKETBALL BACKBOARDS
$74 each

RECTANGULAR GYM MATS
(4 feet by 3 feet)
$77 each

3. Mr. Phillips needs 10 softballs.
   a. How much less will they cost at Playtime than at Sports Plus?
   b. Why should he order more than 10 softballs?

4. Mr. Phillips will order 6 basketball backboards.
   a. How much will it cost to buy them from Playtime?
   b. Which company charges less?

5. Mr. Phillips will order 8 aluminum bats.
   a. How much will they cost from Playtime?
   b. How much does Mr. Phillips save on each bat he buys from Sports Plus instead of Playtime?
   c. How much does he save by buying all 8 bats from Sports Plus instead of Playtime?

6. Mr. Phillips has 12 gym mats just like the ones in the catalogs. He wants to arrange them to cover a square area 12 feet on a side. Draw a diagram to show how he can do that.

7. For tumbling practice, Mr. Phillips wants to use mats to cover a rectangle 30 feet long and 20 feet wide.
   a. Draw a diagram to show how the mats could be placed.
   b. How many more mats does Mr. Phillips need to order?

DIVISION PATTERNS

Patterns can help you to multiply mentally.
For example:

$$4 \times 6 = 24$$
$$4 \times 60 = 240$$
$$4 \times 600 = 2400$$
$$4 \times 6000 = 24{,}000$$

Patterns can also help you divide mentally.

$24 \div 4 = 6$	$48 \div 6 = 8$	$10 \div 2 = 5$
$240 \div 4 = 60$	$480 \div 6 = 80$	$100 \div 2 = 50$
$2400 \div 4 = 600$	$4800 \div 6 = 800$	$1000 \div 2 = 500$
$24{,}000 \div 4 = 6000$	$48{,}000 \div 6 = 8000$	$10{,}000 \div 2 = 5000$

Think

• How are the division patterns and
multiplication patterns alike? How are
they different?

You can mentally divide tens, hundreds, and
thousands. For example, divide 2000 by 4.

$2000 \div 4 = $ ▪

Use the division fact:
$20 \div 4 = 5$

$2000 \div 4 = 500$

Check with mental
multiplication:
$4 \times 500 = 2000$

GUIDED PRACTICE

Write the quotient.

1. $80 \div 4$ 2. $500 \div 5$ 3. $350 \div 7$ 4. $16{,}000 \div 4$

5. $200 \div 5$ 6. $1000 \div 2$ 7. $3000 \div 6$ 8. $400 \div 5$

Critical
Thinking 9. In exercises 1–8, does the quotient always
have the same number of zeros as the
dividend? Why or why not?

INDEPENDENT PRACTICE

Write the quotient.

10. 60 ÷ 6 **11.** 140 ÷ 2 **12.** 6000 ÷ 2 **13.** 250 ÷ 5

14. 200 ÷ 4 **15.** 1000 ÷ 5 **16.** 210 ÷ 3 **17.** 12,000 ÷ 4

18. 560 ÷ 7 **19.** 360 ÷ 6 **20.** 2000 ÷ 5 **21.** 300 ÷ 6

22. 3200 ÷ 4 **23.** 490 ÷ 7 **24.** 64,000 ÷ 8 **25.** 2700 ÷ 3

Write the answer.

26. 4 × 70 **27.** 90 ÷ 3 **28.** 6000 ÷ 6 **29.** 8 × 200

30. 3 × 60 **31.** 160 ÷ 4 **32.** 4 × 3000 **33.** 5 × 60

34. 100 ÷ 5 **35.** 300 ÷ 5 **36.** 8 × 50 **37.** 3 × 9000

38. 60 × 6 **39.** 2800 ÷ 7 **40.** 400 × 9 **41.** 420 ÷ 6

PROJECT • Game

Play this game with a partner. Make a set of cards
like the ones shown here.

a. Place the cards in a stack face
down on the table.

b. Each player takes a card and
places it face up in the center.

c. Each player divides the numbers
on the card.

d. The player with the greater
quotient keeps both cards. If the
quotients are equal, the players
keep their own cards.

e. Repeat steps b–d until all the
cards have been played. The
player with more cards wins.

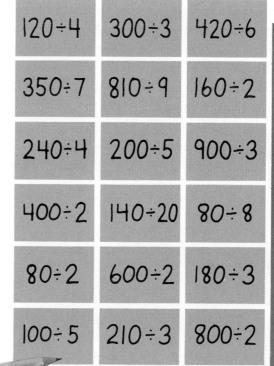

120÷4	300÷3	420÷6
350÷7	810÷9	160÷2
240÷4	200÷5	900÷3
400÷2	140÷20	80÷8
80÷2	600÷2	180÷3
100÷5	210÷3	800÷2

LINE PLOTS

Diane surveyed 12 classmates about how many hours a week they spent reading books. Now she wonders what number of hours is most common.

Alice	25 hours	Nancy	15 hours
Anna	25 hours	Paul	15 hours
Bob	10 hours	Ray	25 hours
Elaine	5 hours	Ron	20 hours
Juan	15 hours	Tawana	10 hours
Maria	20 hours	Wilma	15 hours

Diane makes a **line plot** of her survey results. This makes it easier for her to compare them.

She puts an *X* over the answer each student gave.

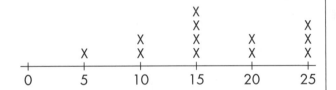

The line is labeled with the hours spent reading each week.

The greatest number of *X*'s is over the number 15. So, 15 is the most common number of hours students read in a week.

INDEPENDENT PRACTICE

Use the line plot above to solve each problem.

1. How many students read for 10 hours each week?

2. Did more students read for 25 hours or for 5 hours?

3. Use the data below to make a line plot.

Number of Brothers and Sisters		
Mark 0	Luis 0	Joe 5
Elaine 3	Barb 4	Nancy 0
Greta 1	Ming 2	Sean 1
Julia 2	John 1	Burt 0

More Practice Set 4.18, p. 436

SECTION REVIEW

for pages 122–142

Write the product.

1. 4×7 2. 8×7 3. 9×9 4. 1×8

5. 7×6 6. 3×9 7. 6×6 8. 5×4

9. 9×10 10. 4×4 11. 10×7 12. 5×5

13. 7×9 14. 8×8 15. 6×5 16. 4×9

17. 10×4 18. 0×7 19. 4×6 20. 8×2

Write the quotient. Then write a related multiplication fact.

21. $36 \div 9$ 22. $64 \div 8$ 23. $42 \div 7$ 24. $81 \div 9$

25. $9 \div 1$ 26. $40 \div 8$ 27. $35 \div 7$ 28. $72 \div 8$

29. $63 \div 7$ 30. $49 \div 7$ 31. $56 \div 7$ 32. $18 \div 6$

33. $45 \div 5$ 34. $50 \div 10$ 35. $24 \div 4$ 36. $32 \div 4$

37. $18 \div 2$ 38. $40 \div 4$ 39. $24 \div 6$ 40. $20 \div 2$

Copy and complete the related sentences.

41. $8 \times 6 = \blacksquare$
    $6 \times \blacksquare = 48$
    $48 \div \blacksquare = 8$
    $\blacksquare \div 8 = 6$

42. $9 \times \blacksquare = 72$
    $\blacksquare \times 8 = 72$
    $\blacksquare \div 9 = 8$
    $72 \div \blacksquare = 9$

43. $\blacksquare \times 10 = 60$
    $6 \times 10 = \blacksquare$
    $60 \div \blacksquare = 6$
    $\blacksquare \div 6 = 10$

Problem Solving

44. Hot dogs come in packages of 8. Sam buys 3 packages for a cookout. Only 2 of the hot dogs were not eaten. How many hot dogs were eaten?

45. Amy put 4 photos on each page in her album. She has 32 photos. How many pages did she fill?

CHAPTER TEST

Write a division sentence for each multiplication sentence.

1. $9 \times 3 = 27$ 2. $2 \times 6 = 12$ 3. $5 \times 10 = 50$ 4. $4 \times 8 = 32$

5. $9 \times 2 = 18$ 6. $5 \times 6 = 30$ 7. $7 \times 4 = 28$ 8. $3 \times 7 = 21$

Copy and complete the number sentence.

9. $149 \times \blacksquare = 149$ 10. $1362 \times \blacksquare = 0$ 11. $\blacksquare \div 1 = 780$

12. $\blacksquare \times 33 = 33 \times 19$ 13. $27 + 27 + 27 = 27 \times \blacksquare$

14. $3 + 3 + 3 = 3 \times \blacksquare$ 15. $\blacksquare \div 20 = 0$ 16. $8 \times 5 = \blacksquare \times 8$

Write the answer.

17.
$$\begin{array}{r} 8 \\ \times\ 5 \\ \hline \end{array}$$

18.
$$\begin{array}{r} 7 \\ \times\ 9 \\ \hline \end{array}$$

19.
$$\begin{array}{r} 10 \\ \times\ 9 \\ \hline \end{array}$$

20.
$$\begin{array}{r} 6 \\ \times\ 3 \\ \hline \end{array}$$

21.
$$\begin{array}{r} 5 \\ \times\ 5 \\ \hline \end{array}$$

22.
$$\begin{array}{r} 10 \\ \times\ 1 \\ \hline \end{array}$$

23.
$$\begin{array}{r} 7 \\ \times\ 6 \\ \hline \end{array}$$

24.
$$\begin{array}{r} 7 \\ \times\ 7 \\ \hline \end{array}$$

25. $5 \div 5$ 26. $40 \div 10$ 27. 6×7 28. 8×2

29. $81 \div 9$ 30. $24 \div 4$ 31. $54 \div 6$ 32. $72 \div 9$

PROBLEM SOLVING

Solve each problem.

33. Poison ivy has 3 leaflets on each stem. How many leaflets would be on 8 stems of poison ivy?

34. A flat of petunias costs $4 each, and a flat of sweet peas costs $6 each. How much will 2 flats of each flower cost?

35. Virginia creeper has 5 leaflets on each stem. If there are a total of 35 leaflets on one creeper plant, how many stems does that plant have?

36. Each student can plant 7 flower plants in an hour. If there are 10 students in Karlena's group, how many flowers can they plant in 2 hours?

CUMULATIVE REVIEW

Write the answer.

1. 362
   $+\ \ 25$

2. 765
   $+\ \ 29$

3. $4.75
   $+\ \ 3.97$

4. 589
   $+\ 431$

5. 14 + 52 + 83 =

6. 145 + 261 + 45 + 182 =

7. 809
   $-\ 253$

8. 3001
   $-\ \ \ 91$

9. 270
   $-\ \ 36$

10. $10.47 − $1.39

Use the line graph.

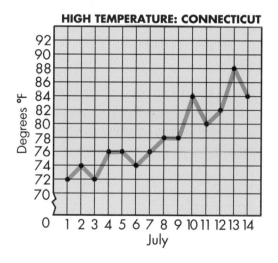

Use the bar graph.

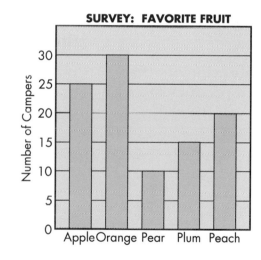

11. When was the temperature the highest?

12. How many degrees higher was the high temperature on July 10 than the high temperature on July 6?

13. Was the temperature at the end of the month higher or lower than the temperature at the beginning of the month?

14. How many campers voted in the survey?

15. How many more campers voted for apples than pears? How did you find your answer?

16. How many votes did the most popular fruit receive?

EXCURSION

NUMBER THEORY

FACTOR TREES

A **prime number** has two different factors: itself and 1. Some prime numbers are 2, 3, 5, 7, 11, 13, and 17.

Other whole numbers have more than two factors.

$18 = 1 \times 18$ or $18 = 2 \times 9$ or $18 = 3 \times 6$

Any whole number can be written as a product of prime numbers. A factor tree can help you.

Write 24 as a product of prime numbers.

Step 1

Find two factors that have a product of 24.

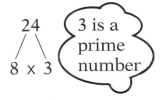

Step 2

Find two factors that have a product of 8. Do not list 1 as a factor.

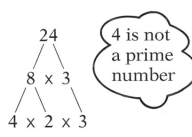

Step 3

Continue to find two factors of any number that is not a prime number.

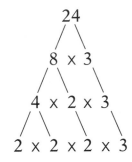

The numbers 2 and 3 are prime numbers. So $2 \times 2 \times 2 \times 3 = 24$ is written as a product of prime factors.

Another factor tree for 24 is:

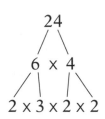

Write *prime* or *not prime* for each number.

1. 5   2. 7   3. 12

4. 8   5. 10   6. 11

7. 20   8. 32   9. 13

10. 27   11. 48   12. 41

Copy and complete each factor tree.

13.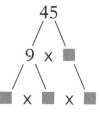

14.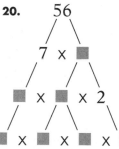

15.

16.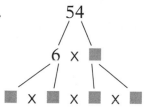

17.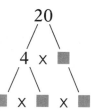

18.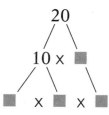

19.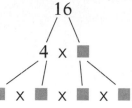

20.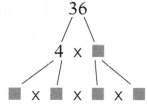

21.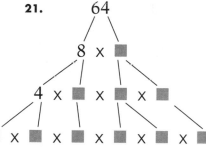

22. Compare the factor trees for exercises 14 and 15, and for 17 and 18. How are they alike? How are they different?

Draw a factor tree to find the prime factors of each.

23. 27   24. 32   25. 40   26. 21

GEOMETRY

Science

A Geometric Design Snowflakes are made of tiny ice crystals. As you can see, each flake has six points and six sides. Some flakes are smooth and rounded. Others have sharp, jagged points. No two snowflakes are exactly alike. Each flake has its own design.

The figure below is called a regular **hexagon.** Notice that it has six equal sides. Trace the outline of the hexagon onto a sheet of white paper. Then draw a snowflake design on your hexagon. Use scissors to cut out the snowflake.

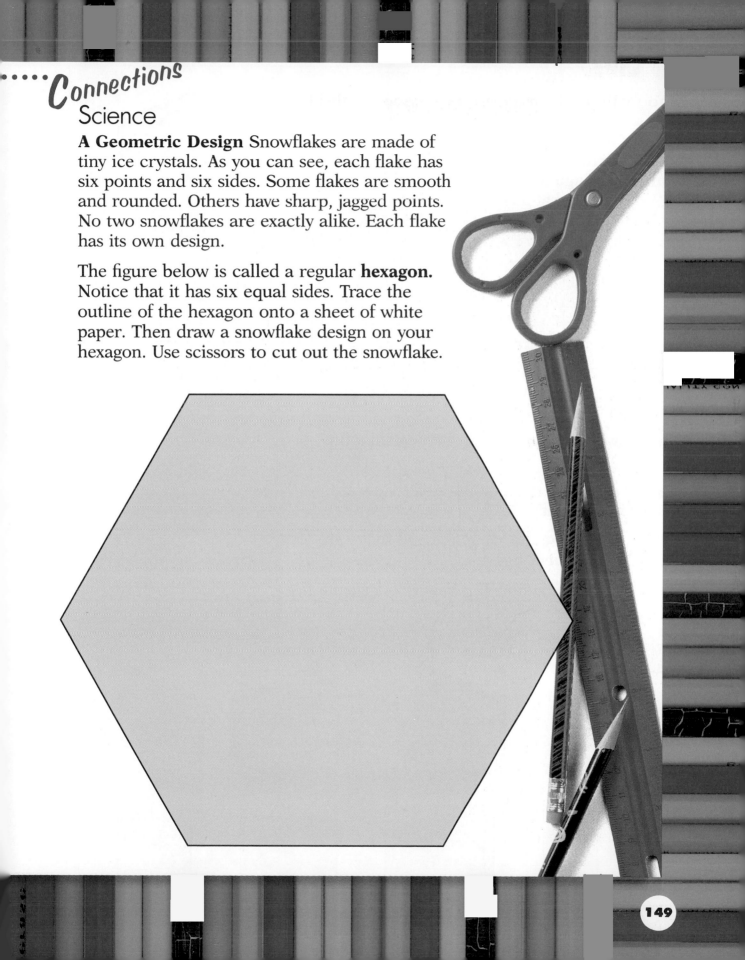

Flips

You will need dot paper and scissors for this lesson.

Gerry and Chris were experimenting with mirrors. They looked at the **mirror image** of a figure. Chris said, "I can show that using two cutouts.

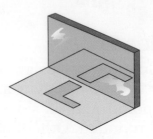

I paste one down.

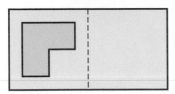

Then flip the other and paste it down."

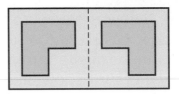

1. If Gerry wanted to check this with a mirror, where do you think he should place the mirror?

2. Why is a mirror image often called a **flip image**?

3. How are the two cutouts alike? How are they different?

Figures that are the same size and shape are called **congruent** figures.

  4. Are a figure and its flip image congruent? Explain.

Match the mirror pictures with the cut-out pictures.

5.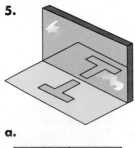

6.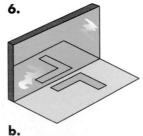

7.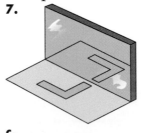

8.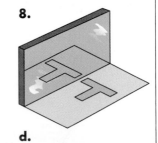

a.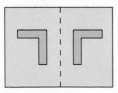

b.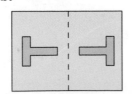

c.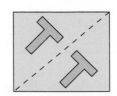

d.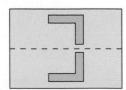

Which of these pictures shows a flip?

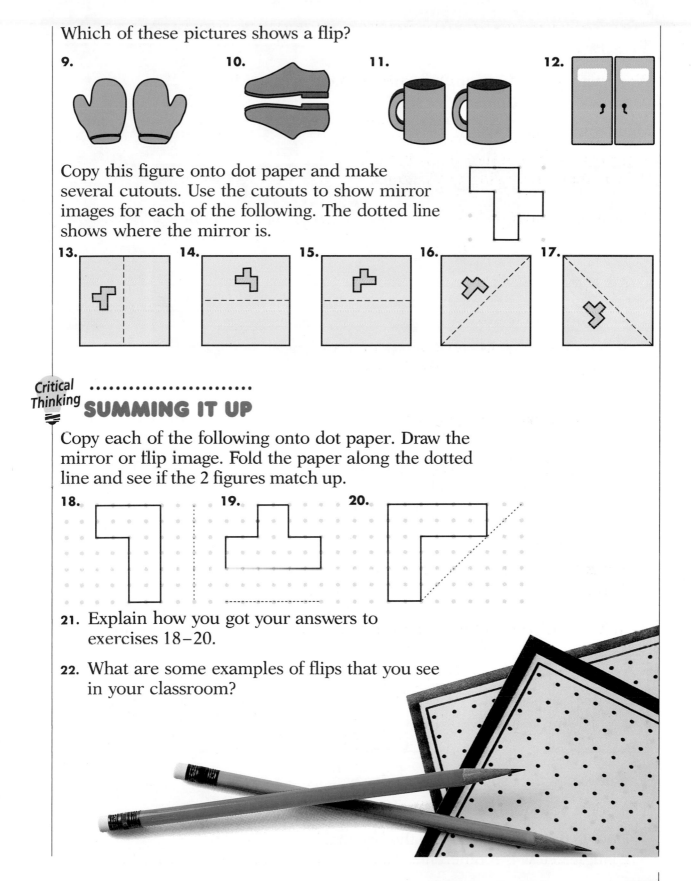

9.   **10.**   **11.**   **12.**

Copy this figure onto dot paper and make several cutouts. Use the cutouts to show mirror images for each of the following. The dotted line shows where the mirror is.

13.   **14.**   **15.**   **16.**   **17.**

SUMMING IT UP

Copy each of the following onto dot paper. Draw the mirror or flip image. Fold the paper along the dotted line and see if the 2 figures match up.

18.   **19.**   **20.**

21. Explain how you got your answers to exercises 18–20.

22. What are some examples of flips that you see in your classroom?

TURNS

Work with a small group. You will need dot paper and tracing paper.

Many things in the world turn.

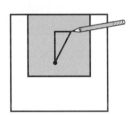

You can turn drawings, too.

On a sheet of paper, draw a triangle.

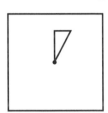

Trace the triangle on a second sheet.

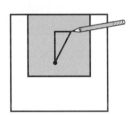

With your pencil, hold one point steady.

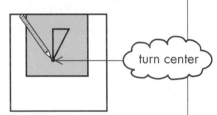

turn center

Turn the tracing.

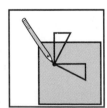

Draw over the tracing. Press down hard with your pencil.

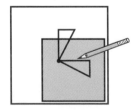

Remove the tracing and draw the triangle in the new position.

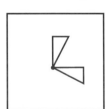

The new position shows the **turn image.**

The point you hold steady is the **turn center.**

1. How is the turn image like the original triangle? How is it different?

Which of these drawings show turns?

2. P

3. B B

4. ㄥ•ㄥ

5. A A

Melinda uses tracing paper and dot paper to make turn images of a triangle. How many turn images does she draw each time?

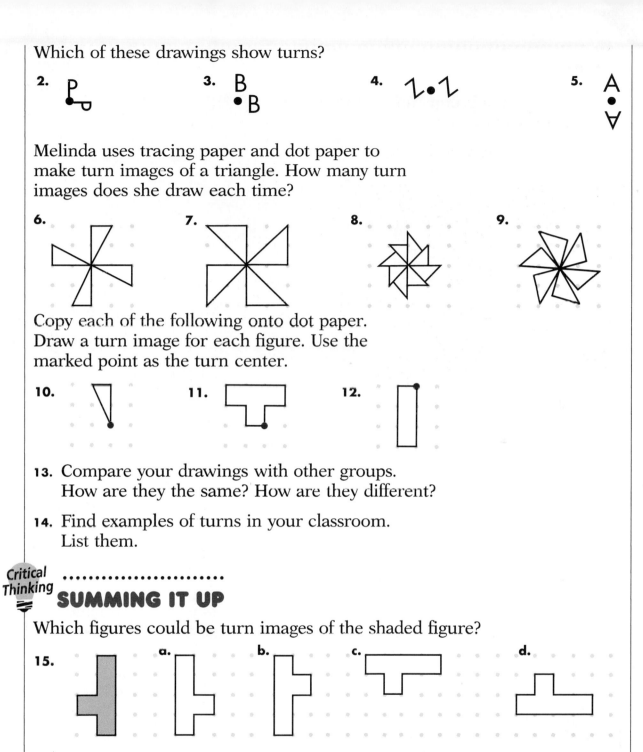

6.

7.

8.

9.

Copy each of the following onto dot paper. Draw a turn image for each figure. Use the marked point as the turn center.

10.

11.

12.

13. Compare your drawings with other groups. How are they the same? How are they different?

14. Find examples of turns in your classroom. List them.

Critical Thinking

SUMMING IT UP

Which figures could be turn images of the shaded figure?

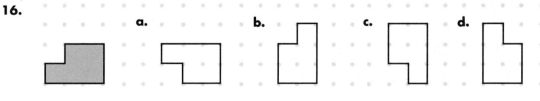

15.

a.   b.   c.   d.

16.

a.   b.   c.   d.

17. Explain how you solved exercises 15 and 16.

153

ANGLES

Start   Finish

Start   Finish

Ruiz and Cristina are practicing marching. Cristina says, "About face!" Ruiz turns to face the opposite direction. He turns halfway around, making a **half turn.**

Then Ruiz says, "Right face!" Cristina turns toward her right hand. She turns only one quarter of the way around. She makes a **quarter turn.**

An **angle** is a figure that can be used to show a turn.

You can use geostrips to show the sides of an angle. Use cardboard and a brass fastener to make a geostrip.

The angle that shows a quarter turn is called a **right angle.** An angle has 2 sides joined at the **vertex.**

A right angle measures 90° (90 degrees).

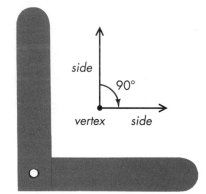

side

90°

vertex   side

Think

- How many degrees in a half turn? How do you know?

- If you turn all the way back to your starting point, through how many degrees will you turn?

GUIDED PRACTICE

Tell which of these angles are right angles.

1.   2.   3.   4.   5.

Critical Thinking 6. How did you decide on your answers to exercises 1–5?

INDEPENDENT PRACTICE

Tell which of these are right angles. Write *yes* or *no*.

7.   8.   9.   10.   11.

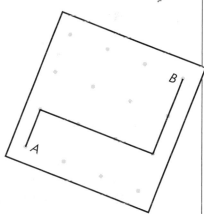

12. Look at the path from *A* to *B* in this drawing. How many right angles appear along the path?

13. On dot paper, mark 4 × 4 squares of dots like the one in exercise 12. Mark points *A* and *B*. Draw a path from *A* to *B* with 3 right angles. Then draw a path with 4 right angles. Next draw a path with 5 right angles.

14. Can you draw a path from *A* to *B* that has 6 right angles? Show how you got your answer.

PROJECT • Circles

Cut out a circle and fold it into fourths. Unfold it. Mark north as shown. Mark east, west, and south. How many angles are formed by the direction lines? What kind of angles are formed?

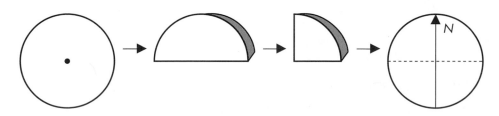

Symmetry

You will need two copies of a recording sheet and a pair of scissors.

▶ Cut out the circle on one recording sheet. When you fold the circle in half, do the two parts of the circle match exactly? When two parts of a figure match exactly, the fold line is a **line of symmetry.**

1. To show a line of symmetry, does it matter where you fold the circle?

2. How many lines of symmetry do you think a circle has?

Another name for a line of symmetry of a circle is a **diameter.**

When you fold the half circle to make a right angle, this fold line is called a **radius.**

▶ There is another kind of symmetry. You can show this with a rectangle. Cut out the rectangle from the recording sheet.

Match the rectangle with the drawing of the rectangle on the second recording sheet.

Turn the rectangle a quarter of the way around.

3. Does the cutout rectangle match the drawing?

Now turn the cutout rectangle so that it is half of the way around.

4. Does the cutout rectangle match the drawing?

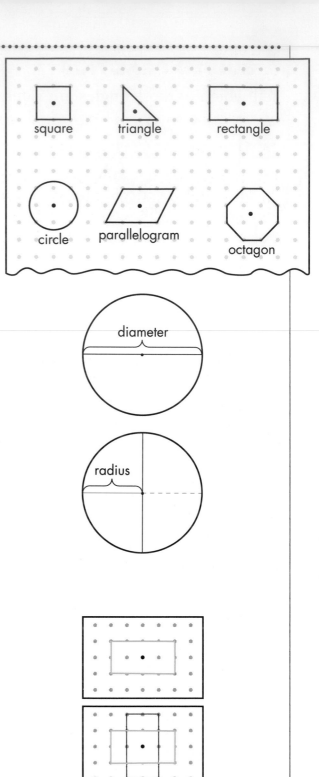

If a cutout matches its drawing when it is turned half way around, the figure has **half-turn symmetry.**

5. Does the rectangle have half-turn symmetry?

6. Does the circle have half-turn symmetry?

▶ Cut out each remaining figure on the recording sheet. Match with the drawing on the second recording sheet. Turn each to find whether or not it has half-turn symmetry. Use the large dot as the turn center.

7. Which figures have half-turn symmetry?

Try to fold each cutout so the two parts match. If the two parts match, open the cutout and mark the line of symmetry. Then mark as many lines of symmetry as you can find.

8. Which of your cutout figures has no lines of symmetry?

9. Does the figure from exercise 8 have half-turn symmetry?

Critical Thinking ·
SUMMING IT UP

Look at the capital letters on the bottom of the recording sheet.

10. Which letters have half-turn symmetry?

11. Which letters have lines of symmetry?

12. Which letters have half-turn symmetry but no line of symmetry?

You may remember that acting out a problem can help you solve it. Once I acted out a problem using a sheet of paper. I made a paper model to help design a new toy.

MY PROBLEM

One part of the toy was a small drum that would have a diameter of 2 inches. I planned to have a metal strip go around the drum. I needed to know the distance around the drum so I would know how long the metal strip would be.

MY SOLUTION

I rolled a sheet of paper to make a model of the drum.

I rolled the paper until my "paper drum" was exactly 2 inches wide across the top. Next, I needed to measure the distance around the drum. So I drew a line around the drum.

I unrolled the paper and measured the line.

How long will the metal strip around the drum be?

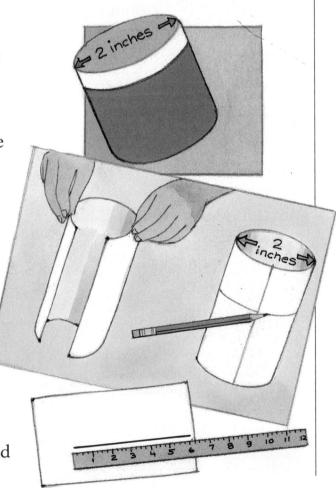

GUIDED PRACTICE

Use the model shown to solve the problem.

1. Ms. Gonyo is planning a design. She wants it to be a circle surrounded by other circles the same size. The circles should touch each other as shown. How many circles can fit around the center one?

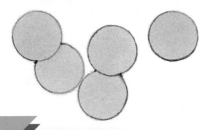

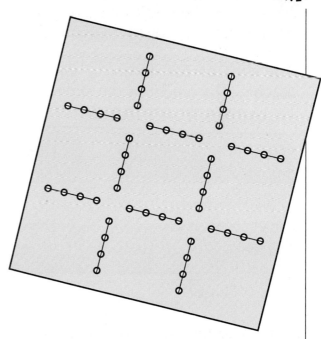

APPLICATION

Work with a small group to solve each problem. Make models when it helps. ·····················

COOPERATIVE • LEARNING

2. A carpenter has a square piece of wood. She wants to cut it into 16 small square pieces. How can she do that by making only 4 cuts? HINT: Use folding, cutting, and stacking with a square piece of paper.

3. At a halftime show, 12 groups of marchers line up in a tic-tac-toe shape. How can they form 3 identical squares if only 3 of the groups move? HINT: The squares touch only at corners.

4. Pat is painting cubes. Each cube is the same size and will have 2 red faces and 4 blue faces. How many different ways can she paint the cubes? HINT: If you make 2 cubes look alike by turning them, the cubes are not different.

SLIDES

You will need dot paper for this lesson.

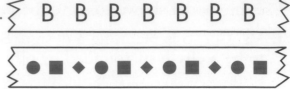

Another type of symmetry is **slide symmetry.** You can see this in repeating patterns.

If you trace part of the pattern and slide it, the tracing will match the pattern farther along.

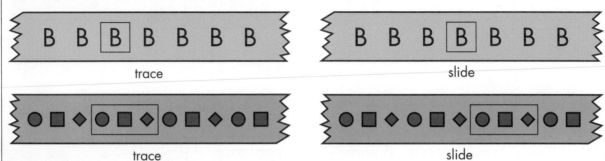

trace

slide

trace

slide

Think

• Will the tracing match no matter what distance you slide it?

The **slide arrow** shows the *direction* to move the tracing. The *length* of the slide arrow tells *how far* to move the tracing.

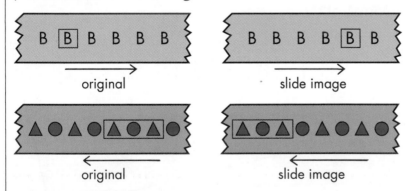

original

slide image

original

slide image

Think

• What do you notice about the original and the slide image?

160

GUIDED PRACTICE

The slide arrow shows the direction and distance to move. Will the slide image match the original? Write *yes* or *no*.

1.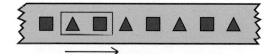

2.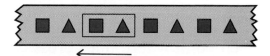

3.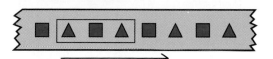

4.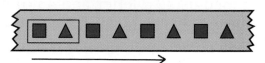

 Critical Thinking 5. Did you write *no* for any exercises? Copy the drawing and draw the slide arrow to make the answer *yes*.

INDEPENDENT PRACTICE

Copy each figure and slide arrow onto dot paper. Draw the slide image for the given slide arrow.

6.   7.   8.   9.

Copy each slide pattern onto dot paper. Mark a slide arrow for each to show slide symmetry.

10.    11.

12.    13.

Maintain • Mixed Practice

Write the answer.

1. 8×9 2. 6×7 3. $64 \div 8$ 4. $56 \div 7$

5. 3×10 6. 5×8 7. $49 \div 7$ 8. $40 \div 10$

ORDERED PAIRS

When one set of lines is drawn over another set as shown, the lines cross each other to make a grid. Usually, we want to show only part of a grid, so we draw only parts of lines, or **line segments.**

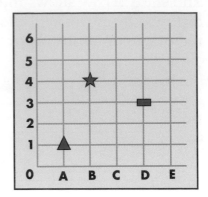

Each point where lines cross can be named using a letter and a number. There is a triangle at (A,1), where lines A and 1 cross. There is a star at (B,4). What is at (D,3)?

Grid lines, or line segments, are often named with numbers only. Then the point where 2 segments cross is named with a pair of numbers. There is a circle at (2,3). There is a square at (3,2).

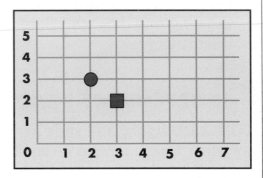

Because we write the number along the bottom line segment first, we call this an **ordered pair.**

Think
- • Does order matter when the ordered pair is a letter and a number?

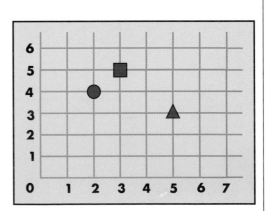

Find out what figure is at (3,5).

Start at 0.
Move 3 lines to the right.
Move 5 lines up.

The square is at the point (3,5).

Think
- • In what direction do you read to name the first number of an ordered pair?

GUIDED PRACTICE

An octagon is at point (*E*,4) in the grid shown.
Name the figure at each of the following points.

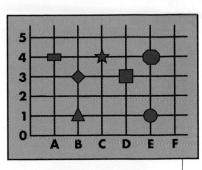

1. (*E*,1)   2. (*B*,1)   3. (*C*,4)

4. (*D*,3)   5. (*A*,4)   6. (*B*,3)

Use the grid at the right to answer each question.

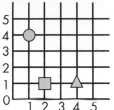

7. What figure is at point (1,4)?

8. What figure is at point (4,1)?

Critical Thinking 9. Is the order of the numbers in an ordered pair important? Why?

INDEPENDENT PRACTICE

Problem Solving You will need squared paper.

A classroom has 4 rows with 5 desks in each row. The desks in each row are called *A*, *B*, *C*, *D*, and *E*. Mary sits at desk (*B*,2). Where does each of the following sit?

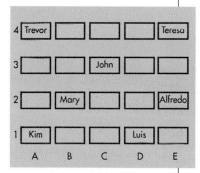

10. Trevor   11. John   12. Alfredo

13. Luis   14. Teresa   15. Kim

16. Copy the grid at the right onto squared paper. Join these following points in order: (1,3) (3,6) (5,3) (3,0) (1,3). What figure did you make?

17. Copy the grid at the right onto squared paper. Join these points in order: (4,4) (3,6) (2,4) (2,1) (4,1) (4,4) (2,4). What figure did you make?

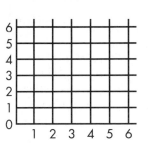

CHALLENGE • Problem Formulation

Critical Thinking Make up a problem with ordered pairs like problems 16 or 17. Give to a friend to solve. Did your friend draw what you expected? Explain.

QUADRILATERALS AND OTHER POLYGONS

You will need a geoboard and geoboard dot paper for this lesson.

a.    b.    c.

Figures like the one in *b* are called *open figures*.
Figures like the ones in *a* and *c* are called *closed figures*.

1. Which of these are open figures?

a.    b.    c.

A closed figure made up of **line segments** that do not cross each other is called a **polygon.**

Here are several polygons:

Square   Rectangle   Triangle   Parallelogram   Hexagon   Pentagon   Octagon

2. Which of the polygons have 4 sides?

3. Which of these figures are not a polygon?
   Explain.

a.   b.   c.   d.

Another name for a 4-sided polygon is a **quadrilateral.**

One corner of a polygon is a **vertex.** A square has 4 **vertices,** or corners. In this square, the vertices are named *A, B, C,* and *D.*

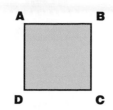

Line segments *AB* and *CD* are **parallel.** They are always the same distance apart.

Two lines that cross to form right angles are **perpendicular.** Line segments *AB* and *BC* are perpendicular.

4. **a.** On geoboard dot paper, copy the following figures:

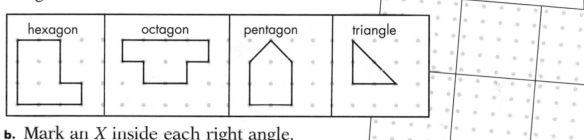

hexagon   octagon   pentagon   triangle

b. Mark an *X* inside each right angle.

5. Make each of the following on a geoboard. Record on geoboard dot paper.

    a. A hexagon with at least one right angle.
    b. A quadrilateral with only two right angles.
    c. A pentagon with two parallel sides.
    d. A triangle with one pair of perpendicular sides.

CHALLENGE • Visualization

Mark a box of 3 x 3 dots onto geoboard dot paper. It is possible to draw 16 different (not congruent) quadrilaterals in the squares. Three are shown on the right.

There are 13 more. Draw as many as you can. Use the geoboard to help you.
    a. How many have pairs of parallel sides?
    b. How many have right angles?

USING STRATEGIES

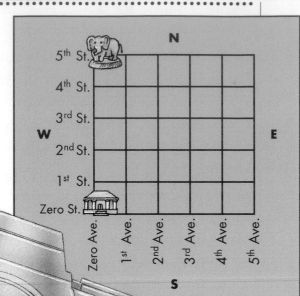

Pam and Paul are planning a treasure hunt for their friends in Gridville. They are using a map of the town to make their plans. They have already written directions to the treasure, which is a camera.

Solve each problem.

1. Follow directions A, B, and C.
   a. Where are you?
   b. Which way are you facing?

2. Which way are you facing after you have followed directions D and E?

3. Follow direction F. Where is the camera?

4. Write directions from Town Hall to the camera so that the treasure hunters have to turn only once.

5. Which path is shorter, yours or Pam and Paul's?

6. Make up your own treasure hunt. Decide where you will hide the treasure. Write directions. Trade with another pair.

Directions to Treasure

A. Start at Town Hall. Face toward the Elephant Statue.

B. Go 1 block in the direction you are facing.

C. Turn right a quarter turn.

D. Go 1 block in the direction you are facing.

E. Turn left a quarter turn.

F. Follow directions B through E 2 more times.

SECTION REVIEW

for pages 150–166

Look at the diagrams below.

a.   b. 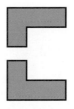   c.

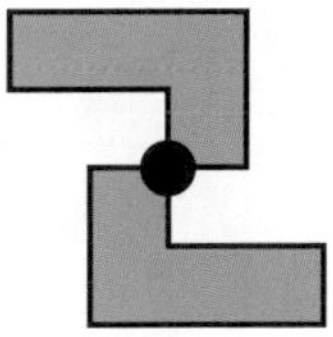

1. Which diagram shows a slide?

2. Which diagram shows a flip?

3. Which diagram shows a turn?

4. Write the letter of each figure below that shows a right angle.

a.   b.    c.    d.

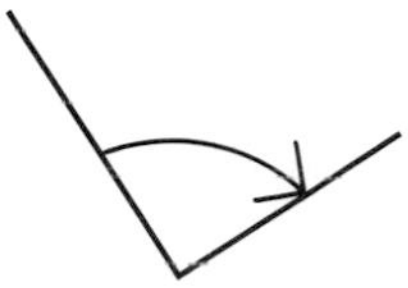

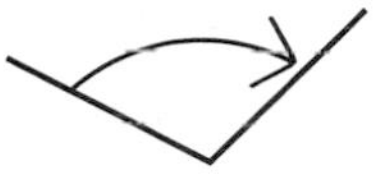

Name the ordered pair for each figure.

5. circle

6. triangle

7. rectangle

8. square

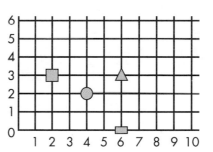

Use the grid to answer each question.

9. What figure is at point (0,2)?

10. What figure is at point (2,0)?

11. What figure is at point (3,4)?

12. What figure is at point (4,3)?

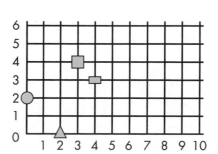

COUNTING SQUARES

You will need square dot paper for this lesson.

It is possible to make different figures using only four square blocks. The blocks must all be connected along whole sides.

These figures are possible.

 or

These figures are not possible.

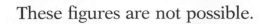 or

The figures at the right are the same. Why?

If you can flip or turn a figure to match another, the two figures are the same.

 and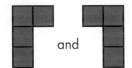

Five different figures are possible.

1. How are all five figures alike? How are they different?

2. Which of the figures below contain the same number of squares?

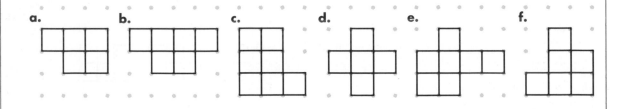

a.   b.   c.   d.   e.   f.

Some figures contain parts of squares as well as whole squares. For example:

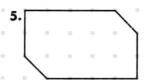

Number of squares:

$5 + \frac{1}{2}$
or
$5\frac{1}{2}$

$4 + \frac{1}{2} + \frac{1}{2} =$
$4 + 1 =$
5

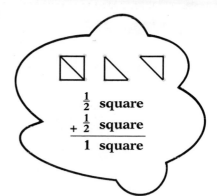

$\frac{1}{2}$ square
$+ \frac{1}{2}$ square
———
1 square

Use square dot paper for exercises 3–9. Copy each figure onto dot paper. Tell how many squares each one contains.

3. **4.** **5.** **6.**

7. The figure at the right contains $6\frac{1}{2}$ squares. Draw three different figures, each containing $6\frac{1}{2}$ squares.

8. Draw a rectangle containing:
   a. 2 squares   **b.** 4 squares   **c.** 8 squares
   d. 3 squares   **e.** 6 squares   **f.** 12 squares

9. Draw three different rectangles, each containing 16 squares.

Critical Thinking

SUMMING IT UP

10. How many figures containing $7\frac{1}{2}$ squares do you think are possible? Explain.

PROJECT • Estimating

The figure at the right contains about 18 squares. Draw another figure without straight sides that contains about 18 squares. Which one is bigger? How can you tell?

AREA

The rectangle at the right contains
12 squares. You could say that the
area of the rectangle is 12 squares.

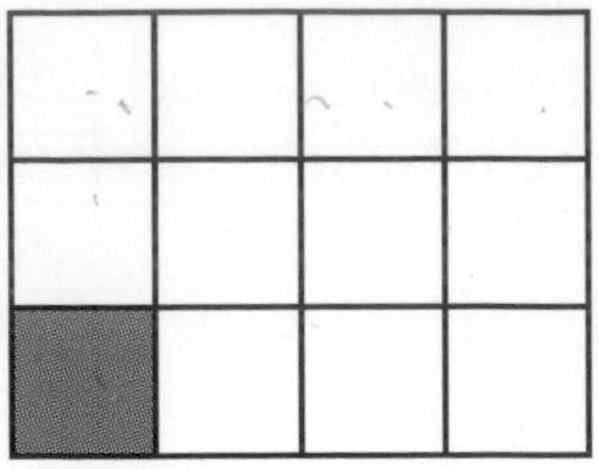

Think

• Which figures below have an area of
  12 squares?

a.   **b.** 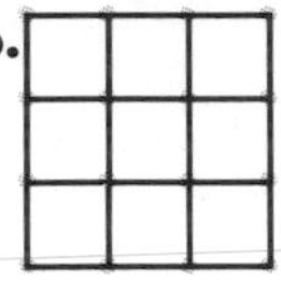   **c.**

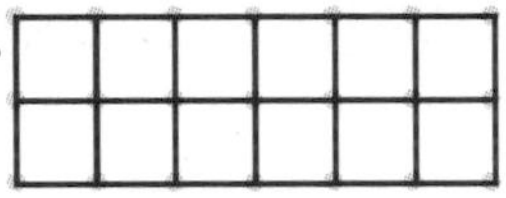

The **area** of a figure is a measure of how much
surface is covered by the figure.

Area is usually measured in units such as
square inches or **square centimeters.**

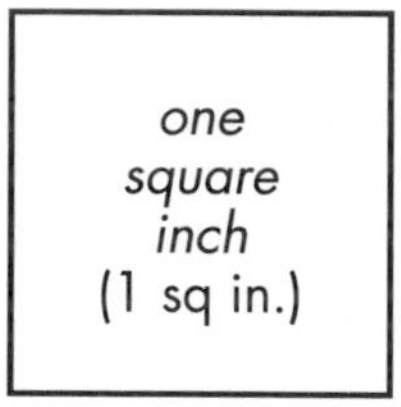

one
square
inch
(1 sq in.)

one square
centimeter
(1 sq cm)

It is not necessary for an area of one square
centimeter to be square in shape. Each of
the figures below has an area of one
square centimeter.

Think

• How can you tell that all the figures
  above have the same area?

GUIDED PRACTICE

Draw the following figures on squared paper.

1. A figure with an area of 6 squares.

2. A figure with an area of 10 squares.

Critical Thinking 3. Three different rectangles, each with an area
   of 18 squares.

170

More Practice Set 5.11, p. 438

The three squares below are drawn on centimeter squared paper. Give the area of each one in square centimeters.

4.

5.

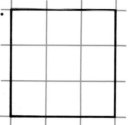

6.

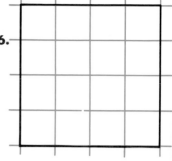

Write which pairs of figures below have the same area.

7.

8.

9.

10.

11.

12.

13. Draw three different figures on centimeter squared paper. Each figure should have an area of two square centimeters.

14. Copy and complete the chart. Use the rectangles at the right.

Figure	Length in Centimeters	Width in Centimeters	Area in Square Centimeters
A			
B			
C			
D			

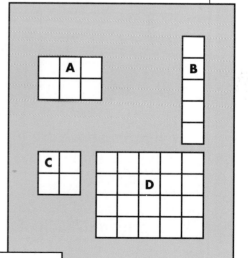

15. **Data Book** Go to page 470. Write the area in squares for each of the four rooms.

MATH LOG

How can knowing the length and width of a rectangle or square help you find the area of the figure?

CONGRUENCE AND SIMILARITY

You will need two copies of geoboard dot paper and one copy of dot paper. Look at each figure.

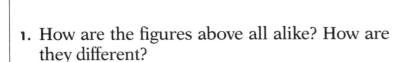

a.   b.   c.

d.   e.   f.

1. How are the figures above all alike? How are they different?

Congruent figures have the same size and shape.

2. Which figures above are congruent?

3. How are the figures below alike? How are they different?

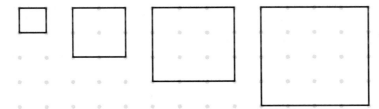

The figures above are not congruent. They do have the same shape, but they are not the same size.

4. Use geoboard dot paper. Color a figure congruent to each of the following.

a.   b. 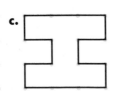   c.

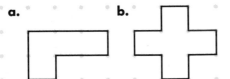

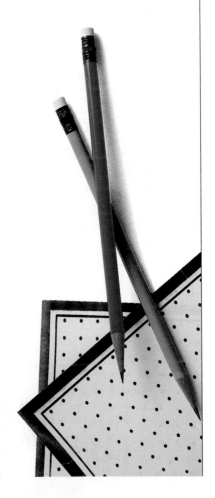

5. On geoboard dot paper, draw as many rectangles as you can find congruent to this one.

6. Mark a box of 3 × 3 dots on geoboard dot paper. Draw as many triangles as you can that are congruent to this one.

7. Mark a box of 3 × 3 dots on geoboard dot paper. Draw as many triangles as you can that are *not* congruent to each other.

SUMMING IT UP

8. Are a figure and its image congruent for a flip? a slide? a turn? Explain.

9. How can you tell when figures are congruent?

PROJECT • Similarity

Copy each figure below onto dot paper four times. Cut out each figure. Fit the four congruent figures together. Make a figure that is **similar.** That means, make a figure that is not congruent but that has the same shape.

SOLIDS

Work with a small group. You will need a recording
sheet, tape, and scissors.

Some solids are **pyramids.** Some are **prisms.**

▶ These are pyramids:

These are not pyramids:

 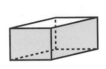

1. Which of the figures below are pyramids?

  a.   **b.**   **c.**   **d.**   **e.**

  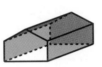

2. How are these pyramids alike?

▶ These are prisms:

 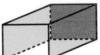 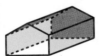

These are not prisms:

3. Which of the figures below are prisms?

  a.   **b.**   **c.**   **d.**   **e.**

4. How are these prisms alike?

▶ Some solids are neither prisms nor pyramids.

  cone   **cylinder**   **sphere**

5. How are these solids different from prisms and pyramids?

Prisms and pyramids all have flat surfaces, or *faces*. Cones and cylinders have curved surfaces.

The faces of pyramids and prisms meet at the edges. The edges meet at the vertices.

The prisms below are named by the shapes of the colored *faces*.

Tell what shape the red face is for each prism.

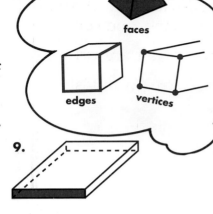

faces

edges   vertices

6.   **7.** 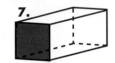 **8.** 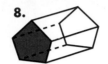 **9.**

10. If exercise 6 shows a triangular prism, which one is a square prism? a rectangular prism? a pentagonal prism?

Pyramids are named by the shapes of their *bases*. The bases are colored in the drawings below.

11. Name each pyramid.

a.   **b.**   **c.** 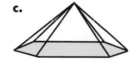 **d.**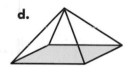

12. The cube is a special solid. What is special about it? Is it a prism or a pyramid?

 Critical Thinking

SUMMING IT UP

13. How do you name a pyramid or prism?

14. What is the difference between pyramids and prisms?

PROJECT • Patterns

A **net** is a pattern that will make a solid. The pattern shown is a net.

Use the recording sheet to cut out the net. Fold on the dotted lines. Tape the edges together to make a figure. Tell what figure you have made.

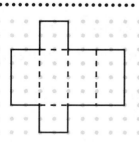

COOPERATIVE • LEARNING

Work with a small group. Your group will need dot paper, triangle dot paper, connecting cubes, and scissors.

Figures made up of 5 squares, like the one shown, are called **pentominoes.**

1. Cut out five 2cm x 2cm paper squares. Make as many different pentominoes as you can. HINT: There are 12 in all. Draw your pentominoes on dot paper.

There are 8 pentominoes that are nets of open boxes. This means that they can be folded to make a cube with one face missing.

You can make a tiling pattern with any pentomino. For example:

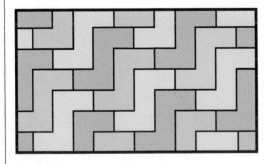

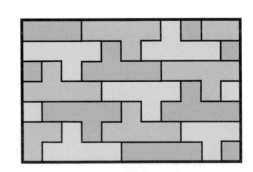

2. Make several copies of one of your pentominoes. Use this set of congruent pieces to make a tiling pattern. Draw your pattern on dot paper.

3. Repeat exercise 2 with a different pentomino.

Instead of using squares to make pentominoes, you can use connecting cubes to make **pentacubes.** Here are some examples:

Use cubes to make the ones above. Then find as many others as you can.

4. How many different pentacubes did you find?

Copy each drawing below onto triangle dot paper. Draw line segments to show each single cube.

5. 　　**6.** 　　**7.** 　　**8.**

9. Which of the drawings above could be pentacubes?

PROJECT • Making Models

You can make this rectangular prism from 3 different pentacubes and the 3-cube solid shown.

Here are the pentacubes you can choose from to make the rectangular prism.

rectangular prism　　　3-cube solid

a. 　　**b.** 　　**c.**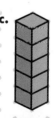

d. 　　**e.** 　　**f.**

Which 3 pentacubes should you choose? Build the pentacubes from connecting cubes and make the prism.

VOLUME

Work with a small group. You may use triangle dot paper, connecting cubes, and a recording sheet.

The number of cubes in a solid is called the **volume** of the solid. There are 5 cubes in a pentacube. So, the volume of a pentacube is 5 cubes.

How many cubes are in each of the following solids if no cubes are hidden?

1.  **2.** 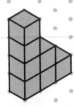 **3.**  **4.**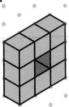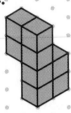

Copy the following solids onto triangle dot paper. Draw line segments to show separate cubes.

5. 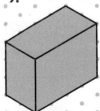 **6.**  **7.** 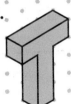 **8.**

How many cubes are in each solid?

Copy these rectangular prisms onto triangle dot paper. Draw line segments to show separate cubes.

9.  **10.** 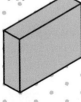 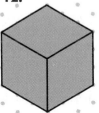 **11.** **12.**

How many cubes are in each solid?

Use a recording sheet like the one below. Record the answers to exercises 13–18 on it.

Number of Cubes (Volume)	Number of Cubes High	Number of Squares on Top	Area on Top
24			

Using connecting cubes, build a prism like the one in exercise 9. Place the prism so it is as tall as possible.

13. How many squares can you see on the top?

14. What is the area of the top?

Place the prism so that it is as short as possible.

15. How many squares can you see on top?

16. What is the area of the top?

Now place the prism another way.

17. How many squares can you see on top?

18. What is the area of the top?

19. Build a prism like the one in exercise 10. Repeat exercises 13–18. Record the answers on the recording sheet.

 Critical Thinking

SUMMING IT UP

20. If two figures have the same volume, do they have to have the same shape? Explain.

PROJECT • Prisms

Make a rectangular prism with 12 cubes. Compare it with the others made in class. How many different ones were made? Sketch your own prism on triangle dot paper.

COOPERATIVE • LEARNING

If you get stuck, remember...

Tips for Problem Solving

on pages 474–475

Mr. Lombardo is making a display to show photos of his family. In a sheet of cardboard, he cuts out openings like windows for his photos to show through.

Help Mr. Lombardo by solving each problem. Show how you get each answer.

1. Mr. Lombardo wants the top row of the display just long enough to show 3 photos that are each 5 inches high and 4 inches wide. He wants to leave 2 inches between photos and 2 inches on each side. How long should the display be?

2. Mr. Lombardo cuts out a circle 5 inches across. Is that large enough to show an entire photo that is 5 inches high and 4 inches wide?

3. Mr. Lombardo cuts out a square that is 4 inches on each side. The photo that Mr. Lombardo decides to use in that spot is 7 inches high and 5 inches wide.
   a. What is the area of the square cutout?
   b. What is the area of the photo?
   c. Will more than half of the photo be seen?

4. To hang the display Mr. Lombardo wants to find its center. The display is 20 inches wide and 18 inches high. On the back, he draws 2 diagonals and marks the point where they meet.
   a. If that point is the center, how far should it be from the edges of the display?
   b. Can you use Mr. Lombardo's method to find the center of any rectangle? Try it.

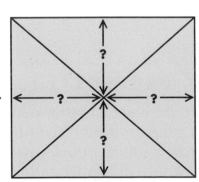

SECTION REVIEW

for pages 168–180

1. Which of the figures below are congruent?

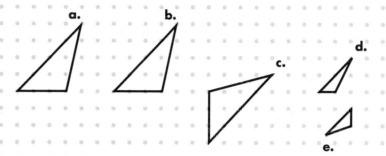

Write how many squares each figure contains.

2.

Key: ☐ =1 square

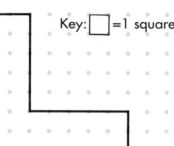

3.

4.

Match each figure with the name.

5. rectangular prism

6. rectangular pyramid

7. triangular prism

8. triangular pyramid

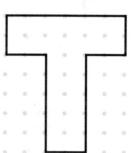

9. Tell how many cubes are in the rectangular prism.

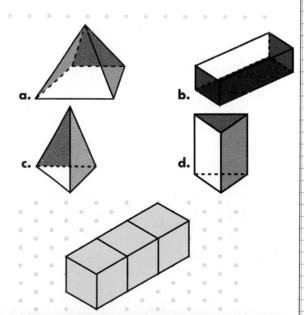

CHAPTER TEST

Tell which of these angles are right angles.

1.   2.   3.   4.   5.

Use the grids at the right. Write the name of the figure that is at each of the following points.

6. (3,2) on grid a   7. (E,5) on grid b

8. (A,4) on grid b   9. (5,2) on grid a

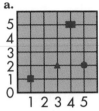
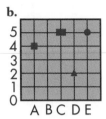

Will the slide image match the original? Write *yes* or *no*.

10. Original:

11. Original:

PROBLEM SOLVING

Solve each problem.

12. Which pair of figures below have the same area? Write *a, b, c,* or *d.*

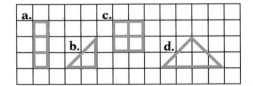

13. Which figure below has an area of 9 squares? Write *a, b, c,* or *d.*

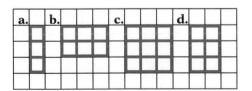

CUMULATIVE REVIEW

Use the spinners and marbles below to answer the questions.

Spinner A

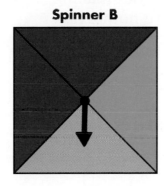

Spinner B

Which is more likely to happen? Write a or b.

1. **a.** Spinner A stops on red.　　**b.** Spinner B stops on red.

2. **a.** picking a red marble　　**b.** picking a yellow marble

3. **a.** Spinner B stops on green.　　**b.** Spinner A stops on yellow.

Write the letter of the exercise that has the same answer.
Then write the answer.

4. 3 × 6　　　　　　　　a. 2 × 8
5. 4 × 5　　　　　　　　b. 5 + 5 + 5 + 5
6. 8 + 8　　　　　　　　c. 6 + 6 + 6

Write a related multiplication fact.

7. 32 ÷ 8　　8. 49 ÷ 7　　9. 30 ÷ 5　　10. 28 ÷ 4　　11. 36 ÷ 9

Copy and complete the number sentence.

12. 2 × 12 = ■ × 2　　　　13. 18 ÷ ■ = 1　　　　14. 32 × 0 = ■

15. ■ ÷ 9 = 0　　　　　　16. 47 × 1 = ■　　　　17. ■ ÷ 1 = 241

EXCURSION
NUMBER THEORY

MODELING SQUARE NUMBERS

You can use what you know about making arrays to find out about square numbers.

You will need dot paper and crayons.

Model 3 × 5.

On dot paper, make an array that has 3 squares down and 5 squares across.

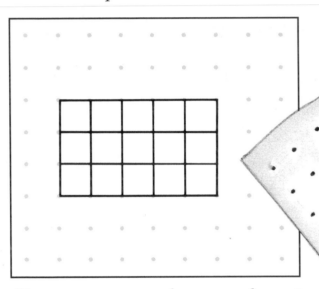

1. How many squares have you drawn?

2. What is the product of 3 × 5?

3. Is the array a square?

Now model 4 × 4.

On dot paper, make an array that has 4 squares across and 4 squares down.

4. How many squares did you draw?

5. What is the product of 4 × 4?

6. Is the array a square?

Make arrays for each. Use dot paper.

7. 1×6 **8.** 6×6 **9.** 3×3 **10.** 3×4

11. 5×5 **12.** 2×4 **13.** 2×5 **14.** 2×2

Answer each question when you are finished with your arrays.

15. For exercises 7–14, which arrays are not squares?

16. For exercises 7–14 which arrays are squares?

17. What do you notice about the factors of the square arrays?

The product shown by a square array is called a **square number.**

18. What square numbers above did you find?

Write *square* or *not square* for each number. Make an array if you need help.

19. 36   **20.** 25   **21.** 40   **22.** 20

23. 49   **24.** 32   **25.** 81   **26.** 54

MULTIPLYING BY 1-DIGIT NUMBERS

Social Studies

Acres of Apples Apples are one of the world's most popular fruits. Each year the United States produces nearly 200 million bushels of apples.

Most of our apples are grown in large orchards like the one shown on page 186. Trees are planted in rows 20 to 30 feet apart. As you can see, this space gives growers room to care for the trees. The space also makes it easier to harvest the fruit.

Orchards are measured in *acres*. An acre is an area of land. Some orchards have 80 to 100 trees for each acre. About how many trees would you find on 2 acres? On 5 acres? Find out where your favorite apples are grown.

ESTIMATING PRODUCTS

Julie earns $36 a month on her paper route. Will she have enough money in 4 months to buy a $100 bicycle?

Estimate: 4 × $36

To get a quick rough estimate, you can use front-end estimation.

4 × $36

4 × $30 = $120

Think

• Will Julie actually earn more than or less than $120 in 4 months? Explain.

Yes, Julie will have enough money.

Front-end estimation was enough to answer this question. But sometimes you will need a closer estimate. Rounding will usually give you a closer estimate.

Estimate: 4 × 295

Front-end
295
× 4
Estimate: 200 × 4 = 800

Rounding
295 → 300
× 4 → × 4
Estimate: 1200

The rounded estimate is much closer to the actual product, since 295 is so close to 300.

	Front-end	Rounding
Estimate: 6 × 45 →	6 × 40 = 240	6 × 50 = 300
Estimate: 4 × 2305 →	4 × 2000 = 8000	4 × 2000 = 8000

GUIDED PRACTICE

Write the letter of the reasonable estimate.

1. 3 × 24
  a. 60
  b. 600
  c. 6000

2. 5 × 676
  a. 350
  b. 3500
  c. 35,000

3. 7 × 98
  a. 70
  b. 700
  c. 7000

4. 6 × 534
  a. 300
  b. 3000
  c. 30,000

Estimate the product. Use the method you like best.

5.   76
     × 4

6.   325
     × 6

7.   578
     × 3

8.   918
     × 4

9.   6498
     × 6

Critical Thinking **10.** Is the actual product in exercise 1 greater than or less than the estimate? Explain.

....
INDEPENDENT PRACTICE

Write the letter of the reasonable estimate.

11. 3 × 32
  a. 90
  b. 900
  c. 9000

12. 6 × 143
  a. 600
  b. 6000
  c. 60,000

13. 5 × 398
  a. 200
  b. 2000
  c. 20,000

14. 4 × 245
  a. 800
  b. 8000
  c. 80,000

Estimate the product. Use the method you like best.

15.   34
      × 5

16.   53
      × 7

17.   278
      × 2

18.   689
      × 4

19.   1989
      × 3

20. 4 × 24

21. 9 × 123

22. 6 × 2567

23. 3 × 8999

24. 5 × 239

25. 6 × 192

26. 2 × 2661

27. 8 × 205

28. Which two numbers in the box have a product of:

  a. about 1500?

  b. about 300?

  c. about 900?

  d. about 5000?

```
314        133
       3
 5         999
```

MULTIPLYING WITH ARRAY DIAGRAMS

The blocks pictured below show 4 × 36.

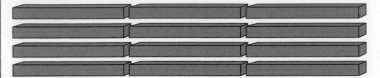

Think

- How could you find the total number of ones?
- How could you find the total number of tens?

You can use a **rectangular array** instead of blocks. The array on the right has 4 rows with 36 squares in each row. It is separated into a tens part and a ones part.

A simpler way to show an array is the **array diagram** at the right.

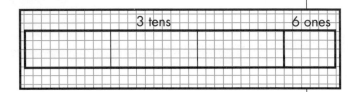

To multiply 36 by 4, first write:

$$\begin{array}{r} 36 \\ \times\ 4 \\ \hline \end{array}$$

30	6
4	4 × 30	4 × 6

- **Multiply the ones.**

$$\begin{array}{r} 36 \\ \times\ 4 \\ \hline 24 \end{array}$$

- **Multiply the tens.**

$$\begin{array}{r} 36 \\ \times\ 4 \\ \hline 24 \\ 120 \end{array}$$

- **Add.**

$$\begin{array}{r} 36 \\ \times\ 4 \\ \hline 24 \\ 120 \\ \hline 144 \end{array}$$

So, 4 × 36 = 144.

GUIDED PRACTICE

Write the product. Use the array diagram to help you multiply.

1. $$\begin{array}{r} 26 \\ \times\ 2 \\ \hline \end{array}$$

20	6
2		

2. $$\begin{array}{r} 57 \\ \times\ 4 \\ \hline \end{array}$$

50	7
4		

3. $$\begin{array}{r} 79 \\ \times\ 3 \\ \hline \end{array}$$

70	9
3		

Draw an array diagram to show the multiplication. Then write the product.

4. 12
    × 3

5. 27
    × 2

6. 21
    × 6

7. 37
    × 4

Critical Thinking **8.** Why can you draw the same-size array diagram for every exercise?

INDEPENDENT PRACTICE

Write the product. Draw an array diagram when it helps.

9. 11
    × 2

10. 36
    × 3

11. 21
    × 5

12. 43
    × 6

13. 8 × 16

14. 5 × 51

15. 7 × 35

16. 6 × 64

17. 4 × 46

18. 6 × 53

19. 9 × 29

20. 3 × 71

Problem Solving

21. Workers are adding new swings to the playground. Each swing uses 23 feet of rope. How much rope do they need for 4 swings?

22. A new park table has 4 legs. Each leg is 36 inches tall. The top of the table is 4 inches thick. How tall is the table?

23. Angelo wants to make 2 muffins for each of the 50 workers. There are 24 muffins in every batch. Will 5 batches be enough?

24. In the park, 6 new rows of trees will be planted. Half of the rows will have 20 trees each. The rest will have 10 trees each. How many trees will be planted?

Maintain • Mixed Practice

Write the answer.

1. 258
    + 229

2. 601
    − 519

3. 3695
    + 489

4. 508
    − 339

5. 400
    − 350

MULTIPLYING 2-DIGIT NUMBERS

Pete's Popcorn Palace has 4 cases of popcorn. Each case contains 36 buckets. How many buckets of popcorn does Pete have?

You can multiply to combine equal groups.

Multiply 36 by 4. You have learned how to multiply using an array diagram.

	30	6
4	4 × 30	4×6

$$\begin{array}{r} 36 \\ \times\ 4 \\ \hline 24 \\ 120 \\ \hline 144 \end{array}$$

Here is a shorter way. Write 4 × 36 like this:

$$\begin{array}{r} 36 \\ \times\ 4 \end{array}$$

● **Multiply the ones. Regroup if necessary.**

$$\begin{array}{r} \overset{2}{3}6 \\ \times\ 4 \\ \hline 4 \end{array}$$

$$\begin{array}{r} 6 \\ \times\ 4 \\ \hline 24 \end{array}$$

● **Multiply the tens.**

$$\begin{array}{r} \overset{2}{3}6 \\ \times\ 4 \\ \hline 4 \end{array}$$

3 tens
× 4
12 tens

● **Add the tens.**

$$\begin{array}{r} \overset{2}{3}6 \\ \times\ 4 \\ \hline 144 \end{array}$$

12 tens
+ 2 tens
14 tens

Think

≡ • How did you show regrouped tens?

• To what number were the 2 tens added?

Pete has 144 buckets of popcorn.

Other Examples

$$\begin{array}{r} \overset{1}{2}4 \\ \times\ 3 \\ \hline 72 \end{array} \qquad \begin{array}{r} 71 \\ \times\ 8 \\ \hline 568 \end{array} \qquad \begin{array}{r} \overset{2}{4}4 \\ \times\ 7 \\ \hline 308 \end{array} \qquad \begin{array}{r} 33 \\ \times\ 2 \\ \hline 66 \end{array}$$

GUIDED PRACTICE

Write the product. Use mental math when you can.

1. 3 × 12   **2.** 6 × 80   **3.** 9 × 72   **4.** 5 × 34 gal

Critical Thinking **5.** For which exercise did you decide to use mental math? Why?

INDEPENDENT PRACTICE

Write the product. Use mental math when you can.

6. 36 × 3	**7.** 19 × 5	**8.** 45 × 6	**9.** 32 × 2	**10.** 32 × 4
11. 98 × 4	**12.** 27 × 7	**13.** 30 × 9	**14.** 60 × 9	**15.** 12 × 8

16. 6 × 56   **17.** 3 × 69   **18.** 1 × 29   **19.** 2 × 54

20. 0 × 83   **21.** 3 × 18   **22.** 6 × 18   **23.** 9 × 26

Problem Solving Use the chart.

Jo and Meg work at Pete's Popcorn Palace. They each earn $5 an hour.

24. Just by looking at the chart, tell who earned more money in April. Then tell exactly how much Jo and Meg each earned in April.

25. Suppose Meg works 11 hours in the first week of May and 6 hours the second week. How much will she earn for those two weeks?

Number of Hours Worked in April				
Week	**1**	**2**	**3**	**4**
Jo	7	9	8	9
Meg	10	10	10	10

MATH LOG

You can multiply in two ways. Which method is easier for you? Explain why.

MULTIPLYING 3-DIGIT NUMBERS

Janice, the manager of Tri-Way Cinema, saw that 8 rolls of tickets were sold last weekend. Each roll has 225 tickets. How many tickets were sold last weekend?

First, estimate the product.

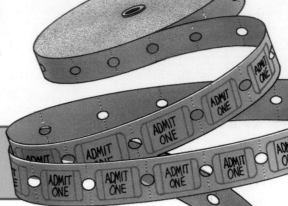

Think
- How did you decide which number to estimate with?

To find the exact product, multiply 225 by 8.

• Multiply the ones. Regroup?	• Multiply the tens. Add tens. Regroup?	• Multiply the hundreds.
$\begin{array}{r} \overset{4}{2}25 \\ \times\ \ 8 \\ \hline 0 \end{array}$	$\begin{array}{r} \overset{24}{2}25 \\ \times\ \ 8 \\ \hline 00 \end{array}$	$\begin{array}{r} \overset{24}{2}25 \\ \times\ \ 8 \\ \hline 1800 \end{array}$

A total of 1800 tickets were sold last weekend.

Think
- Is the answer reasonable? How do you know?

GUIDED PRACTICE

Write the product only for the exercises that have products greater than 1000.

1.	403	2.	312	3.	372	4.	321	5.	124
	× 3		× 2		× 5		× 8		× 4

Critical Thinking 6. How did you decide which exercises to solve?

INDEPENDENT PRACTICE

Write the product.

7.	8.	9.	10.	11.
104 × 6	327 × 3	671 × 8	802 × 9	974 × 6

12.	13.	14.	15.	16.
121 × 4	121 × 8	397 × 7	545 × 3	545 × 6

17. 9 × 729   18. 8 × 777   19. 5 × 829   20. 7 × 222

21. 4 × 336   22. 9 × 271   23. 7 × 602   24. 5 × 650

Problem Solving

25. Janice records the ticket sales for all the shows.
    a. There are 3 theaters. Each theater has 251 seats. How many tickets were sold for the 6 o'clock shows?
    b. How many tickets were sold for the night?

TRI-WAY Cinema

THEATERS	SHOWTIMES
ONE	6:00 P.M. 8:00 P.M. 10:00 P.M.
TWO	6:00 P.M. 8:00 P.M. 10:00 P.M.
THREE	6:00 P.M. 8:00 P.M. 10:00 P.M.

ALL SHOWS SOLD OUT

26. The Tri-Way Cinema Company is conducting a contest among its managers. The table below shows the prizes Janice could win.

Prize Table			
Total Sales	$1500	$2000	$2500
Prize	audio tapes	calculator	radio

    a. Janice sold 407 tickets at $5 a ticket. Is that enough to win the calculator?
    b. Did she sell enough tickets to win the radio?

Critical Thinking 27. Use the prize table to write a word problem of your own. Give it to a friend to solve.

 • **Area**

Tell how many squares are in each shape.

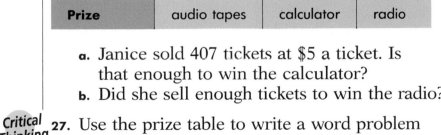

1.   2.   3.

GUESS AND CHECK

Sometimes using guess and check can help you solve a problem.

Here is how guessing and checking helped me mail some boxes.

MY PROBLEM

I brought 5 boxes to the post office. Four of the boxes weighed the same and one weighed 25 pounds. The total weight for all was 93 pounds. I wanted to know the weight of each box. But the scale broke.

MY SOLUTION

I started with a guess that is easy to check. Then I checked to see if the result was too high, too low, or just right.

► My first guess: 10 pounds each

Check: 4 × 10 lb = 40 lb ← **4 small boxes**
$$\begin{array}{r} + \ 25 \text{ lb} \leftarrow \textbf{big box} \\ \hline 65 \text{ lb} \leftarrow \textbf{total} \end{array}$$

10 pounds was too low.

So I made my next guess larger.

► My second guess: 20 pounds each
20 pounds was too high.

Check: 4 × 20 lb = 80 lb
$$\begin{array}{r} + \ 25 \text{ lb} \\ \hline 105 \text{ lb} \end{array}$$

I kept guessing and checking until I had the answer.

Can you figure out what it was?

◤ GUIDED PRACTICE

Use guess and check to solve the problem. The first
guess has already been checked.

1. Sally had only nickels and dimes
   in her pocket. She lost ten coins
   that totaled 85¢. How many of
   each coin did she lose?

First guess: 5 nickels, 5 dimes

Check: $5 \times 10¢ = 50¢$
        $5 \times 5¢ = + 25¢$
        Total $= 75¢$

The total is too low.

....

◤ APPLICATION

Work with a small group. Use guess
and check when it helps.

2. Bolton's is ordering T-shirts.
   Each shirt costs $5. How many
   can they order for $280?

3. Teresa buys 5 ears of corn and
   1 cabbage for a total of $2.60.
   The cabbage costs $1.10. How
   much does each ear of corn cost?

4. At the Whirlygig Fun Park, 6
   people want to ride the Tornado
   Tumbler. Each car can hold up
   to 400 pounds. How can the 6
   people fit into 2 cars?

5. If you subtract 24 from the
   mystery number, the result is
   double 24. Find the mystery
   number.

6. The digits, 1, 2, and 3 are in
   order. They add up to 6. What
   three numbers in order have a
   sum of 6 times 6?

COOPERATIVE • LEARNING

TORNADO TUMBLER

WEIGHT LIMIT
400 lb

176 lb 98 lb   146 lb   151 lb   79 lb   139 lb

EXACT OR ESTIMATE

An estimate tells you *about* how much. Many times that is all you need to know. Other times you need an exact answer. These questions can help you decide which method to use.

Questions to consider:

- Is an estimate enough to solve the problem?

- Is paper and pencil or a calculator available?

- Is it possible to get an exact answer?

- Am I checking if an answer is reasonable?

Think

- Would you estimate or figure out the exact number of people watching a parade? Why?

INDEPENDENT PRACTICE

Solve each problem. Write whether you estimated or computed exactly.

1. Is $10 enough to buy all 3 items?

2. Tim has $567.83 in his checking account. He is writing a check for $124.95. How much will be left in his account?

3. Is the answer reasonable?

$$
\begin{array}{r}
427 \\
\times\ 3 \\
\hline
771
\end{array}
$$

4. *About* how many sit-ups does Jenna do in 1 week?

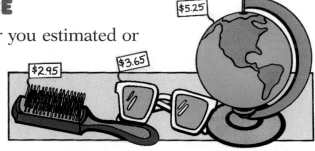

I do 32 sit-ups every day.

SECTION REVIEW

for pages 188–198

Write the letter of the correct answer.

1. 4 × 288
   a. 83,232
   b. 12,442
   c. 1152
   d. 822

2. 7 × 53
   a. 371
   b. 491
   c. 3521
   d. 351

3. 8 × 95
   a. 7240
   b. 760
   c. 720
   d. 1040

4. 7 × 691
   a. 4837
   b. 8437
   c. 42,637
   d. 4237

5. 8 × 304
   a. 24,032
   b. 2642
   c. 2432
   d. 272

6. 5 × 406
   a. 230
   b. 2030
   c. 2150
   d. 20,030

7. 3 × 606
   a. 18,018
   b. 1838
   c. 198
   d. 1818

8. 4 × 403
   a. 1642
   b. 16,012
   c. 1612
   d. 172

9. 8 × 380
   a. 2440
   b. 3040
   c. 466
   d. 24,640

10. 6 × 457
   a. 2742
   b. 2402
   c. 5442
   d. 4245

11. 7 × 509
   a. 6323
   b. 413
   c. 3563
   d. 3503

12. 5 × 635
   a. 3055
   b. 301,525
   c. 4055
   d. 3175

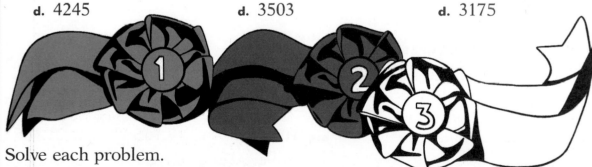

Solve each problem.

13. On field day, there will be 24 different contests. Three ribbons will be awarded for each contest. How many ribbons will be awarded?

14. Teresa plans to place 4 photos on each page of her photograph album. There are 35 pages in the album. How many photos will be in the album?

MULTIPLYING 4-DIGIT NUMBERS

Ellen saw this sign at the airport. She plans to take 3 round-trip flights between New York and Los Angeles in May. Will she earn a free round-trip ticket?

First estimate the product.

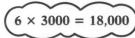

$6 \times 3000 = 18,000$

Think

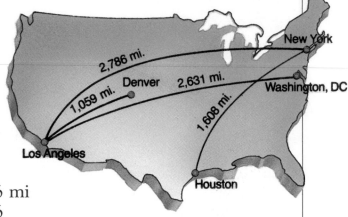

- How many times will Ellen travel between New York and Los Angeles?

- Can you be sure from the estimate that Ellen will earn a free ticket? Explain.

Multiply to find the product of 6 × 2786 miles.

$$\begin{array}{r} 4\,5\,3 \\ 2786 \text{ mi} \\ \times \quad 6 \\ \hline 16,716 \text{ mi} \end{array}$$

Because 16,716 miles > 16,000 miles, Ellen will earn a free round-trip ticket. The product 16,716 is close to the estimate of 18,000.

GUIDED PRACTICE

Choose the product. Estimate when you can.

1. 7 × 6492   a. 45,444   b. 6874   c. 454,740

2. 9 × 2345   a. 2105   b. 17,165   c. 21,105

3. 5 × 1995   a. 10,975   b. 9975   c. 51,995

Write the product.

4. 5 × 5473   5. 6 × 2306   6. 3 × 7555   7. 6 × 1999

Critical Thinking 8. How can estimation help you choose the product in exercises 1–3?

INDEPENDENT PRACTICE

Choose the product. Estimate when you can.

9. 4 × 4792   **a.** 1658   **b.** 19,168   **c.** 1916

10. 6 × 7231   **a.** 43,386   **b.** 433,386   **c.** 4338

11. 8 × 2095   **a.** 1676   **b.** 1776   **c.** 16,760

Write the product. Use mental math when you can.

12.	3412	13.	3017	14.	3000	15.	2999	16.	8000
	× 2		× 6		× 8		× 4		× 7

17. 3 × 3021   18. 2 × 2419   19. 4 × 1372   20. 2 × 4953

21. 8 × 7621   22. 9 × 5008   23. 6 × 7420   24. 2 × 7048

Problem Solving • Data Book Go to page 469 of the Atlas section.

25. Which is a longer distance: 4 round-trips between Chicago and Los Angeles or a 13,000-mile trip halfway around the world?

26. A supersonic plane can fly about 1400 miles in one hour. Would it take more than 3 hours to fly the distance from Seattle to New York? Why or why not?

27. Is the distance from San Antonio to New York shorter than or longer than the distance from San Antonio to Seattle by way of Los Angeles?

28. Wingtip checks its planes every 10,000 miles. A plane flew 2 round-trips from New York to Seattle. Is it time for the plane to be checked?

CHALLENGE • Logical Reasoning

Copy and complete each exercise using numbers from the box. Use each number only once. You may use a calculator.

1		3		9
5	4		6	8
2		0		7

1.	1 1 1	2.	4	3.	3	4.		5.	2
	2■45		20■8		9■		1343		■17
	× 3		× 5		× 6		× ■		× ■
	79■5		1■,090		5■0		26■6		3668

More Practice Set 6.7, p. 442

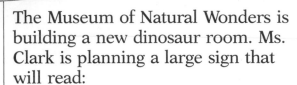

The Museum of Natural Wonders is building a new dinosaur room. Ms. Clark is planning a large sign that will read:

GIANTS OF THE EARTH

The sign will be part of a tile wall. The letters and background will be made of square tiles. The letters will be green. The background will be blue.

Help Ms. Clark plan the sign. Work with a small group to solve each problem. You will need squared paper. You may use a calculator.

1. How many green tiles will be in the letter *G*? HINT: Use multiplication so you do not have to count every tile.

2. Ms. Clark has made a chart to show how many green tiles each kind of letter will need. How many green tiles will be needed for all the *T*'s and *H*'s in the sign?

3. How many green tiles will be needed for the words *THE EARTH*?

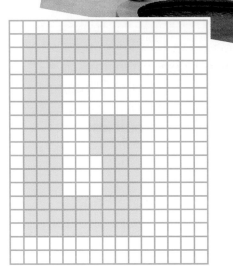

Letters	Number of Green Tiles Each
R	119
E, S, H	99
T	63
I	45
N	120
A, O	108
F	81
G	

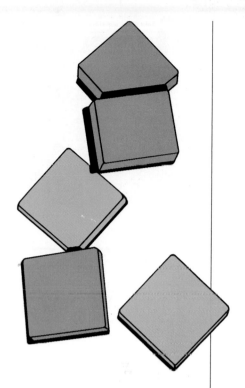

4. Ms. Clark figures 1760 green tiles are needed for all the letters. The sign will be 100 tiles wide and 25 tiles high. How many blue tiles will be needed? HINT: 25 × 100 = 2500

5. The longest dinosaur on display is 60 feet long.
   a. Each tile is 6 inches wide. How long are 2 tiles? HINT: 1 foot = 12 inches
   b. Will the sign be wider than the longest dinosaur?

6. A box of tiles costs $50. There are 24 tiles in each box.
   a. Does each tile cost more than or less than $2?
   b. Will the total cost for all the tiles for the sign be more than or less than $5000? How do you know?

7. The letter *T* will use 63 green tiles. It is supposed to be 15 tiles high and 9 tiles wide. On squared paper, design the letter *T* for the sign. HINT: Look at the thickness of the letters in Ms. Clark's plan below.

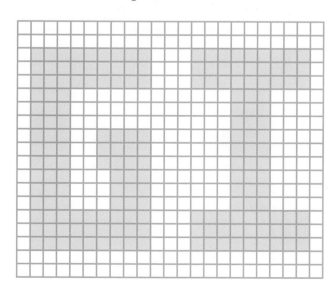

8. The letters *H* and *E* are also supposed to be 15 tiles high and 9 tiles wide. Design those letters. Make sure you use the number of tiles shown on Ms. Clark's chart.

MULTIPLYING MONEY

$8.39

Mrs. Perkins wants to buy a dinosaur kit for each of her 5 grandchildren. She does not want to spend more than $43 for all the kits. Mrs. Perkins decides to estimate to see if $43 will be enough.

Think

• Is an estimated answer enough? Why or why not?

Mrs. Perkins decides to find the exact answer. She uses her calculator to multiply $8.39 by 5.

Mrs. Perkins enters on her calculator:

5 × 8 . 3 9

A calculator does not have a $ key.

This is the answer her calculator displays:

41.95

Mrs. Perkins can buy the dinosaur kits for less than $43.

Other Examples

¹ ⁴ $9.17 × 6 $55.02	Calculator Display: 55.02	

$0.25 × 3 $0.75   Calculator Display: 0.75

³ ² $27.50 × 5 $137.50   Calculator Display: 137.5

GUIDED PRACTICE

Use a calculator to find the product.

1. 7 × $48.23

2. 5 × $3.65

3. 9 × $35.96

4. 8 × $1.98

5. 6 × $0.15

6. 4 × $15.95

Critical Thinking **7.** How did you rewrite the products displayed on the calculator for exercises 5 and 6? Explain your answer.

PROJECT • Decision Making

At the museum, Mrs. Perkins sees the sign at the right. She decides to give her grandson a birthday party at the museum. A clerk at the museum office gives Mrs. Perkins the following information.

> **HAVE A PARTY HERE!**
>
> One Complete Day at Museum Includes:
> - Private Tour with Guide
> - Gift for Each Child
> - Room Reserved for You Only
>
> Ask in Museum Office for Details

Rooms	
Dinosaur Room	$125.00
Bird Room	75.00
Sea Mammal Room	105.00
Planetarium	195.00

Party Favors
(prices are per person)

Dinosaur Kit	$8.39
Rock Collection	2.45
Whale T-Shirt	7.69
Kaleidoscope	5.98
Star Finder	1.59

Menu (prices are per person)

Hamburger	$2.75
Hot Dog	1.50
Tuna Sandwich	2.25
Tacos	2.45
Milk	0.45
Orange Juice	0.95
Apple Juice	0.55
Ice Cream	0.85
Pudding	0.50

Special Dessert

Birthday Cake serves 8	$8.98

Work with your group to help Mrs. Perkins plan the party.

- She has a budget of $400 for the party.

- She will invite no more than 25 people.

- What will the menu be?

You may use pencil and paper or a calculator for your calculations.

Here is what you must decide:

- In which room will the party be held?

- How many people will attend?

- What party favors will you have?

Compare your party plans with those of other groups.

If you get stuck, remember...

Tips for Problem Solving

on pages 474–475

Variety VIDEO

SPECIALS

Rentals: $1.50 per tape
$5.00 for 4 tapes

Sales: Blank KVK-120—$6.95 each
Box of 4—$17.59

Marx Brothers Classics: $24.89 each
Little Rascals Classics: $19.45 each

Solve each problem. Estimate when you can.

1. Simon needs to buy 3 blank tapes. Should he buy 3 tapes or buy a box of 4 tapes? Why?

2. Mrs. Munez wants to rent 4 tapes, buy a box of blank tapes, and also buy 1 Marx Brothers movie. Will her bill be more than $50? Explain.

3. Bart has 3 tapes: a comedy, a sports film, and a science film. In how many different orders can he watch them?

4. Variety Video pays $15 for a full-length movie. How many times do they need to rent the video to pay for the cost of the movie?

5. Lola has a blank tape that can record up to 6 hours of programming. Each episode of her favorite show is 30 minutes long. How many episodes can she record on the tape?

SECTION REVIEW

for pages 200–206

Write the product.

1. 2 × 1200

2. 7 × 237

3. 6 × 4012

4. 5 × $2.20

5. 2 × 4003

6. 6 × 518

Write the letter of the correct answer.

7. 4 × 2880
   a. 14,220
   b. 24,420
   c. 11,520
   d. 1152

8. 7 × $15.30
   a. $107.10
   b. $10,710
   c. $107.1
   d. $10.71

9. 7 × 9520
   a. 6664
   b. 66,640
   c. 67,540
   d. 91,240

10. 8 × 6910
    a. 55,280
    b. 104,280
    c. 5582
    d. 48,280

11. 6 × 1860
    a. 42,660
    b. 13,840
    c. 1116
    d. 11,160

12. 4 × $30.40
    a. $121.6
    b. $12,160
    c. $121.60
    d. $12.160

13. 9 × $4.60
    a. $4.140
    b. $41.40
    c. $4140
    d. $41.4

14. 7 × $2.20
    a. $15.4
    b. $1540
    c. $1.540
    d. $15.40

15. 9 × 3390
    a. 108,810
    b. 30,510
    c. 37,710
    d. 3051

16. 8 × 4530
    a. 3624
    b. 36,040
    c. 36,240
    d. 72,640

17. 4509 × 7
    a. 31,563
    b. 41,563
    c. 3213
    d. 70,323

18. 5 × $4.50
    a. $2.25
    b. $22.5
    c. $2250
    d. $22.50

Solve each problem.

19. Carole buys 2 games for $24.95 each. She gives the clerk $50. How much change should she get back?

20. A camp orders 105 packages of hot dogs. Each package contains 8 hot dogs. There are 420 campers. How many hot dogs are ordered?

CHAPTER TEST

Write the product.

1.	24 $\times\ 7$	**2.**	53 $\times\ 2$	**3.**	49 $\times\ 9$	**4.**	64 $\times\ 5$

5.	23 $\times\ 0$	**6.**	50 $\times\ 8$	**7.**	75 $\times\ 5$	**8.**	91 $\times\ 9$

9.	722 $\times\ 9$	**10.**	182 $\times\ 5$	**11.**	408 $\times\ 3$	**12.**	330 $\times\ 7$

13.	2216 $\times\ 3$	**14.**	6343 $\times\ 7$	**15.**	7003 $\times\ 9$	**16.**	9993 $\times\ 4$

17. 6×15 **18.** 8×34 **19.** 6×19 **20.** 3×31

21. 0×81 **22.** 11×2 **23.** 11×3 **24.** 22×3

25. 2×597 **26.** 9×862 **27.** 6×901 **28.** 4×676

29. 6×4909 **30.** 5×7432 **31.** 8×9038 **32.** 4×8215

PROBLEM SOLVING

Solve each problem.

33. There are 1440 minutes in a day. How many minutes are in a week?

34. It costs $2.99 to rent each video game and $1.99 to rent each movie. Which costs more, renting 2 games or 4 movies?

35. The distance around the track is 440 yards. Tania ran 2 times around the track. Then she rested for 5 minutes. How many yards did she run?

36. At the school fair, Loretta sells 10 packets of raffle tickets. There are 24 tickets in each packet. How many raffle tickets does Loretta sell?

CUMULATIVE REVIEW

Use the line graph to answer each question.

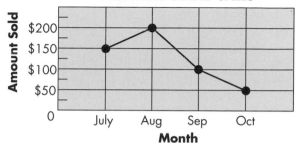

VEGETABLE STAND SALES

1. During what month did sales increase the most?

2. How much did sales decrease from August to September?

Write the answer.

3. 35 ÷ 5   4. 60 ÷ 10   5. 7 × 8   6. 9 × 9

7. 6 × 9   8. 8 × 4   9. 63 ÷ 7   10. 72 ÷ 8

11. 54 ÷ 9   12. 7 × 7   13. 45 ÷ 5   14. 21 ÷ 3

15. 7 × 6   16. 30 ÷ 3   17. 8 × 8   18. 27 ÷ 9

Solve each problem.

19. Janet is putting up a fence around her vegetable garden. Two sides of her garden are each 3 feet long, and the other two sides are each 6 feet long. How much fencing does Janet need? Explain how you solved this problem.

20. Each side of square room is 3 yards long. Is the perimeter of the room more or less than 16 yards? How do you know?

Name the figure at each of the following points.

21. (D,4)

22. (F,1)

23. (A,3)

24. (C,2)

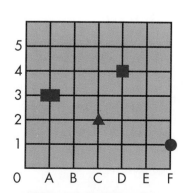

EXCURSION
USING TECHNOLOGY

LOGO

You will need Logo software, a computer, and squared paper.

Here are some commands that tell the Logo turtle how to move.

Logo Command	What You Can Type	What the Turtle Will Do
FORWARD 5	FD 5	move forward 5 steps
BACK 7	BK 7	move back 7 steps
RIGHT 45	RT 45	turn this far to the right
RIGHT 90	RT 90	turn this far to the right
LEFT 45	LT 45	turn this far to the left
LEFT 90	LT 90	turn this far to the left
PENUP	PU	move without drawing
PENDOWN	PD	draw while moving

You can use these commands to write a Logo **procedure**. A procedure is a list of commands that tells the turtle what to draw. Here is one way to write a procedure for a square.

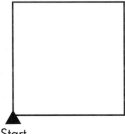

Start

- Type TO and the name of the procedure. → TO SQUARE

- Type the commands. You can type 2 or more commands on each line. → FD 50 RT 90 FD 50 RT 90
→ FD 50 RT 90 FD 50 RT 90

- Type END. → END

To make the turtle begin the procedure, type DRAW and the name of the procedure. → DRAW SQUARE

1. This procedure tells the turtle how to draw two congruent diamonds. Rewrite the procedure so the turtle will draw two diamonds that are the same shape, but not the same size. Type in the procedure.

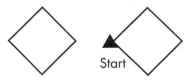

Start

TO DIAMONDS

RT 45 FD 30 RT 90 FD 30 RT 90 FD 30 RT 90 FD

30 PU LT 45 FD 10 RT 45 PD FD 30 LT 90 FD 30

LT 90 FD 30 LT 90 FD 30

END

Tell the turtle to DRAW DIAMONDS.

2. Look at the procedure. Predict what the turtle will draw. Sketch your prediction on squared paper. Type in the procedure.

TO DESIGN

LT 90 FD 40 LT 90 FD 40 RT 90 FD 40 LT 90 FD

40 PU LT 90 FD 20 LT 90 PD FD 20 RT 90 FD 40

LT 90 FD 40 RT 90 FD 20

END

Then tell the turtle to DRAW DESIGN to check your prediction.

3. Write a procedure that tells the turtle how to draw 2 parallel lines. Type in the procedure. Tell the turtle to draw your procedure.

4. Write a procedure to tell the turtle how to draw two congruent rectangles.

5. Write a procedure to tell the turtle how to draw this face. Name the procedure FACE. Type in your procedure. Tell the turtle to DRAW FACE.

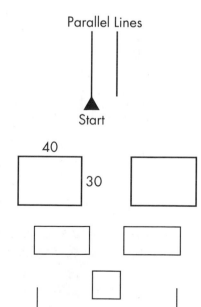

Parallel Lines

Start

40

30

DIVIDING BY 1-DIGIT NUMBERS

Science

Cricket Thermometers What do thermometers and crickets have in common? You may be surprised to learn that both can tell you the temperature.

Have you ever heard crickets chirp? They make the sound by rubbing their front wings together. Crickets chirp when the temperature is between 10°C and 40°C. The hotter it is, the faster they chirp. You can estimate the temperature by counting the number of chirps. Follow these steps.

- First, count the number of chirps in 15 seconds.

- Then, add 5.

- Multiply the sum by 5.

- Then, divide by 9.

The answer gives you the temperature in degrees Celsius. What is the temperature if a cricket chirps 31 times in 15 seconds? What if it chirps 58 times in 15 seconds?

DIVISION WITH REMAINDERS

At his fruit stand, Don puts 7 oranges into each bag. He has 60 oranges. How many bags can he fill? How many oranges are left over?

Divide: $60 \div 7 = \blacksquare$

It asks the same question as $7 \times \blacksquare = 60$.

You know that $7 \times 8 = 56$ and $7 \times 9 = 63$.

So, the quotient is between 8 and 9.

$$
\begin{array}{r}
8 \quad \text{R4} \\
7\overline{)60} \\
-56 \quad \leftarrow 7 \times 8 \\
\hline
4 \quad \leftarrow \text{remainder}
\end{array}
$$

Don can fill 8 bags.
4 oranges left over.

Check the answer:

$8 \times 7 = 56$ oranges in bags $56 + 4 = 60$ oranges in all

The answer checks, because Don started with 60 oranges.

Think

- Why is the answer not 7 R11?
- Why must the remainder always be less than the divisor?

Divide.

1. $7\overline{)43}$ 2. $3\overline{)27}$ 3. $4\overline{)38}$ 4. $5\overline{)43}$ 5. $6\overline{)47}$

6. $32 \div 8$ 7. $28 \div 5$ 8. $33 \div 4$ 9. $29 \div 3$ 10. $57 \div 6$

11. What two multiplication facts could you use to estimate the answer to exercise 4?

INDEPENDENT PRACTICE

Divide.

12. $6\overline{)41}$ 13. $2\overline{)19}$ 14. $4\overline{)29}$ 15. $6\overline{)56}$ 16. $5\overline{)18}$

17. $9\overline{)0}$ 18. $8\overline{)56}$ 19. $7\overline{)54}$ 20. $3\overline{)29}$ 21. $6\overline{)32}$

22. $8 \div 3$ 23. $26 \div 5$ 24. $35 \div 6$ 25. $49 \div 8$ 26. $19 \div 8$

Problem Solving

27. Don sells lemons in packages of 4. He has 23 lemons. How many packages can he make? How many lemons will be left over?

28. One bag of oranges costs $2. Tina buys 8 bags of oranges. She gives Don $20. How much change will she get?

29. Emilio wants to buy a pear for each of the 27 students in his class. Pears come in packages of 6. How many packages does he need to buy? How many extra pears will he have?

30. Don has a piece of paper 28 inches long. He wants to make signs that are 9 inches long. What is the greatest number of signs he can make?

UNDERSTANDING REMAINDERS

When you divide to solve a problem, you sometimes have a remainder. Here are three ways to decide what to do with the remainder.

▶ While at camp, Joey receives a box of 20 oranges from his parents. He shares the oranges equally with 6 friends in his cabin. He gives the rest to his counselor. How many oranges does the counselor get?

Divide: 20 ÷ 6

$$\begin{array}{r} 3\text{ R2} \\ 6\overline{)20} \\ -18 \\ \hline 2 \end{array}$$

Use the remainder. The counselor gets 2 oranges.

▶ Joey's counselor is setting up tents. He needs 8 tent pegs to set up each tent. He has 77 pegs. How many tents can he set up?

Divide: 77 ÷ 8

$$\begin{array}{r} 9\text{ R5} \\ 8\overline{)77} \\ -72 \\ \hline 5 \end{array}$$

Drop the remainder. He can set up 9 tents.

▶ A group of 9 campers and 5 counselors is planning a canoe trip across Lake Shawnee. Each canoe holds 3 people. How many canoes does the group need?

Divide: 14 ÷ 3

$$\begin{array}{r} 4\text{ R2} \\ 3\overline{)14} \\ -12 \\ \hline 2 \end{array}$$

Include the remainder in the answer by writing the next whole number. The group needs 5 canoes.

Think
- How do you decide what to do with the remainder?

GUIDED PRACTICE

Solve each problem. Decide what to do with the remainder.

1. Each canoe needs 2 paddles. There are 17 paddles in the boathouse. How many canoes can the campers use at one time?

2. A group of 29 campers and 3 counselors go on a fishing trip. Can each counselor be in charge of the same number of campers? Explain.

Critical Thinking 3. In exercise 1, how many more paddles are needed for 9 canoes?

INDEPENDENT PRACTICE

Problem Solving

4. At a campfire, 9 campers share a bag of 48 marshmallows. Each camper gets the same number. What is the least number of marshmallows that can be left over?

5. Each table in the dining hall seats 9 campers. If there are 89 campers, how many tables are needed to seat everyone? How many empty seats will there be?

6. Six of the campers hike from Meriden to Bartlett, a distance of 12 miles. How far would it be from Meriden to Bartlett if only 1 of the campers hiked?

7. Sam needs to buy 1 frozen yogurt bar for each of the 35 campers at the cookout. The yogurt bars come in packages of 8. How many packages should Sam buy?

8. Sam is buying 2 hot dog rolls for each of the 35 campers at the cookout. Rolls come in packages of 8. How many packages should he buy?

9. There are 13 campers who will gather wood for the campfire. Show how they can work in groups of 3 and 4.

Critical Thinking 10. Write a division word problem in which the answer has a remainder. Give it to a friend to solve.

ESTIMATING QUOTIENTS

Estimating quotients can help you divide.
Divide: 137 ÷ 3 = ▪
It asks the same question as 3 × ▪ = 137.

- First, decide how many digits are in the quotient.

  3 × 10 = 30

  3 × 100 = 300

  ← **137 is between 30 and 300**

  The quotient is between 10 and 100. It has 2 digits.

- To get an estimate, use multiples of 10.

  3 × 30 = 90
  3 × 40 = 120

  3 × 50 = 150

  ← **137 is between 120 and 150**

  So, the quotient is between 40 and 50, because 137 is between 120 and 150.

▶ You can estimate larger quotients.
Divide: 3945 ÷ 5 = ▪
It asks the same question as 5 × ▪ = 3945.

- How many digits?

  5 × 100 = 500

  5 × 1000 = 5000

  ← **3945 is between 500 and 5000**

  The quotient is between 100 and 1000. It has 3 digits.

- To get an estimate, use multiples of 100.

  5 × 600 = 3000
  5 × 700 = 3500

  5 × 800 = 4000

  ← **3945 is between 3500 and 4000**

  So, the quotient is between 700 and 800, because 3945 is between 3500 and 4000.

Think

- Will the quotient of 3945 ÷ 5 be closer to 700 or 800? How do you know?

Look at the blue numbers in each equation. Then write the two numbers the quotient is between.

1. 6)492   6 × 70 = 420
              6 × 80 = 480
              6 × 90 = 540

2. 8)2317   8 × 200 = 1600
               8 × 300 = 2400
               8 × 400 = 3200

Write the letter of the better estimate.

3. 629 ÷ 5   estimate between: **a.** 100 and 200   **b.** 200 and 300

4. 975 ÷ 3   estimate between: **a.** 200 and 300   **b.** 300 and 400

5. 4913 ÷ 7 estimate between: **a.** 600 and 700   **b.** 700 and 800

Critical Thinking **6.** For exercise 2, which multiple of 100 will the quotient be closest to? How do you know?

Estimate the quotient. Write the two multiples of 100 the estimate is between.

7. 847 ÷ 2   **8.** 5999 ÷ 7   **9.** 692 ÷ 3   **10.** 1939 ÷ 8   **11.** 4780 ÷ 8

12. 6)3210   **13.** 9)3292   **14.** 7)5989   **15.** 4)2828   **16.** 5)2963

Estimate the quotient. Write the letter of the better estimate.

17. 2)847   **18.** 3)854   **19.** 6)372   **20.** 5)440   **21.** 9)7978
  a. 400   **a.** 200   **a.** 60   **a.** 80   **a.** 800
  b. 500   **b.** 300   **b.** 70   **b.** 90   **b.** 900

Problem Solving Estimate to solve.

22. The Lings have picked 278 apples. They want to pack them in boxes of 24. About how many boxes do they need?

23. Patsy has collected 135 bottles to recycle. She has boxes that will hold 12 bottles each. Will 10 boxes be enough? How do you know?

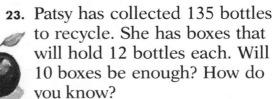

More Practice Set 7.3, p. 444

TWO-DIGIT QUOTIENTS

Tom, Dan, and Kim are starting stamp collections. They have collected 137 stamps. They share the stamps equally. How many stamps does each child get? How many are left over?

Divide: $137 \div 3 = \blacksquare$
It asks the same question as
$3 \times \blacksquare = 137$.

To get an estimate, use multiples of 10.
$3 \times 40 = 120$
$\leftarrow 137$
$3 \times 50 = 150$
So, the quotient is between 40 and 50.

● Write the tens.
Multiply. Subtract.

$$
\begin{array}{r}
4 \\
3\overline{)137} \\
-120 \\
\hline
17
\end{array}
\leftarrow 3 \times 40
$$

● Write the ones.
Multiply. Subtract.

$$
\begin{array}{r}
45 \\
3\overline{)137} \\
-120 \\
\hline
17 \\
-15 \\
\hline
2
\end{array}
$$
$\leftarrow 3 \times 40$
$\leftarrow 3 \times 5$

● Write the remainder if there is one.

$$
\begin{array}{r}
45\,\text{R2} \\
3\overline{)137} \\
-120 \\
\hline
17 \\
-15 \\
\hline
2
\end{array}
$$
$\leftarrow 3 \times 40$
$\leftarrow 3 \times 5$

Check by multiplying and adding.

$$
\begin{array}{r}
45 \leftarrow \text{quotient} \\
\times\ 3 \leftarrow \text{divisor} \\
\hline
135 \\
+\ 2 \leftarrow \text{remainder} \\
\hline
137 \leftarrow \text{dividend}
\end{array}
$$

The quotient with remainder is 45 R2.
Each child gets 45 stamps. There are 2 stamps left over.

Think
• Why was the ones digit not a 4?

Other Examples

```
    17R1
4)69
  -40  ← 4 × 10
   29
  -28  ← 4 × 7
    1
```

```
      99
5)495
  -450  ← 5 × 90
    45
   -45  ← 5 × 9
     0
```

GUIDED PRACTICE

Estimate. Then divide.

1. 3)48 **2.** 5)89 **3.** 4)248 **4.** 8)193 **5.** 6)566

6. 75 ÷ 2 **7.** 340 ÷ 9 **8.** 365 ÷ 7

Critical Thinking **9.** If 7 is the divisor, what is the greatest possible number for the remainder?

INDEPENDENT PRACTICE

Estimate. Then divide.

10. 5)75 **11.** 6)93 **12.** 8)236 **13.** 4)396 **14.** 3)267

15. 2)151 **16.** 7)98 **17.** 9)532 **18.** 6)366 **19.** 4)125

20. 93 ÷ 3 **21.** 129 ÷ 7 **22.** 436 ÷ 5 **23.** 325 ÷ 4

24. 197 ÷ 6 **25.** 864 ÷ 9 **26.** 787 ÷ 8 **27.** 131 ÷ 2

Problem Solving Make diagrams or use other strategies.

28. In two months, Cheryl collects 37 stamps to add to her collection of 45 stamps. She puts 6 stamps on each page of her album. How many pages of her stamp album can Cheryl fill completely?

29. Nicky can fit 8 stamps on each page of his 30-page album. Four of the pages are empty and one page is half filled. The rest are completely filled. How many stamps are in the album? How many more will fit?

MAKE NOTES

Making notes can help you keep track of the information in a problem.

One time, we made notes to help the Science Club plan a trip to the planetarium.

OUR PROBLEM

The bus ride to and from the planetarium for the whole club cost $58. Admission to the planetarium was $4 per person. We wanted to know the total cost for 14 club members.

OUR SOLUTION

We made notes of all the costs.

Costs	
bus	$58 for all
planetarium admission	$4 each

We added to the notes until all the important information was included. Our notes helped us see how to solve the problem.

Costs	
bus	$58 for all
planetarium admission	$4 each
People	
14	

We first found the entire cost of tickets to the planetarium for 14 people. Then we added that to the cost of the bus ride.

The trip was going to cost the Science Club $114.

$14 \times \$4 = \$56$

$56 total cost for planetarium
$+ \ 58$ cost of bus ride
$114 total cost of trip

GUIDED PRACTICE

Copy and complete the notes to help you. Then solve the problem.

1. The Science Club is raising money by selling calendars. Each calendar costs $1.25. So far, 9 calendars have been sold. How much more money needs to be raised to reach the club goal of $75?

> calendar prices $1.25
> calendars sold 9
> club goal

APPLICATION

Work with a partner. Copy and complete the notes. Then solve each problem.

2. One section of the theater in the planetarium has 8 rows of seats. Each row has 15 seats. For the afternoon show, only 7 seats are empty. How many people are in this section?

> 8 rows
> 15 seats in each row
> 7

3. Tracy works in a drugstore 3 afternoons a week. She earns $12.90 each day. From one week's earnings, Tracy spent $8.25 at the movies and $5.00 for lunches. How much money did she have left over from that week's earnings?

> Earns
> $12.90 each day
> for 3 days
> Spends

4. There are 7 members of the Science Club planning to visit the aquarium. It will cost $42 to rent a van. Admission to the aquarium is $3 each. How much will it cost each member for the trip?

> Costs
> Van $42

5. The aquarium opens every day at 10:00 A.M. On Tuesdays and Thursdays it closes at 9:00 P.M. On the other 5 days it closes at 5:00 P.M. How many hours each week is the aquarium open?

> Tuesday, Thursday
> 10 A.M. – 9 P.M.

THREE-DIGIT QUOTIENTS

The Wilsons buy a computer for $3945. They pay for it in 5 equal payments. What is the amount of each payment?

Think

• Can the quotient have 4 digits? Explain.

Divide: $3945 ÷ 5 = ■

It asks the same question as
5 × ■ = $3945.

To get an estimate, use multiples of 100.
5 × 700 = 3500
     ← 3945
5 × 800 = 4000

So, the quotient is between 700 and 800.

● **Write the hundreds. Multiply. Subtract.**

$$\begin{array}{r} 7 \\ 5)\overline{\$3\ 9\ 4\ 5} \\ -3\ 5\ 0\ 0 \quad \leftarrow 5 \times 700 \\ \hline 4\ 4\ 5 \end{array}$$

● **Write the tens. Multiply. Subtract.**

$$\begin{array}{r} 7\ 8 \\ 5)\overline{\$3\ 9\ 4\ 5} \\ -3\ 5\ 0\ 0 \\ \hline 4\ 4\ 5 \\ -4\ 0\ 0 \quad \leftarrow 5 \times 80 \\ \hline 4\ 5 \end{array}$$

● **Write the ones. Multiply. Subtract.**

$$\begin{array}{r} \$7\ 8\ 9 \\ 5)\overline{\$3945} \\ -3500 \\ \hline 445 \\ -400 \\ \hline 45 \\ -45 \quad \leftarrow 5 \times 9 \\ \hline 0 \end{array}$$

Remember to check your answer.
Multiply the divisor by the quotient.
There is no remainder to add.

$$\begin{array}{r} \$789 \\ \times\quad 5 \\ \hline \$3945 \end{array}$$

The amount of each payment is $789.

224

Estimate. Then divide. Use mental math when you can.

1. $6\overline{)728}$ 2. $8\overline{)729}$ 3. $5\overline{)4276}$ 4. $7\overline{)892}$ 5. $3\overline{)298}$

6. $488 \div 4$ 7. $8379 \div 9$ 8. $555 \div 5$ 9. $449 \div 6$

Critical Thinking 10. Which exercises did you solve using mental math?

INDEPENDENT PRACTICE

Write the letter of the best estimate of the quotient.

11. $614 \div 3$
   a. 20
   b. 200
   c. 2000

12. $892 \div 9$
   a. 90
   b. 900
   c. 9000

13. $4263 \div 5$
   a. 80
   b. 800
   c. 8000

14. $787 \div 6$
   a. 10
   b. 100
   c. 1000

Estimate. Then divide. Use mental math when you can.

15. $3\overline{)494}$ 16. $5\overline{)785}$ 17. $7\overline{)987}$ 18. $2\overline{)1578}$ 19. $4\overline{)484}$

20. $4\overline{)526}$ 21. $8\overline{)3385}$ 22. $6\overline{)366}$ 23. $6\overline{)369}$ 24. $5\overline{)384}$

25. $999 \div 3$ 26. $3972 \div 5$ 27. $6839 \div 8$ 28. $547 \div 7$

Problem Solving

29. If the Wilsons bought the computer for $3795 instead of $3945, how much less would each of the five payments be?

30. The Wilsons' printer can print 20 letters each second. How many times can it print the word *MATH* in 1 minute?

CHALLENGE • Logical Reasoning

Critical Thinking Copy and complete.

1.
```
   ■4 R3
5)73
 -■■
  23
 -20
   ■
```

2.
```
   ■■
6)438
 -4■■
  18
 -18
   0
```

3.
```
   96 R2
■)290
 -■■■
  2■
 -18
   ■
```

4.
```
   9■ R■
■)474
 -450
   ■■
 -20
    4
```

PROBLEM SOLVING
USING STRATEGIES

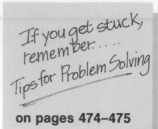
If you get stuck, remember.....
Tips for Problem Solving
on pages 474–475

Solve each problem.

1. Elaine will read two books and write reports. One book has 125 pages. The second book has 140 pages. Elaine plans to read 30 pages every night. At that rate, will she be able to finish reading the two books in 10 days? Explain.

2. Mr. Bishop's class collects 160 used books. They plan to donate half the books to Children's Hospital and sell the rest. If they sell the books at 50¢ each, how much money will they earn?

3. Mr. Bishop's class wrote limericks on index cards that are 5 inches wide and 3 inches high. They want to display them on a bulletin board like the one below. How many cards can fit on the bulletin board?

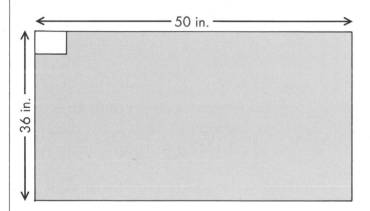

50 in.

36 in.

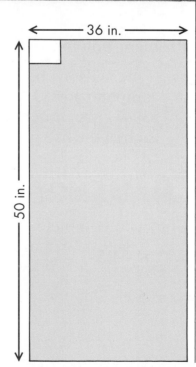

36 in.

50 in.

4. There is a second bulletin board in the classroom like the one at the right.
   a. How many index cards measuring 5 inches wide and 3 inches high can fit on this bulletin board?
   b. Which bulletin board is larger, the first or the second?
   c. Why do more cards fit on the first board?

SECTION REVIEW

for pages 214–226

Divide.

1. $123 \div 3$ 2. $91 \div 8$ 3. $875 \div 4$

4. $763 \div 5$ 5. $200 \div 8$ 6. $205 \div 4$

7. $101 \div 6$ 8. $777 \div 7$ 9. $732 \div 3$

10. $613 \div 8$ 11. $702 \div 9$ 12. $306 \div 6$

Write the letter of the correct answer.

13. $6\overline{)922}$
    a. 153
    b. 154
    c. 153 R4
    d. 157

14. $7\overline{)881}$
    a. 125 R6
    b. 126
    c. 131
    d. 125

15. $5\overline{)662}$
    a. 134
    b. 133
    c. 132
    d. 132 R2

16. $8\overline{)997}$
    a. 125
    b. 124 R5
    c. 124
    d. 129

17. $942 \div 3$
    a. 3042
    b. 303 R5
    c. 314
    d. 600

18. $875 \div 6$
    a. 145 R5
    b. 144 R11
    c. 200
    d. 1455

19. $743 \div 4$
    a. 400
    b. 209 R7
    c. 1853
    d. 185 R3

20. $937 \div 8$
    a. 116 R9
    b. 117 R1
    c. 1171
    d. 200

21. $3\overline{)638}$
    a. 2122
    b. 211 R5
    c. 212 R2
    d. 400

22. $5\overline{)893}$
    a. 178 R3
    b. 179
    c. 181
    d. 178

23. $7\overline{)639}$
    a. 93
    b. 91 R2
    c. 912
    d. 91

24. $6\overline{)475}$
    a. 791
    b. 79
    c. 80
    d. 79 R1

Solve each problem.

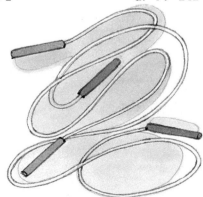

25. Mark uses 9 feet of rope for each jump rope he makes. How many jump ropes can he make from 120 feet of rope?

26. Evan needs 100 hot dog rolls. They come in packages of 8. How many packages will he need to buy?

ZEROS IN THE QUOTIENT

The director of Camp Shawnee needs 435 T-shirts for the campers. The shirts are shipped in boxes of 4. How many boxes should he order?

Divide: 435 ÷ 4 = ■

It asks the same question as
4 × ■ = 435.

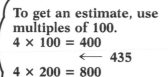

To get an estimate, use multiples of 100.
4 × 100 = 400
         ← 435
4 × 200 = 800

So, the quotient is between 100 and 200.

● **Write the hundreds digit. Multiply. Subtract.**

$$\begin{array}{r} 1 \\ 4)\overline{4\ 3\ 5} \\ -4\ 0\ 0 \quad \leftarrow 4 \times 100 \\ \hline 3\ 5 \end{array}$$

● **Write the tens digit. There are not enough tens. Write a zero in the quotient.**

$$\begin{array}{r} 1\ 0 \\ 4)\overline{4\ 3\ 5} \\ -4\ 0\ 0 \\ \hline 3\ 5 \end{array}$$

● **Write the ones digit. Multiply. Subtract. Is there a remainder?**

$$\begin{array}{r} 108\ \text{R3} \\ 4)\overline{435} \\ -400 \\ \hline 35 \\ -32 \quad \leftarrow 4 \times 8 \\ \hline 3 \end{array}$$

The director should order 109 boxes.

 Think

• Why did the director order 109 boxes?

Other Examples

$$\begin{array}{r} 409\ \text{R4} \\ 5)\overline{2049} \\ -2000 \quad \leftarrow 5 \times 400 \\ \hline 49 \\ -45 \quad \leftarrow 5 \times 9 \\ \hline 4 \end{array}$$

$$\begin{array}{r} 800\ \text{R6} \\ 9)\overline{7206} \\ -7200 \quad \leftarrow 9 \times 800 \\ \hline 6 \end{array}$$

GUIDED PRACTICE

Divide. Use mental math when you can.

1. 6)541   **2.** 8)808   **3.** 5)2516   **4.** 2)1210

5. 705 ÷ 7   **6.** 2762 ÷ 3   **7.** 2480 ÷ 4

Write <, >, or =. Use estimation when it helps.

8. 345 ÷ 8 ● 60   **9.** 5793 ÷ 7 ● 80   **10.** 563 ÷ 4 ● 40

Critical Thinking **11.** Does a zero in the ones place of the quotient mean that there is no remainder? Which of exercises 1–7 proves your answer?

....

INDEPENDENT PRACTICE

Divide. Use mental math when you can.

12. 9)900   **13.** 6)609   **14.** 4)1603   **15.** 5)3500

16. 7)490   **17.** 8)5616   **18.** 3)1891   **19.** 2)1611

20. 254 ÷ 5   **21.** 3607 ÷ 9   **22.** 4270 ÷ 7

23. 803 ÷ 4   **24.** 6300 ÷ 7   **25.** 5463 ÷ 6

Write >, <, or =. Use estimation when it helps.

26. 309 ÷ 3 ● 10   **27.** 400 ÷ 4 ● 80   **28.** 109 ÷ 9 ● 100

29. 1827 ÷ 9 ● 20   **30.** 2265 ÷ 5 ● 40   **31.** 7000 ÷ 7 ● 1000

Problem Solving

32. On an overnight hike, 8 campers will take equal turns keeping watch from 11:00 P.M. to 5:00 A.M. How many minutes should each turn be?

33. Another camper joins the overnight hike. How many minutes less will each turn be?

More Practice Set 7.8, p. 445

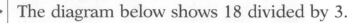

COOPERATIVE LEARNING

DIVISIBILITY

In this lesson, you will discover different ways to decide whether one number divides another number exactly. Work with a partner. You will need counters and a recording sheet.

▶ The diagram below shows 18 divided by 3.

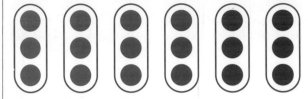

1. Does 3 divide into 18 exactly? How can you tell?

▶ The diagram below shows 17 divided by 3.

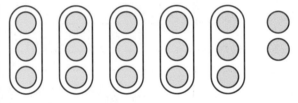

2. Does 3 divide into 17 exactly? How can you tell?

▶ The number 3 divides 9 exactly. You say that 9 **is divisible by** 3.

3. Which numbers below are divisible by 3 exactly? Write *yes* or *no* on the recording sheet. Make a diagram when it helps.

| 7 | 15 | 14 | 29 | 72 | 321 |
| 43 | 37 | 84 | 42 | 32 | 235 |

4. **a.** Choose a number from exercise 3 that is divisible by 3.
   b. Find the sum of all the digits in the number.
   c. Divide that sum by 3.

5. Repeat the steps in exercise 4 for every number in your list that is divisible by 3. What pattern do you notice?

Number	Divisible by 3
7	
15	
14	
29	
72	
321	
43	
37	
84	
42	
32	
235	

► A pattern can help you tell if a number is divisible by 2.

6. Which numbers below are divisible by 2? Write *yes* or *no* on the recording sheet. Make a diagram when it helps.

43	86	57	117	71	32
33	64	29	120	98	56

7. What pattern do you notice in the numbers divisible by 2?

8. Without dividing, list the numbers below that are divisible by 2.

940	631	5892	564
203	555	88	486

► A pattern can help you tell if a number is divisible by 5.

9. Which numbers below are divisible by 5? Write *yes* or *no* on the recording sheet.

30	55	74	100	27	125
41	86	115	80	130	65

10. What pattern do you notice in the numbers divisible by 5?

Critical Thinking ....

SUMMING IT UP

11. Write a rule about divisibility by 2.

12. Write a rule about divisibility by 5.

13. Write a rule about divisibility by 3.

 MATH LOG

What does divisibility mean?

Number	Divisible by 2
43	
86	
57	
117	
71	
32	
33	
64	
29	
120	
98	
56	

Number	Divisible by 5
30	
55	
74	
100	
27	
125	
41	
86	
115	
80	
130	
65	

MAKE NOTES

When you make notes to help solve a problem, keep the notes as short and simple as you can. But try to include enough information so the notes make sense to you.

Wayne borrows 3 books from the Perusa Public Library. The books are due on January 17. The fine for an overdue book is 10¢ a day. Wayne returns the books on January 25. How much is his fine?

Look at the two sets of notes below.

A.

| 3 | Jan. 17 |
| 10 | Jan. 25 |

B.

```
3 books
Due:     Jan. 17
Return:  Jan. 25
Fine:    10¢ a day per book
(Sundays, holidays do not count)
```

Think

• In what ways are the notes alike? In what ways are they different?

• Which set of notes would help you more in solving the problem? Why?

Use one of the sets of notes to help you solve the problem.

GUIDED PRACTICE

Read the problem. Use one set of notes to solve the problem.

1. There are 5 cashiers in the supermarket. Every morning, the manager gives each cashier the same amount of change in quarters, dimes, nickels, and pennies. This morning the manager has $30 in quarters, $20 in dimes, $15 in nickels, and $10 in pennies. Each cashier already has $50 in bills. How much money will each cashier have after the manager gives out the change?

A.

> 5 cashiers
> Bills: Each has $50
> Change: They will share
> $30 + $20 + $15 + $10

B.

> Place: Supermarket
> Time: Morning
> Title: Manager
> Job: Give out money

....

APPLICATION

Work with a small group. Make notes when it helps.

2. Mr. Chung is building a patio next to his house. To complete the patio, he needs to put down 10 rows of tiles, with 14 tiles in each row. The tiles come in boxes of 8. How many boxes of tiles should Mr. Chung buy?

3. There are 24 girls and 15 boys in the school chorus. For one concert, the chorus leader has the singers form 3 rows. Each of the first 2 rows has 14 members. How many singers are in the third row?

4. Gene has $4.75 to spend at a yard sale. He buys 3 paperback books for 50¢ each and 1 picture frame for 65¢. He also spends $1.50 on stickers. When Gene leaves the sale, he notices a hole in his pocket. Only 1 dime is left. How much money has he lost?

5. Chris and Melanie are helping to set up for a dance. To make a large snack table, they will push small square tables together. Each square table is 2 feet long. How many small tables are needed to make a large table 8 feet long and 4 feet wide?

DIVIDING MONEY

This sign is in the window of a store. Marcy wants to figure out how much one cassette will cost.

THE HOTTEST SOUNDS!
Cassettes
5 for $33.50

Think
- Does one cassette cost more than or less than $6? Explain.

To find the exact cost of each cassette, divide $33.50 by 5.

- Divide as you would with whole numbers.

$$
\begin{array}{r}
6\ 70 \\
5\overline{)\$33.50} \\
-30\ 00 \leftarrow 5 \times 600 \\
\hline
3\ 50 \\
-3\ 50 \leftarrow 5 \times 70 \\
\hline
0
\end{array}
$$

- Write the dollar sign and the decimal point in the quotient.

$$
\begin{array}{r}
\$6.70 \\
5\overline{)\$33.50} \\
-30\ 00 \\
\hline
3\ 50 \\
-3\ 50 \\
\hline
0
\end{array}
$$

Check.
$$
\begin{array}{r}
\$6.70 \leftarrow \text{quotient} \\
\times\quad 5 \leftarrow \text{divisor} \\
\hline
\$33.50 \leftarrow \text{dividend}
\end{array}
$$

Each cassette costs $6.70.

GUIDED PRACTICE

Write the quotient.

1. $4\overline{)\$0.28}$

2. $5\overline{)\$0.90}$

3. $6\overline{)\$2.04}$

4. $2\overline{)\$11.24}$

5. $\$0.60 \div 3$

6. $\$7.14 \div 7$

7. $\$16.08 \div 8$

8. $\$22.00 \div 4$

Critical Thinking
9. In exercise 3, what does the zero in the quotient mean?

234

Write the quotient.

10. $2\overline{)\$0.50}$ 11. $9\overline{)\$0.81}$ 12. $4\overline{)\$1.64}$ 13. $3\overline{)\$3.72}$

14. $\$1.00 \div 4$ 15. $\$5.58 \div 6$ 16. $\$8.06 \div 2$ 17. $\$6.55 \div 5$

18. $\$8.80 \div 2$ 19. $\$10.00 \div 5$ 20. $\$15.47 \div 7$ 21. $\$36.60 \div 6$

Write the letter of the best estimate.

22. $\$27.56 \div 9$
    a. between $1.00 and $2.00
    b. between $2.00 and $3.00
    c. between $3.00 and $4.00

23. $\$15.95 \div 5$
    a. between $0.30 and $1.00
    b. between $3.00 and $4.00
    c. between $30.00 and $31.00

Problem Solving

24. Which store has the better buy for 4 cassettes?

25. Last week, Sal bought 4 cassettes at Stereo City at the regular price. This week Amy bought 4 cassettes at the sale price. How much less did Amy pay for each cassette?

26. **Data Book** Go to the General Information section on page 472. How much does one blank audio cassette cost at Variety Video?

Maintain • Mixed Practice

Write the answer.

1. $\begin{array}{r} 4589 \\ \times\quad 6 \\ \hline \end{array}$ 2. $\begin{array}{r} 97,034 \\ -\ 8,669 \\ \hline \end{array}$ 3. $\begin{array}{r} 3006 \\ \times\quad 5 \\ \hline \end{array}$ 4. $\begin{array}{r} 5543 \\ +\ 629 \\ \hline \end{array}$ 5. $\begin{array}{r} 7999 \\ \times\quad 4 \\ \hline \end{array}$

USING DIVISION SENSE

Mr. O'Donnell owns a hobby shop. He is deciding which company to buy model car kits from. The kits are the same, so he will buy them from the company that charges the least.

▶ To compare, he can divide to find the cost of 1 kit from each company.

Indy:
$$\begin{array}{r} 29 \\ 6\overline{)174} \\ -120 \\ \hline 54 \\ -54 \\ \hline 0 \end{array}$$

Each kit costs $29.

Speedy:
$$\begin{array}{r} 33 \\ 5\overline{)169} \\ -150 \\ \hline 19 \\ -15 \\ \hline 4 \end{array}$$

Each kit costs between $33 and $34.

▶ Mr. O'Donnell could have compared by estimating.

Indy: If 6 kits cost $180, then 1 kit would cost $180 ÷ 6, or $30.

But 6 kits cost less than $180. So, each kit costs *less than* $30.

Speedy: If the kits cost $30 each, then 5 kits would cost $150.

But 5 kits cost more than $150. So, each kit costs *more than* $30.

Think

- Which method gives a correct answer to Mr. O'Donnell's problem?

- Which method is easier for you to use?

GUIDED PRACTICE

Estimate. Write the letter of the correct answer.

1. 376 ÷ 8
   a. 47
   b. 87
   c. 107

2. 387 ÷ 9
   a. 23
   b. 43
   c. 93

3. 924 ÷ 7
   a. 82
   b. 102
   c. 132

4. 576 ÷ 6
   a. 96
   b. 106
   c. 46

Compare. Write <, >, or =.

5. 409 ÷ 7 ● 409 ÷ 9
6. 739 ÷ 3 ● 769 ÷ 3
7. 98 ÷ 1 ● 98 × 1

Solve each problem.

Critical Thinking

8. Mr. O'Donnell has 45 wheel kits and 20 trim kits. If he sells 3 wheel kits and 1 trim kit every day, which will he run out of first?

9. How did you decide on your answer to exercise 5?

INDEPENDENT PRACTICE

Estimate. Write the letter of the correct answer.

10. 455 ÷ 5
   a. 71
   b. 61
   c. 91

11. 896 ÷ 8
   a. 92
   b. 72
   c. 112

12. 1224 ÷ 9
   a. 136
   b. 86
   c. 106

13. 498 ÷ 6
   a. 23
   b. 83
   c. 53

Compare. Write <, >, or =.

14. 985 ÷ 5 ● 1228 ÷ 5
15. 576 ÷ 1 ● 576 × 1
16. 522 ÷ 3 ● 813 ÷ 3

Problem Solving

17. How many tire kits can Mr. O'Donnell buy for $100?

18. How many paint kits can he buy for $100?

Critical Thinking

19. Will he have more money left over if he buys all tire kits or all paint kits? How do you know?

SPECIAL
Tire Kits $9
Paint Kits $7

20. How can Mr. O'Donnell spend exactly $50 on kits?

More Practice Set 7.12, p. 446

FINDING AVERAGES

The table shows the ages of the divers on the school team. What is the average age of the divers?

Hart School Diving Team	
Diver	**Age**
Tammy Burr	14
Joe Carver	15
Alex Kovacs	18
Juan Rivera	18
Diane Weiss	15

▶ You can find the average with counters.

• Put all the counters together in a pile.

• Make 5 equal stacks and count how many are in each stack.

▶ You can find the average by computing.

Ages 14, 15, 18, 18, 15

• Find the total of the ages.

$$14 + 15 + 18 + 18 + 15 = 80$$

• Divide the total by the number of divers on the team.

$$\begin{array}{r} 16 \\ 5\overline{)80} \\ -50 \\ \hline 30 \\ -30 \\ \hline 0 \end{array}$$

The average age of the divers is 16 years old.

Think

• If you know the average age of a group of people, can you tell the exact age of any person in the group? Why or why not?

• If Tammy's scores were 9, 8, 6, and 9, how could you find her average score?

238

Write the number you would divide by to find the average.

1. 242, 187, 300, 271

2. 83, 83, 83

3. 2, 5, 7, 4, 7

Critical Thinking

4. Write the average for each of exercises 1–3.

5. For exercise 2, did you need to compute to find the average? Why or why not?

INDEPENDENT PRACTICE

Write the average.

6. 12, 35, 34, 15

7. 9, 7, 8

8. 235, 469

9. 4, 4, 5, 8, 9

10. 137, 275, 215

11. 10, 20, 40, 60, 80

12. 522, 811, 812

13. 2, 3, 5, 6

14. 25, 26, 27

Problem Solving

15. Sally's scores are 80, 90, and 70. By how much will her average score go up if she gets 100 in her next game?

16. A player has scored 16, 18, and 20 points in the 3 games so far. What does he need to score in the next game to have an average of 19 points per game?

17. The starters on the basketball team list their heights as 67, 73, 72, 75, and 68 inches. How many players are shorter than the average height? How many are taller?

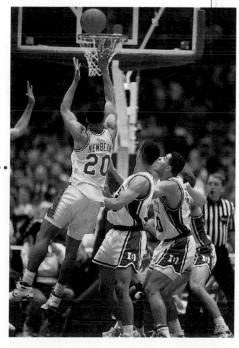

CHALLENGE • Problem Solving

1. Can 4 of 5 basketball players be taller than the average height of the 5 players? Show how. HINT: Try with 4 equally tall players and 1 very short player.

Critical Thinking

2. Can all 5 players be taller than the average team height? Explain.

More Practice Set 7.13, p. 447

PROBLEM SOLVING
USING MATH SENSE

If you get stuck, remember...
Tips for Problem Solving
on pages 474–475

Solve each problem. Estimate when you can.

1. The Starlight Sports Shop sells 11 bowling balls and 8 bowling bags. Does the cost of these 19 items total more than $600? How do you know?

2. Craig needs 3 blank tapes to record music for his bowling party. Which brand costs less?

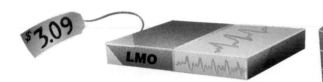

3. Alice works at Starlight Bowling Lanes. She works Mondays and Wednesdays from 5:00 P.M. to 8:00 P.M. She makes $4.30 an hour. How much money does Alice earn in a week?

John and Shawn bowled in a league. The table below shows their weekly scores.

Weeks	1	2	3	4	5
John	43	55	52	58	57
Shawn	70	69	77	79	65

4. Who has a higher average at the end of 5 weeks? HINT: You do not need to figure the averages.

5. What was John's average at the end of 4 weeks?

6. Did John's average go up or down when he bowled the 5th week? By how many points?

7. If Shawn scores a zero in the 6th week, will his average stay the same? Explain your answer.

8. If Shawn is absent the 6th week, will his average stay the same?

SECTION REVIEW

for pages 228–240

Write the letter of the correct answer.

1. $5668 \div 7$
   a. 897 R1
   b. 89 R5
   c. 809 R5
   d. 809

2. $3215 \div 4$
   a. 803 R3
   b. 83 R1
   c. 803
   d. 8382 R2

3. $7234 \div 9$
   a. 803
   b. 83 R7
   c. 837 R7
   d. 803 R7

4. $3652 \div 6$
   a. 68 R4
   b. 608 R4
   c. 686 R4
   d. 608

5. $3235 \div 4$
   a. 808
   b. 88 R3
   c. 887 R2
   d. 808 R3

6. $5633 \div 8$
   a. 74 R1
   b. 704 R1
   c. 741 R2
   d. 704

7. $1542 \div 5$
   a. 380 R2
   b. 38 R2
   c. 308 R2
   d. 308

8. $4962 \div 7$
   a. 708 R6
   b. 78 R6
   c. 708
   d. 788 R4

9. $6359 \div 9$
   a. 76 R5
   b. 706 R5
   c. 706
   d. 786 R5

Solve each problem.

10. Music World usually sells compact discs for $18. The store is having a sale and is selling compact discs at the price of 5 for $65. How much money do you save on each compact disc if you buy 5 of them?

11. A band is renting a studio to record a song. It costs $520 from 9 A.M. to 5 P.M.. How much does it cost for each hour?

12. Carl bowled five games with scores of 120, 130, 100, 135, and 160. Which of his scores were below his average for the five games?

13. Betty bowled 120, 90, and 87 in three of her games. What was her average score?

CHAPTER TEST

Divide.

1. $8\overline{)3264}$ 2. $9\overline{)823}$ 3. $3\overline{)\$3.72}$ 4. $6\overline{)789}$

5. $\$10.50 \div 5$ 6. $678 \div 6$ 7. $\$35.28 \div 4$ 8. $181 \div 9$

9. $8\overline{)7200}$ 10. $4\overline{)\$0.48}$ 11. $6\overline{)5261}$ 12. $5\overline{)47}$

13. $1002 \div 6$ 14. $4921 \div 7$ 15. $309 \div 7$ 16. $328 \div 8$

17. $5\overline{)1190}$ 18. $6\overline{)588}$ 19. $8\overline{)644}$ 20. $5\overline{)\$42.50}$

21. $287 \div 7$ 22. $\$9.18 \div 9$ 23. $753 \div 7$ 24. $3725 \div 4$

Write the average.

25. 3, 7, 8   26. 457, 127   27. 16, 19, 38, 17, 45

28. 142, 129, 131, 250   29. 6, 8, 7   30. 20, 40, 10, 50

31. 8, 12, 15, 25   32. 200, 400, 100, 500   33. 142, 144

34. 75, 21, 51   35. 18, 55, 24, 15   36. 750, 210, 510

PROBLEM SOLVING

Solve each problem.

37. Jessica needs 8-inch lengths of ribbon for a project. If she cuts as many as she can from a 108-inch roll, how many inches will the leftover piece be?

38. Kate is setting up tennis groups. Each group must have 4 players. Thirty-five children want to play. How many groups of 4 players can be formed?

39. Bev bowled five games with scores of 120, 125, 100, 150, and 155. What was her average score?

40. Calvin plays a game where he gets 5 points for each blue truck he counts. He scores 635 points. How many blue trucks does Calvin count?

CUMULATIVE REVIEW

Write the answer.

1. 18 ÷ 2　　　**2.** 7 × 6　　　**3.** 63 ÷ 7　　　**4.** 7 × 7

5. 3 × 8　　　**6.** 45 ÷ 9　　　**7.** 4 × 9　　　**8.** 64 ÷ 8

Find the area of each figure in square centimeters.

9. 　　　**10.**

Tell which of these are right angles. Write *yes* or *no*.

11. 　　　**12.** 　　　**13.** 　　　**14.**

Use the chart to solve each problem.

15. Steve bought a 175 square foot carpet remnant on sale. If he cuts up the remnant, which room could he carpet completely? Explain how you got your answer.

Room	Area In Square Feet
Living Room	300
Dining Room	250
Bedroom 1	200
Bedroom 2	150

16. Two other carpet remnants were on sale. One was 60 square feet and the other was 80 square feet. Could Steve carpet any of the rooms completely by combining these two remnants? Why or why not?

Write the product.

17. 43　　**18.** 63　　**19.** 70　　**20.** 38　　**21.** 62
　　× 2　　　　× 3　　　　× 7　　　　× 5　　　　× 9

22. 2 × 243　　　**23.** 5 × 751　　　**24.** 7 × 583　　　**25.** 8 × 486

Excursion

USING TECHNOLOGY

LOGO

You will need Logo software, a computer, and squared paper.

Look at this Logo procedure for a rectangle.

TO RECTANGLE
FD 30 RT 90 FD 60 RT 90 FD 30 RT 90 FD 60
RT 90
END

Notice that the commands FD 30 RT 90 FD 60 RT 90 repeat twice. You can use the REPEAT command to write the procedure in a shorter way.

TO RECTANGLE
REPEAT 2 [FD 30 RT 90 FD 60 RT 90]

Number of times the command repeats

Commands that repeat

Sometimes a procedure does not work because it has a **bug,** or mistake, in it.

1. Type in this procedure, TO OCTAGON.

TO OCTAGON
FD 30 RT 45 FD 30 RT 45 FD 30 RT 45 FD 30
RT 45 FD 30 LT 45 FD 30 LT 45
END

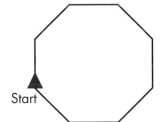

Start

a. Tell the turtle to DRAW OCTAGON. Did the procedure work?
b. Find the bugs and fix them. Tell the turtle to DRAW OCTAGON again.
c. Now write your procedure using the REPEAT command. Type it in and tell the turtle to DRAW OCTAGON.

2. Use the REPEAT command to write a procedure for this drawing at the right. Name the procedure MOUNTAINS. HINT: Start with RT 45. Tell the turtle to DRAW MOUNTAINS.

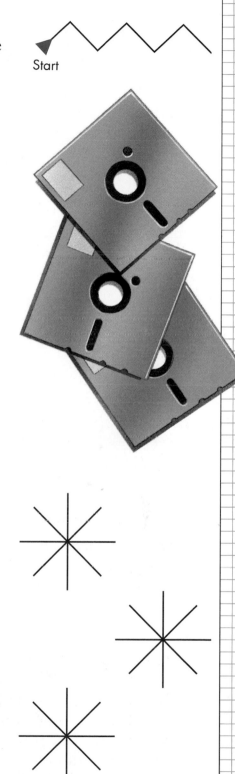

3. Look at the procedure below. Predict what the turtle will draw. Sketch your prediction on squared paper. Type in the procedure.

TO DESIGN
RT 45 REPEAT 4 [FD 40 LT 90] RT 90 FD 30
LT 45 FD 30
END

    a. Tell the turtle to DRAW DESIGN. Does it match your sketch?

4. Type in the procedure below.

TO FRAME
REPEAT 4 [FD 60 RT 90] FD 20 LT 90 FD 20
REPEAT 4 [FD 20 LT 90]
END

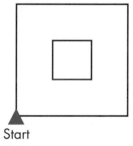

Start

    a. Tell the turtle to DRAW FRAME. Does it work?

    b. Correct the bugs in the procedure. Try it again.

5. Write a procedure to draw the stars at the right. HINT: To draw one segment of each star, move the turtle FD 10 BK 10 RT 45. Name the procedure TO STARS.

    a. Type in the procedure. Tell the turtle to DRAW STARS.

Language Arts

Tuesday I Was Ten

Tuesday I was ten, and though
The fact delights me plenty,
It sort of startles me to know
I'm now a half of twenty.

It's nice to own a bigger bike
With brakes along the wheels
And figure skates (the kind I like)
And shoes with little heels
And have a real allowance, too,
To make me wise and thrifty;
But still, I can't believe (can you?)
I'm now a fifth of fifty!

Although an age like ten appears
Quite young and un-adventure-y,
My gosh! In only ninety years,
My age will be a century!

by Kaye Starbird

FRACTIONS

Look at this Fraction Bar.

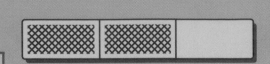

Think

• How many equal parts are there? What is each part called? How many parts are shaded?

Two thirds of the Fraction Bar is shaded.

Using symbols, we write $\frac{2}{3}$.

number of shaded parts $\longrightarrow$ $\underline{2}$ $\longleftarrow$ **numerator**
number of parts $\longrightarrow$ 3 $\longleftarrow$ **denominator**

We can show the fraction $\frac{3}{5}$ by drawing a Fraction Bar.

The Fraction Bar is divided into five equal parts. Three parts are shaded.

Other Examples

four fourths

$\frac{4}{4}$

zero sixths

$\frac{0}{6}$

GUIDED PRACTICE

Write what fraction of each bar is shaded.

1.  2.  3.  4.

Draw a Fraction Bar for each fraction.

5. $\frac{5}{12}$ 6. $\frac{2}{5}$ 7. $\frac{4}{10}$ 8. $\frac{3}{4}$

Write the fraction.

9. five sixths   10. one fourth   11. five fifths

Critical Thinking 12. What is the numerator in exercise 2?

Write what fraction of each bar is shaded.

13. **14.** **15.**

16. **17.** **18.**

Draw a Fraction Bar for each fraction.

19. $\frac{6}{12}$ **20.** $\frac{2}{4}$ **21.** $\frac{12}{12}$ **22.** $\frac{0}{3}$

23. $\frac{3}{10}$ **24.** $\frac{4}{5}$ **25.** $\frac{8}{10}$ **26.** $\frac{4}{6}$

Write the fraction.

27. seven eighths **28.** zero thirds **29.** two halves

Match each bar with the fraction.

30. 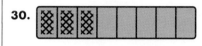 **31.**  **32.**

a. $\frac{9}{12}$ **b.** $\frac{8}{10}$ **c.** $\frac{3}{8}$

Problem Solving

33. One fourth of a Fraction Bar is shaded. What fraction is not shaded?

34. What fraction of the days this week do you come to school?

35. One half of Simon's hats are red. His other 3 hats are blue. How many hats does he have?

36. Jamie ran $\frac{1}{3}$ of the way to school. He walked the rest of the way. Did he walk farther or run farther?

Maintain • Mixed Practice

Write the answer.

1. $\begin{array}{r} 356 \\ \times\ \ 9 \end{array}$ **2.** $\begin{array}{r} 2500 \\ \times\ \ \ 4 \end{array}$ **3.** $4\overline{)1000}$ **4.** $7\overline{)333}$ **5.** $3\overline{)798}$

FRACTIONS AND EQUIVALENCE

Groups:

- small groups

You will need:

- set of Fraction Bars
- Fraction Bars recording sheet

For each exercise, write the fraction of the bar that is shaded.

1. Find a one-half bar.

   a. Find a fourths bar that has an equal amount shaded.

   b. Find a sixths bar that has an equal amount shaded.

   c. Find a twelfths bar that has an equal amount shaded.

2. Find a two-thirds bar.

   a. Find a sixths bar that has an equal amount shaded.

   b. Find a twelfths bar that has an equal amount shaded.

Fraction Bars that have equal amounts of shading are **equivalent.**

The fractions that name them are **equivalent fractions.**

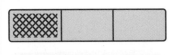

$$\frac{1}{3} = \frac{2}{6}$$

3. Find a one-third bar.

   a. Find all the other Fraction Bars that are equivalent.

4. Find a three-sixths bar.

   a. Find all other Fraction Bars that are equivalent.

5. Find the three-thirds bar.

   a. Find all the other Fraction Bars that are equivalent.

Use the recording sheet with Fraction Bars.

▶ Find the fourths bar. Color in three fourths of the bar. Divide each part of the bar into 2 equal parts.

6. How many parts are in the fourths bar after you divide it?

7. What fraction of the bar is shaded?

▶ Find the fifths bar. Color one fifth of it. Divide each part of the bar into 2 equal parts by drawing a line segment.

8. How many parts are in the fifths bar after you divide it?

9. What fraction of the bar is shaded?

▶ Find the sixths bar. Color five sixths of the bar. Draw a segment to divide each part of this bar into 2 equal parts.

10. How many parts are in the sixths bar after you divide it?

11. What fraction of the bar is shaded?

 Critical Thinking

SUMMING IT UP

12. How do you know when two fractions are equivalent?

13. What does a Fraction Bar name when all the parts are shaded?

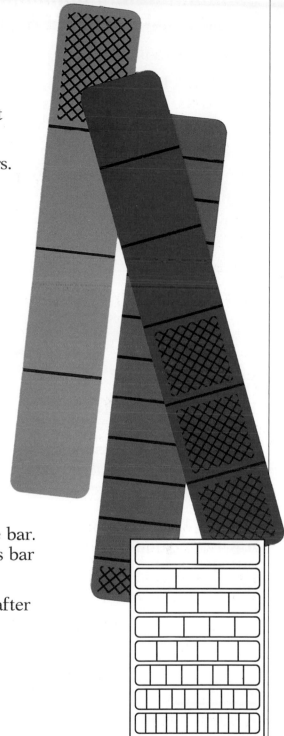

251

EQUIVALENCE AND SIMPLEST FORM

▶ Here is a two-thirds bar.

The dotted line segments have divided the thirds bar into six parts. The total number of parts doubled.

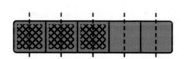

$\frac{2}{3} = \frac{4}{6}$

Think

- What happened to the number of shaded parts?

- What happened to the size of each shaded part?

▶ Here is a three-fifths bar.

The dotted segments have divided the fifths bar into ten parts.

$\frac{3}{5} = \frac{6}{10}$

You can find some equivalent fractions by *multiplying* the numerator and denominator by the same number.

$$\frac{3}{4} = \frac{9}{12}$$

(× 3)

You can find other equivalent fractions by *dividing* the numerator and denominator by the same number.

$$\frac{8}{12} = \frac{2}{3}$$

(÷ 4)

▶ A fraction is in **simplest form** when the only number that divides both the numerator and denominator exactly is 1.

These fractions are in simplest form.

$$\frac{3}{5} \quad \frac{2}{3} \quad \frac{3}{10} \quad \frac{5}{6} \quad \frac{1}{4}$$

These fractions are *not* in simplest form.

$$\frac{3}{9} \quad \frac{4}{10} \quad \frac{6}{8} \quad \frac{2}{6} \quad \frac{6}{12}$$

Match the Fraction Bar with an equivalent Fraction Bar.

1.  **2.**  **3.**

a.  **b.**  **c.**

Copy and complete. Draw a picture of a Fraction Bar to check your answer.

4. $\dfrac{1}{3} = \dfrac{\blacksquare}{6}$ **5.** $\dfrac{2}{4} = \dfrac{\blacksquare}{12}$ **6.** $\dfrac{2}{5} = \dfrac{\blacksquare}{10}$ **7.** $\dfrac{3}{3} = \dfrac{\blacksquare}{6}$

8. $\dfrac{1}{2} = \dfrac{\blacksquare}{\blacksquare}$ **9.** $\dfrac{2}{6} = \dfrac{\blacksquare}{\blacksquare}$ **10.** $\dfrac{3}{4} = \dfrac{\blacksquare}{\blacksquare}$ **11.** $\dfrac{3}{5} = \dfrac{\blacksquare}{\blacksquare}$

Critical Thinking 12. Is $\dfrac{2}{4}$ in simplest form? Explain.

Match the Fraction Bar with an equivalent Fraction Bar.

13.  **14.**  **15.**

a. **b.** **c.**

Copy and complete. Draw a picture of a Fraction Bar to check your answer.

16. $\dfrac{1}{3} = \dfrac{\blacksquare}{12}$ **17.** $\dfrac{2}{4} = \dfrac{\blacksquare}{8}$ **18.** $\dfrac{4}{5} = \dfrac{\blacksquare}{10}$ **19.** $\dfrac{2}{3} = \dfrac{\blacksquare}{6}$

20. $\dfrac{4}{4} = \dfrac{\blacksquare}{\blacksquare}$ **21.** $\dfrac{3}{6} = \dfrac{\blacksquare}{\blacksquare}$ **22.** $\dfrac{1}{5} = \dfrac{\blacksquare}{\blacksquare}$ **23.** $\dfrac{5}{6} = \dfrac{\blacksquare}{\blacksquare}$

CHALLENGE • Patterns

Write the next three equivalent fractions.

1. $\dfrac{2}{3}, \dfrac{4}{6}, \dfrac{6}{9}, \blacksquare, \blacksquare, \blacksquare$

2. $\dfrac{1}{5}, \dfrac{2}{10}, \dfrac{3}{15}, \blacksquare, \blacksquare, \blacksquare$

3. $\dfrac{2}{4}, \dfrac{4}{8}, \dfrac{6}{12}, \blacksquare, \blacksquare, \blacksquare$

4. $\dfrac{4}{5}, \dfrac{8}{10}, \dfrac{12}{15}, \blacksquare, \blacksquare, \blacksquare$

EXPLORING ORDER OF FRACTIONS

Groups:

• small groups

You will need:

• set of Fraction Bars

• Fraction Bars recording sheet

• a blue, a red, a yellow, and a green crayon

▶ Look at these two Fraction Bars.

1. Which Fraction Bar has more shading?

▶ Look at these two Fraction Bars.

2. Which Fraction Bar has more shading?

Use the Fraction Bar recording sheet. Answer each question.

3. Starting with halves, look at the first part of each bar. What can you say about the size of the parts as you go down the sheet?

4. Color $\frac{2}{3}$ of the thirds bar red. Color $\frac{3}{6}$ of the sixths bar red. Which bar has more shading?

5. Color $\frac{1}{2}$ of the halves bar blue. Color $\frac{5}{8}$ of the eighths bar blue. Which has more shading?

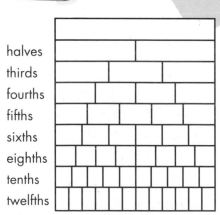

halves
thirds
fourths
fifths
sixths
eighths
tenths
twelfths

6. Color $\frac{2}{6}$ of the sixths bar yellow. Color $\frac{3}{12}$ of the twelfths bar yellow. Which bar has less yellow shading?

7. Color $\frac{1}{5}$ of the fifths bar green. Color $\frac{1}{10}$ of the tenths bar green. Color $\frac{1}{4}$ of the fourths bar green. Compare the green shading. What is the order of the fractions from least to greatest?

Use Fraction Bars and your recording sheet. Put each set of fractions in order from least to greatest.

8. $\frac{7}{8}, \frac{5}{8}, \frac{2}{8}$

9. $\frac{1}{3}, \frac{1}{4}, \frac{1}{6}$

10. $\frac{1}{10}, \frac{2}{5}, \frac{5}{10}$

11. $\frac{2}{12}, \frac{2}{3}, \frac{2}{6}$

12. $\frac{2}{3}, \frac{1}{2}, \frac{2}{6}$

13. $\frac{7}{12}, \frac{5}{6}, \frac{3}{4}, \frac{1}{2}$

14. $\frac{3}{3}, \frac{4}{6}, \frac{0}{2}, \frac{9}{12}$

15. $\frac{1}{8}, \frac{1}{2}, \frac{2}{8}, \frac{3}{4}$

Critical Thinking SUMMING IT UP

16. If three fractions have the same denominator, how can you order them?

17. If three fractions have the same numerator, how can you order them?

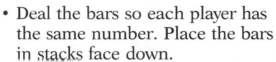

PROJECT • Game

Play this game with a small group. You will need a set of Fraction Bars.

• Deal the bars so each player has the same number. Place the bars in stacks face down.

• Each player turns over the top bar and compares it with the other players' bars.

• The player with the bar representing the largest fraction wins the turned-over bars. Continue until all the bars are turned over.

• The player with the most bars wins the game.

COOPERATIVE • LEARNING

COMPARING AND ORDERING FRACTIONS

Patti, Mark, and Jamal walk to school every day. Patti walks $\frac{5}{8}$ mile. Mark walks $\frac{7}{8}$ mile. Jamal walks $\frac{3}{4}$ mile. Who has the longest walk? Who has the shortest walk?

▶ Fraction Bars can help to compare and order fractions.

$\frac{5}{8}$

$\frac{7}{8}$

$\frac{3}{4}$

▶ Using equivalent fractions is another way to compare and order fractions.

Patti: $\frac{5}{8} = \frac{5}{8}$

Mark: $\frac{7}{8} = \frac{7}{8}$

Jamal: $\frac{3}{4} = \frac{6}{8}$

> **Dotted lines divide the fourths bar into eighths.**

$\frac{3}{4}$ $\frac{6}{8}$

Think

- How does it help to write fourths as eighths?

- Why can you not change the $\frac{5}{8}$ bar and the $\frac{7}{8}$ bar to fourths?

From least to greatest, the fractions are $\frac{5}{8}, \frac{3}{4}, \frac{7}{8}$.

Patti has the shortest walk to school. Mark has the longest walk to school.

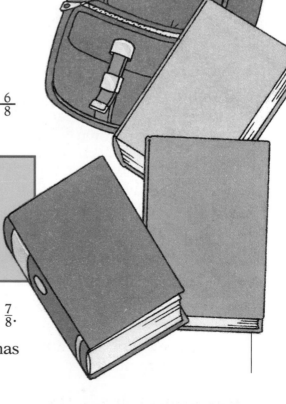

GUIDED PRACTICE

Copy and complete the number sentence. Write
<, >, or =. Use Fraction Bars when it helps.

1. $\frac{2}{4}$ 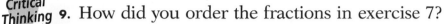 $\frac{4}{12}$
2. $\frac{1}{2}$ ● $\frac{5}{10}$
3. $\frac{2}{6}$ ● $\frac{5}{12}$
4. $\frac{3}{4}$ ● $\frac{7}{8}$
5. $\frac{6}{10}$ ● $\frac{2}{5}$

Write the fractions from least to greatest. Use Fraction
Bars when it helps.

6. $\frac{6}{6}, \frac{1}{6}, \frac{3}{6}$
7. $\frac{2}{4}, \frac{1}{8}, \frac{6}{8}$
8. $\frac{2}{10}, \frac{2}{5}, \frac{7}{10}, \frac{3}{5}$

Critical Thinking 9. How did you order the fractions in exercise 7?

INDEPENDENT PRACTICE

Copy and complete the number sentence. Write
<, >, or =. Use Fraction Bars when it helps.

10. $\frac{1}{2}$ ● $\frac{9}{12}$
11. $\frac{7}{8}$ ● $\frac{1}{4}$
12. $\frac{6}{6}$ ● $\frac{3}{3}$
13. $\frac{3}{6}$ ● $\frac{8}{12}$
14. $\frac{5}{5}$ ● $\frac{7}{10}$

Write the fractions from least to greatest. Use Fraction
Bars when it helps.

15. $\frac{5}{6}, \frac{2}{3}, \frac{12}{12}$
16. $\frac{3}{4}, \frac{1}{2}, \frac{7}{8}$
17. $\frac{4}{5}, \frac{1}{10}, \frac{10}{10}$
18. $\frac{10}{12}, \frac{3}{4}, \frac{1}{12}$
19. $\frac{1}{2}, \frac{2}{2}, \frac{6}{8}, \frac{1}{8}$
20. $\frac{1}{3}, \frac{3}{6}, \frac{3}{12}, \frac{4}{6}$

Problem Solving

21. At the Harley School, $\frac{2}{3}$ of the band
members are boys. Are there more boys or
girls in the band?

22. Harry walks $\frac{1}{2}$ mile to school. Tom walks $\frac{3}{10}$
of a mile to school. Who has the shorter walk?

23. In the band, $\frac{1}{2}$ of the instruments are horns,
$\frac{1}{8}$ are woodwinds, and $\frac{3}{8}$ are drums. Order
the types of instruments from most to fewest.

24. **Data Book** Go to page 472. Look at the
chart on bean stem growth. On day 2, which
plant was taller, plant 1 or plant 2?

More Practice Set 8.5, p. 448

PROBLEM SOLVING
USING MATH SENSE

We went $\frac{2}{3}$ of the way to the soccer game in our boat. Then my Dad saw that we would not have enough gas to get there. So, we went back home.

That doesn't make sense. You would not have enough gas to get back home.

Think

• What fraction would make sense in the story?

Read each story. Does the underlined sentence make sense? Tell why or why not.

1. Andy, Kate, and Pat are on the Eagles. <u>In one game, Andy scored $\frac{1}{2}$ of the Eagles' goals, Kate scored $\frac{1}{2}$ of them, and Pat scored $\frac{1}{2}$ of them.</u>

2. The Eagles played against the Falcons. <u>Andy played in half of the game, and so did Kate and Pat.</u>

3. At the team party, Andy ate $\frac{1}{2}$ of a small cupcake. Pat ate $\frac{1}{4}$ of a large cake. <u>Pat said to Andy, "I ate less than you because $\frac{1}{4}$ is less than $\frac{1}{2}$."</u>

4. Half of the players on the Eagles are in fourth grade. The other 8 players are in fifth grade. <u>So, there must be 16 players on the Eagles.</u>

SECTION REVIEW

for pages 248–258

Write the fraction for each bar.

1.    2.    3.   4.

Write the fraction.

5. three thirds   6. five sixths   7. seven twelfths

Write the letter of the answer.

8. $\frac{1}{2} = \frac{\blacksquare}{4}$
   a. 3
   b. 2
   c. 1

9. $\frac{1}{5} = \frac{\blacksquare}{10}$
   a. 2
   b. 1
   c. 3

10. $\frac{3}{6} = \frac{\blacksquare}{12}$
    a. 5
    b. 3
    c. 6

11. $\frac{6}{6} = \frac{\blacksquare}{12}$
    a. 8
    b. 12
    c. 6

12. $\frac{1}{3} = \frac{\blacksquare}{6}$
    a. 2
    b. 3
    c. 1

13. $\frac{3}{4} = \frac{\blacksquare}{8}$
    a. 3
    b. 7
    c. 6

14. $\frac{1}{2} = \frac{\blacksquare}{12}$
    a. 1
    b. 6
    c. 7

15. $\frac{2}{3} = \frac{\blacksquare}{12}$
    a. 8
    b. 6
    c. 2

Copy and complete. Write >, <, or =.

16. $\frac{1}{6} \bullet \frac{3}{12}$

17. $\frac{1}{2} \bullet \frac{7}{8}$

18. $\frac{2}{3} \bullet \frac{5}{6}$

19. $\frac{1}{4} \bullet \frac{1}{8}$

20. $\frac{5}{5} \bullet \frac{1}{10}$

21. $\frac{5}{10} \bullet \frac{1}{2}$

22. $\frac{9}{12} \bullet \frac{2}{6}$

23. $\frac{2}{5} \bullet \frac{2}{10}$

Solve each problem.

24. In one day, Tom's plant grew $\frac{3}{4}$ of an inch. Sam's plant grew $\frac{1}{2}$ of an inch. Whose plant grew less?

25. Jerry ran $\frac{4}{10}$ of a mile. Pam ran $\frac{1}{2}$ of a mile. Who ran a longer distance?

EXPLORING FRACTIONAL PARTS OF A NUMBER

Groups:

• small groups

You will need:

• 36 counters

• 3 paper plates

• recording sheet

▶ Separate the counters into three equal groups.

Place each group of counters on its own paper plate.

1. How many paper plates are there?

2. What fractional part of the group of plates is one plate?

3. How many counters are there in all?

4. How many counters are on each plate?

5. What fractional part of the group of counters is 12?

6. What is $\frac{1}{3}$ of 36?

▶ Try this without plates. Use 24 counters.

7. Find each fractional part of 24 by separating the counters into equal groups. Record your results on the recording sheet.

8. For $\frac{1}{3}$ of 24, how did you decide how many groups to make?

Chart A
$\frac{1}{2}$ of 24: ▨
$\frac{1}{3}$ of 24: ▨
$\frac{2}{3}$ of 24: ▨
$\frac{1}{4}$ of 24: ▨
$\frac{3}{4}$ of 24: ▨
$\frac{1}{6}$ of 24: ▨
$\frac{1}{8}$ of 24: ▨
$\frac{3}{8}$ of 24: ▨

▶ Next, use 20 counters.

9. Find each fractional part of 20. Record your results on the recording sheet.

10. For $\frac{1}{5}$ of 20, how did you decide how many equal groups to make with the counters?

Critical Thinking ···

SUMMING IT UP

11. What does the denominator of a fraction tell you about the number of groups?

12. What is a way to find $\frac{1}{5}$ of 25 without using counters?

13. What is a way to find $\frac{2}{5}$ of 25 without using counters?

Chart B
$\frac{1}{2}$ of 20: ▨
$\frac{1}{4}$ of 20: ▨
$\frac{3}{4}$ of 20: ▨
$\frac{1}{5}$ of 20: ▨
$\frac{2}{5}$ of 20: ▨
$\frac{1}{10}$ of 20: ▨
$\frac{10}{10}$ of 20: ▨

CHALLENGE • Problem Solving

Work with a small group.

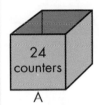
24 counters
A

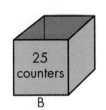
25 counters
B

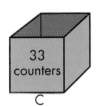
33 counters
C

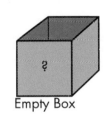
?
Empty Box

You have four boxes. Three boxes contain counters. You want to take enough counters from each box to put 20 counters in the fourth box.

These are the rules:
• You must take some counters from each box.
• The counters you take must be: $\frac{1}{6}$ of box A; $\frac{1}{5}$ of box B; $\frac{1}{3}$ of box C.

How many counters are left in boxes A, B, and C?

Record your answer and share it with another group. Discuss how your group solved the problem.

FRACTIONAL PARTS OF A NUMBER

Harvey orders 12 bicycles for his sports shop. Two thirds of them are dirt bikes. How many dirt bikes does Harvey order?

You can find $\frac{2}{3}$ of 12 with counters. You could also draw a picture like the one below.

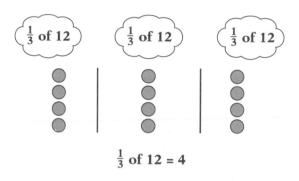

$\frac{1}{3}$ of 12 = 4

Think

• How could you use division to find $\frac{1}{3}$ of 12?

Two thirds is two of the three groups.

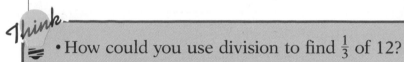

Harvey orders 8 dirt bikes.

Think

• You want to find $\frac{3}{4}$ of 20. How many groups would you divide 20 into?

• How many of those groups make $\frac{3}{4}$ of 20?

GUIDED PRACTICE

Write the answer. Use objects or draw a picture to check your answer.

1. $\frac{1}{3}$ of 18
2. $\frac{2}{3}$ of 18
3. $\frac{3}{6}$ of 30
4. $\frac{5}{5}$ of 15

Critical Thinking 5. How can the answer to excrcise 1 help you find the answer to exercise 2?

INDEPENDENT PRACTICE

Write the answer. Use objects or draw a picture to check your answer.

6. $\frac{1}{2}$ of $10
7. $\frac{1}{2}$ of 20
8. $\frac{1}{6}$ of 18
9. $\frac{2}{6}$ of 18

10. $\frac{1}{8}$ of 32
11. $\frac{2}{8}$ of 32
12. $\frac{1}{4}$ of 20
13. $\frac{2}{4}$ of 20

14. $\frac{1}{5}$ of 30
15. $\frac{2}{5}$ of 30
16. $\frac{1}{12}$ of 24
17. $\frac{2}{12}$ of 24

18. $\frac{1}{10}$ of 40
19. $\frac{2}{10}$ of 40
20. $\frac{5}{10}$ of 40
21. $\frac{10}{10}$ of 40

Problem Solving

22. During Harvey's clearance sale, ski gloves are half price. What does one pair cost?

23. Harvey decides to take $\frac{1}{3}$ off the price of an NFL uniform kit. What will the new price be?

24. Harvey had 40 bowling balls. He sold $\frac{1}{4}$ of them. How many were sold?

25. Harvey had 30 footballs. He sold $\frac{2}{3}$ of them. How many footballs are left?

Critical Thinking 26. Write a word problem for $\frac{1}{3}$ of 18.

 MATH LOG

Explain how to find a fractional part of a number. Use the example $\frac{5}{6}$ of 30.

FULL CIRCLE

2 in.

12 in. length

6 in. width

Beth, Chris, Ray, and Terry are recording 12 songs for their new release, *Full Circle*. Their friend Barbara is designing the compact disc cover. A sketch of the cover is shown at the left.

Work with a small group. Use squared paper when it helps.

1. Barbara wants the title to appear in a colored strip across the cover. She wants it to be 2 inches high. What fraction of the cover will be left for pictures of the band?

2. On the cover, Barbara plans to use two colors. The band members give her the following choices: red, blue, yellow, and purple. Name the color combinations she can choose.

3. The cover will have 3 photos all the same size, side by side. How many inches wide is each photo?

4. Records Galore wants to display the compact discs in the store window. They plan to place 5 discs on each shelf. Will the discs cover more than half of the window? Explain your answer. (Use the picture to help you.)

FULL CIRCLE

1 ft

← ½ ft →

Got to Have an Angle	6 min
Rockin' Radius	8 min
Going in Circles	5 min
De-nom, De-nom-inator	4 min
Diagonal Dancing	3 min
A Matter of Factor	7 min
Array of Sunshine	5 min
I'd Slide, Flip, and Turn for You	4 min
Wrecked Tango	9 min
Divided Heart	6 min

5. *Full Circle* is also sold as a cassette. The table at the right lists all the songs on the compact disc. How would you arrange the songs so that each side of the cassette has under 30 minutes of music?

PROJECT • Using Fractions

COOPERATIVE • LEARNING

Work with a small group. Design a cover for a compact disc. Make up a title for the cover. Sketch your design. The cover should measure 12 inches high and 6 inches wide. Color the cover about one half red, one third blue, and one sixth green. Share your design with the class.

IXED NUMBERS

► Look at the total shaded part of the three Fraction Bars. What do the Fraction Bars below represent?

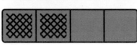

Two whole Fraction Bars and $\frac{1}{6}$ of a bar are shaded. Altogether, two *and* one-sixth bars are shaded.

A number that has a whole number part and a fraction is called a **mixed number**.
Two and one sixth is written $2\frac{1}{6}$.

$2\frac{1}{6}$ is between 2 and 3.

Think

- • How many sixths are shaded?
- • What fraction tells how many sixths are shaded?

► Look at these Fraction Bars. $3\frac{2}{4}$ bars are shaded.

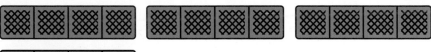

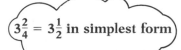

$3\frac{2}{4}$ is between 3 and 4. $3\frac{2}{4} = 3\frac{1}{2}$ in simplest form

Think

- • How many fourths are shaded?
- • What fraction tells how many fourths are shaded?

266

GUIDED PRACTICE

How many bars are shaded? Write your answer as a
fraction and as a mixed number.

1. ▨▨▨▨▨ ▨▨□□□

2. ▨ ▨ ▨ ▨ ▨ □

3. ▨ ▨ ▨ ▨ ▨ □

4. ▨▨▨▨▨ ▨▨▨▨▨
▨▨▨▨▨ ▨□□□□

 5. Between which two whole numbers is the
answer to exercise 4?

INDEPENDENT PRACTICE

How many bars are shaded? Write your answer as a
fraction and as a mixed number.

6. ▨▨▨▨▨ ▨▨▨▨▨

7. ▨▨▨▨▨▨▨▨▨▨ ▨▨□□□□□□

8. ▨▨▨▨▨ ▨▨▨▨□

9. ▨▨▨▨▨▨▨ ▨▨▨□□□□

10. ▨▨▨▨▨▨▨▨▨ ▨▨▨▨▨▨▨□□

11. ▨▨▨▨▨▨▨▨▨ ▨▨▨▨▨▨▨▨▨

Name the two whole numbers each mixed number is between.

12. $5\frac{5}{6}$

13. $14\frac{2}{10}$

14. $10\frac{5}{12}$

15. $25\frac{3}{8}$

Problem Solving Write a mixed number.

16. Emily studies from 8:00 to 9:15.
How many hours does she study?

17. Pepe is 5 years old today. How
old will he be in 6 months?

18. Jerry's ride to the store is 2
miles. He has ridden $\frac{1}{2}$ mile.
How many miles does he have
left to go?

19. Bob and Jim want to share 5
oranges equally. How can they
do this by making only 1 cut?

Maintain • Mixed Practice

1. 2×4080

2. $5\overline{)4505}$

3. $8\overline{)763}$

4. 5×333

5. $6\overline{)276}$

USING STRATEGIES

If you get stuck, remember....
Tips for Problem Solving

on pages 474-475

	First	Second	Third	Fourth	Total
BISONS	2	7	10	6	25
LEOPARDS	7	14	0	0	21

Solve each problem.

1. Which team scored one third of all its points in the first quarter? How do you know?

2. Which team scored more than one half of its points in a single quarter? Which quarter?

3. Look at the scoreboard. In which quarter did one team score half as many points as the other team?

4. At halftime, the band marched in 8 rows of 3 players each. Half the marchers wore red. How many marchers wore red?

5. Which team was ahead after three fourths of the game had been played?

6. The game began at 1:15 and ended at 3:45. How many hours did the game last?

7. Each quarter of the game is 15 minutes of playing time. Did playing time make up more than or less than half of the game time? Explain your answer. Remember, the game began at 1:15 and ended at 3:45.

8. Millie's car had a full tank of gas when she left home for the game. Without stopping for gas, she arrived at the game with three-fourths of a tank left. Does she have enough gasoline to drive straight home? Explain your answer.

SECTION REVIEW

for pages 260–268

Write the letter of the answer.

1. $\frac{1}{2}$ of 16
   a. 2
   b. 8
   c. 9

2. $\frac{2}{3}$ of 9
   a. 5
   b. 3
   c. 6

3. $\frac{1}{4}$ of 20
   a. 5
   b. 6
   c. 4

4. $\frac{1}{6}$ of 12
   a. 6
   b. 3
   c. 2

5. $\frac{1}{5}$ of 20
   a. 6
   b. 5
   c. 4

6. $\frac{2}{4}$ of 12
   a. 6
   b. 5
   c. 4

7. $\frac{3}{4}$ of 12
   a. 4
   b. 9
   c. 6

8. $\frac{4}{4}$ of 12
   a. 7
   b. 4
   c. 12

9. $\frac{1}{3}$ of 15
   a. 5
   b. 6
   c. 3

10. $\frac{2}{3}$ of 15
    a. 3
    b. 10
    c. 7

11. $\frac{3}{3}$ of 15
    a. 15
    b. 8
    c. 3

12. $\frac{5}{6}$ of 18
    a. 6
    b. 8
    c. 15

Write the mixed number.

13.

14.

15.

16.

Solve each problem.

17. Sally's book has 30 pages. She is on page 25. Has she read more than $\frac{2}{3}$ of the book?

18. Simon's Sporting Goods Store has 24 batting helmets. They sell $\frac{1}{4}$ of them. How many batting helmets are left in the store?

CHAPTER TEST

Write what fraction of each bar is shaded.

1.

2.

Copy and complete the number sentence.

3. $\frac{3}{3} = \frac{\blacksquare}{9}$ **4.** $\frac{2}{4} = \frac{\blacksquare}{12}$ **5.** $\frac{4}{5} = \frac{\blacksquare}{10}$ **6.** $\frac{4}{6} = \frac{\blacksquare}{12}$

Write >, <, or =. Use Fraction Bars when it helps.

7. $\frac{2}{3} \bullet \frac{5}{6}$ **8.** $\frac{1}{5} \bullet \frac{2}{10}$ **9.** $\frac{3}{8} \bullet \frac{1}{4}$ **10.** $\frac{1}{4} \bullet \frac{4}{12}$

Write the fractions from least to greatest.

11. $\frac{1}{5}, \frac{4}{10}, \frac{3}{10}, \frac{3}{5}$ **12.** $\frac{7}{8}, \frac{1}{4}, \frac{3}{4}, \frac{1}{2}$ **13.** $\frac{2}{3}, \frac{1}{6}, \frac{5}{6}, \frac{3}{3}$

Write the answer. Use objects or draw a picture to check.

14. $\frac{1}{3}$ of 30   **15.** $\frac{8}{8}$ of 40   **16.** $\frac{3}{4}$ of 36   **17.** $\frac{2}{12}$ of 24

Write the number of shaded bars as a fraction and as a mixed number.

18.

19.

PROBLEM SOLVING

Solve each problem.

20. The cafe has 36 pizzas to sell. Max baked $\frac{1}{3}$ of the pizzas. How many pizzas did Max bake?

21. Sarah watched the Taft School parade from 2:00 to 3:20. José watched it for $1\frac{3}{4}$ hours. Who watched the parade longer?

CUMULATIVE REVIEW

Copy each figure and slide arrow onto dot paper. Draw the slide image for the given slide arrow.

1.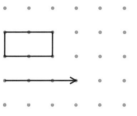

2.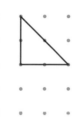

3.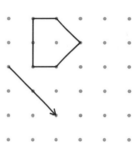

4.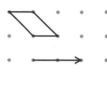

Write the product. Use mental math when you can.

5.	6.	7.	8.	9.
2310 × 7	4652 × 4	7000 × 9	8665 × 5	7042 × 8

10. 6 × 2680   11. 3 × 8998   12. 7 × 4077   13. 6 × 3456

Solve each problem.

14. 3000 people entered and completed a 6-mile walkathon. If each walker raised $1 for every mile he or she walked, how much money was raised altogether? How did you get your answer?

15. Walking shoes are on sale for $29.95 a pair. Is $100 enough to pay for 3 pairs of shoes? How do you know?

Divide.

16. 4)38   17. 7)55   18. 9)63   19. 6)47   20. 8)42

21. 5)157   22. 6)309   23. 8)408   24. 7)499   25. 4)329

26. 572 ÷ 9   27. 349 ÷ 6   28. 830 ÷ 9   29. 777 ÷ 8

30. 291 ÷ 3   31. 456 ÷ 8   32. 672 ÷ 7   33. 414 ÷ 8

EXCURSION

USING TECHNOLOGY

LOGO

Look at the procedure. It tells the turtle how to draw a square. Type it in.

TO SQUARE
REPEAT 4 [FD 40 RT 90]
END
DRAW SQUARE

Start

The design shown is made up of 8 squares.

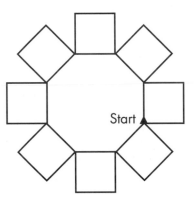

Start

You can write a procedure to draw this design. You can use SQUARE as part of the procedure. A procedure that is part of another procedure is called a **subprocedure**.

1. Type in this procedure.
   TO DESIGN
   REPEAT 8 [SQUARE FD 40 LT 45]
   END
   DRAW DESIGN

> These commands tell the turtle where to begin drawing the next square.

2. The procedure PINWHEEL uses the subprocedures SQUARE and RECTANGLE. Type in both subprocedures.

   TO SQUARE   TO RECTANGLE
   REPEAT 4 [FD 40 RT 90]   REPEAT 2 [FD 20 LT 90 FD 60 LT 90]
   END   END

3. Type in this procedure. Fill in what is missing.
   TO PINWHEEL
   SQUARE LT 45 RECTANGLE RT 45 ____ RT 45
   RECTANGLE RT 45 FD 40 RT 45
   _____ RT 45 ____ RT 45 RECTANGLE
   RT 45 ____ LT 90 FD 90

   ____

Tell the turtle to DRAW PINWHEEL.

Start

272

4. Type this subprocedure into the computer.

TO OCTAGON
REPEAT 8 [FD 15 RT 45]
END

5. Write a procedure to draw a stop sign. First, type in the subprocedures for each drawing at the right. Fill in what is missing for each subprocedure.

TO OCTAGON
REPEAT 8 [FD 50 RT 45]
END

TO S
RT 90 FD 10 ____ FD 10 LT 90 ____ RT 90
FD 10 RT 90 FD 10
END

TO T
RT 90 FD 10 BK 5 RT 90 FD 20
____

TO O
REPEAT _ [FD 20 LT 90 FD 10
____]
END

TO P
FD 20 RT 90 FD 10 RT 90 ____
____ FD 10
END

6. Write a procedure named **SIGN**. Use all of the subprocedures above. Type in the procedure. Tell the turtle to **DRAW SIGN**.

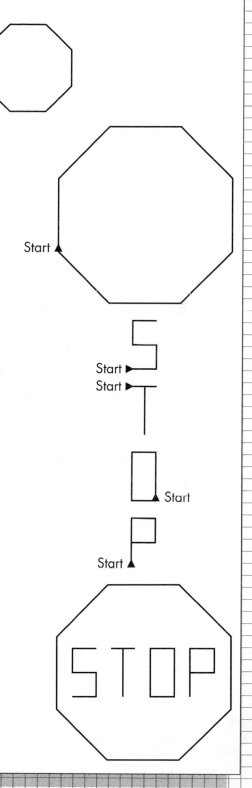

ADDITION AND SUBTRACTION OF FRACTIONS

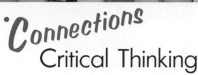

Connections

Critical Thinking

A Fraction Riddle Tiffany's family is riding to the next town, a distance of about 8 miles. They estimate that the trip will take about an hour.

After about 30 minutes, they stop for a snack and a drink of water. The children ask, "How much farther?" Father answers, "We are halfway there."

They continue riding and after another 15 minutes Will asks, "How much farther?" Their mother answers, "We are halfway there."

Tiffany is a bit confused. So, in a little while, she asks one last time, "How much farther?" Once more Father answers, "We are halfway there."

Use the story to answer each question.

- How far were they from the next town when they stopped for a snack?

- How far were they from the next town when Will asked?

- How far were they from the next town when Tiffany asked?

What fraction helps you answer each of these questions? Draw a diagram to explain your answer.

ADDING AND SUBTRACTING LIKE FRACTIONS

▶ Gina has $\frac{1}{8}$ yard of red ribbon and $\frac{5}{8}$ yard of green ribbon. How much ribbon does Gina have? To find the total, you can add $\frac{1}{8}$ and $\frac{5}{8}$. To show $\frac{1}{8} + \frac{5}{8}$ using Fraction Bars, follow these steps:

• Line up the $\frac{1}{8}$ bar and the $\frac{5}{8}$ bar as shown.

• Count the number of shaded parts.

• Write the number sentence.

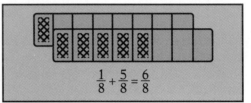

$$\frac{1}{8} + \frac{5}{8} = \frac{6}{8}$$

Think

• What other fraction is the same amount as $\frac{6}{8}$?

▶ How much more green ribbon than red ribbon does Gina have?

Since you are comparing, you want to subtract.

To show $\frac{5}{8} - \frac{1}{8}$ using Fraction Bars, follow these steps:

• Line up the $\frac{5}{8}$ bar and the $\frac{1}{8}$ bar as shown.

• Count the difference between the two shaded amounts.

• Write the number sentence.

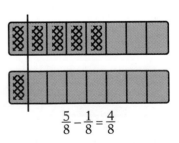

$$\frac{5}{8} - \frac{1}{8} = \frac{4}{8}$$

Think

• What other fraction is the same amount as $\frac{4}{8}$?

276

GUIDED PRACTICE

Write the answer. Use Fraction Bars when it helps.

1. $\frac{1}{6} + \frac{2}{6}$

2. $\frac{5}{8} - \frac{2}{8}$

3. $\frac{3}{8} + \frac{2}{8}$

4. $\frac{4}{5} - \frac{1}{5}$

5. $\frac{1}{3} + \frac{2}{3}$

6. What is another way to write the answer to exercise 5?

Critical Thinking

INDEPENDENT PRACTICE

Write the answer.

7. $\frac{1}{2} + \frac{1}{2}$

8. $\frac{5}{6} - \frac{3}{6}$

Write the answer. Use Fraction Bars when it helps.

9. $\frac{1}{4} + \frac{1}{4}$

10. $\frac{2}{6} + \frac{3}{6}$

11. $\frac{7}{8} - \frac{2}{8}$

12. $\frac{9}{10} - \frac{4}{10}$

13. $\frac{2}{5} + \frac{1}{5}$

14. $\frac{7}{12} - \frac{2}{12}$

15. $\frac{5}{6} - \frac{1}{6}$

16. $\frac{3}{5} - \frac{1}{5}$

Problem Solving

17. Marcella makes $\frac{3}{5}$ of her basketball throws. What fraction of her throws do not go into the basket?

18. John and Joe can swim halfway across the pool. If they swim next to each other, how far across the pool can they swim?

19. In 5 minutes, Mark ran $\frac{1}{4}$ mile. Luis ran $\frac{2}{4}$ mile.

  a. Who ran farther?
  b. How much farther did he run?
  c. Who ran faster?

20. Kristen wants to swim 1 mile in 3 days. She swims $\frac{3}{8}$ mile on Monday and $\frac{2}{8}$ mile on Tuesday. How far must she swim on Wednesday?

Maintain • Comparing Fractions

Copy and complete. Write >, <, or =.

1. $\frac{7}{8} \bigcirc \frac{3}{4}$

2. $\frac{4}{5} \bigcirc \frac{8}{10}$

3. $\frac{5}{6} \bigcirc \frac{12}{12}$

4. $\frac{1}{2} \bigcirc \frac{5}{8}$

5. $\frac{2}{3} \bigcirc \frac{5}{6}$

USING FRACTIONS

In art class, Lani and her friends are working on projects. One project is a banner.

Work with a partner. Use the picture to solve each problem.

1. About what fraction of the banner is red?

2. About what fraction is blue?

3. About what fraction of the banner is not red?

4. Nancy is drawing a line across the chalkboard from one end to the other. About what fraction of the line has she drawn so far?

5. Michael has a bag of beads. Half of the beads in the bag have holes. The other 6 do not. How many beads are in the bag?

6. Jody is making necklaces. There are some green beads in $\frac{2}{3}$ of the necklaces. There are some yellow beads in $\frac{2}{3}$ of the necklaces. Draw a picture of Jody's necklaces to show how this can be.

7. The paint cost three and a half dollars. The beads cost $3.69.
   a. Which cost more?
   b. How much more?

8. Jesse, Jon, and Jennifer are each covering a sheet of cardboard with squares. Which of them has covered about $\frac{2}{3}$ of the sheet?

JESSE

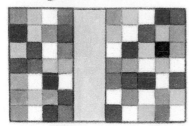

JON

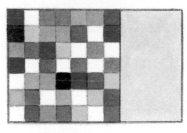

JENNIFER

9. Art class started $\frac{1}{2}$ hour ago. It ends at 2:00.

   a. Look at the clock on page 278. What time did art class start?
   b. What fraction of an hour is left until class ends?
   c. What fraction of the class time has passed so far? HINT: How many minutes long is the class?

Critical Thinking 10. Make up your own fraction problem about the picture of Lani's art class on page 278.

PROJECT • **Problem Solving**

Use squared paper. Design a banner that is

• $\frac{1}{8}$ red   • $\frac{2}{8}$ blue   • $\frac{3}{8}$ green   • the rest yellow

What fraction of your banner is yellow?

ADDING AND SUBTRACTING FRACTIONS

You can use Fraction Bars to show the addition and subtraction of fractions with different denominators.

Groups:

- small groups

You will need:

- set of Fraction Bars

▶ Use Fraction Bars to add $\frac{2}{3}$ and $\frac{1}{6}$.

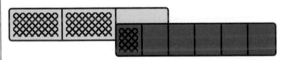

1. Can you name the total shaded thirds? Find the sixths bar that has the same amount shaded as the $\frac{2}{3}$ bar.

2. How many sixths are equal to $\frac{2}{3}$? Because $\frac{4}{6} = \frac{2}{3}$, you can replace $\frac{2}{3}$ with $\frac{4}{6}$ to add the fractions. Use Fraction Bars to show $\frac{4}{6} + \frac{1}{6}$.

3. How many sixths do you have when you add $\frac{4}{6}$ and $\frac{1}{6}$?

Use Fraction Bars to subtract $\frac{1}{12}$ from $\frac{3}{4}$.

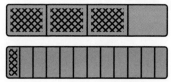

Find the twelfths bar that has the same amount shaded as the $\frac{3}{4}$ bar.

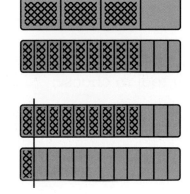

4. How many twelfths are equal to $\frac{3}{4}$?

Because $\frac{9}{12} = \frac{3}{4}$, you can replace $\frac{3}{4}$ with $\frac{9}{12}$ to subtract the fractions. Use Fraction Bars to show $\frac{9}{12} - \frac{1}{12}$.

5. What is the difference in the amount of shading?

6. How many twelfths do you have when you subtract $\frac{1}{12}$ from $\frac{9}{12}$?

Use Fraction Bars to add.

7. $\frac{2}{12} + \frac{1}{6}$ **8.** $\frac{1}{3} + \frac{1}{6}$ **9.** $\frac{3}{4} + \frac{1}{12}$ **10.** $\frac{2}{6} + \frac{1}{2}$

Use Fraction Bars to subtract.

11. $\frac{1}{2} - \frac{2}{6}$ **12.** $\frac{3}{6} - \frac{1}{12}$ **13.** $\frac{11}{12} - \frac{3}{4}$ **14.** $\frac{2}{3} - \frac{1}{6}$

· · · · · · · · · · · · · · · · · · · ·

SUMMING IT UP

15. How did your Fraction Bars help you to add and subtract fractions with different denominators?

16. How do you think you can add and subtract fractions with different denominators without using Fraction Bars?

CHOOSE A COMPUTATION METHOD

The Outdoor Club is on a rafting trip. They need help solving the math problems they find on the trip. There are many tools to help you solve these problems: mental math, estimation, calculator, or paper and pencil. These questions can help you decide which tool to choose:

Think

- Will I have a calculator with me?
- Is an exact answer needed?
- Can I work with the numbers mentally?

INDEPENDENT PRACTICE

Solve each problem. Write whether you used mental math, estimation, calculator, or paper and pencil.

1. The Outdoor Club raised $100 for the trip. Renting the rafts costs $3 per person. Will the club have enough money to rent rafts for all 27 members?

2. The Outdoor Club is taking a bus ride to the river. The bus trip is 75 miles long. The bus can cover 50 miles in one hour. How long will the bus trip be?

3. There are 27 members of the Outdoor Club on the rafting trip. Each raft holds 4 people.
   a. How many rafts are needed?
   b. How many people will be on the raft with fewer than 4 people?

4. The rafting trip was 12 miles long. Halfway down the river, the club stopped for a picnic. Then halfway between the picnic stop and the end of the trip, the rafters saw a deer. How many miles was the deer from the start of the trip?

5. The rafting trip started at 1:15 and ended at 4:45. How many hours did the trip last?

6. After the trip, the club stopped for juice. Each glass of juice cost $0.45. How much did 27 glasses cost?

SECTION REVIEW

for pages 276–282

Write the letter of the correct answer.

1. $\frac{5}{8} + \frac{1}{8}$

   a. $\frac{6}{16}$

   b. $\frac{5}{16}$

   c. $\frac{6}{8}$

2. $\frac{5}{12} + \frac{3}{12}$

   a. $\frac{8}{24}$

   b. $\frac{8}{12}$

   c. $\frac{5}{24}$

3. $\frac{9}{10} - \frac{4}{10}$

   a. $\frac{5}{0}$

   b. $\frac{5}{10}$

   c. $\frac{5}{20}$

4. $\frac{3}{8} + \frac{5}{8}$

   a. $\frac{8}{16}$

   b. $\frac{8}{8}$

   c. $\frac{3}{16}$

5. $\frac{11}{12} - \frac{7}{12}$

   a. $\frac{4}{12}$

   b. $\frac{4}{0}$

   c. $\frac{4}{24}$

6. $\frac{5}{8} - \frac{1}{8}$

   a. $\frac{4}{16}$

   b. $\frac{4}{0}$

   c. $\frac{4}{8}$

Write the answer.

7. $\begin{array}{r} \frac{1}{3} \\ + \frac{1}{3} \\ \hline \end{array}$

8. $\begin{array}{r} \frac{4}{10} \\ + \frac{3}{10} \\ \hline \end{array}$

9. $\begin{array}{r} \frac{9}{10} \\ - \frac{3}{10} \\ \hline \end{array}$

10. $\begin{array}{r} \frac{7}{8} \\ - \frac{3}{8} \\ \hline \end{array}$

11. $\begin{array}{r} \frac{6}{12} \\ + \frac{5}{12} \\ \hline \end{array}$

12. $\begin{array}{r} \frac{6}{8} \\ + \frac{2}{8} \\ \hline \end{array}$

13. $\begin{array}{r} \frac{7}{10} \\ - \frac{2}{10} \\ \hline \end{array}$

14. $\begin{array}{r} \frac{11}{12} \\ - \frac{5}{12} \\ \hline \end{array}$

15. $\begin{array}{r} \frac{1}{3} \\ - \frac{1}{3} \\ \hline \end{array}$

16. $\begin{array}{r} \frac{5}{8} \\ - \frac{1}{8} \\ \hline \end{array}$

Solve each problem.

17. Maria has $\frac{3}{8}$ yard of blue silk and $\frac{4}{8}$ yard of white silk. How much silk does she have?

18. Angela is making pancakes. The recipe calls for 1 cup of milk. She pours in $\frac{1}{3}$ cup of milk. How much more milk does she need to add?

19. Jan walks $\frac{3}{8}$ mile to school. She walks the same way home. Harry walks $\frac{7}{8}$ mile to school and rides home. Who walks farther? How much farther?

ADDING UNLIKE FRACTIONS

You can use Fraction Bars to add $\frac{2}{3}$ and $\frac{1}{6}$.

- Can you name the total shading as thirds?

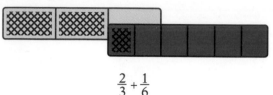

$$\frac{2}{3} + \frac{1}{6}$$

- Find a sixths bar equivalent to the $\frac{2}{3}$ bar.

$$\frac{2}{3} = \frac{4}{6}$$

- Add the sixths.

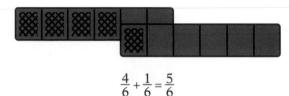

$$\frac{4}{6} + \frac{1}{6} = \frac{5}{6}$$

Think

- How is adding fractions with different denominators different from adding fractions with the same denominator?

GUIDED PRACTICE

Write the sum. Use Fraction Bars when it helps.

1. $\begin{array}{r} \frac{1}{10} = \ \ \frac{1}{10} \\ + \frac{2}{5} = + \frac{4}{10} \\ \hline \end{array}$

2. $\begin{array}{r} \frac{1}{3} = \ \ \frac{4}{12} \\ + \frac{3}{12} = + \frac{3}{12} \\ \hline \end{array}$

3. $\begin{array}{r} \frac{3}{10} \\ + \frac{4}{10} \\ \hline \end{array}$

4. $\begin{array}{r} \frac{3}{10} \\ + \frac{1}{2} \\ \hline \end{array}$

5. $\begin{array}{r} \frac{2}{3} \\ + \frac{1}{6} \\ \hline \end{array}$

Critical Thinking 6. Frank wrote $\frac{4}{12}$ as the answer to exercise 4. What do you think he did wrong?

INDEPENDENT PRACTICE

Write the sum. Use Fraction Bars when it helps.

7. $\frac{1}{8}$
    $+ \frac{3}{4}$

8. $\frac{7}{10}$
    $+ \frac{2}{10}$

9. $\frac{2}{3}$
    $+ \frac{1}{6}$

10. $\frac{1}{5}$
    $+ \frac{3}{10}$

11. $\frac{1}{12}$
    $+ \frac{1}{6}$

12. $\frac{1}{3}$
    $+ \frac{1}{6}$

13. $\frac{4}{12}$
    $+ \frac{5}{12}$

14. $\frac{1}{12}$
    $+ \frac{3}{4}$

15. $\frac{1}{6}$
    $+ \frac{5}{12}$

16. $\frac{4}{5}$
    $+ \frac{1}{5}$

17. $\frac{1}{4} + \frac{7}{12}$

18. $\frac{2}{3} + \frac{1}{12}$

19. $\frac{5}{12} + \frac{3}{12}$

20. $\frac{3}{8} + \frac{1}{2}$

21. $\frac{5}{6} + \frac{1}{12}$

22. $\frac{1}{4} + \frac{3}{8}$

23. $\frac{1}{6} + \frac{1}{2}$

24. $\frac{1}{5} + \frac{1}{10}$

25. $\frac{2}{6} + \frac{1}{3}$

Problem Solving

26. Raquel has a box of marbles. One fourth of the marbles are purple and $\frac{3}{8}$ of the marbles are white. What part of the marbles are purple or white?

27. Marty is helping to make costumes for the class play. One costume needs $\frac{3}{4}$ yard of fabric. Marty has two pieces of fabric. One is $\frac{1}{4}$ yard and one is $\frac{3}{8}$ yard. Does he have enough?

Maintain • Ordering Fractions

Order the fractions from least to greatest.

1. $\frac{2}{8}, \frac{6}{8}, \frac{5}{8}$

2. $\frac{7}{12}, \frac{5}{12}, \frac{10}{12}$

3. $\frac{5}{6}, \frac{2}{3}, \frac{5}{12}$

4. $\frac{9}{10}, \frac{2}{5}, \frac{6}{10}$

5. $\frac{1}{4}, \frac{1}{12}, \frac{1}{6}$

SUBTRACTING UNLIKE FRACTIONS

Linda's mother has $\frac{7}{8}$ yard of silk. She gives Linda $\frac{1}{4}$ yard for a scarf. How much silk does Linda's mother have left?

You need to subtract $\frac{1}{4}$ yd from $\frac{7}{8}$ yd.

You can use Fraction Bars to help you subtract fractions.

- Can you name the difference in shading as fourths?

- How many eighths are equivalent to $\frac{1}{4}$?

- What is the difference in the amount of shading?

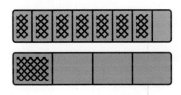

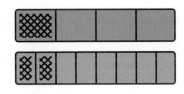

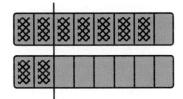

The difference in the amount of shading is $\frac{5}{8}$.
Linda's mother has $\frac{5}{8}$ yard of silk left.

 Think

- Does Linda's mother have more than or less than $\frac{1}{2}$ yard left?

Other Example

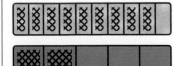

$$
\begin{array}{r}
\frac{9}{10} = \frac{9}{10} \\
-\frac{2}{5} = -\frac{4}{10} \\
\hline
\frac{5}{10} = \frac{1}{2}
\end{array}
$$

286

GUIDED PRACTICE

Write the difference. Use Fraction Bars when it helps.

1.
$$\frac{5}{6} = \frac{5}{6}$$
$$-\frac{1}{3} = -\frac{2}{6}$$

2.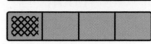
$$\frac{7}{12} = \frac{7}{12}$$
$$-\frac{1}{4} = -\frac{3}{12}$$

Write the difference. Use Fraction Bars when it helps.

3. $\frac{7}{10}$ $-\frac{3}{5}$

4. $\frac{2}{3}$ $-\frac{1}{6}$

5. $\frac{1}{2}$ $-\frac{1}{4}$

6. $\frac{5}{8}$ $-\frac{1}{2}$

7. $\frac{6}{12}$ $-\frac{1}{3}$

8. What other fraction is the same as the answer to exercise 2?

INDEPENDENT PRACTICE

Write the difference. Use Fraction Bars when it helps.

9.
$$\frac{5}{8}$$
$$-\frac{1}{4}$$

10.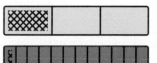
$$\frac{1}{3}$$
$$-\frac{1}{12}$$

Write the difference. Usc Fraction Bars when it helps.

11. $\frac{3}{4}$ $-\frac{5}{12}$

12. $\frac{7}{10}$ $-\frac{1}{5}$

13. $\frac{11}{12}$ $-\frac{5}{6}$

14. $\frac{5}{6}$ $-\frac{2}{3}$

15. $\frac{9}{10}$ $-\frac{3}{5}$

16. $\frac{4}{4}$ $-\frac{1}{2}$

17. $\frac{3}{6}$ $-\frac{1}{3}$

18. $\frac{5}{12}$ $-\frac{1}{3}$

19. $\frac{11}{12}$ $-\frac{2}{6}$

20. $\frac{2}{3}$ $-\frac{2}{6}$

 MATH LOG

How can you use what you know about adding fractions to check your answers when you subtract fractions?

ADDING AND SUBTRACTING MIXED NUMBERS

▶ Beth is making bread. She uses $5\frac{1}{4}$ cups of whole wheat flour and $2\frac{1}{4}$ cups of white flour. How much flour does she use?

You know how to add and subtract whole numbers and fractions.

Add $5\frac{1}{4}$ cups to $2\frac{1}{4}$ cups.

● **Are the denominators the same?**

$$5\frac{1}{4} \text{ c}$$
$$+ \ 2\frac{1}{4} \text{ c}$$

● **Add the fractions. Add the whole numbers.**

$$5\frac{1}{4} \text{ c}$$
$$\underline{+ \ 2\frac{1}{4} \text{ c}}$$
$$7\frac{2}{4} \text{ c}$$

● **Is the answer in simplest form?**

$$5\frac{1}{4} \text{ c}$$
$$\underline{+ \ 2\frac{1}{4} \text{ c}}$$
$$7\frac{2}{4} \text{ c or } 7\frac{1}{2} \text{ c}$$

Beth uses $7\frac{1}{2}$ cups of flour.

▶ You can also subtract mixed numbers. Subtract $3\frac{4}{10}$ from $6\frac{7}{10}$.

Think

• What does the difference between the whole numbers tell you about the difference between the mixed numbers?

● **Are the denominators the same?**

$$6\frac{7}{10}$$
$$- \ 3\frac{4}{10}$$

● **Subtract the fractions. Subtract the whole numbers.**

$$6\frac{7}{10}$$
$$\underline{- \ 3\frac{4}{10}}$$
$$3\frac{3}{10}$$

● **Is the answer in simplest form?**

$$6\frac{7}{10}$$
$$\underline{- \ 3\frac{4}{10}}$$
$$3\frac{3}{10}$$

$3\frac{3}{10}$ is the simplest form.

Write the answer.

1. $1\frac{5}{8}$
   $-1\frac{2}{8}$

2. $2\frac{3}{8}$
   $+6\frac{1}{8}$

3. $5\frac{5}{6}$
   $-4\frac{1}{6}$

4. 7
   $+1\frac{9}{10}$

5. $2\frac{1}{2}$
   $-1\frac{1}{2}$

Critical Thinking 6. How did you solve exercise 4?

INDEPENDENT PRACTICE

Write the answer.

7. $6\frac{1}{4}$
   $+2\frac{1}{4}$

8. $3\frac{1}{8}$
   $+3\frac{3}{8}$

9. $8\frac{3}{4}$
   $-1\frac{3}{4}$

10. $5\frac{2}{3}$
    $-1\frac{1}{3}$

11. $7\frac{2}{6}$
    $+3\frac{2}{6}$

12. $3\frac{1}{6}$
    $+5$

13. $3\frac{2}{5} - 2\frac{1}{5}$

14. $8\frac{7}{8} - \frac{2}{8}$

15. $6\frac{5}{12} + \frac{3}{12}$

16. $1\frac{3}{6} + 2\frac{1}{6}$

17. $3\frac{7}{10} - 1\frac{6}{10}$

18. $6\frac{3}{4} - 2\frac{1}{4}$

19. $4\frac{1}{2} + 1$

20. $3\frac{4}{8} - 1\frac{1}{8}$

Problem Solving

21. For a muffin recipe, Beth must mix $5\frac{1}{2}$ cups of flour and $2\frac{1}{4}$ cups of oat bran. Beth's mixing bowl can hold 8 cups. Is the bowl large enough?

22. **Data Book** Go to page 471 of the General Information section. Beth has $\frac{3}{4}$ cup of flour for the pumpkin muffin recipe. How many more cups of flour does she need?

CHALLENGE • Mixed Numbers

Write the answer.

1. $3\frac{1}{2} + 1\frac{1}{4}$

2. $6\frac{7}{8} - 2\frac{3}{4}$

3. $8\frac{1}{2} + 3\frac{1}{2}$

4. $9\frac{3}{4} - 6\frac{1}{2}$

5. $2\frac{2}{3} + 6\frac{1}{3}$

6. $7\frac{5}{8} - 3\frac{1}{4}$

USE SIMPLER NUMBERS

Some kinds of numbers can make a problem seem hard. You can make the numbers simpler to get an idea of how to solve the problem.

One time, I used simpler numbers to help decide how many hours to work.

MY PROBLEM

I worked 3 days a week at Katz's Pet Shop. I was supposed to work $12\frac{3}{4}$ hours each week. I worked $4\frac{1}{4}$ hours on Monday and $3\frac{1}{4}$ hours on Wednesday. I needed to know how many hours to work on Friday.

MY SOLUTION

To help me come up with a plan, I made the numbers in the problem simpler. I dropped the fraction part and just used whole numbers.

	Actual Numbers	Simpler Numbers
Monday hours	$4\frac{1}{4}$ →	→ 4
Wednesday hours	$3\frac{1}{4}$ →	→ 3
Hours for week	$12\frac{3}{4}$ →	→ 12

The simpler numbers helped me think of a plan. I would add the hours I had worked so far. Then I would subtract that number from the total number of hours I was supposed to work for the week.

Hours worked so far: $4 + 3 = 7$
Hours needed on Friday: $12 - 7 = 5$

Then I used the same plan with the actual numbers.

So, I needed to work $5\frac{1}{4}$ hours on Friday.

Hours so far: $4\frac{1}{4} + 3\frac{1}{4} = 7\frac{2}{4}$
Hours needed: $12\frac{3}{4} - 7\frac{2}{4} = 5\frac{1}{4}$

Solve each problem. Use the simpler numbers to help you.

1. It is feeding time for the five buffalo at the Calamar Zoo. To make lunch for each buffalo, Ms. Clark mixes $7\frac{1}{4}$ pounds of corn and $9\frac{1}{4}$ pounds of oats. She adds wheat until the lunch mix weighs $24\frac{1}{4}$ pounds. How much wheat does she use?

	Actual Numbers	Simpler Numbers
Corn	$7\frac{1}{4}$ →	→ 7
Oats	$9\frac{1}{4}$ →	→ 9
Total Weight	$24\frac{1}{4}$ →	→ 24

2. What other simpler numbers could you have used in the problem?

Work with a small group. Finish choosing simpler numbers. Use them to help you.

3. The Hoot-n-Holler Amusement Park charges $13.25 admission for adults and $9.45 for children. Mr. Simms has $63.67. How much will he have after he buys admission for himself, Mrs. Simms, and their 3 children?

	Actual Numbers	Simpler Numbers
Adult	$13.25 →	> $13
Child	$9.45 →	
Amount Mr. Simms has	$63.67 →	

4. Ming and 2 of his friends chipped in $4.85 each to buy a video to share. The video was on sale and cost only $13.68. How much money should each child get back?

	Actual Numbers	Simpler Numbers
Each share	$4.85 →	
Video cost	$13.68 →	

5. In exercise 4, how much did each person finally pay? Use that amount to check your answer. See if the total amount they paid is equal to $13.68.

USE SIMPLER NUMBERS

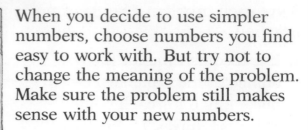

When you decide to use simpler numbers, choose numbers you find easy to work with. But try not to change the meaning of the problem. Make sure the problem still makes sense with your new numbers.

The students at the Pine School voted for a mascot. There were 229 votes for a bear and 307 votes for an eagle. The other $\frac{1}{2}$ of the students voted for a dolphin. How many students voted?

Look at the 2 sets of simpler numbers below.

A.

	Actual Numbers	Simpler Numbers
Number for Bear	229 →	→ 200
Number for Eagle	307 →	→ 300
Fraction for Dolphin	$\frac{1}{2}$ →	→ 1

B.

	Actual Numbers	Simpler Numbers
Number for Bear	229 →	→ 200
Number for Eagle	307 →	→ 300
Fraction for Dolphin	$\frac{1}{2}$ →	→ $\frac{1}{2}$

Think

- How are the two sets different?

- How does using 1 instead of $\frac{1}{2}$ in the problem change the meaning of the problem?

Solve the problem with one of the sets of simpler numbers. Then solve it with the actual numbers.

1. Tanya plans to put 2 logs end to end, along one side of her garden. The side is 14 feet long. One log is 8 feet 9 inches long. The other is 7 feet 9 inches long. Tanya wants the 2 logs to be the same length. How much should she cut off each log?

A.

	Actual Numbers	Simpler Numbers
Total	14 ft →	→ 14 ft
One log	8 ft 9 in. →	→ 8 ft
Other log	7 ft 9 in. →	→ 7 ft

B.

	Actual Numbers	Simpler Numbers
Total	14 ft →	→ 14 ft
One log	8 ft 9 in. →	→ 8 ft 10 in.
Other log	7 ft 9 in. →	→ 7 ft 10 in.

Work in pairs. Use simpler numbers or other strategies you think will help you.

2. The chef at Fred's Fish House needs $16\frac{1}{2}$ pounds of fish to make fish stew. So far, the chef has bought 5 pounds 4 ounces of pike and 4 pounds 4 ounces of halibut. How much more fish does the chef need to buy?
   HINT: 1 pound = 16 ounces

3. Mark is buying 7 containers of yogurt. How much change should he receive if he gives the clerk $5.00?

4. Janet is making a cover for her book report. She wants to draw a $2\frac{1}{2}$ inch square in the center of a sheet of paper that is $8\frac{1}{2}$ inches wide and 11 inches long. How many inches from the edge of the paper should the sides of the square be?

YOGURT
67¢ each
4 for $2.49

293

The map below shows the six time zones of the United States, including Alaska and Hawaii. The clocks show the afternoon time in each zone when it is 4:00 P.M. in the Eastern time zone.

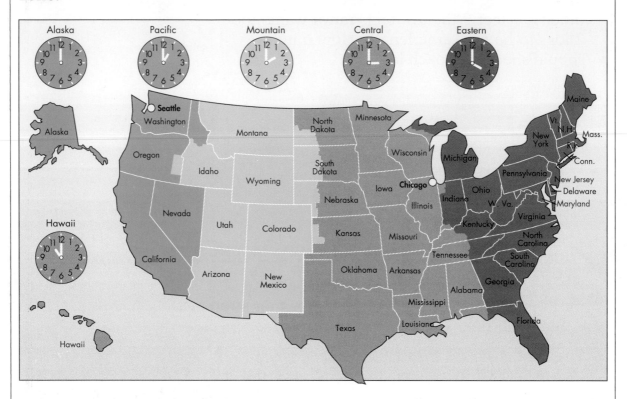

Use the map to answer each question.

1. What time is it in New York?

2. What time is it in Georgia?

3. What time is it in Alaska?

4. What time is it in Hawaii?

5. If it is 6 A.M. in Cleveland, Ohio, what time is it in Reno, Nevada?

6. If it is 12:00 noon in California, what time is it in Alaska?

7. If it is 4:00 P.M. in Albuquerque, New Mexico, what time is it in Phoenix, Arizona?

8. An airplane pilot left Chicago at 2:30 P.M. and arrived in Hawaii at 6:00 P.M. How many hours did she fly?

9. Ramon arrives in Seattle, Washington, at 8:00 P.M. His flight from Portland, Maine, took 7 hours. What time did Ramon leave Portland?

SECTION REVIEW

for pages 284–294

Write the letter of the correct answer.

1. $\frac{1}{2} + \frac{1}{4}$

   a. $\frac{2}{6}$

   b. $\frac{3}{4}$

   c. $\frac{2}{4}$

2. $\frac{11}{12} - \frac{1}{6}$

   a. $\frac{3}{4}$

   b. $\frac{10}{6}$

   c. $\frac{10}{12}$

3. $\frac{9}{10} - \frac{2}{5}$

   a. $\frac{7}{5}$

   b. $\frac{1}{2}$

   c. $\frac{7}{10}$

4. $\frac{5}{12} + \frac{1}{6}$

   a. $\frac{6}{12}$

   b. $\frac{6}{18}$

   c. $\frac{7}{12}$

5. $\frac{3}{8} + \frac{1}{4}$

   a. $\frac{4}{8}$

   b. $\frac{1}{3}$

   c. $\frac{5}{8}$

6. $4\frac{2}{3} - 1\frac{1}{3}$

   a. $4\frac{1}{3}$

   b. $3\frac{1}{3}$

   c. 3

7. $6\frac{5}{8} + 4\frac{1}{8}$

   a. $10\frac{3}{4}$

   b. 10

   c. $6\frac{3}{4}$

8. $\frac{7}{12} + \frac{1}{4}$

   a. $\frac{5}{6}$

   b. $\frac{8}{12}$

   c. $\frac{8}{16}$

9. $5\frac{7}{10} - 2\frac{1}{10}$

   a. 3

   b. $3\frac{3}{5}$

   c. $3\frac{8}{10}$

Solve each problem.

10. Pam and Betty started their homework at the same time. Pam finished in $2\frac{1}{2}$ hours. Betty finished $1\frac{1}{4}$ hours later. How long did it take Betty to finish her homework?

11. Mrs. Wolfe is walking $3\frac{3}{10}$ miles from her house to the library. She has already walked 2 miles. It has taken her $\frac{3}{4}$ hour. How far is she from the library?

CHAPTER TEST

Write the answer.

1. $\frac{3}{8} + \frac{1}{8}$ 2. $\frac{7}{10} - \frac{4}{10}$ 3. $\frac{4}{6} + \frac{1}{6}$ 4. $\frac{5}{12} - \frac{4}{12}$

5. $\begin{array}{r} \frac{5}{12} \\ + \frac{1}{3} \\ \hline \end{array}$ 6. $\begin{array}{r} \frac{3}{5} \\ + \frac{1}{10} \\ \hline \end{array}$ 7. $\begin{array}{r} \frac{1}{12} \\ + \frac{1}{6} \\ \hline \end{array}$ 8. $\begin{array}{r} \frac{1}{3} \\ + \frac{1}{12} \\ \hline \end{array}$

9. $\begin{array}{r} \frac{3}{8} \\ - \frac{1}{4} \\ \hline \end{array}$ 10. $\begin{array}{r} \frac{3}{5} \\ - \frac{1}{10} \\ \hline \end{array}$ 11. $\begin{array}{r} \frac{7}{12} \\ - \frac{1}{6} \\ \hline \end{array}$ 12. $\begin{array}{r} \frac{1}{2} \\ - \frac{1}{8} \\ \hline \end{array}$

13. $\frac{4}{5} - \frac{1}{10}$ 14. $\frac{3}{4} - \frac{1}{8}$ 15. $\frac{3}{10} - \frac{1}{5}$ 16. $\frac{5}{6} - \frac{7}{12}$

17. $\begin{array}{r} 4\frac{6}{8} \\ - 3\frac{1}{8} \\ \hline \end{array}$ 18. $\begin{array}{r} 4\frac{5}{8} \\ + 3\frac{2}{8} \\ \hline \end{array}$ 19. $\begin{array}{r} 5\frac{3}{8} \\ - 2\frac{1}{8} \\ \hline \end{array}$ 20. $\begin{array}{r} 3\frac{2}{8} \\ - 1\frac{1}{8} \\ \hline \end{array}$

21. $6\frac{2}{12} - 3\frac{1}{12}$ 22. $3\frac{1}{6} + 2\frac{3}{6}$ 23. $4\frac{3}{5} - 2\frac{2}{5}$ 24. $5\frac{3}{10} + 1\frac{1}{10}$

PROBLEM SOLVING

Solve each problem.

25. Paul lives 1 mile from school. This morning he ran $\frac{3}{4}$ of the way to school and walked the rest. How far did he walk?

26. Shirley had some flour for baking muffins. She used $2\frac{1}{2}$ cups and has $1\frac{1}{2}$ cups left. How much flour did she start with?

27. Maria is riding her bike to school, which is a distance of $2\frac{3}{4}$ miles. She has already gone $1\frac{1}{4}$ miles. How many miles does she still need to go?

28. Juan worked $1\frac{1}{2}$ hours on Monday. He worked $\frac{1}{2}$ hour more than that on Tuesday. Altogether, how many hours did he work in the 2 days?

CUMULATIVE REVIEW

Write the product.

1. $\begin{array}{r} 433 \\ \times\ \ \ 2 \end{array}$	2. $\begin{array}{r} 721 \\ \times\ \ \ 7 \end{array}$	3. $\begin{array}{r} 300 \\ \times\ \ \ 4 \end{array}$	4. $\begin{array}{r} 782 \\ \times\ \ \ 5 \end{array}$
5. $\begin{array}{r} 709 \\ \times\ \ \ 8 \end{array}$	6. $\begin{array}{r} 654 \\ \times\ \ \ 5 \end{array}$	7. $\begin{array}{r} 457 \\ \times\ \ \ 3 \end{array}$	8. $\begin{array}{r} 594 \\ \times\ \ \ 6 \end{array}$

9. 3×2132 10. 4×2114 11. 5×2003

12. 7×6701 13. 9×4000 14. 4×6545

15. How did you solve exercises 3 and 13?

Divide.

16. $5\overline{)250}$ 17. $7\overline{)631}$ 18. $8\overline{)644}$ 19. $6\overline{)606}$

20. $4\overline{)2428}$ 21. $9\overline{)6755}$ 22. $6\overline{)5045}$ 23. $3\overline{)2720}$

24. $\$0.35 \div 5$ 25. $\$0.48 \div 6$ 26. $\$2.84 \div 4$

27. $\$6.68 \div 2$ 28. $\$49.00 \div 7$ 29. $\$13.68 \div 3$

Write what fraction of each bar is shaded.

30. ▨▨▨ | | | | | 31. ▨▨ | | | | | 32. ▨▨▨ | | |

33. ▨▨▨▨ | | | 34. | | | | | 35. ▨▨▨▨ |

Copy and complete. Use Fractions Bars when helpful.

36. $\frac{1}{5} = \frac{\blacksquare}{10}$ 37. $\frac{2}{3} = \frac{\blacksquare}{6}$ 38. $\frac{3}{4} = \frac{\blacksquare}{8}$ 39. $\frac{2}{6} = \frac{\blacksquare}{12}$

40. $\frac{1}{2} = \frac{\blacksquare}{4}$ 41. $\frac{4}{6} = \frac{\blacksquare}{12}$ 42. $\frac{3}{5} = \frac{\blacksquare}{10}$ 43. $\frac{2}{4} = \frac{\blacksquare}{8}$

EXCURSION
CULTURAL DIVERSITY

MEAN, MODE, AND MEDIAN

The Carolina Sea Islands dot the Atlantic coast from Florida to North Carolina. Most of the people who live on these tiny, rural islands are African-American, and their language and culture are similar to those of some West African villages.

On Edisto Island, one of the islands off South Carolina, most people farm or fish for a living. Therefore, they pay close attention to weather and climate. The chart on the right shows Edisto Island's average high temperatures for the month of June.

Edisto Island's Average High Temperatures (°F) for June	
Year 1	86°F
Year 2	93°F
Year 3	89°F
Year 4	86°F
Year 5	81°F

▶ The **mean** is the average of a set of numbers. To find the mean, add the numbers. Then divide the sum by the number of addends.

So, the mean temperature is 87 degrees Fahrenheit.

Notice that the mean is based on the *average* temperature each June.

$$
\begin{array}{r}
86 \\
93 \\
89 \\
86 \\
+\ 81 \\
\hline
435
\end{array}
\qquad
\begin{array}{r}
87 \\
5)\overline{435} \\
-400 \\
\hline
35 \\
-35 \\
\hline
0
\end{array}
$$

▶ The **mode** is the number that occurs most often in a set of numbers.

   86   93   89   86   81

So, the mode of the temperatures is 86.

▶ The **median** is the number that falls exactly in the middle when a set of numbers is arranged in order from least to greatest.

   81   86   86   89   93

So, the median temperature is 86.

Aneatha and Jackson live on Edisto Island and fish in the summer. To attract fish, they beat a drum or a paddle on the side of the boat. At the end of the week, the children count how many fish they have caught. Read the table and answer each question below.

Number of Fish Caught in One Week			
Day	Aneatha	Jackson	Total
Monday	2	6	8
Tuesday	7	2	9
Wednesday	2	2	4
Thursday	5	4	9
Friday	4	1	5

1. Look at the total number of fish caught by both children. How many fish did Aneatha and Jackson catch in all?

2. Look at the total number of fish caught by both children. What is the mean number of fish caught for the week?

3. What is the mode of Aneatha's catch for the week?

4. What is the median of Aneatha's catch for the week?

5. How many fish did Aneatha catch for the week?

6. What is the mean number of fish caught by Aneatha?

7. What is the median of Jackson's catch for the week?

8. How many fish did Jackson catch for the week?

9. What is the mode of Jackson's catch for the week?

10. What is the mean number of fish caught by Jackson?

MEASUREMENT AND TIME

Connections

Science

Sundials Sundials have been used for thousands of years. The dial shows time using shadows. Each morning the sun appears in the eastern sky. Then it seems to move across the sky and disappear in the west. As the sun moves, a shadow moves across the sundial. You can read the shadow like the hands of a clock.

Sundials are not as accurate as clocks, but they are useful to people who have no clocks or watches. Try making your own sundial. You will need a piece of cardboard, a ball of clay, a pencil 6 to 8 inches long, and a crayon. Find a flat spot outdoors away from buildings and large trees. Then set up your sundial as shown below.

The pencil will cast a shadow on the cardboard. Use the crayon to mark the location of the shadow once each hour. The shadows will form a pattern. By remembering the pattern, you can use shadows to estimate the time of day.

INCH, HALF INCH, AND QUARTER INCH

In the United States we usually use the customary system of measurement. The **inch (in.)** is a customary unit used to measure length.

The crayon below is 4 inches long, **to the nearest inch**.

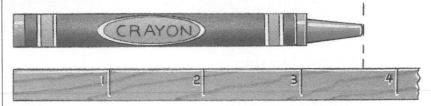

If you use a ruler marked in half inches, you can see that the crayon is a little more than $3\frac{1}{2}$ inches long. It is $3\frac{1}{2}$ inches long **to the nearest half inch**.

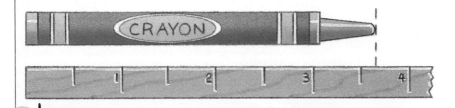

Think

- Suppose you measured a pencil to the nearest inch and to the nearest half inch. Could the two answers be the same? Explain.

Now measure the crayon with a ruler marked in quarter inches. Its length is $3\frac{3}{4}$ inches **to the nearest quarter inch**.

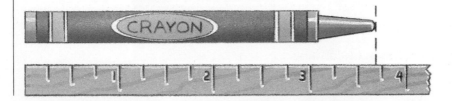

GUIDED PRACTICE

Measure the length to the nearest inch, half inch, and quarter inch.

1.

2.

Draw line segments of the following lengths. Use a ruler.

3. $5\frac{1}{2}$ inches   **4.** $6\frac{1}{4}$ inches   **5.** $5\frac{1}{4}$ inches

 Critical Thinking **6.** Compare the segment you drew for exercise 5 with the one a friend drew. Are they exactly the same? Explain.

INDEPENDENT PRACTICE

Measure the length to the nearest inch, half inch, and quarter inch.

7.

8.

9.

10.

11. your pencil

12. length of a book

Draw line segments of the following lengths. Use a ruler.

13. $9\frac{1}{2}$ inches   **14.** $15\frac{1}{4}$ inches   **15.** 7 inches

Maintain • Ordering Fractions

Order the fractions from least to greatest.

1. $\frac{3}{5}, \frac{5}{5}, \frac{1}{5}$ **2.** $\frac{11}{12}, \frac{1}{3}, \frac{5}{12}$ **3.** $\frac{3}{5}, \frac{2}{10}, \frac{8}{10}$ **4.** $\frac{3}{4}, \frac{4}{8}, \frac{1}{4}, \frac{7}{8}$

FOOT, YARD, AND MILE

To measure longer lengths in the customary system, you use the units **foot (ft)**, **yard (yd)**, and **mile (mi)**.

Equivalent Units	
1 ft = 12 in.	1 mi = 5280 ft
1 yd = 3 ft	1 mi = 1760 yd
1 yd = 36 in.	

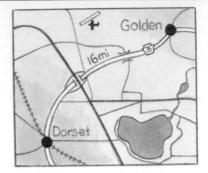

A sheet of notebook paper is about 1 foot long.

A doorway is about 1 yard wide.

Distances between cities are measured in miles.

▶ Lee needs 60 inches of wire for an art project. The store sells wire only by the foot. Lee made a table to help him decide how much wire to buy.

ft	1	2	3	4	5
in.	12	24	36	48	60

The table shows that 60 inches is the same as 5 feet. Lee needs 5 feet of wire.

Think

• How many inches are in half a foot?

▶ Three students are measuring an art project. Jan reports that it is 42 inches wide. Pedro says it is 3 feet 6 inches wide, and Emi thinks it is $3\frac{1}{2}$ feet wide. How can you tell if these are the same?

You can write all three measures as inches:

42 inches

3 feet 6 inches = 36 inches + 6 inches
$\qquad\qquad\qquad\qquad$ = 42 inches

$3\frac{1}{2}$ feet = 36 inches + 6 inches = 42 inches

The three measures show the same width. They are **equivalent measures**.

GUIDED PRACTICE

Tell which unit you would use to measure each. Write
foot, yard, or *mile.*

1. distance from Miami, Florida to
Austin, Texas

2. length of your desk

Tell which measure is the better estimate.

3. height of a basketball player
   a. 7 yards   **b.** 7 feet

4. length of your leg
   a. 2 feet   **b.** 2 inches

Write each measure as feet and inches. Make a table
when it helps.

5. 33 inches   **6.** $2\frac{1}{2}$ feet   **7.** 77 inches   **8.** 28 inches

Critical Thinking **9.** How did you decide on your answer to
exercise 3? Explain.

INDEPENDENT PRACTICE

Tell which unit you would use to measure each. Write
foot, yard, or *mile.*

10. height of your classroom

11. a city bus route

12. length of a football field

13. height of a tall tree

Tell which measure is the better estimate.

14. length of a kitchen table
   a. 4 feet   **b.** 4 inches

15. width of a highway bridge
   a. 50 miles   **b.** 50 feet

16. length of a moving truck
   a. 10 yards   **b.** 10 inches

17. width of the Atlantic Ocean
   a. 3000 yards   **b.** 3000 miles

Match the equivalent measures.

18. 65 inches

a. 10 feet

19. 8 feet 9 inches

b. 5 feet 6 inches

20. 120 inches

c. 5 feet 5 inches

21. $5\frac{1}{2}$ feet

d. 105 inches

PERIMETER

Mrs. Kelley's class is decorating the room for Parents' Night. They decide to put a painted paper border around a small rectangular bulletin board. To find out how much border they need to make, they find the **perimeter** of the bulletin board.

The perimeter of the board is the distance around it.

They found that one long side is 3 feet and one shorter side is 2 feet.

Think

• You know that the bulletin board is a rectangle. Do you have to measure all four sides to find the perimeter? Explain.

Other Examples

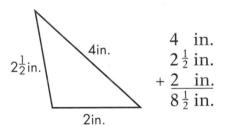

8 in.
8 in.
4 in.
+ 4 in.
24 in.

4 in.
2 ½ in.
+ 2 in.
8 ½ in.

GUIDED PRACTICE

1. Measure the green rectangle around this Guided Practice to the nearest quarter inch. Record the measurements.

2. Write the perimeter of the rectangle.

3. Compare the measurements with those of a friend. Do you think a measurement with a ruler is exact? Explain your answer.

INDEPENDENT PRACTICE

Write the perimeter.

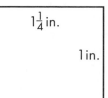

4.
$1\frac{1}{4}$ in.

1 in.

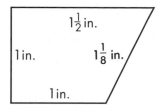

5.
$1\frac{1}{2}$ in.

1 in. $1\frac{1}{8}$ in.

1 in.

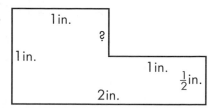

6.
1 in.

?

1 in.

1 in. $\frac{1}{2}$ in.

2 in.

Measure each diagram to the nearest quarter inch.
Write the perimeter.

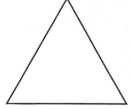

7.

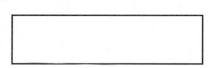

8.

9.

10. You need to measure the ribbon. Your ruler
is broken. How can you still use the ruler to
find the length of the ribbon? About how
long is the ribbon?

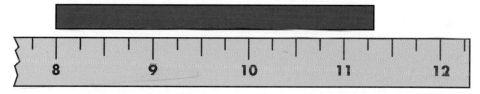

PROJECT • Estimation

Work with a partner. You will need a ruler or a yardstick.

• Choose three things in your classroom, for
  example a desk.

• Estimate whether the perimeter is less than 1
  yard, about 1 yard, or more than 1 yard.
  Record the estimate.

• Then measure and record the perimeter to
  check your estimates.

MEASUREMENT LAB

Groups:
• small groups

You will need:
• 12-inch ruler
• yardstick
• recording sheet

1. Use the ruler and then the yardstick to measure each item below. Record the measure on your recording sheet.

Item	12-inch ruler	Yardstick
Height of door		
Perimeter of desktop		
Width of window		

2. Now choose five more items in your classroom. Measure with the inch ruler and the yardstick. Record your measurements on the recording sheet. Be sure to state whether you are measuring the height, length, width, or perimeter of each item.

3. Which ruler was easier to use for the items you measured? Discuss with your group.

4. Now choose five more items in the classroom to measure. First estimate the measure of each one. Decide which ruler is better for measuring each item. Record your results on the recording sheet.

Item	Estimate	Actual Measure	Ruler Used

Critical Thinking

SUMMING IT UP

5. How did you decide which ruler is better for measuring a particular item?

6. How did you report your answers for the 12-inch ruler?

7. How did you report your answers for the yardstick?

COOPERATIVE · LEARNING

PROJECT • Using Measurement

Work with a small group to map out a plan for building a 3-shelf bookcase.

• Find a place in the classroom where you would like to put the bookcase. Decide how big your bookcase will be. Decide which unit of measure to use.

• Make a drawing of the bookcase. Label all measurements.

• Compare your drawing with the drawing of another group.

Next week, the Oak Glen School is having a field day. Jordan and Manuela need to measure the track on the playground for some of the races.

Work with a small group. Help Jordan and Manuela by solving each problem. Show how you get each answer.

1. The track will be an oval $\frac{1}{4}$ mile around.

   a. How many yards are in 1 mile?

   b. How many yards are in $\frac{1}{4}$ mile?

2. Each straight section of the track will be 110 yards long.

   a. Is 110 yards more or less than the length of your classroom?

   b. Is 110 yards more than or less than $\frac{1}{10}$ mile?

   c. Will the straight sections be more than or less than 110 yards apart?

3. The playground is a rectangle 215 yards long and 170 yards wide. Will the track fit in the playground?

4. Jordan and Manuela are laying out a straight section of the track.

   a. How many feet in 110 yards?

   b. How can they measure out that distance if their tape measure is only 50 feet long?

5. Jordan thinks about using his footsteps to measure each 110-yard curved section of the track. It takes Jordan 15 footsteps to walk 30 feet.

   a. How many feet long will one curved section be?

   b. How many feet long is each of Jordan's steps?

   c. How many steps would Jordan take to measure a curved section of the track?

6. Jordan and Manuela can roll a wheel to measure the curved sections. The wheel turns 10 times as it rolls 10 yards.

   a. How many turns will the wheel make when it rolls the 110 yards?

   b. Which method do you think would be more accurate, using the wheel or using footsteps to measure the track? Explain your answer.

7. Manuela runs 110 yards in 15 seconds. Suppose she kept running at that rate.

   a. How long would it take her to run $\frac{1}{4}$ mile?

   b. How long would it take to run 1 mile?

   c. How many miles would she run in 1 hour?

   d. Do you think she could run a mile at the same rate she ran the first 110 yards? Why or why not?

CUSTOMARY UNITS OF CAPACITY

Equivalent Units	
1 cup (c)	= 8 fl oz
1 pint (pt)	= 16 fl oz
1 quart (qt)	= 32 fl oz
1 half gallon	= 64 fl oz
1 gallon (gal)	= 128 fl oz

The **fluid ounce (fl oz)** is the basic unit for measuring liquid capacity in the customary system. Every other unit is a multiple of 8 fluid ounces.

Here are some familiar capacities.

a measuring **cup** of water

a **pint** of juice

a **quart** of milk

a **gallon** of paint

Think

- In school, milk is served in half-pint containers. What is another name for this amount of milk?

GUIDED PRACTICE

Copy and complete this table.

1.

qt	1	2	3	4
pt	2	4		
c	4			

Make each statement true. Write <, >, or =.

2. 12 quarts ● 12 pints

3. 3 pints ● 3 cups

4. 8 cups ● 2 quarts

5. 48 fl oz ● 1 half gallon

Copy and complete. Make a table or use mental math when it helps.

6. 6 pt = ■ c   **7.** 5 gal = ■ qt   **8.** ■ qt = 6 pt   **9.** 2 c = ■ fl oz

Critical Thinking **10.** How did you solve exercise 6?

INDEPENDENT PRACTICE

Make each statement true. Write <, >, or =.

11. 6 gallons ● 6 quarts

12. 18 cups ● 18 pints

13. 8 pints ● 16 cups

14. 5 quarts ● 2 gallons

Copy and complete. Make a table or use mental math when it helps.

15. 5 qt = ▪ pt

16. ▪ qt = 3 gal

17. 48 fl oz = ▪ pt

PROJECT • Capacity Lab

Work with a small group. You will need water, a measuring cup, and three containers of different shapes.

a. Copy the chart and use it to record your work.

b. Estimate which container will hold the most water.

c. Estimate which will hold the least amount of water.

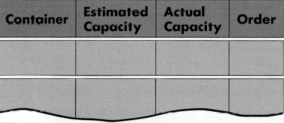

Container	Estimated Capacity	Actual Capacity	Order

d. Arrange the containers in order of size according to your estimates, from smallest to largest.

e. Using the measuring cup, fill the container that you think has the least capacity.

f. Repeat with the container that you think has the second largest capacity.

g. Measure the capacity of the last container.

h. Arrange the containers in order of actual capacity, from least to greatest.

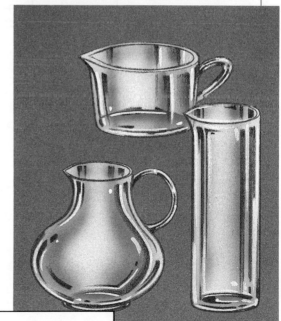

 MATH LOG

Explain why the height of the container does not tell you which container has the largest capacity.

OUNCE, POUND, AND TON

The **ounce (oz)**, **pound (lb)**, and **ton (T)**
are units of weight in the customary system
of measure.

Equivalent Units
1 lb = 16 oz
1 T = 2000 lb

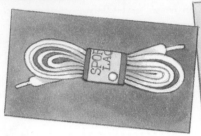

about 1 ounce   about 1 pound   about 1 ton

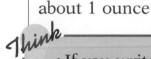

Think

• If you write 2 pounds as ounces, will the
  number of ounces be greater than or
  less than 2? Explain.

INDEPENDENT PRACTICE

Make each statement true. Write <, >, or =. Make a
table or use mental math when it helps.

1. 48 oz ● 4 lb

2. 2 lb ● 32 oz

3. 3800 lb ● 2 T

Problem Solving

4. Which weighs more, 32 ounces
of rice or 4 pounds of apples?

5. Which weighs less, 18 ounces of
marshmallows or 1 pound of
bananas?

PROJECT • Estimating Weight

COOPERATIVE • LEARNING

Work with a small group. You will need a pan balance, a
pound weight, and five objects.

• Estimate the weight of each object. Sort them
  into three groups: less than a pound, about a
  pound, or greater than a pound.

• Check your estimates by weighing each object.

• Put a star beside each correct estimate.

314

More Practice Set 10.7, p. 453

SECTION REVIEW

for pages 302–314

Measure the length to the nearest quarter inch.

1.
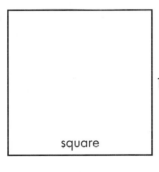

2.

3.
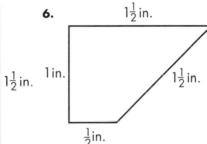

4.

Write the perimeter of each figure.

5.
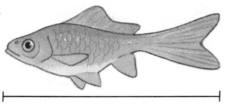
square

6.
$1\frac{1}{2}$ in.
1 in.
$1\frac{1}{2}$ in.
$\frac{1}{2}$ in.

7.
1 in.
$2\frac{1}{2}$ in.
rectangle

Make each statement true. Write <, >, or =.

8. 3 gallons ● 10 quarts

9. 4 pints ● 2 quarts

10. 3 pounds ● 20 ounces

11. 2 yards ● 8 feet

Copy and complete. Make a table or use mental math when it helps.

12. ■ ft = 6 yd

13. ■ in. = 1 yd

14. 2 gal = ■ qt

15. 4 pt = ■ qt

16. 3000 lb = ■ T

17. 16 fl oz = ■ c

18. 3 ft = ■ in.

19. 2 qt = ■ c

CENTIMETER AND MILLIMETER

Much of the world uses the metric system of measure. The **centimeter (cm)** and the **millimeter (mm)** are metric units for measuring length.

Equivalent Units
1 cm = 10 mm

The drawing below shows some objects that measure about a centimeter or a millimeter.

There are 10 millimeters in 1 centimeter.

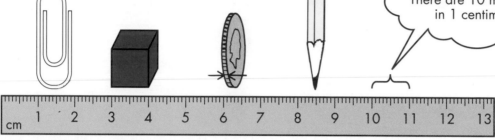

Look at the rectangle. What is its length to the nearest centimeter?

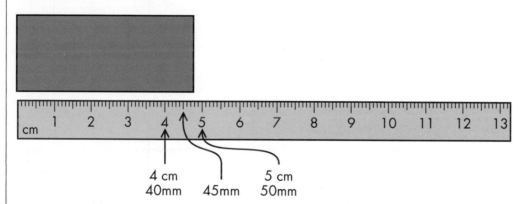

4 cm
40mm   45mm   50mm
                  5 cm

Notice that the length of the rectangle is closer to 5 cm than to 4 cm. So, the length is 5 cm to the nearest centimeter. What is the length to the nearest millimeter?

Think
- Is the length more than or less than 50 millimeters?

To the nearest millimeter, the length of the rectangle is 48 mm.

GUIDED PRACTICE

Measure the length of each to the nearest centimeter and the nearest millimeter.

1.

2.

Critical Thinking **3.** If you know the length in centimeters, how can you find the length in millimeters without measuring?

INDEPENDENT PRACTICE

Measure the length of each to the nearest centimeter and the nearest millimeter.

4.

5.

6.

7.

Write the perimeter of each figure.

8.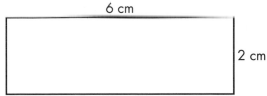
6 cm
2 cm

9.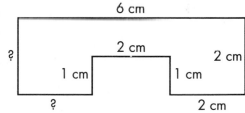
6 cm
2 cm
2 cm
1 cm
1 cm
?
?
2 cm

10. On centimeter squared paper, draw a square with sides 6 centimeters long.
  a. Write its perimeter.
  b. Draw another square whose sides are twice as long.
  c. Write its perimeter.
  d. How do the perimeters compare?

11. Draw a square whose sides are half as long as the original one you drew.
  a. Write its perimeter.
  b. How does the perimeter compare with the perimeter of the original square?

DECIMETER, METER, AND KILOMETER

Equivalent Units
1 cm = 10 mm
1 dm = 10 cm
1 m = 10 dm
1 m = 100 cm
1 km = 1000 m

The **decimeter (dm)**, **meter (m)**, and **kilometer (km)** are other metric units of length. Kilometers are used to measure longer distances.

A paperback book is about 1 decimeter (dm) wide.

A school door is about 1 meter (m) wide.

Kim can walk 1 kilometer (km) in about 15 minutes.

The table shows how the kilometer and meter are related.

km	1	2	3	4	5
m	1000	2000	3000	4000	5000

Think

- Which is easier to compute: the number of inches in 15 feet or the number of decimeters in 15 meters? Why?

▶ Kim has a bookcase that is 15 decimeters wide. She wants to fit it into a space that is 2 meters wide. Will it fit? To decide, you have to know how many decimeters are in 2 meters.

You can make a table to find the answer.

The table shows that 15 decimeters is between 1 and 2 meters. So there is enough space for the bookcase.

m	1	2	3
dm	10	20	30

GUIDED PRACTICE

Choose the better estimate.

1. length of a nail
   a. 8 cm   **b.** 8 m

2. width of a lake
   a. 1 m   **b.** 1 km

3. the height of a book
   a. 15 m   **b.** 15 cm

4. the width of a door
   a. 1 m   **b.** 1 dm

Copy and complete. Make a table or use mental math.

5. 30 dm = ▒ m

6. ▒ cm = 40 mm

7. 3 km = ▒ m

Critical Thinking **8.** Which method did you use to solve exercise 7?

INDEPENDENT PRACTICE

Choose the better estimate.

9. The width of a chair is about
   a. 3 dm   **b.** 30 dm

10. An hour's walk is about
   a. 4 km   **b.** 40 km

11. The height of a bush is about
   a. 1 m   **b.** 100 m

12. An adult's height is about
   a. 2 m   **b.** 20 m

Copy and complete. Make a table or use mental math.

13. ▒ m = 600 cm

14. 40 cm = ▒ dm

15. 4 m = ▒ cm

16. 8 dm = ▒ cm

17. ▒ km = 3000 m

18. 7 cm = ▒ mm

Problem Solving

19. When Mr. Russell jogs, each step measures about 1 meter. If he jogs about 900 steps, is this more than 1 kilometer? How do you know?

Critical Thinking **20.** Kim is 142 centimeters tall. Can she walk through a doorway $1\frac{1}{2}$ meters high without stooping? How do you know?

METRIC UNITS OF CAPACITY

The **milliliter (mL)** and **liter (L)** are metric units used for measuring liquid capacity.

How many liter bottles would it take to hold 4000 milliliters of springwater?

You can make a table to find how many liters are equal to 4000 milliliters.

L	1	2	3	4
mL	1000	2000	3000	4000

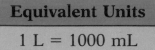

Equivalent Units

1 L = 1000 mL

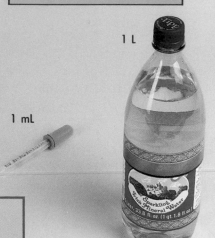

Think

• How is the table above like the table for meters and kilometers?

You can see that 4 liters are equal to 4000 milliliters.

GUIDED PRACTICE

Estimate the capacity of each container. Write *true* or *false*.

1. A washing machine holds about 1 liter.

2. A glass holds about 1 milliliter.

Make each statement true. Write <, >, or =.

3. 9 L ● 9 mL

4. 5000 mL ● 5000 L

5. 3000 mL ● 3 L

Write the unit you would use to measure the capacity of each. Write *liter* or *milliliter*.

6. punch bowl

7. teaspoon

8. car gas tank

Copy and complete. Make a table or use mental math when it helps.

9. 6 L = ▇ mL

10. 2000 mL = ▇ L

11. ▇ L = 500 mL

Critical Thinking 12. Explain how you solved exercise 4.

INDEPENDENT PRACTICE

Estimate the capacity of each container.
Write *true* or *false* for each statement.

13. The bathtub holds about 1 liter.

14. The perfume bottle holds more than 1 liter.

15. The bathtub holds much more than 1 liter.

16. The bathtub holds less than 1 liter.

17. There is about 1 liter of springwater.

18. The perfume bottle holds much less than 1 liter.

Choose the unit you would use to measure the capacity of each of these.

19. a medium-size fish tank

    a. liters   **b.** milliliters

20. a vitamin bottle

    a. milliliters   **b.** liters

Make each statement true. Write <, >, or =.

21. 5 L ● 5 mL

22. 30 mL ● 3 L

23. 8000 mL ● 8000 L

24. 2000 mL ● 20 L

25. 80,000 mL ● 8 L

26. 10 L ● 10,000 mL

Copy and complete. Make a table or use mental math when it helps.

27. ■ L = 4000 mL

28. 10 L = ■ mL

29. ■ mL = 8 L

Maintain • Mixed Practice

Write the answer.

1. $\frac{1}{8} + \frac{3}{8}$

2. $\frac{7}{12} - \frac{5}{12}$

3. $\frac{1}{2} + \frac{1}{4}$

4. $\frac{3}{6} + \frac{3}{6}$

5. $3\frac{1}{2} + \frac{1}{2}$

6. $4\frac{1}{6} + 2\frac{4}{6}$

7. $6\frac{1}{10} - 3$

8. $7\frac{3}{5} - 2\frac{1}{5}$

GRAM AND KILOGRAM

The **gram (g)** and **kilogram (kg)** are metric units of mass.

Equivalent Units
1 kg = 1000 g

A baseball card has a mass of about 1 gram.

Your math book has a mass of about 1 kilogram.

The table shows how kilograms and grams are related.

kg	1	2	3
g	1000	2000	3000

Think

• Which is easier to compute, the number of grams in 14 kilograms or the number of ounces in 14 pounds? Why?

INDEPENDENT PRACTICE

Choose the better estimate of the mass.

1. truckload of coal
   a. 3000 g
   b. 3000 kg

2. kitten
   a. 1 kg
   b. 10 kg

3. dime
   a. 2 kg
   b. 2 g

4. bicycle
   a. 10 kg
   b. 10 g

Copy and complete. Make a table or use mental math.

5. 6 kg = ■ g

6. ■ kg = 8000 g

7. $\frac{1}{2}$ kg = ■ g

PROJECT • Estimation

Work with a small group. You will need a pan balance, metric masses, and a recording sheet.

• Choose four small objects. Estimate each mass in grams. On the pan balance use gram masses to balance the objects.

Object	Estimate	Actual

COOPERATIVE • LEARNING

More Practice Set 10.11, p. 455

PROBLEM SOLVING
USING STRATEGIES

If you get stuck, remember...
Tips for Problem Solving

on pages 474–475

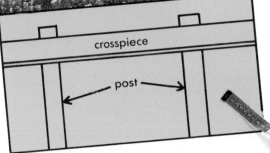

crosspiece

post

Solve each problem.

1. Gretchen is building a wooden fence around a field. The field is 16 meters long and 12 meters wide.
   a. How many meters of fencing does Gretchen need?
   b. Each crosspiece is 2 meters long. How many crosspieces does she need?
   c. How many posts does she need?

2. Gretchen has a second field that is the same width as the first but twice as long. How many crosspieces will she need for this fence?

3. Is your answer to exercise 2 double your answer to exercise 1b? Why or why not?

4. Gretchen has a third field that is twice as long as it is wide. Its perimeter is about 150 meters. About how long and wide is this field?

323

TEMPERATURE

Temperature is measured in **degrees Fahrenheit (°F)** in the customary system and in **degrees Celsius (°C)** in the metric system.

The thermometer at the right shows both scales. Comfortable room temperature is about 70°F or about 21°C.

Think

- Which is colder, 0°C or 0°F? Explain.
- If the temperature goes up by 1°C, does it go up by more than or less than 1°F?

In both scales, it is possible to write temperatures below zero. Degrees below zero are written with a minus sign. You read ⁻6° as *6 degrees below zero*.

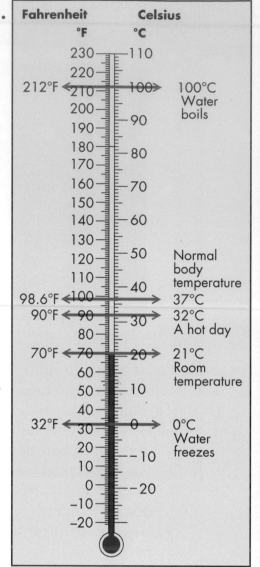

GUIDED PRACTICE

Choose the better estimate.

1. The temperature inside a freezer.
   a. 10°F   **b.** 10°C

2. The temperature on a spring day.
   a. 15°F   **b.** 15 °C

Write the temperature in degrees Celsius and in degrees Fahrenheit.

3.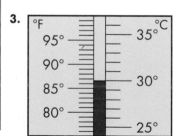

4.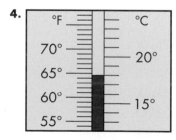

5.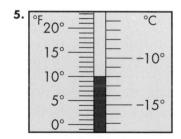

Critical Thinking 6. Which temperature is better for outdoor ice skating, 28°F or 28°C? How do you know?

324

INDEPENDENT PRACTICE

Write the temperature in degrees Fahrenheit and in degrees Celsius.

7.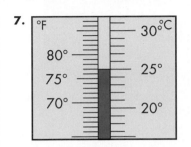

8.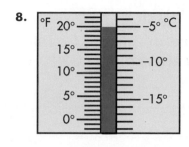

9.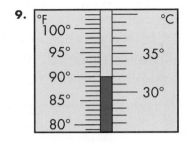

Choose the better estimate. Use the thermometer on page 324 if you need to.

10. You could make a snowman.
  a. 25°F
  b. 25°C

11. You could swim outdoors.
  a. 30°C
  b. 30°F

12. Your soup would boil.
  a. 100°C
  b. 100°F

13. Your room would be comfortable.
  a. 65°C
  b. 65°F

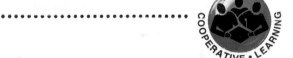

PROJECT • Temperature Change

Work with a small group. Your group will need a thermometer, a bowl, a spoon, warm water, and 12 ice cubes.

a. Fill a bowl halfway with warm water.
b. Put the thermometer into the water. Watch what happens. Record the temperature.
c. Drop 12 ice cubes into the bowl.
d. After one minute, read the thermometer and record the temperature. Be careful not to move the thermometer.
e. Read and record the temperature once a minute for ten minutes. Notice when the temperature remains the same.
f. Make a line graph of the temperature changes. Write a paragraph about what you saw.

ELAPSED TIME

Elapsed time is time that has gone by.

Joel's flight took off from Boston, Massachusetts, at 11:15 in the morning (11:15 A.M.). When it arrived in Atlanta, Georgia, his watch read 1:32 in the afternoon (1:32 P.M.). How long was the flight?

Equivalent Units
1 min = 60 s
1 h = 60 min
1 day = 24 h

Think

• About how many hours was his flight?

Look at a clock.

 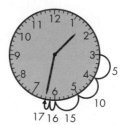

Count the number of hours from 11:15 to 1:15. It is 2 hours.

Count by 5's and 1's to count the minutes from 1:15 to 1:32. It is 17 minutes.

The flight was 2 hours and 17 minutes long.

GUIDED PRACTICE

Write how much time has passed.

1.
11:40 A.M.
12:05 P.M.

2.
9:45 P.M.
10:22 P.M.

3.

Critical Thinking 4. For exercise 1, explain how you decided how much time passed.

INDEPENDENT PRACTICE

Write the elapsed time.

5.

| 12:10 A.M. |
| 12:45 A.M. |

6.

7.

| 11:55 A.M. |
| 1:30 P.M. |

8. from 8:15 P.M. to 8:35 P.M.

9. from 9:22 P.M. to 12:35 A.M.

10. from 3:20 A.M. to 3:20 P.M.

11. from 6:40 A.M. to 7:28 A.M.

How much time has passed? Choose the better estimate.

12.

13.

14.

| 3:17 P.M. |
| 3:37 P.M. |

a. more than 1 hour

b. less than 1 hour

a. about a half hour

b. about an hour

a. more than a half hour

b. less than a half hour

Problem Solving • Data Book Use the flight guide on page 470 to answer each question.

15. Is TWA Flight 187 from New York City to Miami about 3 hours? How can you tell?

16. What is the flight time from Miami to New York City on Pan Am flight 360?

CHALLENGE • Elapsed Time

··

Write the end time.

Start Time	Time Elapsed	End Time
10:31 P.M.	3 h 20 min	
2:15 P.M.	1 h 30 min	
7:10 A.M.	4 h 50 min	
11:45 A.M.	1 h 30 min	

More Practice Set 10.14, p. 455

USING A CALENDAR

Work with a partner. You will need your recording sheet. Fill in the three calendars with the dates for this year. Write important dates and reminders on your calendars to help you answer each question.

1. Rehearsals will begin on the second Monday in March. The first performance of the play will take place exactly 6 weeks later. What day of the week will that be? What is the date of the first performance?

2. The play will be performed for 4 nights in a row. There will be a party after the last performance. What date is the party?

3. Nancy is in charge of renting eight costumes. The costumes are needed for the dress rehearsal 3 days before the first performance. By what date must she pick up the costumes?

4. The costumes must be returned not later than 15 days after the last performance. If it takes 1 week to dry clean them, what is the latest date the costumes must be sent to the cleaners?

5. Joan and Alvin are on the advertising committee. They need 2 weeks to get sponsors for the playbill. It will take another 2 weeks to print the playbill. What is the latest date they should begin finding sponsors?

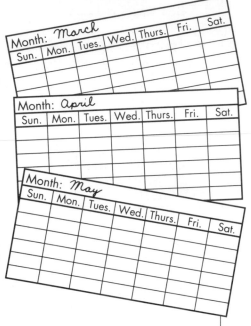

Month: March						
Sun.	Mon.	Tues.	Wed.	Thurs.	Fri.	Sat.

Month: April						
Sun.	Mon.	Tues.	Wed.	Thurs.	Fri.	Sat.

Month: May						
Sun.	Mon.	Tues.	Wed.	Thurs.	Fri.	Sat.

6. The advertising committee also wants to put advertisements in the local newspaper, which is published every Thursday. An ad must be received 3 days before the paper is published. The committee wants to advertise 3 weeks in a row before the performance. When must they send the advertisement to the newspaper?

7. The committee plans to put up posters around the school 2 weeks before the performance. It takes 5 days to print the posters. The printer works only Mondays through Fridays. When must the group finish designing the poster in time to have it printed?

8. Tickets will go on sale 3 weeks before the first performance. It takes 2 weeks to print the tickets. By what date must the printing begin?

9. The students will make all the scenery for the play. It will take 1 month to make the scenery. What is the latest date the students should begin making the scenery?

10. Props can be rented for only 7 days. When is the earliest date the props can be picked up if they are returned the day after the last performance?

If you get stuck, remember....

Tips for Problem Solving

on pages 474–475

The graphs below show the height of two seedling trees from March to October. The trees were measured on the first day of each month.

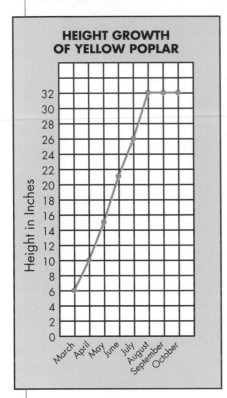

HEIGHT GROWTH OF YELLOW POPLAR

HEIGHT GROWTH OF WHITE ASH

Use the two graphs to help you answer each question.

1. At the beginning of June, how tall was the white ash? The yellow poplar?

2. Which tree was taller at the beginning of April? At the beginning of July?

3. Which tree grew more from April to July?

4. How much did each tree grow from March to August?

5. How much did the yellow poplar grow from August to October?

6. During which month did the white ash grow the most? The least?

7. Which tree stops growing the earliest in the year?

SECTION REVIEW

for pages 316–330

Copy and complete. Make a table or use mental math.

1. 5000 g = ▧ kg
2. ▧ cm = 40 mm
3. 5 m = ▧ cm

4. ▧ m = 40 dm
5. 1500 mL = ▧ L
6. 5 km = ▧ m

Make each statement true. Write <, >, or =.

7. 2 L ⬤ 2 mL
8. 3 cm ⬤ 50 mm

9. 400 cm ⬤ 5 m
10. 4000 g ⬤ 4 kg

11. 5 dm ⬤ 5 cm
12. 4 L ⬤ 3500 mL

Write the elapsed time.

13.
| 2:20 P.M. |
| 4:40 P.M. |

14.
| 11:30 A.M. |
| 2:20 P.M. |

15.
| 3:18 P.M. |
| 8:28 P.M. |

Choose the better estimate.

16. You could make a snowball at about   **a.** 30°C.   **b.** 30°F.

17. You could swim in water that is about   **a.** 75°C.   **b.** 75°F.

Solve each problem.

18. The Little League season begins on the first Saturday in April. The first doubleheader is scheduled 5 weeks later. What date is that?

19. The Little League playoffs begin 2 weeks before the last Sunday in June. What date is that?

April						
Sun	Mon	Tue	Wed	Thu	Fri	Sat
						1
2	3	4	5	6	7	8
9	10	11	12	13	14	15
16	17	18	19	20	21	22
23	24	25	26	27	28	29
30						

May						
Sun	Mon	Tue	Wed	Thu	Fri	Sat
	1	2	3	4	5	6
7	8	9	10	11	12	13
14	15	16	17	18	19	20
21	22	23	24	25	26	27
28	29	30	31			

June						
Sun	Mon	Tue	Wed	Thu	Fri	Sat
				1	2	3
4	5	6	7	8	9	10
11	12	13	14	15	16	17
18	19	20	21	22	23	24
25	26	27	28	29	30	

CHAPTER TEST

Write the perimeter.

1.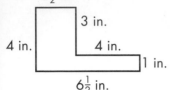

2.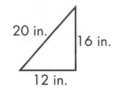

3.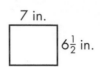

4.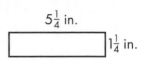

Measure the length of each segment to the nearest centimeter or nearest millimeter.

5. ___ centimeters |⊢———————————————————⊣|

6. ___ millimeters |⊢————————⊣|

Tell which measure is the better estimate. Write *a* or *b*.

7. length of a dining room table

   a. 6 ft **b.** 6 in.

8. mass of a puppy

   a. 1 kg **b.** 1 g

Copy and complete. Make a table or use mental math.

9. 4 qt = ▧ gal

10. 6000 lb = ▧ T

11. ▧ yd = 9 ft.

12. ▧ cm = 9 m

13. ▧ mL = 2 L

14. 24 in. = ▧ ft

Choose the better estimate.

15. Icicles would form.

   a. 20°F **b.** 20°C

16. The weather is very warm.

   a. 30°F **b.** 30°C

PROBLEM SOLVING

Solve each problem.

17. The soccer team tryouts begin at 1:00 P.M. They are over at 3:15 P.M. How long do the tryouts last?

18. Pedro arrived at the ballpark 65 minutes before the 1:00 P.M. starting time. At what time did Pedro arrive at the ballpark?

CUMULATIVE REVIEW

Write the average.

1. 14, 23, 44

2. 5, 8, 6, 9

3. 145, 100, 220, 87

4. 18, 11, 26, 13, 32

5. 300, 200, 500, 100, 400

Solve each problem.

6. How much would 2 tank tops cost? Explain how you found your answer.

7. What is the price of 1 sweatshirt? How did you find your answer?

T-shirts 3 for $40.00   Tank Tops 4 for $30.00   Sweatshirts 2 for $50.00

Copy and complete the number sentence. Write >, <, or =. Use Fraction Bars to check.

8. $\frac{2}{3}$ ● $\frac{1}{3}$

9. $\frac{6}{10}$ ● $\frac{4}{5}$

10. $\frac{3}{4}$ ● $\frac{6}{8}$

11. $\frac{1}{2}$ ● $\frac{2}{6}$

12. $\frac{3}{5}$ ● $\frac{6}{10}$

Write the fractions from least to greatest. Use Fraction Bars when it is helpful.

13. $\frac{3}{8}, \frac{5}{8}, \frac{1}{8}, \frac{7}{8}$

14. $\frac{3}{4}, \frac{1}{8}, \frac{1}{4}, \frac{3}{8}$

15. $\frac{1}{6}, \frac{2}{3}, \frac{5}{6}, \frac{1}{3}$

Write the answer. Use objects or draw a picture.

16. $\frac{1}{3}$ of 45

17. $\frac{5}{5}$ of 40

18. $\frac{2}{10}$ of 30

19. $\frac{1}{12}$ of 36

20. $\frac{2}{3}$ of 75

21. $\frac{1}{2}$ of 48

22. $\frac{4}{4}$ of 60

23. $\frac{1}{10}$ of 50

Write the answer.

24. $\frac{6}{8} + \frac{2}{8}$

25. $\frac{7}{10} + \frac{2}{10}$

26. $\frac{6}{5} - \frac{4}{5}$

27. $\frac{9}{10} - \frac{6}{10}$

Write the sum. Use Fraction Bars when it is helpful.

28. $\begin{array}{r} \frac{2}{3} \\ +\frac{1}{6} \end{array}$

29. $\begin{array}{r} \frac{3}{8} \\ +\frac{1}{4} \end{array}$

30. $\begin{array}{r} \frac{5}{6} \\ +\frac{1}{12} \end{array}$

31. $\begin{array}{r} \frac{2}{5} \\ +\frac{3}{10} \end{array}$

EXCURSION
CULTURAL DIVERSITY

DECISION MAKING

Price is not the only thing to think about when you buy something. Making a decision depends upon what you need, when you need it, and how you will use it. Read the ads on the right for two martial arts classes. Decide which class would be better for you.

Before you decide which class to sign up for, here are some things for you to think about.

- How far away is each martial arts class?

- How will I get to the class? Can I walk or ride my bike?

- How much will a round-trip bus ride cost?

- How much will it cost to attend classes for several months?

- What time does each class begin?

- Do I know much about martial arts? Would I rather learn about several different martial arts or just focus on one?

- How experienced are the instructors at the studio compared to the instructors at the center?

- Do I have brothers and sisters who are interested in taking classes too? Could we take advantage of a family rate?

What else might you need to think about? Make a list of all the factors that will affect your decision. You may use a calculator to help you figure and compare costs.

After considering cost and other factors, which class would you choose? Explain your reasons.

YUKIO'S AIKIDO STUDIO

日本

Try aikido, the gentle Japanese martial art. Exercise for the mind as well as the body! Children's classes meet two times each week.

$35.00 per month
Family rate:
$130 per month

Free introductory lesson.

Springfield Community Center Classes for Young People

Introduction to Martial Arts
This class introduces students to several different martial arts, including the ancient Chinese art of t'ai chi, the Japanese art of aikido, and the art of tae kwon do from Korea

Cost:
$58.00 per person
for 10 weeks

Suppose you have just been given aikido lessons as a birthday present. Group lessons will be paid for, but you will have to pay for equipment, fees, and extra classes. There are two aikido studios downtown. Consider the choices and decide which would be best for you.

AIKIDO WEST

No membership fee

Insurance fee _____ $2.50 per month

Exercise mats provided by the studio

Sweatpants and sweatshirt
with studio emblem _____ $17.95

Judo or Karate gi _____ $25.00

Hakama to be worn over gi _____ $13.50
(Students must wear hakamas for tournaments)

Tournament fee _____ $15.00 per year

Private classes _____ $7.50 per class

(Private classes recommended once a month
for students who wish to enter competition)

SCHOOL OF AIKIDO

Youth membership fee:
$5.00

Insurance fee:
$23.00 per year

Exercise mat:
$16.00

Sweatpants and sweatshirt
with school emblem:
$15.39

Judo or karate gi:
$28.00

Semi-private classes available:
$4.50 per class

(Students of this school do not
participate in tournaments)

Before you make your decision, make a list of things to think about. Use your list and, if you wish, your calculator to help you decide. Explain your decision.

CHAPTER 11

DECIMALS

Estimation

Decimals at the Deli Evan waited in line at the deli to buy sandwich meat for lunch. His mother gave him $2.00 and told him to buy one half pound of sliced turkey.

At the deli, sliced turkey sells for $3.99 per pound. Evan watches as the sliced turkey is weighed. He notices that the scale reads 0.49 pound. Use this information to answer each question.

- Is there more than or less than one pound on the scale?

- Does Evan have enough money with him?

- Should Evan let the man put one more slice of turkey on the scale?

Discuss your answers with your classmates.

EXPLORING TENTHS

Groups:
• pairs

You will need:
• Decimal Squares (tenths)
• a recording sheet
• a crayon

Take out the Decimal Square card shown to the right.

1. How many sections is the square divided into?

2. What fraction of the square is 1 section?

You can write **one tenth** as a fraction or a decimal.

$$\frac{1}{10} = 0.1$$

3. On the one tenth card, is more than or less than one half of the square shaded?

4. Find a card where more than one half of the square is shaded. Write in words how much of the card is shaded. Write a decimal for how much of the card is shaded.

5. Look at the table on your recording sheet. Sort all your cards into three groups, one group for each column in the table. Then fill in the table.

Less Than One Half Shaded		Exactly One Half Shaded		More Than One Half Shaded	
Words	Decimal	Words	Decimal	Words	Decimal
three tenths	0.3				

6. Suppose you had a card like the one shown at the right. What number would the card stand for? Why?

▶ You can use decimals to write numbers greater than one. Look at these squares.

Two and seven tenths squares are shaded.
2.7 squares are shaded.

7. How many whole squares are shaded?

8. What part of the last square is shaded?

▶ On your recording sheet, color in whole squares and partial squares to show each amount listed below.

9. one and nine tenths   **10.** two and four tenths

11. 3.1   **12.** 1.3   **13.** 4.9

14. Write a decimal for each amount in exercises 9 and 10.

15. Look at your drawings for exercises 11 through 13. Write the decimals in order from least to greatest.

Critical Thinking

SUMMING IT UP

16. Write three and seven tenths as a mixed number and as a decimal. How are the mixed number and decimal alike? How are they different?

17. Without drawing pictures, how can you tell that the number 2 is greater than the number 0.9?

EXPLORING TENTHS AND HUNDREDTHS

Groups: pairs

You will need:
- Decimal Squares
  (tenths and hundredths)
- a recording sheet
- a crayon

1. Take out any green Decimal Square.
   How many small squares is the large square
   divided into? How did you figure that out?

Each small square on a green Decimal Square is
one hundredth of the large square. You can
write **one hundredth** as a fraction or a decimal.

$$\frac{1}{100} = 0.01$$

Take out the 3 green Decimal Squares shown
below. For each Decimal Square, write how
many hundredths of the square are shaded.

2.   3.   4.

Find the Decimal Square shown below.
Thirty-five hundredths of the square is shaded.
You can use fractions or decimals to describe this square.

$\frac{35}{100}$

of the large
square is shaded.

0.35
of the large
square is shaded.

$$\frac{35}{100} \quad = \quad \text{thirty-five hundredths} \quad = \quad 0.35$$

5. Is more than half of the square above shaded?

6. Is 0.35 greater than or less than one half?

7. Find the Decimal Square for each decimal in the chart. Use the Decimal Square to help you fill in the chart on your recording sheet.

Decimal	Greater or Less Than One Half?
0.75	
0.25	
0.95	
0.45	
0.50	

On each of the 2 cards below, the same part is shaded.

$$0.3 = 0.30$$
$$\frac{3}{10} = \frac{30}{100}$$

8. Find 2 other pairs of red and green Decimal Squares that show the same part shaded. Draw a picture of each pair on your recording sheet. Then write the decimal that describes each card.

9. Find the Decimal Squares for each pair of decimals listed in the chart. Use the cards to help you fill in the chart.

Red Square	Green Square	Compare
0.6	0.25	0.6 > 0.25
0.5	0.05	
0.5	0.55	
0.3	0.30	
0.8	0.75	

 Critical Thinking ·

SUMMING IT UP

10. Since 30 is greater than 3, why isn't 0.30 greater than 0.3?

12. Suppose the large square on this Decimal Square stands for one dollar. Use a decimal to write the amount of money represented by the shaded part.

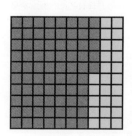

PLACE VALUE AND DECIMALS

A place value chart shows what each digit
in a decimal stands for.

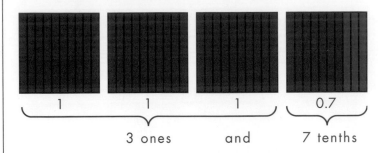

		1		1		1		0.7

3 ones   and   7 tenths

Hundreds	Tens	Ones	Tenths	Hundredths
		3	7	

three and seven tenths

3.7

> The decimal point separates
> the whole number places from
> the decimal places.

Hundreds	Tens	Ones	Tenths	Hundredths
		0	4	5

forty-five hundredths

0.45

> The zero shows
> there are no ones.

Think

- In the mixed number $3\frac{5}{100}$, how do you
  know the 5 stands for 5 hundredths?

- In the decimal 3.05, how do you know
  the 5 stands for 5 hundredths?

342

GUIDED PRACTICE

Write the decimal.

1. four and eight hundredths
2. ten and one tenth
3. thirty-two and fifty-six hundredths
4. one hundred five and ten hundredths

What does the blue digit in the number stand for?

5. 43.36
6. 247.08
7. 0.14
8. 196.02

Write in words.

9. 3.28
10. 26.54
11. 15.90
12. 15.09

 Critical Thinking 13. In exercise 11, is the decimal closer to 15 or 16? Explain.

INDEPENDENT PRACTICE

Write the decimal.

14. thirty and thirty hundredths
15. six and six hundredths
16. twenty-five and three tenths
17. one hundred twelve and forty-two hundredths

What does the blue digit in the number stand for?

18. 205.16
19. 19.05
20. 0.33
21. 42.90

Write in words.

22. 458.08
23. 26.80
24. 30.9
25. 30.09

CHALLENGE • Patterns

Press 2 + 0 . 1 =
If you keep pressing =, your calculator will count by tenths.
Copy the number line. Use your calculator to fill in the missing numbers.

2.5 2.6 ▥ 2.8 ▥ 3.0 ▥ 3.2 ▥ ▥ 3.5 3.6 ▥ 3.8 ▥ ▥ ▥ 4.2 ▥ ▥ 4.5

COMPARING DECIMALS

▶ Compare 0.8 and 0.69.

 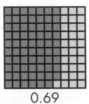

0.8   0.69

Tenths square   **Hundredths square**

Replace the tenths square with an equivalent hundredths square.

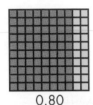

0.80   0.69

The Decimal Square 0.80 has more shaded. So, 0.8 > 0.69.

▶ Here is another way to compare 0.8 and 0.69.

Look at the tenths place. Compare the digits.

$$0.8 \bullet 0.69$$

Since 0.8 > 0.6, then 0.8 > 0.69.

▶ Some decimals have the same digit in the tenths place, for example, 0.58 and 0.50:

If the tenths are the same, compare hundredths.

$$0.58 \bullet 0.50$$

Since 0.08 > 0.00, then 0.58 > 0.50.

Think

- Which is greater, 0.4 or 0.04? How do you know?

- How is comparing 0.4 and 0.04 like comparing 4 dimes and 4 pennies?

GUIDED PRACTICE

Copy and complete. Write <, >, or =.

1.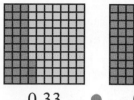

0.33 ● 0.53

2.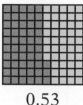

0.7 ● 0.48

3. 0.17 ● 17 **4.** 9.17 ● 10.17 **5.** 4.8 ● 4.08 **6.** 5.5 ● 5.50

Critical Thinking **7.** In exercise 4, is it necessary to look at the decimal places? Explain.

INDEPENDENT PRACTICE

Copy and complete. Write <, >, or =.

8.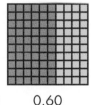

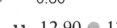

0.75 ● 0.60

9.

0.7 ● 0.70

10. 0.31 ● 0.3 **11.** 12.90 ● 12.89 **12.** 0.1 ● 0.10 **13.** 15.29 ● 16.29

14. 0.7 ● 0.70 **15.** 9.60 ● 9.6 **16.** 13.06 ● 13.60 **17.** 7.00 ● 7.10

Problem Solving

18. Which is heavier, 4.56 pounds or 4.32 pounds?

19. Which is less, 10 liters of gas or 10.7 liters of gas?

Maintain • Elapsed Time

Write the elapsed time.

1.
| 3:25 P.M. |

| 4:30 P.M. |

2.
| 11:45 A.M. |

| 2:20 P.M. |

3.
| 8:05 A.M. |

| 11:55 A.M. |

4.
| 6:15 A.M. |

| 6:15 P.M. |

More Practice Set 11.4, p. 456

ORDERING DECIMALS

Libraries that use the Dewey Decimal System label their books with decimals. The librarian compares the decimals. The books are placed on the shelves by their numbers. The numbers are arranged from least to greatest. What is the correct order of the decimals on the books?

Donnelly — Poodles — 636.72

Silverstein — DOGS, All About Them — 636.7

Woodhouse — The Arco Color Book of Dogs — 636.71

To order decimals from least to greatest, first compare.

● Line up the decimal points.	● Compare the digits from left to right.	● Compare the digits that are not the same.	● Write the decimals from least to greatest.
636.72 636.70 (636.7 = 636.70) 636.71	636.72 636.70 636.71 the same	636.72 636.70 $0 < 2$ 636.71 $0 < 1$	636.70 636.71 636.72

The order of the decimals from least to greatest is 636.7, 636.71, 636.72.

 Think

- Do you need to look at the tenths place when you compare 11.25 and 9.7? Why or why not?

- Do you need to look at the hundredths place to compare 1.35 and 1.87? Explain.

GUIDED PRACTICE

Write the numbers in order from least to greatest.

1. 1.4, 1.08, 1.80

2. 0.04, 0.01, 0.4

3. 3.3, 3.25, 3.88

4. 18.05, 18.50, 18.4, 18

5. 24.98, 24.89, 24.9, 24.8

Critical Thinking **6.** Explain how you solved exercise 2.

....

INDEPENDENT PRACTICE

Write the numbers in order from least to greatest.

7. 4.0, 4.01, 4.10

8. 13.31, 13.21, 13.30

9. 1.78, 1.2, 1.4

10. 1.8 m, 1.85 m, 1.82 m

11. 6.5, 6.05, 6.06

12. 0.56, 0.41, 0.6

13. 17.83, 17.7, 17, 17.69

14. 29.3, 29.29, 29.99, 29.6

....

PROJECT • Ordering Decimals

COOPERATIVE • LEARNING

Play this game with a partner. You will need Decimal Squares.

a. Deal 5 Decimal Squares in a row, face up. Leave them in the order they are dealt. Place the remaining squares face down in a pile.

b. Take turns taking the top square from the pile. Use it to replace one of the squares in the row. Put the extra square at the bottom of the pile.

c. The winner is the first player to get 5 squares in least to greatest order.

PROBLEM SOLVING
···
USING STRATEGIES

*If you get stuck, remember...
Tips for Problem Solving
on pages 474–475*

Television ratings give us an idea of how popular different shows are. If a TV show gets a high rating, it means that people were watching that show in a lot of homes.

The table below lists the ratings for some of the top sports shows one year.

TOP SPORTS SHOWS OF THE YEAR	
Program	**Rating**
Super Bowl	41.9
World Series	32.6
AFC Championship Game	28.7
NFC Playoff	27.7
NFC Championship Game	27.6
Winter Olympics— Ladies' Figure Skating Finals	26.4

Work in pairs to solve each problem. Use the data from the table.

1. Name the TV shows listed that had a rating over 30.

2. The most popular weekly show that year had a rating of 32.3. If it were listed with the sports shows, between which two shows would it be placed?

Use the data from the table on page 348 and this number line to solve each problem.

3. Which show had a higher rating, *Super Bloopers* or *Ladies' Figure Skating Finals*?

4. Suppose all ten shows were listed on the same chart. In what place would the *Academy Awards* be?

5. How many of the ten shows had a rating between 25 and 30?

6. What was the rating of each?

   a. *Barbara Walters Special*

   b. *Tonight Show Anniversary Special*

7. A rating of 50 means that people watched the show in half of the homes with televisions. Were more than or less than half the homes with televisions tuned into the *Super Bowl*?

8. Which of the shows had a rating closest to 24.0?

9. What fraction of the sports shows listed had a lower rating than the *Academy Awards*?

TOP SPECIALS FOR THE YEAR

30.0

← *Academy Awards*

29.0

28.0

27.0

26.0

25.0

24.0 ← *Tonight Show Anniversary Special*

23.0

22.0 ← *Barbara Walters Special*

← *Super Bloopers*

21.0

PROJECT • Statistics

Find out about the shows last week that had the highest ratings. Look in television magazines or the TV section of the newspaper for the data. Make a chart to display that data.

Find out which shows the students in your class like the most. Are they the same shows that had the highest ratings? Why or why not?

COOPERATIVE • LEARNING

CALCULATOR OR MENTAL MATH

You will need a calculator.

The calculator is a good tool to help you compute. But sometimes it is even faster and easier to do a problem mentally.

Questions for you to consider:

- Can I compute quickly in my head?

- Will entering the problem into a calculator take too much time?

INDEPENDENT PRACTICE

Write each answer. Write whether or not you used a calculator to find your answer.

1. $1.36
    + 2.79

2. $\frac{3}{4}$
    $+ \frac{1}{4}$

3. 834
    + 497

4. 78
    × 8

5. 9875
    − 5000

6. 6 + 3 + 7 + 4   7. 30 − 19   8. 72 ÷ 3   9. 7 × 100   10. 207 + 300

Problem Solving

11. Last year, 7798 people attended the Sports Day events. This year there were 10,942 people at the events. How many more people were at the events this year?

12. Lynn has saved $33.57 to buy a skateboard. The skateboard costs $37.25. How much more money does Lynn need to buy the skateboard?

13. There are 6 buses driving to the circus. Each bus can hold 40 students. How many students can go to the circus?

14. *Critical Thinking* Which problems did you solve using a calculator? Explain.

Section Review

for pages 338–350

Write the decimal.

1.

2.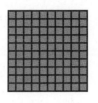

3. sixty-five and nine hundredths

4. thirty-three and five tenths

5. ten and forty hundredths

6. five and twenty-two hundredths

7. six and seven hundredths

8. twenty and two hundredths

9. 3 tenths + 4 hundredths

10. 0 tenths + 7 hundredths

11. 8 tenths + 0 hundredths

12. one + 4 tenths

13. $4\frac{3}{10}$

14. $\frac{6}{100}$

15. $14\frac{2}{10}$

16. $7\frac{16}{100}$

17. $1\frac{12}{100}$

18. $11\frac{8}{100}$

19. $\frac{18}{100}$

20. $\frac{25}{100}$

Write in words.

21. 4.90

22. 4.09

23. 73.8

24. 24.62

Copy and complete. Write <, >, or =.

25. 9.1 ● 9.11

26. 0.1 ● 0.09

27. 32.1 ● 32.10

28. 0.90 ● 0.9

29. 0.7 ● 1.0

30. 12.07 ● 12.7

31. 0.1 ● 0.10

32. 1.1 ● 1.05

33. 8.1 ● 8.14

Write the numbers in order from least to greatest.

34. 6.1, 6.01, 6.11

35. 3.02, 3.1, 3.03

36. 0.9, 0.99, 0.93

37. 23.5, 23.35, 23, 23.49

38. 15.78, 15.63, 15.8, 16.63

USING ROUNDING TO ESTIMATE

You already know how to round whole numbers. You can also round decimals.

▶ Round 4.79 to the nearest whole number. Use a number line.

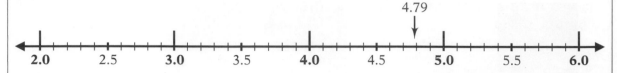

4.79

You can see that 4.79 is closer to 5 than to 4. So, 4.79 rounds to 5.

Think

• What whole number does 4.28 round to?

▶ Joanne buys two packages of meat. One weighs 6.18 pounds. The other weighs 3.77 pounds. About how many pounds of meat did she buy?

Estimate the sum: 6.18 lb + 3.77 lb

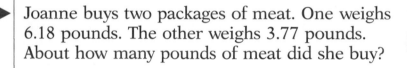

3.77   6.18

6.18 lb + 3.77 lb
↓   ↓
6 lb   +   4 lb   = 10 lb   So, 6.18 lb + 3.77 lb is about 10 lb.

▶ Sergio has $5.20 and spends $3.95. About how much money does he have left?

Estimate the difference: $5.20 − $3.95

  $5.20 — rounds to → $5.00
− 3.95 — rounds to → − 4.00
      Estimate: $1.00

$3.95 $5.20

So, Sergio has about $1 left.

GUIDED PRACTICE

Round to the nearest whole number. Draw a number
line when it helps.

1. 3.9   **2.** 8.2   **3.** $5.87   **4.** $6.39   **5.** 4.62

Use rounding to estimate. Draw a number line
when it helps.

6.	**7.**	**8.**	**9.**	**10.**
5.9	$6.19	8.2	$7.35	7.95
+ 8.4	+ $2.63	− 4.4	− $4.89	+ 6.89

Critical Thinking

11. Is the exact answer to exercise 10 more than
or less than the estimate? How do you know?

....

INDEPENDENT PRACTICE

Round to the nearest whole number. Draw a number
line when it helps.

12. 7.1   **13.** 4.8   **14.** 3.7   **15.** 9.9   **16.** $6.03

17. $4.77   **18.** 3.92   **19.** 0.82   **20.** $3.49   **21.** 2.66

Use rounding to estimate. Draw a number line
when it helps.

22.	**23.**	**24.**	**25.**	**26.**
$4.22	3.17	$5.25	9.6	6.69
+ 1.29	+ 2.88	− 2.38	− 3.8	− 2.86

27. 7.68 + 3.56   **28.** $6.78 + $1.89   **29.** 9.47 − 6.08

Problem Solving Estimate to solve. Explain each answer.

30. Terry needs to buy at least 15 kg
of dog food. Will two bags
be enough?

31. Can Terry buy one bag of dog
food and a collar with $13?

32. Can Terry buy two cans of flea
spray and one collar with $20?

More Practice Set 11.8, p. 457

ADDING DECIMALS

Gerard plans to go on a bike tour from Morton to Lane by way of Silverton and Lindburg. How many miles will he ride?

Add: 20.75 mi + 29.5 mi + 32 mi

Sometimes the decimals do not have the same number of places. Write them as equal decimals by writing zeros.

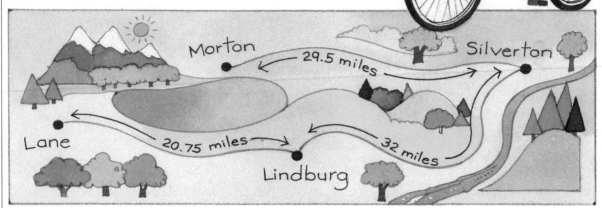

● **Line up the places. Write zeros if necessary.**

20.75 mi
29.50 mi
+ 32.00 mi

(29.5 = 29.50
32 = 32.00)

● **Add as you would with whole numbers.**

  1 1
20.75 mi
29.50 mi
+ 32.00 mi
82 25

● **Write the decimal point in the sum.**

  1 1
20.75 mi
29.50 mi
+ 32.00 mi
82.25 mi

Gerard will ride 82.25 miles.

Think

• How can you tell if your answer is reasonable?

Other Examples

12.34
+ 6
18.34

  1 1 1
$55.71
+ 14.29
$70.00

  2 1 1
12.75
9.22
+ 18.14
40.11

GUIDED PRACTICE

Write the sum.

1. 9.4
    + 8.61

2. 9.66
    + 4

3. 4.1
    3.2
    + 7.3

4. 97.65
    + 72.44

5. $1.19
    .44
    + 3.89

6. 4.8 m + 13.5 m

7. 0.13 + 4.02 + 8

8. 0.88 + 16 + 5.7

Critical Thinking 9. Why is it important to line up the places when you add decimals?

INDEPENDENT PRACTICE

Write the sum.

10. 1.88
     + 7.91

11. 16.9
     + 12

12. 88
     + 22.09

13. 7.54
     + 5.93

14. 28
     + 32.04

15. 33.7 + 14.08

16. 6.3 m + 2.7 m

17. 0.9 + 8.9 + 6

18. $0.81 + $0.12

19. $0.79 + $1.50 + $2

20. 30.4 + 8.75

21. 12.91 + 3

22. 56.4 + 7.29

23. 97.65 + 72.4 + 21

Problem Solving

Clover Bicycle Tours		
Name of Trip	Distance	Cost
Quick Rider	49.7 mi	$6.29
Road Rider	62.1 mi	$8.75
Advanced	108.7 mi	$12.49
Super Biker	124.3 mi	$14.98

24. Is the Advanced tour longer than the Quick Rider and Road Rider tours combined? Explain your answer.

25. Susan wants to sign up for both the Quick Rider and Road Rider tours. Will that cost more than the Super Biker Tour? Explain your answer.

26. What combination of tours would let you ride the greatest distance for under $20?

Maintain • Mixed Practice

Write the answer.

1. 7 × 246

2. 4)‾568

3. 9 × 507

4. 5)‾500

5. 3 × 689

SUBTRACTING DECIMALS

André Phillips of the United States won the Olympic gold medal for the 400-meter hurdles in 1988. How much faster was he in 1988 than Edwin Moses was in 1984?

Olympic Gold Medalists Men's 400-Meter Hurdles		
1976	Edwin Moses (United States)	47.64 s
1980	Volker Beck (E. Germany)	48.70 s
1984	Edwin Moses (United States)	47.75 s
1988	André Phillips (United States)	47.19 s
1992	Kevin Young (United States)	46.78 s

▶ Subtract: 47.75 s − 47.19 s

● Line up the places.

47.75 s
− 47.19 s

● Subtract as you would with whole numbers.

```
      6 15
  4 7.7 5 s
− 4 7.1 9 s
  0 5 6 s
```

● Write the decimal point in the difference.

```
      6 15
  4 7.7 5 s
− 4 7.1 9 s
  0.5 6 s
```

Check by adding.
```
  47.19 s
+  0.56 s
  47.75 s
```

André Phillips was 0.56 second faster than Edwin Moses.

▶ Sometimes the decimals do not have the same number of places. Write them as equal decimals by writing zeros.

Subtract: 42.8 − 26.53

● Line up the places. Write zeros if necessary.

42.80
− 26.53

42.8 = 42.80

● Subtract as you would with whole numbers.

```
  3 12 7 10
  4 2.8 0
− 2 6.5 3
  1 6 2 7
```

● Write the decimal point in the difference.

```
  3 12 7 10
  4 2.8 0
− 2 6.5 3
  1 6.2 7
```

Think

● How can you check to see if your answer is reasonable?

GUIDED PRACTICE

Write the difference.

1. 4.2
    − 0.08

2. 7.8
    − 3.92

3. 71.4 m
    − 60.5 m

4. 13
    − 6.8

5. 44.32
    − 3.76

6. 12.11 − 7

7. 0.84 − 0.7

8. 19.45 − 11.81

Critical Thinking 9. How does knowing how to write equal decimals help you subtract hundredths from tenths?

INDEPENDENT PRACTICE

Write the difference.

10. 42.99
     − 20.43

11. 0.91 km
     − 0.37 km

12. 12.6
     − 4

13. 18.04
     − 6

14. 22
     − 4.8

15. 4.9 − 3.5

16. 11.76 − 5.7

17. 38 − 17.1

18. 8.2 − 5.47

19. 5 − 0.89

20. 4.94 − 1.6

21. 18.75 − 9

22. 6.26 − 4.9

23. 17.81 − 4.65

Problem Solving Use mental math when you can.

24. How many years after the slowest time was the fastest time recorded?

25. In 1988, Florence Griffith-Joyner set the Olympic record. How much faster was her time than Gail Dever's time in 1992?

OLYMPIC GOLD MEDALISTS WOMEN'S 100-METER DASH		
1968	Wyomia Tyus (U.S.)	11.00 s
1972	Renate Stecher (E. Germany)	11.07 s
1976	Annegret Richter (W. Germany)	11.08 s
1980	Ludmila Kondratyeva (USSR)	11.06 s
1984	Evelyn Ashford (U.S.)	10.97 s
1988	Florence Griffith-Joyner (U.S.)	10.54 s
1992	Gail Devers (U.S.)	10.82 s

26. Who was faster: the 1968 winner or the 1972 winner? By how much?

27. Which two times were separated by 0.52 of a second?

MATH LOG

How are adding and subtracting decimals like adding and subtracting whole numbers?

USING DECIMALS

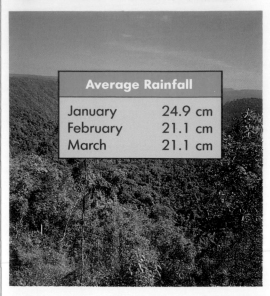

Average Rainfall	
January	24.9 cm
February	21.1 cm
March	21.1 cm

▶ The chart at the left shows the rainfall in Brazil for the first three months of one year. What was the total rainfall for the three months?

First, estimate the sum.

Think
- How did you estimate?

To find the exact answer, add 24.9, 21.1, and 21.1 on the calculator.

This is the answer the calculator displays:　　　　　67.1

Think
- Is this answer close to your estimate?

The total rainfall for the first three months was 67.1 cm.

▶ In April, the average rainfall in Brazil was 10.2 cm. What was the difference in rainfall between January and April?

To find the exact answer, subtract 10.2 from 24.9 on the calculator.

This is the answer the calculator displays:　　　　　14.7

INDEPENDENT PRACTICE

Data Book Use the data on page 464. Use pencil and paper, calculator, or mental math to answer each question.

1. Did more rain fall in the desert in California in the first 3 months of the year or the last 9 months? How did you find out?

2. In which months did Brazil's tropical forest have at least 10 centimeters of rain more than California's desert?

3. How much rain fell in the desert in California:
   a. for the first 5 months of the year?
   b. for the first 8 months of the year?

4. Is the total rainfall for June, July, and August in Brazil's tropical forest more than 5 centimeters? How can you tell without using your calculator or paper and pencil?

5. Did more rain fall in the desert in California in the first half of the year or the second half? How much more?

6. How many months of the year was there no rain at all in the desert in California? What fraction of the year is this?

7. In which month was there the least rainfall in the tropical forest in Brazil?

8. Was the total rainfall for the year in the desert in California more than or less than 1 meter?

9. What was the yearly difference in average rainfall between the tropical forest in Brazil and the desert in California?

10. During which month did Brazil's tropical forest rainfall for the year go over 80 cm? How did you find out?

11. Which place had a higher average monthly rainfall for the year, the tropical forest in Brazil or the desert in California? How can you tell without computing each average?

Critical Thinking 12. Write a word problem about the data. Give it to a friend to solve.

PROJECT • Graphs

Round each decimal to the nearest whole number. Make a line graph of the data on rainfall in Brazil and California. How are the trends in rainfall in the two places alike? How are they different?

COOPERATIVE • LEARNING

PROBLEM SOLVING
USING MATH SENSE

If you get stuck, remember...

Tips for Problem Solving

on pages 474–475

I had some pennies, nickels, dimes, and quarters in my pocket. I heard 3 of my coins drop and roll away. I wonder how much money I lost.

The least it can be is 3 pennies. The most it can be is 3 quarters.

So, we can tell you lost at least 3 cents, but no more than 75 cents.

Think
- How do you know that the amount must be between 3¢ and 75¢?

Work with a small group. Read each story to answer each question.

1. In the gymnastics contest, the lowest score John got was 6.5. His highest score was 8.8. What can you tell about the average of his scores?

2. Jack's average score so far is 8.9. Suppose he gets 9.5 for his next score. What can you tell about his new average?

3. Erica rode her horse along a trail for 6.8 miles. Then she turned and rode 4.7 miles. What can you tell about how far she is from where she started?

4. Joe ran between 2 and 3 miles yesterday. He ran between 3 and 4 miles today. What can you tell about the total distance he ran in the two days?

5. Some numbers are missing from the scoreboard. What can you tell about the number of points the Giants scored in the third quarter?

	QUARTERS				
	1ST	2ND	3RD	4TH	FINAL
GIANTS	7	10		14	31
BEARS		20		10	

6. The Giants won the game. What can you tell about the number of points the Bears scored in the third quarter?

7. Mr. Chung has 7 bills in his wallet. The smallest is a one-dollar bill. The largest is a twenty-dollar bill. What can you tell about how much money is in Mr. Chung's wallet?

8. Jason, Jan, and Joe ran for team captain. Jason received $\frac{1}{4}$ of the votes. Jan received $\frac{1}{8}$ of the votes. What can you tell about who won?

9. Jason received 10 votes. This was $\frac{1}{4}$ of the votes. What can you tell about the number of people who voted?

10. A circular pie is in a box 30 centimeters on each side. What can you tell about the size of the top of the pie?

11. The movie began sometime between 2:00 P.M. and 3:00 P.M. It ended sometime between 4:00 P.M. and 5:00 P.M. What can you tell about the length of the movie?

ESTIMATING WITH MONEY

Pedro has $10 to buy the groceries shown. Is that enough money?

You can use front-end estimation to solve this problem.

- Make a front-end estimate:

Chicken:	$4.89
Lettuce:	1.29
Ice Cream:	2.45

  Rough estimate: $7.00

- Adjust, using the cents parts:

  $4.89 ⟶ About $1
  1.29
  2.45 ⟶ About $0.50

  Adjusted estimate:
  $7 + $1 + $0.50 = $8.50

Pedro has enough money.

Think

- How do you know the estimate of $8.50 is close enough to the exact sum, so that Pedro will have enough money?

- How could you use rounding to solve this problem?

INDEPENDENT PRACTICE

Is the amount of money shown below enough to buy the items? Write *yes* or *no*. Then explain how you found the answer. Use any estimation method you wish.

1. $5.00 **2.** $12.00 **3.** $10.00 **4.** $20.00

More Practice Set 11.13, p. 458

SECTION REVIEW

for pages 352–362

Write the letter of the correct answer.

1. 2.8 + 3.75
   a. 4.03
   b. 655
   c. 6.55
   d. 5.155

2. 5.3 + 7.98
   a. 13.28
   b. 1328
   c. 12.128
   d. 8.51

3. 6.7 + 4.38
   a. 10.108
   b. 1108
   c. 5.05
   d. 11.08

4. 7.27 + 5.8
   a. 1307
   b. 13.07
   c. 7.85
   d. 12.107

5. 6.28 − 3.5
   a. 5.93
   b. 2.7
   c. 2.78
   d. 3.33

6. 5.63 − 1.8
   a. 3.83
   b. 3.8
   c. 4.23
   d. 5.45

7. 6.53 − 4.8
   a. 2.33
   b. 1.7
   c. 6.05
   d. 1.73

8. 27.07 − 5.8
   a. 21.2
   b. 21.27
   c. 26.49
   d. 22.87

9. 12.18 − 7.5
   a. 11.43
   b. 4.6
   c. 4.68
   d. 5.48

10. 15.63 + 7.8
    a. 23.43
    b. 2343
    c. 22.143
    d. 16.41

11. 16.53 − 14.8
    a. 2.33
    b. 1.7
    c. 15.05
    d. 1.73

12. 7.97 + 5.8
    a. 1377
    b. 13.77
    c. 8.55
    d. 12.177

Solve each problem.

13. Tracy lives 2.5 kilometers from school and 1.7 kilometers from the library. How far is it for her to walk straight to school and back home?

14. George needs 5 kilograms of dog food. The food comes in 3.3 kilogram bags. If George buys 2 of the bags how much extra dog food will he have?

CHAPTER TEST

Write each decimal in words.

1. 4.8

2. 9.6

3. 5.01

4. 67.12

5. 98.35

6. 373.03

7. 50.70

8. 307.9

What does the blue digit in the number stand for?

9. 82.37

10. 14.05

11. 621.96

12. 307.82

13. 25.8

14. 702.66

15. 100.02

16. 78.30

Write in order from least to greatest.

17. 0.45, 0.51, 0.5

18. 93.4, 93.04, 93.5

19. 11.10, 10.11, 11.01

20. 20.3, 30.2, 23.2, 20.2

21. 14.5, 14.49, 14.44, 14.05

22. 50.05, 55.05, 50.50, 55.50

Write the answer.

23.
```
   0.5
  12.1
+  6.07
```

24.
```
   0.93
 − 0.8
```

25.
```
   7.21
   9.2
+ 26
```

26.
```
   9
 − 3.07
```

PROBLEM SOLVING

Solve each problem. Use the chart for exercises 27 and 28.

27. How much less rain fell in May than in April?

28. Suppose the total rainfall for January, February, and March had been the same as the total for April, May, and June. How much rain would have fallen from January to June?

Average Rainfall in Seattle, Washington	
April	17.9 cm
May	15.4 cm
June	15.3 cm

CUMULATIVE REVIEW

How many bars are shaded? Write your answer
as a fraction and as a mixed number.

1.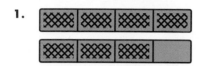

2.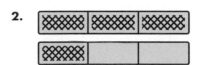

Solve each problem.

3. How much does a backpack
cost on sale? Is that a lower
price than the sale price of the
sports bag?

4. By the end of the first day, $\frac{1}{3}$ of
the 30 backpacks in stock were
not sold. How many backpacks
were sold? Explain your answer.

SUMMER SALE

SALE ITEMS	REGULAR PRICE
Backpacks: $\frac{1}{2}$ off	$20.00
Sports bags: **$5.00 off**	$20.00

Write the difference. Use Fraction Bars when it is
helpful.

5. $\frac{4}{5} - \frac{3}{10}$
6. $\frac{2}{4} - \frac{1}{8}$
7. $\frac{11}{12} - \frac{1}{3}$
8. $\frac{1}{2} - \frac{1}{12}$

Write the answer.

9. $\begin{array}{r} 2\frac{3}{8} \\ +\ 1\frac{1}{8} \end{array}$
10. $\begin{array}{r} 9\frac{7}{12} \\ -\ 7\frac{5}{12} \end{array}$
11. $\begin{array}{r} 6\frac{5}{6} \\ -\ 4\frac{1}{6} \end{array}$
12. $\begin{array}{r} 3\frac{3}{4} \\ +\ 6\frac{1}{4} \end{array}$
13. $\begin{array}{r} 7\frac{2}{3} \\ -\ 3\frac{2}{3} \end{array}$
14. $\begin{array}{r} 5\frac{1}{5} \\ +\ 4\frac{3}{5} \end{array}$

Measure each diagram to the nearest quarter inch.
Write the perimeter.

15. **16.** 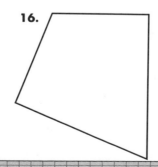 **17.**

EXCURSION
CULTURAL DIVERSITY

ALGEBRA

Have you ever played caroms? This game, similar to pocket billiards, probably originated in North Africa. But it is enjoyed in many parts of the world, including India, Pakistan, Yemen, and the United States.

Caroms is played on a square board by two players, each with nine disks. An extra disk is called the queen. Points are earned by striking a disk into a pocket. The queen counts for extra points.

▶ How many points is the queen worth? Look at the table.

Player A's score without the queen	Rule	Player A's score with the queen
6	+5	11
3	+5	8
4	+5	9

A player's score is 5 points more with the queen. So the queen is worth 5 points. The rule, then, is to add 5.

▶ Use the table below to help you find out how many games are in a match of caroms.

Matches played	Games played
5	15
3	9
9	27
2	6

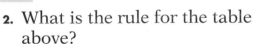

1. How many games are there in each match?

2. What is the rule for the table above?

3. If you played in 4 matches, how many games of caroms would you have played?

4. If you played 18 games of caroms, how many matches would you have played in?

Copy and complete each table. Then write the rule.

5.

3	18
6	36
■	60
■	24
12	■

6.

16	4
24	6
44	11
96	■
■	20

7.

6	26
8	28
19	39
20	■
■	20
42	■

8.

30	25
25	20
18	13
16	■
32	■
■	40

9. Make up a rule. Use it to make a table. Have a friend try to guess the rule.

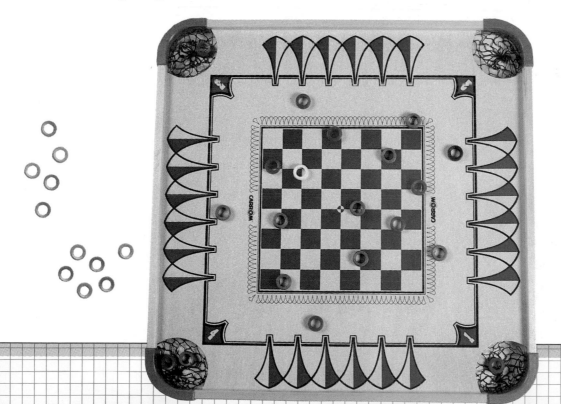

MULTIPLYING BY 2-DIGIT NUMBERS

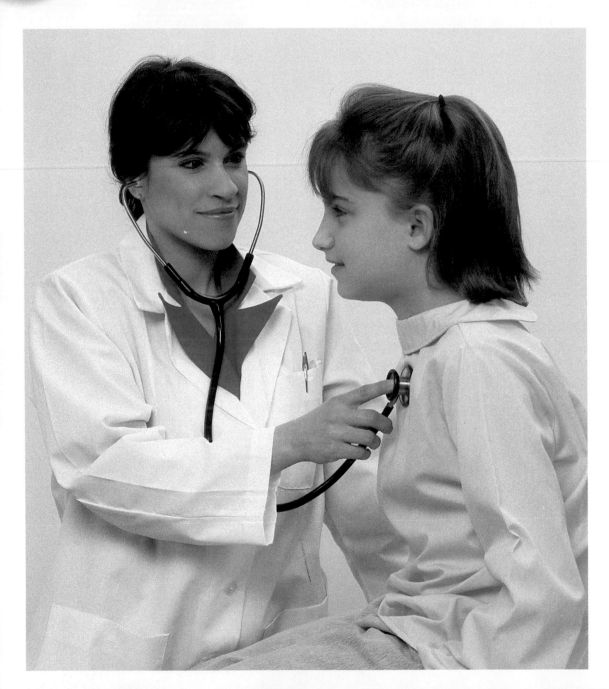

Science

Heartbeats The heart is an amazing organ. It is a powerful muscle that pumps blood to all parts of your body. It beats constantly throughout your life.

At your age, the heart beats about 70 times each minute. You can count the number of heartbeats by checking your pulse. Press your fingers against the side of your neck to feel your pulse. Count the number of beats that you feel in 15 seconds. Then multiply by 4. Your answer is the number of times your heart beats in one minute.

How many times does your heart beat in one hour? In one day? You may be surprised by the answers.

USING PATTERNS

You already know how to multiply a single digit by tens, hundreds, and thousands. For example:

$$4 \times 30 = 120$$

$$2 \times 400 = 800$$

$$9 \times 1000 = 9000$$

Now you will learn to multiply a multiple of 10 by tens, hundreds, and thousands.

▶ Look for patterns in the multiplication sentences below.

a. $2 \times 10 = 20$
   $20 \times 10 = 200$
   $20 \times 100 = 2000$
   $20 \times 1000 = 20,000$

b. $7 \times 40 = 280$
   $70 \times 40 = 2800$
   $70 \times 400 = 28,000$
   $70 \times 4000 = 280,000$

c. $6 \times 50 = 300$
   $60 \times 50 = 3000$
   $60 \times 500 = 30,000$
   $60 \times 5000 = 300,000$

Think

- What patterns do you see in examples a and b?

- How is the pattern in example c the same as examples a and b? How is it different from examples a and b?

▶ Compare the mental math rules for multiplication and addition.

Multiply: 20×30

First, multiply the non-zero digits. Then, place as many zeros at the end of the product as there are in both factors together.

$$20 \times 30 = 600$$
   ↑   ↑   ↑↑

1 zero + 1 zero = 2 zeros

Add: $20 + 30$

First, add the non-zero digits. Then, place as many zeros at the end of the sum as there are in each addend.

$$20 + 30 = 50$$
   ↑   ↑   ↑

1 zero in each number

GUIDED PRACTICE

Write the product. Use mental math.

1. 6×20 2. 70×80 3. 20×40 4. 60×700

5. 80×3000 6. 50×500 7. 20×50 8. 8×50

Critical Thinking
9. Which products have more zeros than the total number of zeros in their two factors? Explain why.

INDEPENDENT PRACTICE

Write the product. Use mental math.

10.	60	11.	30	12.	50	13.	700	14.	100
	$\times\ 3$		$\times 40$		$\times 60$		$\times\ 50$		$\times\ 10$

15. 8×80 16. 30×70 17. 40×40 18. 20×80

19. 40×100 20. 60×600 21. 10×400 22. 20×3000

Write the answer. Use mental math.

23. 20×20 24. 30×70 25. $20 + 20$ 26. $30 + 50$

27. 30×40 28. 30×800 29. $500 + 400$ 30. 20×400

31. $30 + 30$ 32. 10×90 33. 30×30 34. $300 + 300$

Problem Solving

35. The floor plan on the right shows how Shopper's Mart is being tiled. How many tiles of each color are needed?

36. Shopper's Mart is open from 6 A.M. to 2 A.M., 7 days a week. How many hours is it open in a 30-day month?

37. There are 30 Shopper's Marts in southern California and 40 Shopper's Marts in the rest of the state. How many Shopper's Marts are there in California?

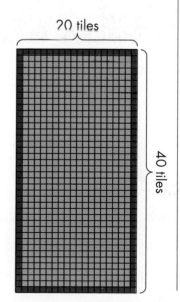

20 tiles

40 tiles

More Practice Set 12.1, p. 458

ESTIMATING PRODUCTS

Mr. Langley's art class is making a mosaic using colored paper. Each student will make one large square with 32 triangles. The finished mosaic will have 28 large squares. The class has cut out almost 600 triangles. Will that be enough?

Estimate: 28 × 32

To get a quick, rough estimate, you can use front-end estimation.

28 × 32   (20 × 30 = 600)

Since 28 is greater than 20 and 32 is greater than 30, 28 × 32 is greater than 600.

600 triangles will not be enough for the mosaic.

▶ About how many triangles will the class need to cut out for the mosaic?

To get a closer estimate of 28 × 32, round each number. Then multiply.

$$28 \times 32$$
$$\downarrow \qquad \downarrow$$
$$30 \times 30 = 900$$

Mr. Langley's class needs about 900 triangles.

Think

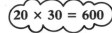

- Why does rounding 28 × 32 give a closer estimate?

Write the letter of the most reasonable estimate.

1. 3 × 34	**2.** 62 × $9.97	**3.** 23 × 85	**4.** 48 × 53
a. 90	**a.** $620	**a.** 16	**a.** 250
b. 900	**b.** $6200	**b.** 160	**b.** 2500
c. 9000	**c.** $62,000	**c.** 1600	**c.** 25,000

Estimate. Use any method you wish.

5. 72	**6.** 398	**7.** 46	**8.** $9.75	**9.** 67
× 53	× 3	× 47	× 28	× 31

10. Is the actual product in exercise 7 greater than or less than 2500? Explain.

Estimate. Use any method you wish.

11. 47	**12.** 628	**13.** 32	**14.** 36	**15.** 54
× 24	× 4	× 21	× 34	× 54

16. 42 × 35   **17.** 56 × $3.08   **18.** 66 × 21   **19.** 32 × $9.89

20. $10.25 × 12   **21.** 220 × 5   **22.** 44 × 15   **23.** 13 × 28

24. Which two numbers in the box have a product of about:

a. 300?   **b.** 2400?

c. 1800?   **d.** 1200?

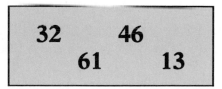

32   46

61   13

Problem Solving Estimate to solve each problem. Use the illustration on page 372.

25. Each of the triangles in the mosaic has 12 pieces of paper. Does one large square with 32 triangles contain more than or fewer than 300 pieces of paper?

26. The class worked from 1 P.M. to 4 P.M. to complete one large square. Can they finish all 28 squares in less than 90 hours?

MULTIPLYING BY MULTIPLES OF TEN

One year, the month of February had 20 school days. If Brian was in school 365 minutes each day, how many minutes was he in school for the month?

- Multiply by the ones. Record the zero in the ones place.

$$\begin{array}{r} 365 \text{ min} \\ \times\ 20 \\ \hline 0 \end{array}$$ (0 × 365 = 0)

- Multiply by the tens. Regroup.

$$\begin{array}{r} {\scriptstyle 1\ 1} \\ 365 \text{ min} \\ \times\ 20 \\ \hline 7300 \text{ min} \end{array}$$

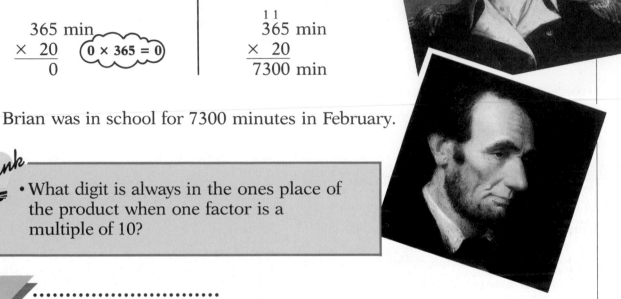

Brian was in school for 7300 minutes in February.

Think

- What digit is always in the ones place of the product when one factor is a multiple of 10?

GUIDED PRACTICE

Write the letter of the most reasonable estimate.

1. 60 × 325
   a. 180
   b. 1800
   c. 18,000

2. 75 × 78
   a. 640
   b. 6400
   c. 64,000

3. 40 × 212
   a. 8000
   b. 80,000
   c. 800,000

4. 41 × 63
   a. 2400
   b. 24,000
   c. 240,000

Estimate. Then write the product.

5. $\begin{array}{r} 34 \\ \times\ 20 \\ \hline \end{array}$

6. $\begin{array}{r} 25 \\ \times\ 40 \\ \hline \end{array}$

7. $\begin{array}{r} 111 \text{ mL} \\ \times\ 50 \\ \hline \end{array}$

8. $\begin{array}{r} 144 \\ \times\ 20 \\ \hline \end{array}$

9. $\begin{array}{r} 144 \\ \times\ 40 \\ \hline \end{array}$

10. $30 × 72

11. 20 × 463

12. 50 × 425

13. 60 × 315

Critical Thinking

14. Look at the product in exercise 9. Will the product of 80 × 144 be more than or less than 10,000? How can you tell?

INDEPENDENT PRACTICE

Write the letter of the most reasonable estimate.

15. 60 × 149
  a. 60
  b. 600
  c. 6000

16. 80 × 78
  a. 640
  b. 6400
  c. 64,000

17. 50 × 62
  a. 300
  b. 3000
  c. 30,000

18. 90 × 875
  a. 720
  b. 7200
  c. 72,000

Estimate. Then write the product.

19.   33
      × 30

20.   45 in.
      × 20

21.   54
      × 40

22.   124
      × 20

23.   116 m
      × 50

24.   849
      × 40

25.   349
      × 30

26.   349
      × 60

27.   24
      × 50

28.   478
      × 30

29. 20 × 78

30. 21 × 40

31. 60 × 71

32. 70 × 77

33. 60 × 827

34. 30 × 123

35. 20 × 276

36. 40 × 525

Problem Solving

37. There are 185 days in the school year. Math class meets every day from 10:40 A.M. to 11:30 A.M. How many minutes does math class meet in one school year?

38. Gym class meets Monday, Wednesday, and Friday from 11:30 A.M. to 12:10 P.M. During one school year, 108 gym classes are scheduled. How many minutes a year will a student spend in gym class?

Maintain • Comparing Decimals

Copy and complete. Write >, <, or =.

1. 7.3 ● 7.29

2. 0.68 ● 0.49

3. 14.49 ● 15.49

4. 12.5 ● 12.50

5. 5.09 ● 5.90

6. 35.25 ● 35.1

If you get stuck, remember....

Tips for Problem Solving

on pages 474–475

The Sunpower Company makes purple squares that change the sun's rays into electricity. Pieces of the squares are used to run calculators.

To make electricity for cars, boats, and space stations, the squares are arranged to form large panels. Ms. Smith designs these panels for the Sunpower Company.

Help Ms. Smith by solving each problem. Work with a small group.

1. Ms. Smith is designing a panel for a solar boat.
   a. How many square sections are needed for this panel?
   b. What is the area of each square?
   c. What is the area of the panel?

2. Ms. Smith is also working on a panel for a solar car. To produce enough electricity, the area of the panel will be 8000 square centimeters.
   a. How many squares will be needed?
   b. How can the squares be arranged to make a rectangle?

3. A thin metal frame must go completely around each solar panel. How many centimeters of frame are needed for the panel for the solar boat in exercise 1?

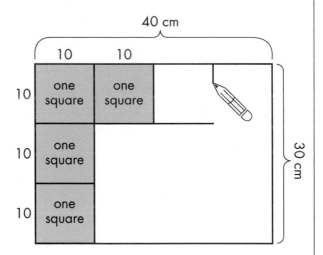

Use the company's cost chart to help solve
problems 4–7.

4. The panel for a solar lamp will
be 50 cm long and 40 cm wide.
How much will the squares for
this panel cost?

5. How much will the frame cost
for the solar-lamp panel?

6. Ms. Smith is working on two
different plans for a solar panel.
a. Which plan will produce
more electricity?
b. Which plan will cost the
Sunpower Company less to
build? HINT: include the cost
of the frame.
c. How much less?

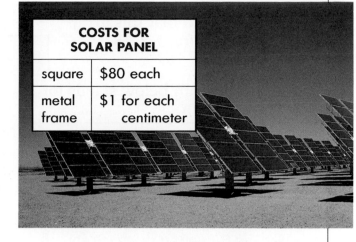

COSTS FOR SOLAR PANEL	
square	$80 each
metal frame	$1 for each centimeter

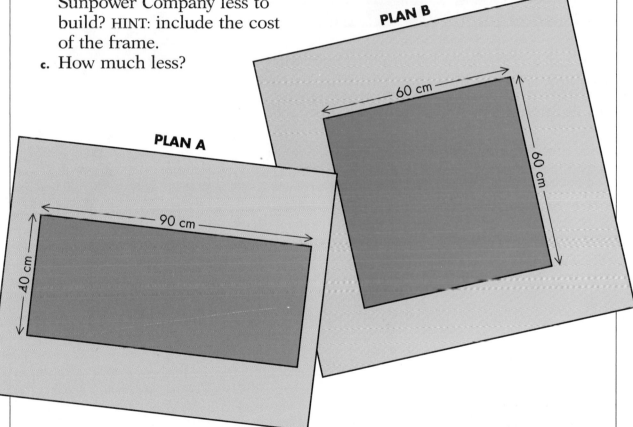

PLAN B

60 cm

60 cm

PLAN A

90 cm

40 cm

7. Design a panel for a solar scooter. The area
must be at least 6000 square centimeters.
What will be the total cost for the frame and
the squares for your panel?

MULTIPLYING WITH ARRAY DIAGRAMS

You have learned that this array diagram stands for 3 × 18.

	10	8
3	3 × 10 = 30	3 × 8 = 24

The array diagram below stands for 23 × 18.

	10	8
20	20 × 10 = 200	20 × 8 = 160
3	3 × 10 = 30	3 × 8 = 24

Think

• How is the array diagram for 23 × 18 similar to the array diagram for 3 × 18?

You can use the array diagram to help you multiply. Here is how to record what you do.

To multiply 18 by 23, write it like this:
```
  18
× 23
```

● Multiply by the ones.

```
   18
 × 23
   24  ← 3 × 8
   30  ← 3 × 10
```

● Multiply by the tens.

```
    18
  × 23
    24
    30
   160  ← 20 × 8
   200  ← 20 × 10
```

● Add.

```
    18
  × 23
    24
    30
   160
   200
   414
```

The product of 23 × 18 is 414.

GUIDED PRACTICE

Write the product. Use the array diagram to help you multiply.

1.
```
   12
 × 12
```
	10	2
10		
2		

2.
```
   24
 × 15
```
	20	4
10		
5		

3.
```
   26
 × 34
```
	20	6
30		
4		

Draw an array diagram for the multiplication. Write the product.

4. 13×27 **5.** 34×43 **6.** 28×64 **7.** 11×88

 8. Why is it helpful to separate the factors into tens and ones?

INDEPENDENT PRACTICE

Write the product. Use the array diagram to help you multiply.

	10	3
10		
1		

9. $\begin{array}{r} 13 \\ \times\ 11 \end{array}$

	60	3
10		
2		

10. $\begin{array}{r} 63 \\ \times\ 12 \end{array}$

	50	6
20		
6		

11. $\begin{array}{r} 56 \\ \times\ 26 \end{array}$

Write the product. Draw an array diagram when it helps.

12. $\begin{array}{r} 12 \\ \times\ 41 \end{array}$ **13.** $\begin{array}{r} 13 \\ \times\ 12 \end{array}$ **14.** $\begin{array}{r} 36 \\ \times\ 71 \end{array}$ **15.** $\begin{array}{r} 28 \\ \times\ 43 \end{array}$ **16.** $\begin{array}{r} 25 \\ \times\ 25 \end{array}$ **17.** $\begin{array}{r} 62 \\ \times\ 52 \end{array}$

18. 25×15 **19.** 41×41 **20.** 16×35 **21.** 81×23

Problem Solving

22. Shay's Department Store has 16 display windows. Each display is changed twice a month. How many displays must be planned for one year?

23. The store ordered 48 boxes of photo albums. Each box has 15 albums. How many albums were ordered?

 24. There are 17 display cases on the first floor. The manager wants to put 12 lights in each case. She orders 200 lights. Is that enough? How do you know?

25. For the summer sale, Shay's will decorate the store with balloons. They need 190 balloons. Will 20 bags of 10 balloons each be enough? Why or why not?

MATH LOG

How does using the array diagram help you multiply?

MULTIPLYING 2-DIGIT NUMBERS

Mr. O'Hara takes 23 fourth-graders to the State Fair. Each student receives 18 tickets for the exhibits and the rides. How many tickets does Mr. O'Hara order for the students?

You can multiply 18 by 23. You have already learned how to multiply using an array diagram.

	10	8
20	20 × 10 = 200	20 × 8 = 160
3	3 × 10 = 30	3 × 8 = 24

$$
\begin{array}{r}
18 \\
\times\ 23 \\
\hline
24 \\
30 \\
160 \\
200 \\
\hline
414
\end{array}
$$

Here is a shorter way.

● **Multiply by the ones.**

$$
\begin{array}{r}
18 \\
\times\ 23 \\
\hline
54 \leftarrow 3 \times 18
\end{array}
$$

● **Multiply by the tens.**

$$
\begin{array}{r}
18 \\
\times\ 23 \\
\hline
54 \\
360 \leftarrow 20 \times 18
\end{array}
$$

● **Add.**

$$
\begin{array}{r}
18 \\
\times\ 23 \\
\hline
54 \\
360 \\
\hline
414
\end{array}
$$

Mr. O'Hara orders 414 tickets.

Think

• How is this method of multiplication the same as multiplying with an array diagram?

GUIDED PRACTICE

Write the product.

1. 32 × 12	**2.** 13 pt × 33	**3.** 25 × 22	**4.** 35 × 33	**5.** 47 ft × 23	**6.** 50 × 90

7. 11 × 77   **8.** 23 × 32 kg   **9.** 24 × 66   **10.** 55 × 65

Copy and complete. Write >, <, or =.

11. 55 × 16 ● 54 × 18   **12.** 70 × 50 ● 68 × 48   **13.** 30 × 65 ● 20 × 85

Critical Thinking **14.** How did you solve exercise 12?

INDEPENDENT PRACTICE

Write the product.

15.	11	**16.**	15 lb	**17.**	24	**18.**	60	**19.**	27 oz	**20.**	35
	× 19		× 22		× 28		× 20		× 27		× 45

21. 12 × 24   **22.** 14 × 54   **23.** 10 × 70   **24.** 15 × 67

25. 27 × 45   **26.** 80 × 80   **27.** 30 × 93   **28.** 39 × 43

Copy and complete. Write >, <, or =.

29. 9 × 11 ● 10 × 10   **30.** 20 × 40 ● 22 × 32   **31.** 13 × 12 ● 11 × 14

32. 34 × 12 ● 33 × 13   **33.** 3 × 21 ● 21 × 40   **34.** 40 × 22 ● 38 × 24

Problem Solving

35. Two quilting clubs will exhibit quilts at the fair. The diagrams on the right show two quilts. Which one has more squares?

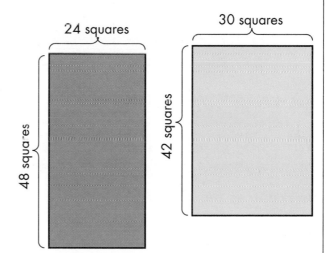

24 squares

30 squares

48 squares

42 squares

Critical Thinking **36.** There are 35 school buses parked at the fairground. Each bus seats 45 people. Use this information to write a word problem of your own. Have a friend solve it.

Maintain • Mixed Practice

Write the answer.

1.	42.34	**2.**	76.7	**3.**	53.09	**4.**	60.5	**5.**	$45.00
	+ 9.9		− 23.85		+ 53.91		− 2.98		− 4.50

More Practice Set 12.6, p. 460

LOGICAL REASONING

You can use the words *all, some,* or *none* to help you describe a set of objects.

Statements A, B, and C are true statements about the set pictured below. Statement D is false.

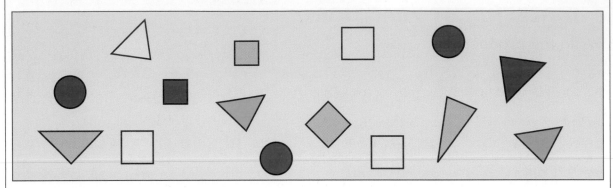

A. *All* of the circles are red.
c. *None* of the squares are green.

B. *Some* of the triangles are blue.
D. *All* of the red figures are circles.

Think

- Why is statement D false?

- How could you change statement D to make it true?

INDEPENDENT PRACTICE

Write *true* or *false* for each statement. Use the picture above.

1. Some of the circles are yellow.

2. Some of the squares are blue.

3. All of the green figures are triangles.

4. None of the yellow figures are circles.

5. Some of the triangles are green.

6. Some of the yellow figures are squares.

7. All of the green triangles are congruent.

Critical Thinking **8.** Write a true statement and a false statement about the set of objects in the picture.

SECTION REVIEW

for pages 370–382

Write the product.

1. 30 × 53
2. 45 × 60
3. 50 × 83
4. 20 × 68
5. 52 × 60
6. 70 × 76
7. 20 × 81
8. 30 × 97
9. 54 × 70
10. 80 × 89
11. 34 × 60
12. 60 × 99

Write the letter of the correct answer.

13. 34 × 57
    a. 171,228
    b. 399
    c. 1938
    d. 2138

14. 66 × 96
    a. 6636
    b. 1152
    c. 576,576
    d. 6336

15. 16 × 39
    a. 1124
    b. 624
    c. 39,234
    d. 273

16. 43 × 74
    a. 296,222
    b. 518
    c. 3182
    d. 3282

17. 47 × 88
    a. 4136
    b. 4636
    c. 376,376
    d. 752

18. 65 × 73
    a. 455,195
    b. 650
    c. 4745
    d. 4845

19. 34 × 56
    a. 374
    b. 168,224
    c. 2104
    d. 1904

20. 83 × 94
    a. 7802
    b. 7902
    c. 1034
    d. 747,332

21. 38 × 57
    a. 171,456
    b. 2166
    c. 627
    d. 2666

22. 46 × 87
    a. 4402
    b. 870
    c. 368,322
    d. 4002

23. 55 × 64
    a. 640
    b. 3720
    c. 3520
    d. 320,320

24. 48 × 63
    a. 3024
    b. 252,504
    c. 756
    d. 3224

Solve each problem.

25. The members of the Garden Club have $1000 to spend on plants. They buy 32 shrubs for $27 each. How much money do they have left?

26. They also buy 18 boxes of flowers. Each box contains 24 flowers and costs $7.75. How many flowers did they buy?

MULTIPLYING 3-DIGIT NUMBERS

The garden center orders 405 bags of tulip bulbs, with 25 bulbs in each bag. How many tulip bulbs are there?

First estimate the product.

Think

- Which numbers did you estimate with?

To find how many tulip bulbs the garden center orders, you can multiply 405 by 25.

	400	5
20	20 × 400 = 8000	20 × 5 = 100
5	5 × 400 = 2000	5 × 5 = 25

$$
\begin{array}{r}
405 \\
\times\ 25 \\
\hline
2025 \quad \leftarrow\ 5 \times 405 \\
8100 \quad \leftarrow\ 20 \times 405 \\
\hline
10{,}125
\end{array}
$$

The garden center orders 10,125 tulip bulbs.

Think

- How can you tell if your answer is reasonable?

GUIDED PRACTICE

Estimate. Then write the product.

1. 111 qt
    × 78

2. 122
    × 40

3. 122
    × 80

4. 600
    × 50

5. 372 m
    × 34

6. 12 × 104

7. 34 in. × 333

8. 56 × 236

Critical Thinking 9. How can the product of exercise 2 help you solve exercise 3?

INDEPENDENT PRACTICE

Write the product.

10. 411
       × 10

11. 232 ft
       × 23

12. 306
       × 50

13. 427
       × 64

14. 762
       × 28

15. 300
       × 26

16. 401 in.
       × 31

17. 865
       × 65

18. 735
       × 37

19. 907
       × 71

20. 82 × 225

21. 73 × 687

22. 46 × 684

Estimate. Then write the letter of the correct product.

23. 13 × 227
   a. 1453
   b. 2951
   c. 8891

24. 32 × 513
   a. 2565
   b. 164,160
   c. 16,416

25. 48 × 676
   a. 8112
   b. 32,448
   c. 7352

Problem Solving Look for shortcuts.

26. The garden center orders 225 packages of string bean seeds. Each package has 30 seeds. Is that enough for 50 planters if each planter will have 100 seeds?

27. The garden center has a display of tulips. There are 18 rows of red tulips and 12 rows of yellow tulips. Each row has 120 tulips. How many tulips are on display?

CHALLENGE • Measurement

Every room on the floor plan is a rectangle. How many square feet of carpet will you need to cover each room?

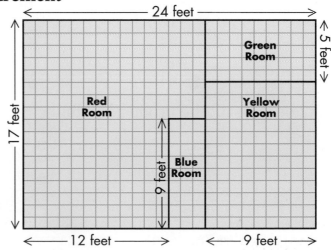

MULTIPLYING MONEY

Juana orders bulbs to plant in her garden from a flower catalog. She orders tulips, daffodils, and crocuses.

Juana fills in each column of the order form. What should she put at the bottom of the order form for the total cost?

Flower	Color	Item No.	Price
Tulip	Red	TX–15	$0.38 ea
	Yellow	TX–16	$0.38 ea
	Purple	TX–17	$0.38 ea
Daffodil	White	DX–12	$0.47 ea
	Yellow	DX–13	$0.47 ea
Crocus	Purple	CX–14	$0.19 ea
	Yellow	CX–15	$0.19 ea
	White	CX–16	$0.19 ea
Hyacinth	Purple	HX–19	$0.61 ea
	Pink	HX–20	$0.61 ea
	White	HX–21	$0.61 ea

Quantity	Item No.	Type of Flower	Color	Unit Price	Total
12	TX-16	Tulip	Yellow	$0.38	
12	DX-12	Daffodil	White	$0.47	
24	CX-14	Crocus	Purple	$0.19	
				Total	

Think

- What must Juana find out before she can fill in the total?

Juana multiplies to find the total cost of each type of flower.

Tulips	Daffodils	Crocuses
$0.38	$0.47	$0.19
× 12	× 12	× 24
76	94	76
380	470	380
$4.56	$5.64	$4.56

Then Juana adds all the products to find the total.

$$\begin{array}{r} \$4.56 \\ 5.64 \\ +\ 4.56 \\ \hline \$14.76 \end{array}$$

Juana's total is $14.76.

INDEPENDENT PRACTICE

Write the product.

1.	$45.99	2.	$2.45	3.	$8.50	4.	$8.50	5.	$32.45
	× 15		× 36		× 12		× 24		× 25

....

PROJECT • Problem Solving

The Tyson City Garden is planning a Community Children's Garden to be planted by the local children. Mr. Greenberg, the groundskeeper, is ordering bulbs for the garden.

With your group, help Mr. Greenberg decide which bulbs to order. Use the catalog shown on page 386. You may use paper and pencil or a calculator to compute.

Here is what you need to know:

- Mr. Greenberg has a budget of $75.

- He wants to have as many different kinds and colors of flowers as possible.

- He wants no less than twelve of each different flower that is ordered.

Here is what you must decide:

- Which kinds and colors of flowers should be ordered?

- How many of each kind of flower should be ordered?

When you have made your decisions, use your recording sheet to complete the order form.

Quantity	Item No.	Type of Flower	Color	Unit Price	Total
				Total	

MULTIPLYING THREE FACTORS

Julia ordered 15 cartons of flower bulbs for the garden center. Each carton holds 6 boxes. In each box are 12 bulbs. How many bulbs did Julia order?

You can multiply 12 by 6 by 15.

● Multiply two factors.

$$
\begin{array}{r}
12 \\
\times\ 6 \\
\hline
72
\end{array}
$$

● Multiply the product by the third factor.

$$
\begin{array}{r}
72 \\
\times\ 15 \\
\hline
360 \\
720 \\
\hline
1080
\end{array}
$$

Julia ordered 1080 flower bulbs.

Think

- How many ways can you group the factors to multiply 12 by 6 by 15? List them.

- Is there a way of grouping that makes the multiplication easier?

GUIDED PRACTICE

Explain how you would group the factors to multiply. Look for an easy way.

1. $5 \times 6 \times 2$ **2.** $2 \times 9 \times 30$ **3.** $4 \times 16 \times 5$ **4.** $10 \times 11 \times 7$

Write the product.

5. $11 \times 2 \times 12$ **6.** $22 \times 8 \times 40$ **7.** $22 \times 0 \times 75$ **8.** $15 \times 36 \times 10$

 Critical Thinking 9. How did you find the product for exercise 7?

INDEPENDENT PRACTICE

Explain how you would group the factors to multiply.

10. $12 \times 4 \times 10$ **11.** $21 \times 11 \times 3$ **12.** $11 \times 5 \times 13$ **13.** $5 \times 12 \times 8$

Write the product.

14. $11 \times 6 \times 10$ **15.** $7 \times 23 \times 12$ **16.** $45 \times 15 \times 0$

17. $42 \times 17 \times 2$ **18.** $16 \times 5 \times 16$ **19.** $4 \times 54 \times 14$

20. $18 \times 8 \times 13$ **21.** $0 \times 19 \times 36$ **22.** $25 \times 25 \times 3$

Problem Solving

23. The garden center orders 5 cartons of flower pots. Each carton has 12 boxes, with 4 flower pots in each box. How many flower pots does the garden center order?

24. Julia earns $9 per hour at the garden center. Last month she worked from 9 A.M. to 3 P.M. each day for 18 days. How much did she earn last month?

25. **Data Book** Go to page 472. Look at the garden center price list. How much do four 18-inch country vases cost?

CHALLENGE • Problem Solving

In a multiplication magic square, every row, column, and diagonal has the same product. Copy and complete the magic square using three factors from the Number Box.

Critical Thinking Make a new multiplication magic square and a number box. Give it to a friend to solve.

?	4	18
36	6	?
2	?	12

Number Box

	3	
5		2
	0	
9		1

USING MATH SENSE

If you get stuck, remember....
Tips for Problem Solving
on pages 474–475

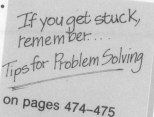

Solve each problem. Explain how you got your answer.

1. **a.** Look at the notebooks at the right. At which store do a dozen notebooks cost less?

   b. Pablo has a ten-dollar bill. Is that enough to buy a dozen notebooks?

2. Mrs. O'Reilly is supposed to be in Springfield at 1:30 P.M. It is 11:30 A.M. and she is 135 miles away. If she drives at an average speed of 55 miles per hour, will she make it to Springfield on time? How can you tell?

3. The diagrams below show plans for two gardens.
   a. Which garden has more area?
   b. Which garden needs less fence to go completely around its edge?
   c. How much less?

Cal's Corner Store $1.69

NOTEBOOK

Everybody's Market $1.49

PLAN A   PLAN B

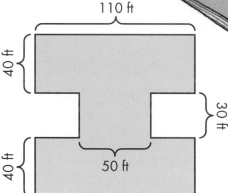

110 ft

110 ft

110 ft

40 ft

30 ft

40 ft

50 ft

4. Are there more seconds in an hour or hours in a year?

5. How many days old are you? HINT: There are 365 days in a year.

6. Every fourth year is a leap year with 366 days. The year 1992 was a leap year. How does this change your answer to problem 6?

SECTION REVIEW

for pages 384–390

Write the product.

1. 2×124
2. 17×237
3. 26×412
4. 5×20
5. 42×400
6. 66×815
7. 30×33
8. 8×586
9. 77×797

Write the letter of the correct answer.

10. 24×288
    a. 5062
    b. 1728
    c. 6912
    d. 9302

11. 37×153
    a. 5661
    b. 10,181
    c. 1530
    d. 5481

12. 74×952
    a. 95,648
    b. 70,448
    c. 10,472
    d. 17,948

13. 38×692
    a. 26,296
    b. 14,236
    c. 35,966
    d. 7612

14. 16×186
    a. 3226
    b. 1302
    c. 6126
    d. 2976

15. $14 \times \$3.55$
    a. $56.30
    b. $17.75
    c. $49.70
    d. $42.80

16. $63 \times 12 \times 9$
    a. 1323
    b. 6804
    c. 675
    d. 171

17. $22 \times 23 \times 7$
    a. 513
    b. 315
    c. 660
    d. 3542

18. $33 \times 28 \times 9$
    a. 1176
    b. 8316
    c. 285
    d. 549

19. $45 \times 26 \times 8$
    a. 568
    b. 1178
    c. 9360
    d. 1378

20. $37 \times 62 \times 7$
    a. 16,058
    b. 693
    c. 2728
    d. 2301

21. $52 \times 74 \times 6$
    a. 3854
    b. 4292
    c. 756
    d. 23,088

Solve each problem.

22. Eddie buys 3 rolls of film with 36 pictures each. The 3 rolls cost $18. How many pictures will Eddie be able to take?

23. Eddie also buys 4 photo albums. Each album has 24 pages that hold 6 pictures each. How many pictures can the albums hold?

CHAPTER TEST

Write the product. Use the array diagram to help you multiply.

1. 15
    × 14

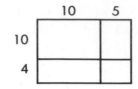

2. 46
    × 25

Write the product.

3. 21
    × 30

4. 44
    × 20

5. 686
    × 70

6. 85
    × 40

7. 50 × 229

8. 59 × 40

9. 30 × 478

10. 66 × 331

11. 72 × 249

12. 11 × 101

13. 18 × 4 × 16

14. 54 × 13 × 7

15. 76 × 22 × 0

16. 38 × 8 × 12

17. 4 × 75 × 19

18. 7 × 88 × 14

PROBLEM SOLVING

Solve each problem.

19. Music class lasts 1 hour. During one school year, 110 music classes are scheduled. How many minutes will a student spend in music class during the year?

20. The auditorium has 42 rows of seats. Each row has 32 seats. Are there more than 1000 seats in the auditorium?

21. There are 15 school buses coming to the fairgrounds. Five of the buses carry 40 children each. The rest carry 45 children each. How many children are riding in the 15 buses?

22. The garden center orders one box of carrot seeds for $39.00. There are 300 packages of carrot seeds in a box. Each package contains 25 seeds. How many seeds are there in the box?

CUMULATIVE REVIEW

Solve each problem.

1. A recipe for pumpkin bread calls for $2\frac{3}{4}$ cups of flour. Sue has $2\frac{1}{2}$ cups. Is that enough flour to make the pumpkin bread? How do you know?

2. A drink recipe calls for $\frac{3}{4}$ cup of yogurt, $1\frac{1}{2}$ cups of milk, and $1\frac{1}{4}$ cups of orange juice. Is a 4-cup container large enough to hold this recipe?

Choose the better estimate.

3. The length of a house is about
   a. 65 ft.   **b.** 65 in.

4. A postage stamp has a mass of about
   a. 1 kg   **b.** 1 g

Copy and complete. Make a table or use mental math.

5. ■ T = 6000 lb   6. 36 ft = ■ yd   7. 70 cm = ■ dm   8. ■ mL = 9 L

9. 24 in = ■ ft   10. 1 qt = ■ c   11. ■ cm = 50 mm   12. 2 L = ■ mL

Choose the better estimate.

13. Water would boil.
    a. 100°C   **b.** 100°F

14. You could go swimming.
    a. 25°C   **b.** 25°F

Write the elapsed time.

15. 10:05 A.M.
    10:25 A.M.

16. 7:30 P.M.
    9:45 P.M.

17. 11:57 A.M.
    12:35 P.M.

18. 6:33 A.M.
    6:33 P.M.

Write in words the number of shaded squares.

19.

20.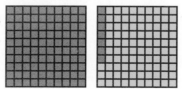

21.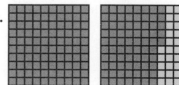

EXCURSION

CULTURAL DIVERSITY

AREA

The Agricultural Training Center is a special school in Senegal, Africa. Here students learn new methods of farming a dry region called the Sahel. Built in 1977, the Center is a reflection of its environment. The sand to make the bricks of the rectangular buildings comes from nearby soil.

When you plan buildings, you need to calculate area. To find the area of a rectangle, you multiply the length by the width. Notice that the rectangles below have different lengths and widths, but they have the same area.

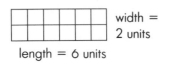 width = 2 units
length = 6 units

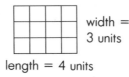 width = 3 units
length = 4 units

2 × 6 = 12 square units   3 × 4 = 12 square units

You can also find the length and width of a rectangle if you know the area. Find the lengths and widths of two different rectangles with an area of 16 square feet.

- Try a width of 2 feet. Divide the area by the width.   `1 6 ÷ 2 =`

- Try a width of 4 feet. Divide.    **8.**

So, two rectangles with an area of 16 square feet are as follows: `1 6 ÷ 4 =`

2 ft × 8 ft and 4 ft × 4 ft    **4.**

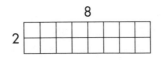
8
2

4
4

Look at the floor plan drawing below. It shows how the buildings of the Agricultural Training Center are arranged.

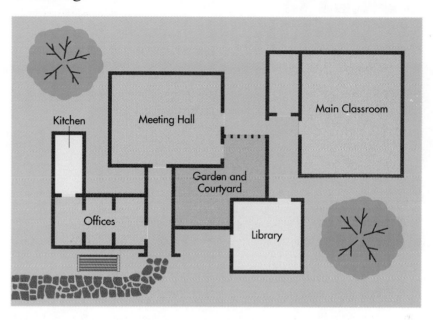

 Use your calculator to solve each problem. Every answer is in whole numbers.

1. The main classroom has an area of 120 square meters. What is the length and width of the room?

2. What is the perimeter of the main classroom?

3. The library has an area of 49 square meters. What is the length and width of the room?

4. The meeting hall has an area of 99 square meters. What is the length and width of the hall?

5. The kitchen has an area of 18 square meters. What is the length and width of the room? What is the perimeter?

6. Altogether, the offices have an area of 45 square meters. What is the length and width of the office area?

7. There are three separate offices within the 45 square meter office area. Each one has the same area. They also have the same dimensions. What is the length and width of each office?

8. Work with a partner. Estimate how many students would fit comfortably in the main classroom. How many would fit in the meeting hall? Explain your estimates.

CHAPTER 13

DIVIDING BY 2-DIGIT NUMBERS

Connections

Social Studies

Signatures Schoolbooks are printed on a large press like the one pictured on page 396. The press uses huge rolls of paper up to 5 miles long. The press may use up to one thousand feet of paper per minute and often runs day and night.

The piece of paper the pressman is pulling out of the printer is called a signature. Each signature is a large piece of paper with 32 of your textbook's pages printed on it. After all the signatures are printed, they are sewn and glued into the cover.

You can compute the number of signatures in your book. First, find the total number of book pages. Make sure to count the pages in the front, as well as any blank pages in the back. Then divide the total number of pages by 32. Your answer gives you the number of signatures in your book.

Check your answer by counting the number of signatures in the spine of your book.

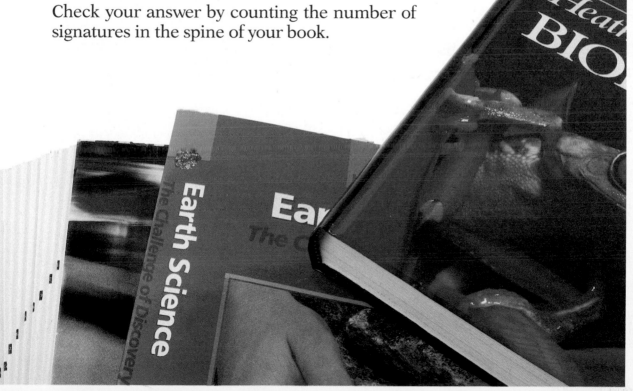

USING PATTERNS

You have used patterns to multiply mentally.

$$30 \times 2 = 60$$

$$30 \times 20 = 600$$

$$30 \times 200 = 6000$$

$$30 \times 2000 = 60,000$$

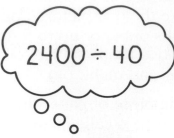

2400 ÷ 40

Multiplication patterns can help you divide tens, hundreds, and thousands.

Divide: $2400 \div 40 = \blacksquare$

It asks the same question as $40 \times \blacksquare = 2400$.

Remember the rule for multiplying:

> **First multiply the non-zero digits. Then place as many zeros at the end of the product as there are in both factors together.**

This rule can help you find the missing factor.

$$40 \quad \times \quad \blacksquare \quad = \quad 2400$$
$$40 \quad \times \quad 60 \quad = \quad 2400$$
$$\uparrow \qquad \uparrow \qquad \uparrow\uparrow$$

4 × 6 = 24

1 zero + 1 zero = 2 zeros

Since $40 \times 60 = 2400$, then $2400 \div 40 = 60$.

Think

- How are the division patterns like the multiplication patterns? How are they different?

Other Example

$$2000 \div 50 = 40$$

GUIDED PRACTICE

Write the quotient. Use mental math.

1. 120 ÷ 4   2. 120 ÷ 40   3. 1200 ÷ 40   4. 3600 ÷ 60

5. 2400 ÷ 4   6. 1000 ÷ 20   7. 600 ÷ 30   8. 35,000 ÷ 50

Write the missing factor.

9. 70 × ■ = 140   10. ■ × 40 = 240   11. ■ × 50 = 300

Critical Thinking 12. Explain how you can use multiplication to check a quotient in exercises 1–8.

....

INDEPENDENT PRACTICE

Write the letter of the correct quotient.

13. 2400 ÷ 8   14. 420 ÷ 60   15. 350 ÷ 70   16. 1600 ÷ 4
    a. 3   a. 7   a. 5   a. 40
    b. 30   b. 70   b. 50   b. 400
    c. 300   c. 700   c. 500   c. 4000

Write the quotient. Use mental math.

17. 800 ÷ 4   18. 800 ÷ 40   19. 1500 ÷ 30   20. 4900 ÷ 70

21. 3600 ÷ 60   22. 2000 ÷ 50   23. 3000 ÷ 50   24. 16,000 ÷ 40

25. 180 ÷ 90   26. 1800 ÷ 90   27. 18,000 ÷ 90   28. 2400 ÷ 60

Write the missing factor. Use mental math.

29. 30 × ■ = 600   30. 20 × ■ = 600   31. 40 × ■ = 8000

32. ■ × 60 = 1200   33. 40 × ■ = 2800   34. ■ × 20 = 1000

Problem Solving Use mental math.

35. Ralph sold Little League tickets for $1.00 each. The grand prize of $250 was shared equally by 5 friends. When they divided up the prize money how much did they each receive?

36. There are 30 students selling bags of popcorn at the Little League game. A bag costs 25¢. If each student sells 20 bags of popcorn, how many will they sell?

More Practice Set 13.1, p. 461

ESTIMATING QUOTIENTS

▶ Estimating quotients can help you divide.

Divide: $170 \div 24 = $ ▨

It asks the same question as $24 \times$ ▨ $= 170$.

● First, decide how many
digits are in the quotient.

$24 \times 1 = 24$

⟵ 170 is between 24
and 240

$24 \times 10 = 240$

So, the quotient is between 1
and 10. It has one digit.

● Estimate.

$$\begin{array}{r} 24 \\ \times\ 7 \\ \hline 168 \end{array} \qquad \begin{array}{r} 24 \\ \times\ 8 \\ \hline 192 \end{array}$$

170 is between 168 and 192

So, the quotient is between 7
and 8.

▶ You can estimate larger quotients.

Divide: $1198 \div 45 = $ ▨

It asks the same question as $45 \times$ ▨ $= 1198$.

● How many digits are in the quotient?

$45 \times 10 = 450$

⟵ 1198 is between 450
and 4500

$45 \times 100 = 4500$

So, the quotient is between 10
and 100. It has two digits.

● To estimate, use multiples of 10.

$$\begin{array}{r} 45 \\ \times\ 20 \\ \hline 900 \end{array} \qquad \begin{array}{r} 45 \\ \times\ 30 \\ \hline 1350 \end{array}$$

1198 is between 900 and 1350.

So, the quotient is between 20
and 30.

Think

- Will the quotient of $1198 \div 45$ be closer
to 20 or to 30? How do you know?

Look at the blue number in each multiplication exercise.
Then write the two numbers the quotient is between.

1. 38)754

38	38	38
×10	×20	×30
380	760	1140

2. 14)99

14	14	14
× 6	× 7	× 8
84	98	112

Write the letter of the better estimate.

3. 783 ÷ 85   Estimate between: **a.** 8 and 9   **b.** 9 and 10

4. 63 ÷ 20   Estimate between: **a.** 3 and 4   **b.** 4 and 5

Estimate the quotient. Write the two multiples of 10 the estimate is between.

5. 25)752   **6.** 63)684   **7.** 47)4538   **8.** 35)2750

Critical Thinking **9.** For exercise 2, will the quotient be closer to 7 or 8? How do you know?

Write the letter of the better estimate.

10. 76 ÷ 12   Estimate between: **a.** 5 and 6   **b.** 6 and 7

11. 576 ÷ 98   Estimate between: **a.** 5 and 6   **b.** 6 and 7

Estimate the quotient. Write the two multiples of 10 the estimate is between.

12. 64)3425   **13.** 21)753   **14.** 59)944   **15.** 42)3214

16. 32)500   **17.** 39)1876   **18.** 41)4001   **19.** 34)480

20. 843 ÷ 22   **21.** 680 ÷ 26   **22.** 1763 ÷ 18   **23.** 753 ÷ 42

MATH LOG

How can estimating quotients help you divide?

USING STRATEGIES

COOPERATIVE • LEARNING

The Moon Valley Fruit Farm grows and sells strawberries. Some people buy the berries already picked. Some people pick their own berries.

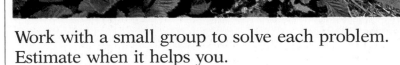

Moon Valley Fruit Farm			
OUR STRAWBERRIES ARE THE BERRY BEST!			
Container Size	Approximate number of strawberries in container	Cost per container	
		We pick	You pick
small	12	$0.95	$0.75
medium	24	$1.80	$1.50
large	48	$3.25	$2.75
giant	96	$5.75	$4.75

Work with a small group to solve each problem. Estimate when it helps you.

1. Andrew buys 1 container of each size already picked.

   a. About how many berries will he get?

   b. How much will that cost?

   c. Without picking them, how could Andrew have bought more berries for less money?

2. Joan wants to buy about 60 berries in containers.

   a. What are the different combinations of containers she can buy?

   b. Which of these will be cheapest?

3. Jamie picks enough berries to fill a large container. Is it more than or less than 5¢ a berry? HINT: Think of $2.75 as 275 cents.

4. One giant container has about as many berries as 2 large containers.

   a. Does a giant container cost more than or less than 2 large containers?

   b. Which container is the better buy?

5. Write which container is the better buy. Explain how you get each answer. HINT: Use the same method used in exercise 4.

   a. A medium container or a large container.

   b. A small container or a large container.

   c. A medium container you pick yourself or a large container already picked.

6. Ms. Sanchez buys 4 large containers and 4 giant containers of berries already picked.

   a. How much will that cost?

   b. How much would 1 large container and 1 giant container cost?

   c. Multiply your answer to part b by 4.

   d. Compare your answers to parts a and c. Which answer was easier to get?

7. Mr. Kowalski bought some small and some medium containers of berries already picked. He spent a total of $7.30. Figure out how many containers of each size he bought.

ONE-DIGIT QUOTIENTS

The table shows how many flowers the gardeners at the Dutch Treat Flower Farm cut on Monday. They want to separate the tulips into bunches of 24. How many bunches of tulips can they make? How many will be left over?

FLOWERS CUT ON MONDAY	
Type of Flower	**Number Cut**
carnation	190
daffodil	140
tulip	170

You can divide to find the number of bunches of tulips.

Divide: $170 \div 24 = \blacksquare$

It asks the same question as $24 \times \blacksquare = 170$.

● **Decide how many digits are in the quotient.**

$24 \times 1 = 24$

$\longleftarrow 170$

$24 \times 10 = 240$

So, the quotient has one digit.

● **Estimate.**

$$\begin{array}{cc} 24 & 24 \\ \times\ 7 & \times\ 8 \\ \hline 168 & 192 \end{array}$$

$168 \ \uparrow \ 192$

170

So, the quotient is between 7 and 8.

● **Write the ones. Multiply. Subtract. Is there a remainder?**

$$\begin{array}{r} 7\ \text{R2} \\ 24\overline{)170} \\ -168 \leftarrow 24 \times 7 \\ \hline 2 \end{array}$$

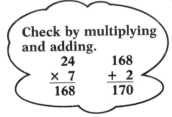

Check by multiplying and adding.

$$\begin{array}{cc} 24 & 168 \\ \times\ 7 & +\ 2 \\ \hline 168 & 170 \end{array}$$

The quotient with remainder is 7 R2.

They can make 7 bunches of tulips. There will be 2 tulips left over.

Think

• With a divisor of 24, could you have a remainder of 24? Explain your answer.

Estimate. Then divide.

1. $46\overline{)92}$ .2. $19\overline{)84}$ 3. $56\overline{)447}$ 4. $63\overline{)504}$

5. $53 \div 53$ 6. $73 \div 18$ 7. $210 \div 24$ 8. $182 \div 32$

Critical Thinking 9. What should you do if your remainder is larger than your divisor?

INDEPENDENT PRACTICE

Estimate. Then divide.

10. $38\overline{)87}$ 11. $14\overline{)56}$ 12. $22\overline{)96}$ 13. $49\overline{)95}$

14. $55\overline{)275}$ 15. $82\overline{)536}$ 16. $68\overline{)250}$ 17. $76\overline{)547}$

18. $25\overline{)50}$ 19. $25\overline{)75}$ 20. $25\overline{)150}$ 21. $25\overline{)225}$

22. $288 \div 72$ 23. $288 \div 36$ 24. $288 \div 48$ 25. $288 \div 32$

Problem Solving

26. Alex has 144 daffodil bulbs. Each box can hold 16 bulbs. How many boxes will he need?

27. The flower market sells 37 bunches of roses for a total of $353. Does each bunch of roses cost more than $10?

28. Ninety children visit the flower farm. Only 25 can go into the greenhouse at one time. How many groups will go into the greenhouse?

29. Gina has 300 bunches of daisies and 22 boxes. Each box holds 14 bunches. How many more bunches of daisies does Gina need to fill the 22 boxes?

Maintain • Multiplication

Write the product.

1. $\begin{array}{r} 35 \\ \times\ 18 \\ \hline \end{array}$ 2. $\begin{array}{r} 98 \\ \times\ 36 \\ \hline \end{array}$ 3. $\begin{array}{r} 491 \\ \times\ 50 \\ \hline \end{array}$ 4. $\begin{array}{r} 254 \\ \times\ 64 \\ \hline \end{array}$ 5. $\begin{array}{r} 762 \\ \times\ 82 \\ \hline \end{array}$

TWO-DIGIT QUOTIENTS

The Lowell basketball team played 21 games. They scored a total of 1365 points. What is the team's average number of points per game?

You can divide to find the average.
Divide: 1365 ÷ 21 = ■

It asks the same question as 21 × ■ = 1365.

● **Decide how many digits are in the quotient.**

$$21 × 10 = 210$$
$$\longleftarrow 1365$$
$$21 × 100 = 2100$$

So, the quotient has two digits.

● **To estimate, use multiples of 10.**

$$\begin{array}{cc} 21 & 21 \\ \times\ 60 & \times\ 70 \\ \hline 1260 & 1470 \end{array}$$
$$\uparrow$$
$$1365$$

So, the quotient is between 60 and 70.

Think

- How do you know where to place the first digit in the quotient?

● **Write the tens digit. Multiply. Subtract.**

$$\begin{array}{r} 6 \\ 21\overline{)1365} \\ -1260 \longleftarrow 21 × 60 \\ \hline 105 \end{array}$$

● **Write the ones digit. Multiply. Subtract. Is there a remainder?**

$$\begin{array}{r} 65 \\ 21\overline{)1365} \\ -1260 \\ \hline 105 \\ -105 \longleftarrow 21 × 5 \\ \hline 0 \end{array}$$

Check by multiplying.
$$\begin{array}{r} 65 \\ \times\ 21 \\ \hline 65 \\ 1300 \\ \hline 1365 \end{array}$$

The quotient is 65. The team's average is 65.

Other Examples

$$\begin{array}{r} 17 \\ 21\overline{)357} \\ -210 \\ \hline 147 \\ -147 \\ \hline 0 \end{array}$$

$$\begin{array}{r} 22\ \text{R20} \\ 34\overline{)768} \\ -680 \\ \hline 88 \\ -68 \\ \hline 20 \end{array}$$

GUIDED PRACTICE

Estimate. Then divide.

1. 14)1176   2. 43)2259   3. 27)2098   4. 45)1484

5. 1364 ÷ 31   6. 5149 ÷ 76   7. 2212 ÷ 82   8. 458 ÷ 36

Critical Thinking

9. Can the quotient of a 4-digit number divided by a 2-digit number ever be a 4-digit number? How do you know?

INDEPENDENT PRACTICE

Estimate. Then divide.

10. 24)52   11. 17)51   12. 19)152   13. 37)217

14. 42)966   15. 58)725   16. 29)938   17. 17)927

18. 25)325   19. 25)425   20. 25)525   21. 25)625

22. 98 ÷ 31   23. 462 ÷ 66   24. 404 ÷ 59   25. 739 ÷ 67

26. 360 ÷ 15   27. 360 ÷ 18   28. 360 ÷ 24   29. 360 ÷ 45

Problem Solving Use the data on page 406 to answer exercise 30.

30. The Lowell basketball team played its 22nd game. They won 50 to 45. Did the team's average number of points per game go up or down?

31. A basketball backboard set sells for $180 at Sue's Sporting Goods. Jill's parents will pay for half the set. Jill saves $15 a month. When can she buy the set?

Maintain • Mixed Practice

1.	2.	3.	4.	5.
46 − 29	245 + 96	856 − 648	5342 + 498	976 − 689

PROBLEM SOLVING
USING STRATEGIES

If you get stuck, remember....
Tips for Problem Solving
on pages 474–475

Gina makes cartoons. A cartoon is made up of single pictures called frames. When the frames are shown on a movie screen, the pictures seem to move.

One second of a cartoon contains 24 frames.

Gina is working on a cartoon called *Jumping Jack*. Help Gina by solving each problem.

1. In one scene, the character Jumping Jack bounces to the top of a building. The scene contains 480 frames. How long does the scene last?

2. Before Jumping Jack bounces, he does jumping jacks for 5 seconds. How many frames does that take?

3. It takes 6 frames to show one jumping jack. In the first frame of the scene, Jumping Jack is drawn in Position A. What is the letter of the position in which he is drawn in the
   a. sixth frame?
   b. seventh frame?
   c. ninth frame?
   d. fifteenth frame?
   e. twenty-fifth frame?

4. How many jumping jacks does Jumping Jack do in 1 second? REMEMBER: 24 frames is 1 second.

5. Can people do jumping jacks as fast as Jumping Jack? Try it. About how many jumping jacks can you do in a second?

408

SECTION REVIEW

for pages 398–408

Divide.

1. $180 \div 30$ 2. $320 \div 20$ 3. $612 \div 30$ 4. $463 \div 50$

5. $8000 \div 80$ 6. $2000 \div 40$ 7. $7200 \div 60$ 8. $707 \div 7$

Write the letter of the correct answer.

9. $73\overline{)231}$
   a. 3
   b. 4
   c. 3 R12
   d. 2 R85

10. $27\overline{)481}$
    a. 17 R22
    b. 18
    c. 16 R49
    d. 17

11. $25\overline{)462}$
    a. 17 R37
    b. 19
    c. 18
    d. 18 R12

12. $18\overline{)997}$
    a. 56
    b. 55 R7
    c. 55
    d. 54 R25

13. $17\overline{)549}$
    a. 335
    b. 30 R25
    c. 32 R5
    d. 326 R6

14. $36\overline{)870}$
    a. 24 R6
    b. 20 R46
    c. 222 R6
    d. 246

15. $14\overline{)635}$
    a. 441 R5
    b. 40 R55
    c. 4 R55
    d. 45 R5

16. $21\overline{)907}$
    a. 40 R34
    b. 43 R4
    c. 434
    d. 439 R4

17. $35\overline{)531}$
    a. 356
    b. 10 R56
    c. 15 R6
    d. 114 R6

18. $41\overline{)803}$
    a. 19 R24
    b. 20
    c. 18 R65
    d. 19

19. $14\overline{)389}$
    a. 27
    b. 27 R11
    c. 28
    d. 26 R25

20. $57\overline{)918}$
    a. 151 R6
    b. 166
    c. 10 R66
    d. 16 R6

Solve each problem.

21. Each pizza has 8 slices. Eight pizzas were ordered for the 23 children in Mr. Kent's class. Will there be enough pizza for each child to have 3 slices?

22. Mr. Kent wants 10 ounces of fruit punch for each of his 20 guests. How many cans does he need if each can contains 46 ounces?

USING DIVISION

Melanie needs to buy stationery and supplies for her stay at summer camp. Which box of envelopes would be a better buy?

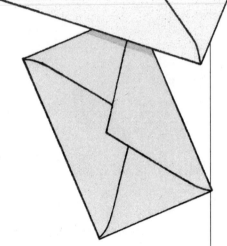

Each box contains a different amount of envelopes. You can divide to find the cost of one envelope in each box. Then you can compare to find the better buy.

Divide $3.99 by 36.

```
        $0.11
   36)$3.99
      -3 60  ← 36 × 10
         39
        -36  ← 36 × 1
          3
```

Divide $1.99 by 24.

```
        $0.08
   24)$1.99
      -1 92  ← 24 × 8
          7
```

The envelopes in the box of 36 cost about $0.11 each. The envelopes in the box of 24 cost about $0.08 each.

Since $0.11 is greater than $0.08, the box of 24 is the better buy.

- Do you need to consider the remainder to decide which box of envelopes is the better buy? Explain your answer.

- How could you decide the better buy without dividing?

Problem Solving

1. Todd is in charge of the day trip to Blueberry Island. There will be 59 campers on the trip and there are 13 rowboats. Can Todd put the same number of campers in each rowboat?

2. There will be 78 people at the camp chicken barbecue. If chicken pieces come 32 to a bag, how many bags should the cook order to have at least 4 pieces for each person?

Lauren wants to go to a summer camp. She shows her parents each of these ads to decide which camp to attend.

CAMP GRANADA

8 WEEKS OF FUN
3 PAYMENTS OF $399 EACH

Camp Paloma
Summer Session
July 5 to August 30
$999

3. How many weeks long is Camp Paloma's summer session? Use the calendars on the right to help you.

4. Which camp costs less money per week? How do you know?

JULY

Sun	Mon	Tues	Wed	Thurs	Fri	Sat
		1	2	3	4	5
6	7	8	9	10	11	12
13	14	15	16	17	18	19
20	21	22	23	24	25	26
27	28	29	30	31		

5. Lauren's parents are driving her to summer camp, which is 220 miles from home. A camper's welcome party begins at 3:00 P.M. Lauren's family leaves home at 10:30 A.M. They drive an average of 55 miles per hour, and stop once for 15 minutes. Will Lauren arrive at camp in time for the party? How early or late will she be?

AUGUST

Sun	Mon	Tues	Wed	Thurs	Fri	Sat
					1	2
3	4	5	6	7	8	9
10	11	12	13	14	15	16
17	18	19	20	21	22	23
24	25	26	27	28	29	30
31						

6. On the first day of camp, Lauren enters a relay race. Each runner on a team will run 2.5 kilometers. Lauren and 3 other runners are on one team. What is the total distance they will run?

USING DIVISION FOR AVERAGES

The Spartans just completed another basketball season. Tom has kept a graph of all their scoring. He wants to get an idea of the team's average number of points per game.

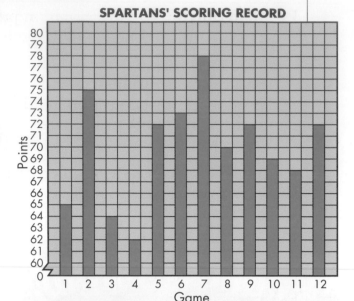

SPARTANS' SCORING RECORD

Think

- Could the average be more than 80? How do you know?

- Could it be less than 60? How do you know?

Tom estimates that the Spartans' point average was between 62 and 78 points a game. He calculates to find the exact average.

To find the average:

- Add the numbers.

- Divide by the number of addends.

Tom adds all of the scores and gets a sum of 840 total points scored. To find the average number of points per game, he divides the total points by the number of games played.

$$
\begin{array}{r}
70 \\
12\overline{)840} \\
-840 \quad \leftarrow 12 \times 70 \\
\hline
0
\end{array}
$$

The Spartans' average was 70 points a game.

Think

- Is Tom's answer reasonable? How do you know?

INDEPENDENT PRACTICE

Problem Solving Use the graph on page 412 to help solve problems 1–3. Remember some problems do not have enough information.

1. In how many games did the Spartans score above the team average?

2. In how many games did the Spartans score below the team average?

3. How many games did the Spartans win this season?

Use the chart to answer problems 4–8. You may want to use a calculator.

4. What was Sam's point average after the first 3 games? How did you get your answer?

5. Look at Sam's points for the fourth game. Without calculating, was his average for the first 4 games higher or lower than for the first 3 games? Estimate by how much. Then find the average.

6. Sam played in all 12 games. Was his point average for all 12 games between 10 and 20 points or between 20 and 30 points? How do you know?

SAM'S GAME POINTS			
Game	Points	Game	Points
1	24	7	24
2	24	8	0
3	24	9	12
4	20	10	20
5	21	11	18
6	23	12	18

7. What was Sam's point average for the 12 games?

8. Why might Sam have scored 0 points in game 8?

9. **Data Book** Go to the Almanac section on page 466. What was Julius Erving's yearly average for free throws?

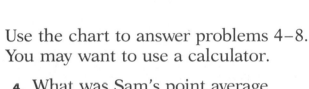

10. *Critical Thinking* Use the graph and the chart to write your own word problem. Give it to a friend to solve.

PROPLEM SOLVING
USING STRATEGIES

If you get stuck, remember....
Tips for Problem Solving
on pages 474–475

Solve each problem.

1. Warren Pizza Parlor has four toppings for their pizzas: mushrooms, sausage, onions, and peppers. They have a special today: any two toppings on a pizza for $2.50. How many different combinations of the two toppings are there?

2. It's a pizza war! Pepé's Pizza Parlor is battling Warren Pizza for customers. The owner of Pepé's Pizza offers four toppings too, but he decides to offer this special: any three toppings for $3.75. How many different three-topping combinations are there?

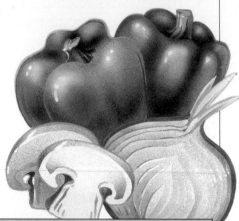

3. All of the music stores in the four towns around Elviston get their compact discs and tapes delivered by truck from Elviston. What is the shortest route the driver can take from Elviston to the four towns and back to Elviston?

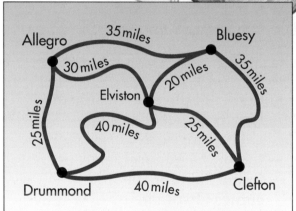

Allegro — 35 miles — Bluesy
30 miles
25 miles
Elviston
20 miles
35 miles
40 miles
25 miles
Drummond — 40 miles — Clefton

4. Cheryl found a smudged coded message. A key to the code was on a piece of torn paper. Figure out how the code works and use it to complete the message.

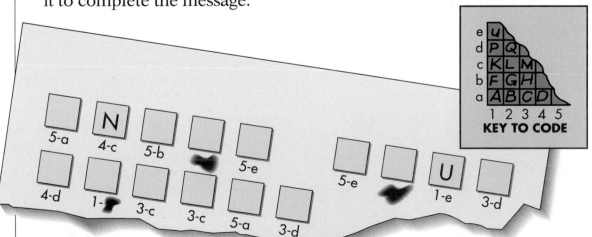

5-a | N 4-c | 5-b | | 5-e
4-d | 1- | 3-c | 3-c | 5-a | 3-d | 5-e | | U 1-e | 3-d

KEY TO CODE

e u
d P Q
c K L M
b F G H
a A B C D
  1 2 3 4 5
KEY TO CODE

SECTION REVIEW

for pages 410–414

Solve each problem.

1. Mindy worked 80 hours last month and received a check for $480. How much money does Mindy earn for an hour of work?

2. Decorations at the Holiday Company are packed 40 to the box. How many boxes will be needed to pack 3000 ornaments?

3. Carolyn decided to sell her collages at a crafts fair for $12. How many collages does she need to make $500?

4. Cindy is making bunches of cut roses to sell at her parents' store. How many bunches of 12 can she make from 750 roses?

5. The cut roses first come in boxes of 50. If Cindy decides that she wants 1200 roses, how many boxes should she order?

6. There are 192 people who want to be in Alice's play. They will try out in groups of 16. How many groups will there be?

7. Nine performances were given of Alice's play. The theater can hold 100 people. On 3 of the nights, the play was sold out. On the other 6 nights, there were 9 empty seats each night. What was the total number of people attending the 9 performances?

8. The total amount of money made at the box office for 9 nights was $6345. On the average, how much money was made each night?

9. Philip spent $16 on his costume, while the other 4 members of the cast each spent twice that amount. What was the total amount spent on costumes by the cast?

10. On week nights, the play began at 7:00 P.M. and ended at 9:30 P.M. On weekends, it began at 7:30 P.M. and ended at 10:00 P.M. What was the average length of time of each performance?

CHAPTER TEST

Divide.

1. $37\overline{)357}$
2. $29\overline{)77}$
3. $17\overline{)828}$
4. $22\overline{)154}$

5. $31\overline{)99}$
6. $49\overline{)804}$
7. $67\overline{)262}$
8. $25\overline{)775}$

9. $32\overline{)69}$
10. $11\overline{)944}$
11. $14\overline{)56}$
12. $18\overline{)990}$

13. $567 \div 63$
14. $895 \div 51$
15. $247 \div 19$
16. $85 \div 17$

17. $462 \div 77$
18. $918 \div 23$
19. $726 \div 33$
20. $197 \div 40$

21. $713 \div 31$
22. $475 \div 25$
23. $663 \div 26$
24. $90 \div 18$

Write the average of each set of numbers.

25. $19, $38, $7, $15, $16

26. $74, $75, $62, $51

27. 142, 99, 56, 108, 65, 46, 88, 93, 140

28. 600, 513, 991, 1000, 711, 485, 838

PROBLEM SOLVING

Solve each problem.

29. The fourth grade gave concerts last week. On Wednesday night, 93 people attended. On Thursday night, 81 people attended. A total of 210 people attended on Friday and Saturday nights. What was the average number of people attending each performance?

30. One fourth-grade class decides to sell bunches of flowers at each school concert to raise money for the school band. The children include a dozen flowers in each bunch. How many whole bunches can be made from 500 flowers?

31. The 87 fourth-graders at the Pinewood School are chipping in to buy the school a computer that costs $348. How much will each student's share be?

32. One teacher orders 8 bags of apples for the 35 children in the class. Each bag has 8 apples in it. Will there be enough for each child to have 2 apples?

CUMULATIVE REVIEW

Solve each problem.

1. Emma arrives at soccer tryouts at 1:45 P.M. She is called to play at 2:05 P.M. Did Emma wait more than half an hour to be called to play? How do you know?

2. Baseball tryouts begin at 9:15 A.M. and are supposed to last 4 hours. They end at 2:00 P.M. Did the tryouts last longer than they were supposed to? How do you know?

Write the numbers in order from least to greatest.

3. 2.0; 2.01; 2.1

4. 15.51; 15.41; 15.5

5. 3.45; 3.2; 3.5

6. 8.4; 8.04; 8.06

7. 0.68; 0.6; 0.8

8. 36.6; 3.66; 3.6

Write the sum.

9.
```
  56.17
+ 19.3
```

10.
```
  84.8
  21.79
+  6.1
```

11.
```
   0.2
  10.38
+  9
```

12.
```
  40.51
  77.4
+  3.09
```

13. 24.63 + 4.6 + 31.7

14. 17.9 + 2.85 + 31.77

Write the difference.

15.
```
  74.55
- 30.23
```

16.
```
  0.72
- 0.48
```

17.
```
  21.8
-  4
```

18.
```
  37.52
-  6
```

19.
```
  85
-  9.7
```

20. 6.3 − 4.29

21. 18 − 0.81

22. 32.54 − 3.77

Write the product.

23.
```
   423
×   43
```

24.
```
   659
×   20
```

25.
```
   453
×   42
```

26.
```
  $8.56
×    19
```

27.
```
  $4.25
×    76
```

28. 43 × 717

29. 26 × $5.05

30. 39 × $7.55

31. 4 × 7 × 9

32. 8 × 18 × 20

33. 49 × 9 × 26

EXCURSION

CULTURAL DIVERSITY

BETTER BUY

When you look for the better buy, you need to be able to find the **unit price** of an item. Figuring out the unit price is especially important when you have many tempting choices, as the shoppers do in this *mercado* (mare-kah-doe), or market, in San Antonio, Texas.

One Saturday, Carmen goes to the *mercado* with her grandfather. There she finds one of her favorite foods—tamales (tah-mah-lays) filled with meat and spices. Look at the two packages of tamales at the right. Which one is the better buy?

▶ To find the unit price for the tamales, divide the total cost by the number of items in each bag.

0.5

Each tamale costs $0.50.

0.63

Each tamale costs $0.63.

▶ So, 20 tamales for $10.00 is the better buy.

Many items are sold by weight. To find the unit price for an 8-pound bag of *papas*, or potatoes, divide the total cost by the number of pounds in the bag.

0.36

So, the unit price is $0.36 per pound for an 8-pound bag.

Use a calculator. Find unit prices or use other strategies. Write the better buy.

1.

3 lb for $1.20   5 lb for $1.90

2.

16 oz for $0.59   10 lb for $4.40

3.

8 for $14.24   5 for $9.75

4.

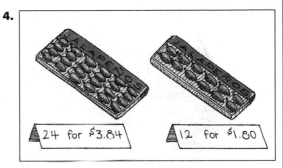

24 for $3.84   12 for $1.80

5.

5 lb for $3.70   3 lb for $2.52

6.

3 for $0.96   6 for $1.80

7. A pound of *queso* (cheese) for $1.59, or 8 ounces for $0.85?

8. Two mangoes for $1.98, or 3 mangoes for $2.89?

9. Two pounds of tomatillos for $0.78, or 3 pounds for $1.65?

10. A quart of *leche* (milk) for $1.09 or a half-gallon for $1.99?

11. Suppose you find pineapples at two shops. One shop sells them at $0.30 per pound. The other shop sells pineapples for $1.25 each. What information do you need to find the better buy?

12. Look at the pattern in the unit price throughout this lesson. Is the unit price usually more or less for larger packages of the same item?

More Practice

SET 1.3, USE WITH PAGES 6–7.

Write the answer.

1. 9 + 2   2. 6 + 8   3. 7 + 7   4. 5 + 9

5. 18 − 6   6. 22 − 11   7. 15 − 5   8. 9 − 6

9. 70 + 20 + 10   10. 15,000 − 5000   11. 600 + 800

12. 130 − 60   13. 9000 + 9000   14. 1200 − 800

SET 1.5, USE WITH PAGES 10–11.

Write in standard form.

1. three thousand, ten   2. 7000 + 500 + 40 + 7

3. four hundred twenty-five   4. 1000 + 600 + 9

Write in words.

5. 450   6. 500   7. 6910   8. 8322   9. 1244

Write the value of the blue digit.

10. 531   11. 2009   12. 3294   13. 9326   14. 5639

SET 1.6, USE WITH PAGES 12–13.

Write the number that is halfway between each
pair of numbers.

1. 10, 30   2. 140, 180   3. 600, 800   4. 1000, 2000

Write the number you estimate the arrow is
pointing to.

5.
6.

SET 1.9, USE WITH PAGES 18–19.

Write in standard form.

1. five hundred three thousand, sixty-one

2. nine hundred fifty-two thousand

3. six hundred thousand, seven

4. eighty-two thousand, twenty-nine

5. fifty thousand, one hundred five

6. one hundred thousand, seven hundred

7. three hundred thousand, forty-six

Write in words.

8. 871,072   9. 500,120   10. 120,000

Write the value of the blue digit.

11. 799,031   12. 609,414   13. 253,119   14. 716,947,513

SET 1.11, USE WITH PAGES 22–23.

Round to the nearest ten.

1. 24   2. 61   3. 78   4. 57   5. 46
6. 44   7. 88   8. 16   9. 32   10. 93

Round to the nearest hundred.

11. 360   12. 874   13. 201   14. 619   15. 849
16. 178   17. 243   18. 514   19. 790   20. 496
21. 923   22. 371   23. 622   24. 488   25. 146

Round to the nearest thousand.

26. 6511   27. 8930   28. 4299   29. 1999   30. 3299
31. 2978   32. 5489   33. 7216   34. 9160   35. 6349

SET 1.12, USE WITH PAGES 24–25.

Write < or >.

1. 4329 ● 4339

2. 3566 ● 1566

3. 1763 ● 763

4. 9319 ● 7913

5. 9376 ● 4376

6. 7701 ● 7710

7. 2894 ● 2904

8. 7616 ● 7606

Write the numbers in order from least to greatest.

9. 27,321; 67,100; 7672

10. 11,004; 8999; 10,004

11. 34,681; 3468; 43,681

12. 9807; 78,090; 4567

13. 29,061; 48,065; 2940

14. 33,471; 23,681; 54,970

SET 1.13, USE WITH PAGES 26–27.

Write the amount of money.

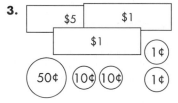

Find the pattern. Write the next three numbers.

4. 25¢, 35¢, 45¢, ▓, ▓, ▓

5. $13, $15, $17, ▓, ▓, ▓

6. $3.10, $3.20, $3.30, ▓, ▓, ▓

7. 10¢, 15¢, 20¢, 25¢, ▓, ▓, ▓

Write the amount, using the dollar sign and decimal point.

8. one dime more than twelve dollars

9. ten dollars less than eighty dollars and fifty cents

10. two nickels more than three quarters

SET 1.15, USE WITH PAGES 30–31.

Write the least number of bills and coins you would receive as change.

1. Cost of item: $0.79
   Amount given: $1.00

2. Cost of item: $4.43
   Amount given: $10.00

3. Cost of item: $13.03
   Amount given: $20.00

4. Cost of item: $12.85
   Amount given: $15.00

5. Cost of item: $1.19
   Amount given: $1.25

6. Cost of item: $18.98
   Amount given: $20.00

7. Cost of item: $0.51
   Amount given: $1.01

8. Cost of item: $21.70
   Amount given: $30.00

9. Cost of item: $36.10
   Amount given: $40.10

10. Cost of item: $4.51
    Amount given: $5.00

11. Cost of item: $89.01
    Amount given: $100.01

12. Cost of item: $0.58
    Amount given: $1.00

13. Cost of item: $44.95
    Amount given: $50.00

14. Cost of item: $9.01
    Amount given: $20.00

15. Cost of item: $3.67
    Amount given: $5.00

SET 1.16, USE WITH PAGES 32–33.

Write the least number of pennies you could have.

1. $1.14
2. $6.56
3. $0.68

4. $0.79
5. $1.24
6. $2.32

7. $3.87
8. $1.98
9. $0.99

10. $1.51
11. $4.44
12. $0.91

13. $5.66
14. $2.72
15. $3.53

Exchange each amount to get as many quarters as you can. Write the number of quarters.

16. 100 pennies
17. 75 dimes
18. 100 nickels

19. $2.25
20. $4.75
21. $3.00

22. $1.50
23. $5.50
24. $6.25

25. $3.25
26. $2.00
27. $1.75

28. $6.00
29. $7.75
30. $4.25

SET 2.1, USE WITH PAGES 42–43.

Copy and complete.

1. $32 + 15 = \blacksquare + 32$

2. $27 + (51 + 49) = (\blacksquare + 51) + 49$

3. $322 - 0 = \blacksquare$

4. $17 - \blacksquare = 0$

5. $(\blacksquare + 500) + 9 = 64 + (500 + 9)$

6. $787 + \blacksquare = 787$

7. $92 + \blacksquare = 7 + 92$

8. $\blacksquare + 55 = 55 + 182$

9. $\blacksquare - 0 = 721$

10. $\blacksquare + 0 = 904$

11. $\blacksquare + 0 = 0 + 45$

12. $0 + 430 = \blacksquare$

13. $32 + 8 + 94 + 6 = (32 + \blacksquare) + (94 + 6)$

14. $(140 + \blacksquare) + 19 = 140 + (11 + 19)$

SET 2.2, USE WITH PAGES 44–45.

Write the answer. Use mental math.

1. $17 + 4$
2. $4 + 57$
3. $5 + 48$
4. $98 + 3$
5. $27 + 8$
6. $63 + 5$
7. $45 + 6$
8. $51 + 9$
9. $34 - 5$
10. $25 - 7$
11. $42 - 3$
12. $65 - 8$
13. $75 - 7$
14. $56 - 6$
15. $38 - 7$
16. $72 - 4$
17. $32 + 9$
18. $84 - 5$
19. $19 + 9$
20. $41 - 4$

SET 2.3, USE WITH PAGES 46–47.

Write the sum. Use mental math.

1. $65 + 10$
2. $30 + 75$
3. $25 + 45$
4. $55 + 55$
5. $225 + 225$
6. $650 + 250$
7. $305 + 125$
8. $415 + 115$
9. $2000 + 3500$
10. $1500 + 1500$
11. $2050 + 3050$
12. $4500 + 2500$
13. $15 + 20 + 25$
14. $30 + 65 + 5$
15. $10 + 45 + 55$
16. $13 + 12 + 19$
17. $88 + 80 + 82$
18. $28 + 25 + 30$

SET 2.5, USE WITH PAGES 50–51.

1. List three number pairs in the box with sums of about 100.

82		56	
	23		31
48		67	

2. List three number pairs in the box with sums of about 1000.

311		240	
	715		688
456		542	

SET 2.6, USE WITH PAGES 52–53.

Write the sum.

1.
$$93 + 893$$

2.
$$56 + 33$$

3.
$$\$0.63 + 0.93$$

4.
$$81 + 64$$

5.
$$\$0.99 + 5.50$$

6.
$$\$8.60 + 5.09$$

7.
$$66 + 919$$

8.
$$568 + 47$$

9.
$$\$0.98 + 6.11$$

10.
$$344 + 23$$

11.
$$839 + 852$$

12.
$$72 + 698$$

13.
$$\$9.83 + 8.93$$

14.
$$\$6.09 + 2.75$$

15.
$$167 + 888$$

SET 2.7, USE WITH PAGES 54–55.

Write the sum.

1.
$$808 + 255 + 551$$

2.
$$\$60.22 + 7.56 + 46.69$$

3.
$$365 + 9961 + 1320$$

4.
$$895 + 491 + 471$$

5.
$$8013 + 840 + 845$$

6.
$$\$0.94 + 0.47 + 0.27 + 0.10$$

7.
$$7569 + 96 + 2184 + 291$$

8.
$$5119 + 7880 + 9258 + 8066$$

9.
$$918 + 7341 + 644 + 32$$

10.
$$\$8.18 + 5.46 + 9.87 + 8.11$$

11. $58 + 47 + 40 + 65 + 71$

12. $\$0.53 + \$0.33 + \$0.45 + \$0.36 + \$0.14$

13. $\$0.16 + \$0.95 + \$0.63 + \$0.89 + \$0.42$

14. $15 + 20 + 16 + 59 + 68$

SET 2.8, USE WITH PAGE 56.

Estimate by rounding to the greatest place.

1. 29 + 53   **2.** 12 + 37   **3.** 19 + 38   **4.** $0.41 + $0.93

5. 282 + 197   **6.** 912 + 320   **7.** 693 + 196   **8.** 621 + 702

9. $1.12 + $3.98   **10.** $4.87 + $1.90   **11.** $0.68 + $0.24   **12.** $8.08 + $0.93

13. 1384 + 1202 + 2009   **14.** 2519 + 1003 + 4988   **15.** 1481 + 1510 + 5990

16. 1103 + 2009 + 1990   **17.** 4500 + 1010 + 5101   **18.** 1786 + 1209 + 1592

Estimate by making a front-end estimate or by rounding.

19. 521 + 304   **20.** 781 + 392   **21.** 279 + 430

22. 677 + 118 + 288   **23.** 813 + 833 + 198   **24.** 321 + 490 + 101

25. $1.01 + $0.21 + $0.98   **26.** $2.10 + $0.12 + $2.86   **27.** $0.79 + $0.89

28. 231 + 321   **29.** $89.01 + $27.95   **30.** $0.58 + $1.65

31. 44 + 95   **32.** 230 + 167 + 123   **33.** $9.02 + $1.99

34. $44.95 + $28.09   **35.** 23 + 89 + 17   **36.** 977 + 355

SET 2.9, USE WITH PAGES 58–59.

Estimate. Use the method you like best.

	1. 787 − 592	**2.** 512 − 288	**3.** 410 − 108	**4.** 691 − 294	**5.** 996 − 389
	6. $12.04 − 10.06	**7.** $7.10 − 2.84	**8.** $9.09 − 4.86	**9.** $6.12 − 4.98	**10.** $25.94 − 21.11
	11. 14,902 − 12,888	**12.** 35,673 − 11,124	**13.** 41,109 − 37,321	**14.** 28,684 − 19,694	**15.** 33,512 − 14,779

SET 2.10, USE WITH PAGES 60-61.

Write the difference.

1. $\begin{array}{r} 39 \\ -16 \end{array}$
2. $\begin{array}{r} 99 \\ -47 \end{array}$
3. $\begin{array}{r} 62 \\ -21 \end{array}$
4. $\begin{array}{r} \$8.58 \\ -0.16 \end{array}$
5. $\begin{array}{r} \$1.55 \\ -0.49 \end{array}$

6. $\begin{array}{r} 747 \\ -76 \end{array}$
7. $\begin{array}{r} \$7.87 \\ -0.78 \end{array}$
8. $\begin{array}{r} 779 \\ -388 \end{array}$
9. $\begin{array}{r} 499 \\ -82 \end{array}$
10. $\begin{array}{r} \$9.27 \\ -7.89 \end{array}$

11. $\begin{array}{r} \$7.24 \\ -3.42 \end{array}$
12. $\begin{array}{r} 824 \\ -49 \end{array}$
13. $\begin{array}{r} \$92.67 \\ -43.10 \end{array}$
14. $\begin{array}{r} \$88.16 \\ -30.31 \end{array}$
15. $\begin{array}{r} 6246 \\ -2989 \end{array}$

16. $\begin{array}{r} 4331 \\ -2297 \end{array}$
17. $\begin{array}{r} 6543 \\ -2651 \end{array}$
18. $\begin{array}{r} \$31.44 \\ -16.55 \end{array}$
19. $\begin{array}{r} \$78.78 \\ -19.95 \end{array}$
20. $\begin{array}{r} 4321 \\ -1234 \end{array}$

21. 6721 − 3004
22. 3985 − 492
23. $84.11 − $29.07

24. $35.52 − $16.99
25. 4226 − 3151
26. 7652 − 3877

SET 2.12, USE WITH PAGES 64-65.

Write the difference.

1. $\begin{array}{r} 470 \\ -39 \end{array}$
2. $\begin{array}{r} 607 \\ -24 \end{array}$
3. $\begin{array}{r} 580 \\ -229 \end{array}$
4. $\begin{array}{r} \$3.05 \\ -1.64 \end{array}$
5. $\begin{array}{r} \$8.20 \\ -1.76 \end{array}$

6. $\begin{array}{r} 505 \\ -329 \end{array}$
7. $\begin{array}{r} 700 \\ -429 \end{array}$
8. $\begin{array}{r} 6530 \\ 419 \end{array}$
9. $\begin{array}{r} 8301 \\ -650 \end{array}$
10. $\begin{array}{r} \$50.50 \\ -3.72 \end{array}$

11. $\begin{array}{r} 6009 \\ -3665 \end{array}$
12. $\begin{array}{r} 4072 \\ -1154 \end{array}$
13. $\begin{array}{r} 4660 \\ -297 \end{array}$
14. $\begin{array}{r} \$70.06 \\ -55.55 \end{array}$
15. $\begin{array}{r} \$80.00 \\ -32.22 \end{array}$

16. $\begin{array}{r} 9260 \\ -8195 \end{array}$
17. $\begin{array}{r} \$94.83 \\ -10.29 \end{array}$
18. $\begin{array}{r} \$865.60 \\ -58.99 \end{array}$
19. $\begin{array}{r} 60,700 \\ -120 \end{array}$
20. $\begin{array}{r} 52,307 \\ -243 \end{array}$

21. $4.10 − $2.56
22. 2070 − 853
23. 6470 − 350

24. 150 − 42
25. 33,800 − 2319
26. $59.60 − $2.27

Write the answer.

1. 9,388 + 48,054	**2.** $73.09 + 78.52	**3.** 4215 + 9093	**4.** 9,975 + 14,034	**5.** $58.83 + 423.69
6. $396.37 − 30.55	**7.** 7065 − 3526	**8.** 4328 − 3782	**9.** 4957 − 3640	**10.** 20,125 − 9,268

11. 1397 − 776

12. $633.22 − $522.84

13. $968.44 − $283.99

14. $40.37 + $83.96

15. 90,450 + 84,090

16. 20,040 + 6,831

Copy the chart. Use the data to complete it.

1.

Students' Favorite Sport		
Sport	**Tally**	**Total**
baseball	////	4

DATA: STUDENTS' FAVORITE SPORT;
baseball—Phil, Patrice, Alex, Marie;
soccer—Matt, Nancy, Jason; swimming—
Larry, Kim; football—Barbara, Jim,
Leonard, Stacey, Kyle

2. What is the least popular sport among students?

3. How many students listed football as their favorite sport?

SET 3.2, USE WITH PAGES 78–79.

Copy and complete the table and bar graph.

1.
**Bundles of Magazines Collected
for Recycling Project**

Class	Tally	Total
Ms. Greene's	~~JHT~~ ~~JHT~~	10
Mr. Kiley's	~~JHT~~	
Ms. Romero's	~~JHT~~ ~~JHT~~	
Mr. Stein's	~~JHT~~ ~~JHT~~ ~~JHT~~	

2.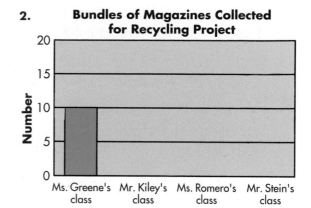
**Bundles of Magazines Collected
for Recycling Project**

3. Which class collected the most bundles?

4. Which class or classes collected 10 bundles?

SET 3.4, USE WITH PAGES 82–83.

Use the pictograph to answer each question.

1. How many bicycles were sold in the first week?

2. Were more than 100 bicycles sold during the month?

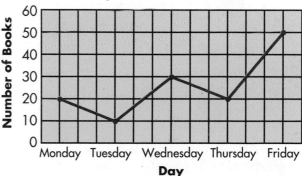

Monthly Bicycle Sales

KEY: = 10 bicycles = 5 bicycles

SET 3.5, USE WITH PAGES 84–85.

Daily Sales at Warren Books

Answer each question.

1. On which day were sales lowest?

2. On which two days did the store sell the same number of books?

3. How many more books were sold on Wednesday than on Tuesday?

4. On which days during the week did sales go above 20?

SET 3.6, USE WITH PAGES 86–87.

Use the circle graph to answer each question.

1. How many students were interviewed for the graph?

2. What fraction of the students do not visit friends?

3. Do more students watch television or help around the house?

4. What is the least popular activity on Saturday morning?

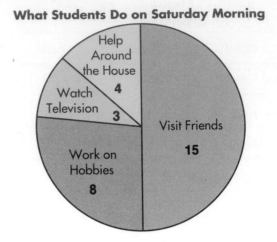

What Students Do on Saturday Morning

Help Around the House **4**

Watch Television **3**

Work on Hobbies **8**

Visit Friends **15**

SET 3.7, USE WITH PAGES 88–89.

Use the graphs to answer each question.

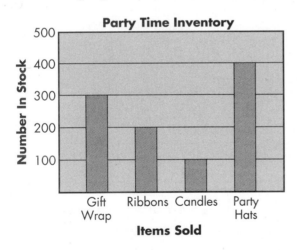

Party Time Inventory

Number In Stock

500, 400, 300, 200, 100

Gift Wrap, Ribbons, Candles, Party Hats

Items Sold

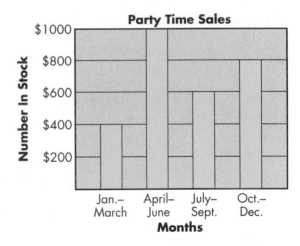

Party Time Sales

Number In Stock

$1000, $800, $600, $400, $200

Jan.–March, April–June, July–Sept., Oct.–Dec.

Months

1. When were Party Time sales the highest?

2. When were Party Time sales $800 or more?

3. How many ribbons are in stock?

4. Which item does Party Time have the least number of in stock?

5. How much greater were sales from October to December than from January to March?

6. How many more party hats than candles are in stock?

SET 3.10, USE WITH PAGES 94–95.

Use the picture to answer each question.

1. What are the chances of picking a red marble from the jar?

2. What are the chances of picking a blue marble?

3. The chances of picking a green marble are the same as the chances of picking what other marble?

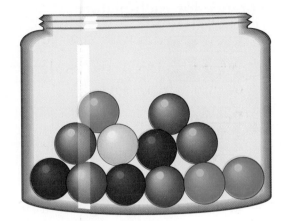

SET 3.13, USE WITH PAGE 100.

Write the answer. Use mental math.

1. 22 + 29	2. 18 + 19	3. 65 + 39
4. 47 + 49	5. 12 + 59	6. 26 + 99
7. 44 + 69	8. 36 + 79	9. 77 + 9
10. 63 + 89	11. 58 + 19	12. 83 + 9
13. 33 + 49	14. 39 + 39	15. 71 + 29
16. 12 + 9	17. 49 + 29	18. 54 + 39
19. 49 + 49	20. 28 + 19	21. 57 − 19
22. 41 − 9	23. 38 − 29	24. 33 − 19
25. 65 − 39	26. 98 − 79	27. 76 − 19
28. 55 − 39	29. 88 − 69	30. 27 − 19
31. 66 − 9	32. 44 − 29	33. 72 − 59
34. 23 − 9	35. 82 − 49	36. 52 − 29
37. 36 − 19	38. 84 − 49	39. 63 − 39
40. 77 − 59	41. 25 − 19	42. 58 − 9
43. 64 − 29	44. 32 − 19	45. 86 − 49

SET 4.1, USE WITH PAGES 108–109.

Write an addition sentence and a multiplication sentence for each picture.

1.
2.
3.
4.
5.
6.

SET 4.2, USE WITH PAGES 110–111.

Write the product.

1.	2.	3.	4.	5.	6.	7.
5×9	10×2	7×5	3×5	8×10	7×10	5×2

8. 4×5
9. 10×1
10. 5×0
11. 9×10

12. 0×10
13. 10×5
14. 8×5
15. 3×10

16. 1×5
17. 5×5
18. 10×4
19. 10×10

SET 4.3, USE WITH PAGES 112–113.

Write a division sentence for each multiplication sentence.

1. $8 \times 2 = 16$
2. $12 \times 3 = 36$
3. $4 \times 8 = 32$
4. $3 \times 5 = 15$

5. $6 \times 7 = 42$
6. $2 \times 10 = 20$
7. $6 \times 3 = 18$
8. $9 \times 4 = 36$

9. $7 \times 2 = 14$
10. $9 \times 2 = 18$
11. $5 \times 4 = 20$
12. $8 \times 5 = 40$

Divide. Use a related multiplication fact to help you.

13. $12 \div 3$
14. $33 \div 11$
15. $42 \div 6$
16. $30 \div 5$

17. $40 \div 4$
18. $50 \div 10$
19. $28 \div 7$
20. $36 \div 3$

21. $24 \div 6$
22. $14 \div 2$
23. $35 \div 5$
24. $18 \div 9$

SET 4.4, USE WITH PAGES 114–115.

Write the quotient.

1. $5\overline{)30}$ 2. $5\overline{)20}$ 3. $10\overline{)80}$ 4. $5\overline{)15}$ 5. $10\overline{)20}$

6. $45 \div 5$ 7. $70 \div 10$ 8. $100 \div 10$ 9. $35 \div 5$ 10. $50 \div 10$

11. $50 \div 5$ 12. $40 \div 5$ 13. $10 \div 10$ 14. $10 \div 5$ 15. $30 \div 10$

16. $5\overline{)5}$ 17. $10\overline{)40}$ 18. $10\overline{)60}$ 19. $5\overline{)25}$ 20. $10\overline{)90}$

SET 4.5, USE WITH PAGES 116–117.

Copy and complete the number sentence.

1. $23 \times 8 = \blacksquare \times 23$

2. $344 \times 0 = \blacksquare$

3. $1898 \times \blacksquare = 1898$

4. $5 \times (\blacksquare \times 9) = 9 \times (5 \times 3)$

5. $\blacksquare \times 348 = 348 \times 45$

6. $\blacksquare \times 1492 = 0$

7. $1 \times 700 = \blacksquare$

8. $12 \times (4 \times 2) = \blacksquare \times (2 \times 12)$

9. $63 \times 24 \times 12 = 12 \times \blacksquare \times 24$

10. $\blacksquare \times 1 = 83$

11. $16 \div 16 = \blacksquare$

12. $\blacksquare \div 412 = 0$

13. $0 \div 420 = \blacksquare$

14. $819 \div \blacksquare = 819$

15. $758 \div \blacksquare = 758$

16. $\blacksquare \div 360 = 1$

17. $\blacksquare \div 280 = 0$

18. $\blacksquare \div 126 = 0$

19. $50 \div 50 = \blacksquare$

20. $75 \div \blacksquare = 1$

21. $\blacksquare \times 3 \times 14 = 3 \times 60 \times 14$

22. $778 \times 0 = \blacksquare$

23. $\blacksquare \times 1 = 45$

24. $(4 \times 8) \times 10 = 4 \times (10 \times \blacksquare)$

25. $315 \div \blacksquare = 315$

26. $0 \div 585 = \blacksquare$

27. $754 \div 754 = \blacksquare$

28. $62 \times \blacksquare = 8 \times 62$

SET 4.7, USE WITH PAGE 120.

Write the answer.

1. $\begin{array}{r} 80 \\ -\ 40 \\ \hline \end{array}$	2. $\begin{array}{r} 428 \\ -\ 319 \\ \hline \end{array}$	3. $\begin{array}{r} 68 \\ +\ 4 \\ \hline \end{array}$	4. $\begin{array}{r} 221 \\ -\ 8 \\ \hline \end{array}$	5. $\begin{array}{r} 23 \\ 42 \\ +\ 12 \\ \hline \end{array}$
6. $\begin{array}{r} \$4.10 \\ +\ \$0.89 \\ \hline \end{array}$	7. $\begin{array}{r} 73 \\ -\ 18 \\ \hline \end{array}$	8. $\begin{array}{r} 913 \\ -\ 111 \\ \hline \end{array}$	9. $\begin{array}{r} 47 \\ +\ 55 \\ \hline \end{array}$	10. $\begin{array}{r} 675 \\ -\ 119 \\ \hline \end{array}$

SET 4.8, USE WITH PAGES 122–123.

Write the product.

1. 8×5	2. 3×4	3. 7×4	4. 9×2
5. 2×2	6. 4×2	7. 8×6	8. 8×3
9. 7×8	10. 2×1	11. 9×2	12. 6×4
13. 8×8	14. 6×2	15. 10×4	16. 4×1
17. 7×2	18. 8×10	19. 4×8	20. 2×5
21. 8×2	22. 5×4	23. 2×3	24. 4×9
25. 4×4	26. 8×1	27. 10×2	28. 9×8

SET 4.9, USE WITH PAGES 124–125.

Write the quotient.

1. $2\overline{)12}$	2. $4\overline{)8}$	3. $2\overline{)16}$	4. $8\overline{)72}$
5. $4\overline{)24}$	6. $2\overline{)14}$	7. $8\overline{)32}$	8. $2\overline{)8}$
9. $18 \div 2$	10. $20 \div 4$	11. $28 \div 4$	12. $56 \div 8$
13. $16 \div 4$	14. $4 \div 2$	15. $32 \div 4$	16. $10 \div 2$
17. $8\overline{)24}$	18. $8\overline{)40}$	19. $8\overline{)64}$	20. $8\overline{)8}$
21. $36 \div 4$	22. $2 \div 2$	23. $16 \div 8$	24. $4 \div 4$

SET 4.11, USE WITH PAGES 128–129.

Write the answer.

1. 6×7
2. $12 \div 6$
3. 3×6
4. $18 \div 3$
5. $42 \div 6$
6. 6×10
7. 5×3
8. $21 \div 3$
9. 1×6
10. 9×6
11. $24 \div 3$
12. $6 \div 3$
13. 5×6
14. 10×3
15. 3×7
16. $6 \div 6$
17. 6×4
18. $15 \div 3$
19. $27 \div 3$
20. 6×6
21. $30 \div 6$
22. 3×2
23. $54 \div 6$
24. $12 \div 3$
25. 8×3
26. $24 \div 6$
27. 3×3
28. $36 \div 6$
29. $3 \div 3$
30. $48 \div 6$
31. 3×4
32. 6×2
33. $60 \div 10$

SET 4.12, USE WITH PAGES 130–131.

Write the answer.

1. 4×7
2. $42 \div 7$
3. $9 \div 9$
4. $56 \div 7$
5. 10×9
6. 7×7
7. $7 \div 7$
8. 10×7
9. $45 \div 9$
10. $14 \div 7$
11. $18 \div 9$
12. 9×9
13. $35 \div 7$
14. 9×7
15. $49 \div 7$
16. 2×7
17. 5×7
18. 2×9
19. $63 \div 9$
20. $21 \div 7$
21. $72 \div 9$
22. 3×7
23. 6×9
24. $81 \div 9$
25. 9×5
26. 3×9
27. 8×7
28. $28 \div 7$
29. $27 \div 9$
30. 8×9
31. $36 \div 9$
32. 6×7
33. $90 \div 9$

SET 4.17, USE WITH PAGES 140–141.

Write the quotient.

1. $1000 \div 10$ 2. $240 \div 6$ 3. $5000 \div 5$

4. $160 \div 2$ 5. $3200 \div 8$ 6. $10,000 \div 2$

7. $360 \div 9$ 8. $2000 \div 4$ 9. $990 \div 3$

10. $1600 \div 8$ 11. $450 \div 5$ 12. $210 \div 7$

13. $28,000 \div 7$ 14. $8800 \div 4$ 15. $6000 \div 3$

Write the answer.

16. 8×20 17. $120 \div 3$ 18. 3×900

19. $2220 \div 2$ 20. 4×6000 21. $810 \div 9$

22. 2×80 23. $1400 \div 7$ 24. 5×500

25. $630 \div 3$ 26. 100×6 27. $12,000 \div 6$

28. 70×7 29. $1500 \div 5$ 30. 9×7000

SET 4.18, USE WITH PAGE 142.

Use the data to make a line plot. Then use the
line plot to solve each problem.

Number of Pets		
Tina 3	Trevor 4	Luis 0
Bev 2	Jim 1	Becky 3
Bill 0	Sandy 3	Rob 1

1. How many students do not have
   a pet?

2. Do more students have 1 pet or
   2 pets?

3. What is the greatest number of
   pets that a student has?

4. How many more students have 3
   pets than 1 pet?

SET 5.3, USE WITH PAGES 154–155.

Tell which of these are right angles.

1.   2.    3.   4.

5.   6. 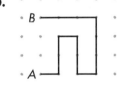   7. 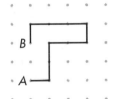   8.

Tell how many right angles appear along the path from
A to *B* in each drawing.

9.    10.

SET 5.6, USE WITH PAGES 160–161.

If the tracing is moved as shown by the slide arrow,
does the tracing match the pattern? Write *yes* or *no*.

1.    2.

3.    4.

Copy each figure and slide arrow on dot paper. Draw
the slide image for the given slide arrow.

5. 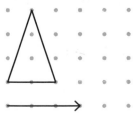   6.    7.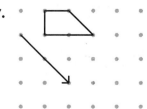

SET 5.7, USE WITH PAGES 162–163.

Name the figure at each of the following points.

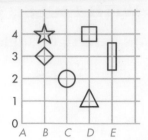

1. D1
2. C2
3. B4
4. B3
5. E3
6. D4

Copy the grid at the right onto squared paper. Join the following points in order. (1,4) (3,2) (6,2) (8,4) (1,4) (4,4) (4,7) (7,4)

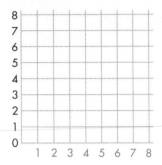

SET 5.11, USE WITH PAGES 170–171.

These figures are drawn on square dot paper. Give the area of each one in square units.

1.
2.
3.

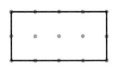
☐ = 1 square unit

Write which of the figures below have the same area.

4.
5.
6.

7.
8.
9.

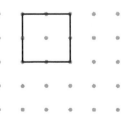
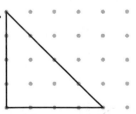
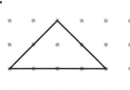

SET 5.14, USE WITH PAGES 176–177.

Trace each drawing below. Draw line segments
to show each single cube.

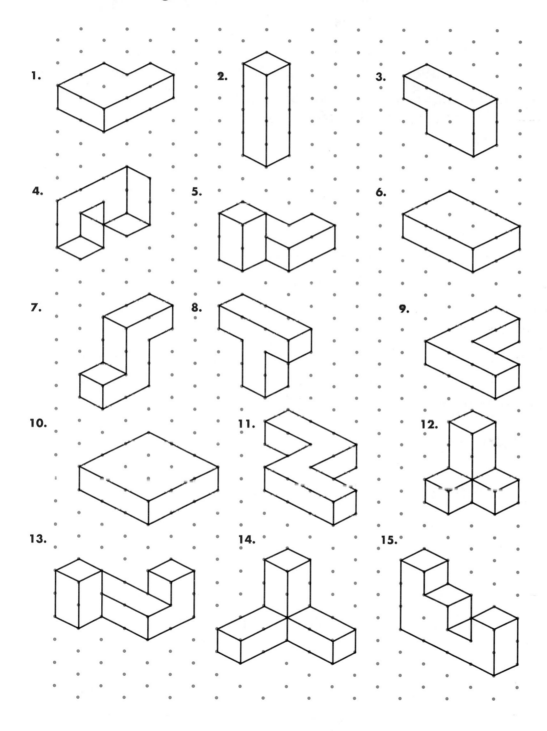

1.

2.

3.

4.

5.

6.

7.

8.

9.

10.

11.

12.

13.

14.

15.

16. Which of the drawings above could be pentacubes?

SET 6.1, USE WITH PAGES 188–189.

Estimate the product.

1. 77 × 4	**2.** 839 × 6	**3.** 4526 × 5	**4.** 27 × 9	**5.** $1.93 × 3
6. 68 × 4	**7.** 398 × 5	**8.** 1854 × 8	**9.** 2625 × 9	**10.** $49.42 × 2
11. 463 × 7	**12.** 35 × 9	**13.** 5978 × 4	**14.** 666 × 3	**15.** 756 × 8
16. 82 × 4	**17.** 612 × 2	**18.** 4087 × 6	**19.** 8080 × 3	**20.** 753 × 5
21. 4242 × 3	**22.** 48 × 9	**23.** 879 × 4	**24.** 143 × 9	**25.** 4294 × 7

SET 6:2, USE WITH PAGES 190–191.

Write the product. Draw an array diagram when it helps.

1. 73 × 4	**2.** 24 × 6	**3.** 45 × 5	**4.** 39 × 3	**5.** 43 × 7
6. 82 × 2	**7.** 67 × 8	**8.** 56 × 9	**9.** 98 × 2	**10.** 77 × 3
11. 35 × 4	**12.** 53 × 5	**13.** 48 × 3	**14.** 79 × 5	**15.** 33 × 8
16. 71 × 6	**17.** 64 × 2	**18.** 21 × 7	**19.** 25 × 9	**20.** 57 × 2

SET 6.3, USE WITH PAGES 192–193.

Write the product.

1. 87 × 3	2. 52 × 5	3. 65 × 1	4. 88 × 5	5. 58 × 6	6. 94 × 1

7. 3 × 77   8. 9 × 88   9. 8 × 69   10. 9 × 89

11. 81 × 7	12. 42 × 2	13. 94 × 4	14. 16 × 2	15. 38 × 1	16. 18 × 4

17. 8 × 86   18. 8 × 92   19. 9 × 22   20. 2 × 78

21. 72 × 9	22. 57 × 8	23. 33 × 7	24. 85 × 1	25. 91 × 3	26. 91 × 5

27. 4 × 73   28. 8 × 12   29. 4 × 39   30. 3 × 18

31. 6 × 91   32. 6 × 38   33. 9 × 25   34. 5 × 96

35. 34 × 2	36. 88 × 9	37. 77 × 8	38. 69 × 5	39. 14 × 8	40. 44 × 7

SET 6.4, USE WITH PAGES 194–195.

Write the product.

1. 301 × 5	2. 191 × 3	3. 538 × 9	4. 828 × 2	5. 865 × 2

6. 356 × 5	7. 511 × 7	8. 773 × 5	9. 878 × 4	10. 999 × 6

11. 3 × 254   12. 5 × 763   13. 3 × 814   14. 9 × 182

15. 4 × 554   16. 6 × 207   17. 7 × 508   18. 2 × 891

SET 6.7, USE WITH PAGES 200–201.

Write the product.

1. 3577×9
2. 9306×7
3. 5418×6
4. 5322×4
5. 7215×8

6. 2042×9
7. 1528×2
8. 3021×7
9. 8697×6
10. 4971×4

11. 2096×6
12. 5527×4
13. 6531×7
14. 7224×2
15. 5668×3

16. 5421×5
17. 8585×8
18. 7006×9
19. 7216×3
20. 9344×4

21. 2×5329
22. 8×7138
23. 5×9188
24. 7×4635

25. 4×8425
26. 5×2021
27. 6×7648
28. 9×9828

SET 6.9, USE WITH PAGES 204–205.

Write the product.

1. $\$8.02 \times 7$
2. $\$7.14 \times 9$
3. $\$1.12 \times 2$
4. $\$8.95 \times 1$
5. $\$4.14 \times 8$

6. $\$1.92 \times 8$
7. $\$4.95 \times 4$
8. $\$2.32 \times 7$
9. $\$4.56 \times 7$
10. $\$3.25 \times 5$

11. $\$19.95 \times 5$
12. $\$42.07 \times 7$
13. $\$30.09 \times 3$
14. $\$27.40 \times 9$
15. $\$83.55 \times 3$

16. $2 \times \$0.12$
17. $6 \times \$0.24$
18. $9 \times \$0.49$
19. $6 \times \$0.75$

20. $6 \times \$27.06$
21. $4 \times \$27.28$
22. $8 \times \$52.18$
23. $9 \times \$26.14$

SET 7.1, USE WITH PAGES 214–215.

Write the quotient and remainder.

1. 9 ÷ 7 **2.** 7 ÷ 2 **3.** 25 ÷ 4 **4.** 35 ÷ 6 **5.** 36 ÷ 5

6. 6)38 **7.** 3)16 **8.** 9)73 **9.** 9)67 **10.** 8)62

11. 36 ÷ 5 **12.** 23 ÷ 3 **13.** 67 ÷ 8 **14.** 25 ÷ 3 **15.** 33 ÷ 6

16. 6)38 **17.** 8)29 **18.** 3)7 **19.** 5)23 **20.** 4)17

21. 20 ÷ 3 **22.** 49 ÷ 5 **23.** 18 ÷ 7 **24.** 26 ÷ 8 **25.** 44 ÷ 9

26. 8)21 **27.** 2)7 **28.** 9)74 **29.** 8)66 **30.** 9)87

31. 71 ÷ 9 **32.** 37 ÷ 4 **33.** 50 ÷ 7 **34.** 30 ÷ 7 **35.** 45 ÷ 6

36. 57 ÷ 9 **37.** 41 ÷ 7 **38.** 39 ÷ 4 **39.** 29 ÷ 3 **40.** 49 ÷ 5

SET 7.2, USE WITH PAGES 216–217.

Solve each problem. Decide what to do with each remainder.

1. In Mrs. Clarke's gym class no more than four students can stretch on a mat. How many mats will a class of 27 students need for warm-ups?

2. The 27 students play soccer. Two teams of 11 players are needed; the remaining players will be substitutes. How many substitutes will each team have?

3. Mrs. Clarke has 25 soccer balls. She's going to have groups of students practice a warm-up drill using 3 balls per group. How many groups of students will there be?

4. At the end of the week Mrs. Clarke must begin giving each one of her 27 students a fitness test that lasts 6 minutes. She'll test one student at a time while the rest of the students play a game. How many students can she test in a 55 minute class period? How many class periods will it take Mrs. Clarke to test all the students?

SET 7.3, USE WITH PAGES 218–219.

Estimate the quotient. Write the two multiples of 10 the estimate is between.

1. $5\overline{)489}$ 2. $7\overline{)364}$ 3. $4\overline{)236}$

4. $106 \div 5$ 5. $187 \div 6$ 6. $579 \div 9$

7. $3\overline{)268}$ 8. $6\overline{)349}$ 9. $4\overline{)110}$

10. $100 \div 7$ 11. $222 \div 5$ 12. $593 \div 8$

Estimate the quotient. Write the two multiples of 100 the estimate is between.

13. $4\overline{)746}$ 14. $6\overline{)5294}$ 15. $5\overline{)2678}$

16. $8\overline{)3803}$ 17. $4\overline{)3492}$ 18. $5\overline{)1890}$

19. $543 \div 3$ 20. $3645 \div 5$ 21. $269 \div 2$

22. $880 \div 3$ 23. $6398 \div 8$ 24. $4655 \div 7$

SET 7.4, USE WITH PAGES 220–221.

Divide.

1. $7\overline{)88}$ 2. $8\overline{)88}$ 3. $3\overline{)48}$ 4. $2\overline{)31}$ 5. $4\overline{)56}$

6. $54 \div 2$ 7. $78 \div 3$ 8. $37 \div 2$ 9. $24 \div 2$ 10. $48 \div 2$

11. $4\overline{)252}$ 12. $9\overline{)398}$ 13. $6\overline{)341}$ 14. $7\overline{)118}$ 15. $5\overline{)495}$

16. $279 \div 4$ 17. $641 \div 7$ 18. $484 \div 9$ 19. $481 \div 7$ 20. $390 \div 6$

21. $2\overline{)177}$ 22. $3\overline{)292}$ 23. $4\overline{)317}$ 24. $7\overline{)497}$ 25. $6\overline{)416}$

26. $777 \div 8$ 27. $312 \div 4$ 28. $329 \div 7$ 29. $474 \div 8$ 30. $367 \div 4$

SET 7.6, USE WITH PAGES 224–225.

Divide.

1. $550 \div 2$ 2. $595 \div 5$ 3. $953 \div 3$

4. $1176 \div 4$ 5. $1342 \div 3$ 6. $4734 \div 5$

7. $3608 \div 8$ 8. $7160 \div 8$ 9. $5346 \div 7$

10. $4\overline{)2455}$ 11. $4\overline{)1007}$ 12. $6\overline{)690}$

13. $7\overline{)3969}$ 14. $7\overline{)1584}$ 15. $5\overline{)857}$

16. $2\overline{)644}$ 17. $8\overline{)2269}$ 18. $9\overline{)8711}$

19. $5\overline{)892}$ 20. $3\overline{)791}$ 21. $7\overline{)6869}$

SET 7.8, USE WITH PAGES 228–229.

Divide.

1. $832 \div 4$ 2. $840 \div 3$ 3. $943 \div 9$

4. $1207 \div 6$ 5. $3015 \div 6$ 6. $1637 \div 8$

7. $903 \div 5$ 8. $7240 \div 8$ 9. $4226 \div 7$

10. $2\overline{)608}$ 11. $4\overline{)682}$ 12. $2\overline{)619}$

13. $6\overline{)644}$ 14. $3\overline{)1820}$ 15. $8\overline{)6452}$

16. $2\overline{)1204}$ 17. $3\overline{)2250}$ 18. $9\overline{)3154}$

19. $2\overline{)606}$ 20. $3\overline{)540}$ 21. $6\overline{)1207}$

22. $7\overline{)1428}$ 23. $3\overline{)326}$ 24. $2\overline{)1122}$

SET 7.11, USE WITH PAGES 234–235.

Write the quotient.

1. 3)$\overline{\$0.18}$ 2. 5)$\overline{\$0.40}$ 3. 8)$\overline{\$0.24}$ 4. 9)$\overline{\$0.45}$

5. 3)$\overline{\$0.45}$ 6. 2)$\overline{\$0.44}$ 7. 3)$\overline{\$0.51}$ 8. 5)$\overline{\$0.80}$

9. 5)$\overline{\$1.40}$ 10. 2)$\overline{\$1.66}$ 11. 8)$\overline{\$3.76}$ 12. 6)$\overline{\$4.92}$

13. 4)$\overline{\$7.12}$ 14. 4)$\overline{\$5.84}$ 15. 6)$\overline{\$9.24}$ 16. 2)$\overline{\$6.30}$

17. $14.13 ÷ 9 18. $58.16 ÷ 8 19. $12.74 ÷ 7

20. $13.26 ÷ 6 21. $27.86 ÷ 7 22. $11.43 ÷ 3

23. $12.80 ÷ 4 24. $25.20 ÷ 6 25. $29.08 ÷ 2

26. $34.00 ÷ 5 27. $17.68 ÷ 8 28. $46.11 ÷ 3

29. $61.20 ÷ 9 30. $11.60 ÷ 4 31. $23.50 ÷ 5

32. $35.60 ÷ 4 33. $49.60 ÷ 8 34. $51.10 ÷ 7

35. $0.90 ÷ 3 36. $46.20 ÷ 6 37. $7.80 ÷ 2

38. $51.30 ÷ 9 39. $1.92 ÷ 4 40. $14.50 ÷ 5

SET 7.12, USE WITH PAGES 236–237.

Divide.

1. 5)$\overline{315}$ 2. 4)$\overline{276}$ 3. 9)$\overline{207}$ 4. 6)$\overline{211}$

5. 648 ÷ 8 6. 523 ÷ 9 7. 462 ÷ 7

8. 2)$\overline{982}$ 9. 3)$\overline{366}$ 10. 5)$\overline{845}$ 11. 3)$\overline{388}$

12. 896 ÷ 8 13. 806 ÷ 3 14. 710 ÷ 4

15. 4)$\overline{777}$ 16. 2)$\overline{271}$ 17. 6)$\overline{448}$ 18. 4)$\overline{358}$

19. 726 ÷ 7 20. 108 ÷ 7 21. 212 ÷ 5

SET 7.13, USE WITH PAGES 238–239.

Write the average.

1. 4, 9, 8
2. 7, 7, 6, 4
3. 9, 5, 3 4, 4

4. 19, 31, 13
5. 45, 90, 84, 21
6. 92, 15, 88, 70, 35

7. 315, 491
8. 112, 208, 211
9. 205, 210, 215, 220, 230

10. 1, 2, 5, 5, 9, 8
11. 22, 18, 32, 31, 10, 13
12. 310, 415, 502

SET 8.1, USE WITH PAGES 248–249.

Write what fraction of each bar is shaded.

1.
2.
3.

4.
5.
6.

SET 8.3, USE WITH PAGES 252–253.

Match the Fraction Bar with an equivalent Fraction Bar.

1.
2.
3.

a
b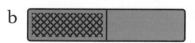
c

Copy and complete.

4. $\frac{3}{3} = \frac{\blacksquare}{12}$
5. $\frac{2}{5} = \frac{\blacksquare}{10}$
6. $\frac{2}{3} = \frac{\blacksquare}{6}$
7. $\frac{3}{4} = \frac{\blacksquare}{12}$

8. $\frac{1}{3} = \frac{\blacksquare}{6}$
9. $\frac{2}{4} = \frac{\blacksquare}{8}$
10. $\frac{4}{6} = \frac{\blacksquare}{12}$
11. $\frac{3}{5} = \frac{\blacksquare}{10}$

12. $\frac{1}{2} = \frac{\blacksquare}{6}$
13. $\frac{5}{6} = \frac{\blacksquare}{12}$
14. $\frac{1}{3} = \frac{\blacksquare}{12}$
15. $\frac{1}{2} = \frac{\blacksquare}{12}$

16. $\frac{1}{6} = \frac{\blacksquare}{12}$
17. $\frac{1}{4} = \frac{\blacksquare}{12}$
18. $\frac{4}{4} = \frac{\blacksquare}{8}$
19. $\frac{1}{5} = \frac{\blacksquare}{10}$

SET 8.5, USE WITH PAGES 256–257.

Copy and complete. Write $>$, $<$, or $=$.

1. $\frac{3}{4}$ ■ $\frac{2}{4}$ 　　2. $\frac{3}{5}$ ■ $\frac{4}{5}$ 　　3. $\frac{1}{3}$ ■ $\frac{5}{12}$ 　　4. $\frac{6}{8}$ ■ $\frac{7}{8}$ 　　5. $\frac{3}{5}$ ■ $\frac{6}{10}$

6. $\frac{1}{4}$ ■ $\frac{1}{2}$ 　　7. $\frac{7}{10}$ ■ $\frac{4}{5}$ 　　8. $\frac{3}{4}$ ■ $\frac{8}{12}$ 　　9. $\frac{2}{3}$ ■ $\frac{3}{6}$ 　　10. $\frac{2}{6}$ ■ $\frac{5}{6}$

11. $\frac{1}{3}$ ■ $\frac{3}{6}$ 　　12. $\frac{4}{5}$ ■ $\frac{2}{10}$ 　　13. $\frac{4}{8}$ ■ $\frac{1}{2}$ 　　14. $\frac{3}{6}$ ■ $\frac{1}{2}$ 　　15. $\frac{3}{4}$ ■ $\frac{1}{2}$

16. $\frac{3}{5}$ ■ $\frac{5}{5}$ 　　17. $\frac{5}{12}$ ■ $\frac{2}{6}$ 　　18. $\frac{5}{5}$ ■ $\frac{10}{10}$ 　　19. $\frac{7}{8}$ ■ $\frac{3}{4}$ 　　20. $\frac{1}{10}$ ■ $\frac{4}{5}$

Order the fractions from least to greatest.

21. $\frac{3}{8}, \frac{7}{8}, \frac{2}{8}$ 　　　　22. $\frac{3}{4}, \frac{1}{2}, \frac{1}{4}$ 　　　　23. $\frac{3}{4}, \frac{1}{4}, \frac{5}{8}$

24. $\frac{2}{10}, \frac{3}{5}, \frac{4}{10}$ 　　　　25. $\frac{1}{3}, \frac{2}{12}, \frac{8}{12}$ 　　　　26. $\frac{3}{10}, \frac{7}{10}, \frac{1}{2}$

27. $\frac{7}{12}, \frac{3}{4}, \frac{2}{3}$ 　　　　28. $\frac{1}{4}, \frac{1}{2}, \frac{3}{8}$ 　　　　29. $\frac{1}{2}, \frac{5}{6}, \frac{2}{3}$

30. $\frac{3}{5}, \frac{1}{2}, \frac{7}{10}, \frac{1}{5}$ 　　　31. $\frac{2}{4}, \frac{3}{12}, \frac{1}{6}, \frac{2}{3}$ 　　　32. $\frac{3}{4}, \frac{5}{8}, \frac{3}{8}, \frac{1}{4}$

33. $\frac{1}{2}, \frac{3}{4}, \frac{1}{4}, \frac{1}{8}$ 　　　34. $\frac{2}{5}, \frac{5}{10}, \frac{3}{10}, \frac{1}{5}$ 　　　35. $\frac{5}{6}, \frac{4}{6}, \frac{5}{12}, \frac{2}{12}$

SET 8.8, USE WITH PAGES 262–263.

Write the answer.

1. $\frac{1}{8}$ of 32 　　2. $\frac{1}{5}$ of 35 　　3. $\frac{2}{5}$ of 35 　　4. $\frac{1}{2}$ of 18 　　5. $\frac{1}{3}$ of 27

6. $\frac{1}{4}$ of $28 　　7. $\frac{1}{12}$ of 48 　　8. $\frac{1}{5}$ of 20 in. 　　9. $\frac{1}{10}$ of 60 　　10. $\frac{5}{10}$ of 16

11. $\frac{10}{10}$ of 10 　　12. $\frac{1}{4}$ of 12 　　13. $\frac{1}{6}$ of 54 　　14. $\frac{1}{5}$ of 5 　　15. $\frac{1}{3}$ of 30

16. $\frac{1}{8}$ of $40 　　17. $\frac{1}{12}$ of 36 　　18. $\frac{5}{12}$ of 36 　　19. $\frac{1}{6}$ of 24 　　20. $\frac{3}{6}$ of 24

21. $\frac{1}{6}$ of 48 　　22. $\frac{1}{5}$ of 25 　　23. $\frac{1}{12}$ of 24 　　24. $\frac{1}{3}$ of 9 　　25. $\frac{3}{4}$ of 8

SET 8.10, USE WITH PAGES 266-267.

How many bars are shaded? Write your answer as a fraction and as a mixed number.

1.

2.

3.

4.

5.

6.

7.

8.

9.

SET 9.1, USE WITH PAGES 276-277.

Write the answer.

1. $\begin{array}{r} \frac{4}{8} \\ + \frac{2}{8} \\ \hline \end{array}$

2. $\begin{array}{r} \frac{3}{4} \\ - \frac{1}{4} \\ \hline \end{array}$

3. $\begin{array}{r} \frac{2}{5} \\ + \frac{2}{5} \\ \hline \end{array}$

4. $\begin{array}{r} \frac{2}{4} \\ + \frac{2}{4} \\ \hline \end{array}$

5. $\begin{array}{r} \frac{5}{10} \\ + \frac{3}{10} \\ \hline \end{array}$

6. $\begin{array}{r} \frac{5}{5} \\ - \frac{4}{5} \\ \hline \end{array}$

7. $\begin{array}{r} \frac{3}{8} \\ - \frac{3}{8} \\ \hline \end{array}$

8. $\begin{array}{r} \frac{8}{12} \\ - \frac{5}{12} \\ \hline \end{array}$

9. $\begin{array}{r} \frac{3}{10} \\ + \frac{2}{10} \\ \hline \end{array}$

10. $\begin{array}{r} \frac{9}{12} \\ - \frac{7}{12} \\ \hline \end{array}$

11. $\begin{array}{r} \frac{1}{5} \\ + \frac{3}{5} \\ \hline \end{array}$

12. $\begin{array}{r} \frac{6}{8} \\ - \frac{3}{8} \\ \hline \end{array}$

13. $\begin{array}{r} \frac{2}{6} \\ + \frac{2}{6} \\ \hline \end{array}$

14. $\begin{array}{r} \frac{4}{4} \\ - \frac{1}{4} \\ \hline \end{array}$

15. $\frac{1}{8} + \frac{3}{8}$

16. $\frac{8}{8} - \frac{2}{8}$

17. $\frac{7}{12} + \frac{3}{12}$

18. $\frac{5}{6} - \frac{1}{6}$

19. $\frac{2}{3} + \frac{1}{3}$

20. $\frac{9}{12} - \frac{3}{12}$

21. $\frac{1}{2} - \frac{1}{2}$

22. $\frac{3}{10} + \frac{2}{10}$

23. $\frac{4}{5} - \frac{1}{5}$

24. $\frac{5}{6} - \frac{4}{6}$

25. $\frac{5}{12} + \frac{2}{12}$

26. $\frac{7}{10} - \frac{4}{10}$

SET 9.2, USE WITH PAGES 278–279.

Solve each problem.

1. Jennie needs $1\frac{1}{2}$ gallons of paint for her playroom. She has $\frac{3}{4}$ of a gallon. Does she have enough paint? Why or why not?

2. Kevin started painting at 1:00. He finished the first wall at 1:45. What fraction of an hour did he spend on the first wall?

3. Fran is making curtains for her bedroom. She needs $\frac{3}{5}$ of a yard of blue fabric and $\frac{2}{5}$ of a yard of white fabric. How much fabric does she need in all?

4. Ron spent $\frac{1}{2}$ of his $10 at the decorating shop. Brenda spend $\frac{3}{4}$ of her $12. Who spent more?

SET 9.5, USE WITH PAGES 284–285.

Write the sum. Use Fraction Bars when it helps.

1. $\frac{2}{12}$
   $+ \frac{5}{6}$

2. $\frac{3}{8}$
   $+ \frac{1}{4}$

3. $\frac{2}{8}$
   $+ \frac{1}{2}$

4. $\frac{1}{10}$
   $+ \frac{1}{5}$

5. $\frac{2}{3}$
   $+ \frac{1}{12}$

6. $\frac{5}{10}$
   $+ \frac{1}{2}$

7. $\frac{1}{3}$
   $+ \frac{1}{12}$

8. $\frac{1}{12}$
   $+ \frac{2}{3}$

9. $\frac{3}{8}$
   $+ \frac{1}{2}$

10. $\frac{8}{10}$
    $+ \frac{1}{5}$

11. $\frac{3}{4}$
    $+ \frac{1}{12}$

12. $\frac{2}{8}$
    $+ \frac{1}{2}$

13. $\frac{3}{10}$
    $+ \frac{3}{5}$

14. $\frac{3}{8}$
    $+ \frac{2}{4}$

15. $\frac{1}{2} + \frac{1}{4}$

16. $\frac{3}{10} + \frac{2}{5}$

17. $\frac{5}{8} + \frac{1}{4}$

18. $\frac{1}{6} + \frac{5}{12}$

19. $\frac{5}{12} + \frac{1}{3}$

20. $\frac{7}{10} + \frac{1}{5}$

21. $\frac{1}{2} + \frac{1}{12}$

22. $\frac{1}{3} + \frac{1}{6}$

23. $\frac{2}{3} + \frac{1}{6}$

24. $\frac{7}{12} + \frac{1}{3}$

25. $\frac{1}{5} + \frac{3}{10}$

26. $\frac{2}{6} + \frac{2}{3}$

27. $\frac{1}{2} + \frac{3}{12}$

28. $\frac{2}{5} + \frac{1}{10}$

29. $\frac{3}{8} + \frac{1}{2}$

30. $\frac{1}{4} + \frac{1}{12}$

SET 9.6, USE WITH PAGES 286–287.

Write the difference. Use Fraction Bars when it helps.

1. $\frac{4}{8}$
    $-\frac{4}{8}$

2. $\frac{10}{10}$
    $-\frac{1}{10}$

3. $\frac{8}{12}$
    $-\frac{1}{6}$

4. $\frac{4}{5}$
    $-\frac{1}{10}$

5. $\frac{3}{10}$
    $-\frac{1}{5}$

6. $\frac{1}{2}$
    $-\frac{3}{8}$

7. $\frac{7}{8}$
    $-\frac{1}{2}$

8. $\frac{3}{4}$
    $-\frac{1}{12}$

9. $\frac{4}{5}$
    $-\frac{3}{5}$

10. $\frac{5}{8}$
    $-\frac{1}{4}$

11. $\frac{3}{5}$
    $-\frac{3}{10}$

12. $\frac{7}{10}$
    $-\frac{1}{5}$

13. $\frac{3}{8}$
    $-\frac{1}{4}$

14. $\frac{3}{4}$
    $-\frac{3}{8}$

15. $\frac{7}{8} - \frac{3}{4}$

16. $\frac{1}{2} - \frac{1}{4}$

17. $\frac{3}{4} - \frac{4}{12}$

18. $\frac{1}{3} - \frac{3}{12}$

19. $\frac{4}{6} - \frac{1}{3}$

20. $\frac{3}{8} - \frac{1}{4}$

21. $\frac{9}{10} - \frac{2}{5}$

22. $\frac{6}{8} - \frac{1}{4}$

23. $\frac{1}{6} - \frac{1}{12}$

24. $\frac{1}{2} - \frac{3}{6}$

25. $\frac{2}{3} - \frac{7}{12}$

26. $\frac{2}{3} - \frac{2}{6}$

SET 9.7, USE WITH PAGES 288–289.

Write the answer.

1. $6\frac{1}{3}$
    $+ 1\frac{1}{3}$

2. $3\frac{2}{8}$
    $+ \frac{2}{8}$

3. $7\frac{1}{2}$
    $- 6$

4. 6
    $+ \frac{3}{8}$

5. $3\frac{1}{8}$
    $- 2\frac{1}{8}$

6. $2\frac{3}{12}$
    $+ 4\frac{6}{12}$

7. $1\frac{7}{8}$
    $- \frac{1}{8}$

8. $3\frac{2}{5}$
    $- 3\frac{2}{5}$

9. $4\frac{9}{12}$
    $- 1\frac{1}{12}$

10. $5\frac{5}{8}$
    $- 3\frac{1}{8}$

11. $1\frac{1}{4} + 2$

12. $3\frac{3}{4} - 2\frac{3}{4}$

13. $1\frac{7}{8} - \frac{3}{8}$

14. $2\frac{2}{10} + \frac{1}{10}$

15. $7\frac{1}{3} + 2$

16. $4\frac{3}{12} + 3\frac{1}{12}$

17. $9\frac{2}{10} - 2\frac{1}{10}$

18. $8\frac{5}{6} - \frac{1}{6}$

19. $1\frac{6}{8} - 1\frac{6}{8}$

20. $3\frac{6}{12} + 2\frac{1}{12}$

21. $1\frac{8}{12} - 1\frac{3}{12}$

22. $7\frac{5}{6} - \frac{3}{6}$

23. $2\frac{2}{10} + 3\frac{3}{10}$

24. $7\frac{1}{8} + 3\frac{2}{8}$

25. $1\frac{2}{4} + \frac{1}{4}$

26. $2\frac{5}{6} - 1\frac{5}{6}$

SET 9.10, USE WITH PAGE 294.

Use the map on page 294 to answer each question.

1. What time is it in Texas?

2. What time is it in North Carolina?

3. If it is 6:00 in Colorado, what time is it in Kansas?

4. If it is 7:00 in Georgia, what time is it in Alabama?

5. Ramon arrives in Arizona at 10:00, after a 6-hour flight from New York. What time did he leave New York?

6. Jessie left Minnesota at 2:00 and arrived in Nevada at 5:00. How long was her flight?

SET 10.1, USE WITH PAGES 302–303.

Write the length to the nearest quarter inch.

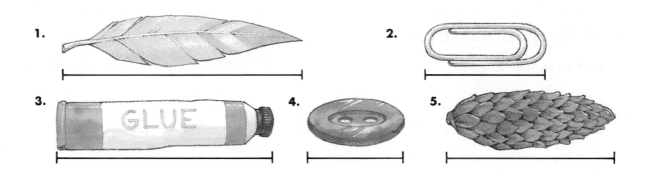

1.

2.

3.

4.

5.

SET 10.2, USE WITH PAGES 304–305.

Tell which unit you would use to measure each. Write *foot, yard,* or *mile.*

1. height of a table
2. width of a garden
3. distance across a parking lot
4. distance to Cuba
5. length of a driveway
6. depth of a pool
7. distance of a marathon
8. height of a fire escape
9. distance around a car
10. mail carrier's route
11. distance you can throw a ball
12. width of a checkers board

SET 10.3, USE WITH PAGES 306–307.

Write the perimeter.

1.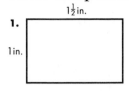

2.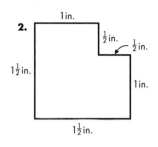

3.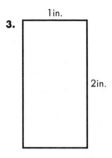

4.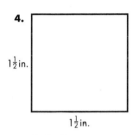

5.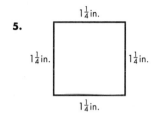

6.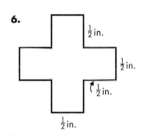

SET 10.6, USE WITH PAGES 312–313.

Make each statement true. Write <, >, or =.

1. 1 half-gallon ▦ 4 cups

2. 1 gallon ▦ 3 quarts

3. 3 quarts ▦ 8 pints

4. 2 quarts ▦ 1 half gallon

5. 16 cups ▦ 1 gallon

6. 4 cups ▦ 1 pint

7. 3 gallons ▦ 14 quarts

8. 5 pints ▦ 18 cups

9. 32 fl oz ▦ 2 pints

10. 2 cups ▦ 12 fl oz

11. 3 gallons ▦ 25 pints

12. 32 fl oz ▦ 3 cups

13. 4 quarts ▦ 128 fl oz

14. 6 pints ▦ 1 half gallon

15. 16 cups ▦ 4 quarts

16. 128 fl oz ▦ 1 half gallon

SET 10.7, USE WITH PAGE 314.

Make each statement true. Write <, >, or =.

1. 2 lb ▦ 36 oz

2. 2 T ▦ 3600 lb

3. 50 oz ▦ 5 lb

4. 4000 lb ▦ 2 T

5. 64 oz ▦ 4 lb

6. 10 lb ▦ 160 oz

7. 14 oz ▦ 1 lb

8. 25 oz ▦ 3 lb

9. 4 T ▦ 6000 lb

SET 10.8, USE WITH PAGES 316–317.

Write the length to the nearest centimeter.

1. 2. 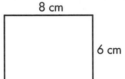 3.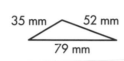

Write in millimeters.

4. 6 cm   5. 14 cm   6. 2 cm   7. 7 cm   8. 12 cm   9. 10 cm   10. 8 cm

Write the perimeter.

11.
8 cm

6 cm

12.

35 mm   52 mm

79 mm

13.
3 cm
2 cm
3 cm
2 cm
?
2 cm
1 cm
8 cm

SET 10.9, USE WITH PAGES 318–319.

Copy and complete. Make a table or use mental math.

1. 3 dm = ▓ cm   2. 4000 m = ▓ km   3. 700 cm = ▓ m

4. 400 cm = ▓ m   5. 20 cm = ▓ dm   6. 6 km = ▓ m

Choose the better estimate.

7. the width of your thumbnail
   a. 1 mm   b. 10 mm

8. the height of a paper cup
   a. 1 dm   b. 10 dm

9. the length of a paper clip
   a. 3 mm   b. 30 mm

10. the height of a giraffe
   a. 5 m   b. 50 m

SET 10.10, USE WITH PAGES 320–321.

Choose the unit you would use to measure the capacity of each of these.

1. a vitamin bottle
   a. liters b. milliliters

2. a baby's spoon
   a. liters b. milliliters

3. a washing machine
   a. liters b. milliliters

4. a bottle of cough medicine
   a. liters b. milliliters

SET 10.11, USE WITH PAGE 322.

Copy and complete. Make a table or use mental math.

1. 3 kg = ■ g   **2.** 7000 g = ■ kg   **3.** ■ kg = 5000 g

Choose the better estimate.

4. the mass of a nickel
  a. 50 g   **b.** 5 kg

5. the mass of a baseball bat
  a. 1 kg   **b.** 1 g

6. the mass of a basketball
  a. 6 g   **b.** 600 g

7. the mass of a polar bear
  a. 30 kg   **b.** 300 kg

SET 10.13, USE WITH PAGES 324–325.

Write the temperature.

1.
50°F
45°F
40°F
35°F
30°F
25°F

2.
10°C
5°C
0°C
-5°C
-10°C
-15°C

3.
20°C
15°C
10°C
5°C
0°C
-5°C

4.
160°F
155°F
150°F
145°F
140°F
135°F

Choose the better estimate.

5. You could wear mittens when it is
  a. 28°C. **b.** 28°F.

6. Food would sizzle on the stove at
  a. 110°C. **b.** 110°F.

7. You would want a fan when it is
  a. 37°C. **b.** 37°F.

8. The weather would be cool at
  a. 50°C. **b.** 50°F.

SET 10.14, USE WITH PAGES 326–327.

Write the elapsed time.

1.
9:25a.m.
10:10a.m.

2.
4:37p.m.
8:45p.m.

3.
3:10a.m.
8:04a.m.

4.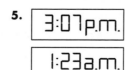
11:49a.m.
1:17p.m.

5.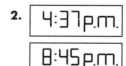
3:07p.m.
1:23a.m.

6.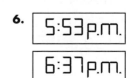
5:53p.m.
6:37p.m.

7. from 4:55 A.M. to 4:55 P.M.

8. from 11:28 P.M. to 4:09 A.M.

SET 11.3, USE WITH PAGES 342–343.

Write the decimal.

1. three tenths   **2.** two and nine tenths   **3.** seven hundredths

4. nine tenths   **5.** five and two tenths   **6.** four and six hundredths

What does the blue digit stand for?

7. 21.4   **8.** 0.12   **9.** 5.2   **10.** 40.8   **11.** 13.64

12. 18.6   **13.** 68.3   **14.** 3.25   **15.** 19.08   **16.** 46.9

Write in words.

17. 0.4   **18.** 7.03   **19.** 20.2   **20.** 0.53   **21.** 14.6

22. 20.01   **23.** 0.7   **24.** 0.29   **25.** 8.15   **26.** 9.6

Write the decimal.

27. $\frac{9}{100}$ **28.** two and eleven hundredths   **29.** $21\frac{17}{100}$

30. $39\frac{4}{10}$ **31.** $18\frac{16}{100}$ **32.** $\frac{37}{100}$ **33.** $5\frac{2}{10}$ **34.** $40\frac{8}{100}$

35. nine and ninety-nine hundredths   **36.** one and forty hundredths

37. four and twelve hundredths   **38.** six tenths

39. seventeen and eight tenths.   **40.** five and three hundredths

---

SET 11.4, USE WITH PAGES 344–345.

Copy and complete. Write >, <, =.

1. 0.8   0.45   **2.** 0.19   0.50   **3.** 0.7   0.7

4. 7.76 ■ 7.80   **5.** 63.42 ■ 63.24   **6.** $14.05 ■ $14.50   **7.** 4.4 ■ 4.40

8. $0.70 ■ $0.70   **9.** 0.6 ■ 0.59   **10.** 93.90 ■ 93.9   **11.** 0.50 ■ 0.7

SET 11.5, USE WITH PAGES 346–347.

Write the numbers in order from least to greatest.

1. 3.02; 3.20; 3.0
2. $57.23; $57.13; $57.20
3. 9.5; 9.89; 9.7
4. 26.5; 25.98; 26.01; 26
5. 40.8; 40.56; 40.09; 40.3
6. 14.8; 13.9; 14; 14.6
7. $32.05; $32.01; $32.10
8. 22.12; 22.06; 22.16; 21.99
9. 0.96; 0.87; 0.69; 0.78
10. $66.53; $65.89; $66.98; $66.82
11. 7.19; 7.04; 7.14; 7; 7.21

SET 11.8, USE WITH PAGES 352–353.

Round to the nearest whole number. Draw a number line when it helps.

1. 6.3
2. 8.6
3. 4.2
4. 2.9
5. 2.7
6. $4.12
7. $3.66
8. $1.10
9. $6.98
10. $4.49

Use rounding to estimate. Draw a number line when it helps.

1. 4.9 − 1.9
2. 8.48 + 9.16
3. 4.46 + 1.29
4. 7.7 − 2.4
5. $9.12 + $9.85
6. $4.22 − $1.88
7. $8.86 + $4.19
8. $6.35 − $4.13

SET 11.9, USE WITH PAGES 354–355.

Write the sum.

1. $\begin{array}{r} 0.23 \\ 0.7 \\ + 6.2 \\ \hline \end{array}$
2. $\begin{array}{r} 68.57 \\ 0.47 \\ + 85.76 \\ \hline \end{array}$
3. $\begin{array}{r} 0.5 \\ + 7.7 \\ \hline \end{array}$
4. $\begin{array}{r} 0.45 \text{ mi} \\ + 0.4 \text{ mi} \\ \hline \end{array}$
5. $\begin{array}{r} 1 \\ 0.69 \\ + 1.8 \\ \hline \end{array}$

6. 0.6 + 0.52 + 6.57
7. $36.36 + $2.30
8. 0.28 + 5.1
9. $7.28 + $0.41
10. 61.6 + 0.3
11. 2.4 cm + 5.2 cm
12. $88 + $0.08
13. 7.7 in. + 71.4 in. + 5.6 in.
14. 0.75 + 0.52 + 0.4

15. $\begin{array}{r} 0 \\ 0.2 \\ + 5.2 \\ \hline \end{array}$
16. $\begin{array}{r} $0.55 \\ + 0.20 \\ \hline \end{array}$
17. $\begin{array}{r} 0.89 \\ 0.03 \\ + 0.87 \\ \hline \end{array}$
18. $\begin{array}{r} 0.4 \\ 0.2 \\ + 7.6 \\ \hline \end{array}$
19. $\begin{array}{r} 8.77 \\ + 0.4 \\ \hline \end{array}$

SET 11.10, USE WITH PAGES 356–357.

Write the difference.

1. $\begin{array}{r} 0.3 \\ -\ 0 \\ \hline \end{array}$

2. $\begin{array}{r} 0.53\ \text{m} \\ -\ 0.47\ \text{m} \\ \hline \end{array}$

3. $\begin{array}{r} 0.6 \\ -\ 0.53 \\ \hline \end{array}$

4. $\begin{array}{r} 6.4 \\ -\ 3.6 \\ \hline \end{array}$

5. $\begin{array}{r} \$47.60 \\ -\ \ \ 6.00 \\ \hline \end{array}$

6. $5 - 0.79$

7. $3.32 - 0.5$

8. $9.3\ \text{mL} - 8\ \text{mL}$

9. $6.5 - 6$

10. $69.3 - 0.22$

11. $52.7 - 0.29$

12. $\$99.92 - \$72$

13. $7.48 - 0$

14. $0.18 - 0.1$

15. $\begin{array}{r} 7.07 \\ -\ 0.97 \\ \hline \end{array}$

16. $\begin{array}{r} 2.4 \\ -\ 0.13 \\ \hline \end{array}$

17. $\begin{array}{r} 8.7\ \ \text{km} \\ -\ 6.37\ \text{km} \\ \hline \end{array}$

18. $\begin{array}{r} 0.2 \\ -\ 0.15 \\ \hline \end{array}$

19. $\begin{array}{r} 3.5 \\ -\ 3.1 \\ \hline \end{array}$

SET 11.14, USE WITH PAGE 362.

Write the estimate. Use any method you wish.

1. $\begin{array}{r} \$8.12 \\ 2.03 \\ +\ \ 2.10 \\ \hline \end{array}$

2. $\begin{array}{r} \$7.98 \\ 5.18 \\ +\ \ 5.20 \\ \hline \end{array}$

3. $\begin{array}{r} \$4.21 \\ 6.18 \\ +\ \ 6.81 \\ \hline \end{array}$

4. $\begin{array}{r} \$8.18 \\ 4.02 \\ +\ \ 2.12 \\ \hline \end{array}$

5. $\begin{array}{r} \$9.45 \\ 1.27 \\ 2.23 \\ +\ \ 4.51 \\ \hline \end{array}$

6. $\begin{array}{r} \$3.80 \\ 5.65 \\ 3.42 \\ +\ \ 1.23 \\ \hline \end{array}$

7. $\begin{array}{r} \$7.14 \\ 2.20 \\ 4.79 \\ +\ \ 1.81 \\ \hline \end{array}$

8. $\begin{array}{r} \$6.36 \\ 4.72 \\ 2.69 \\ +\ \ 2.28 \\ \hline \end{array}$

SET 12.1, USE WITH PAGES 370–371.

Write the answer. Use mental math.

1. 5×30

2. 7×70

3. 4×20

4. 8×50

5. 30×60

6. 40×90

7. 20×80

8. 60×70

9. 50×400

10. 70×500

11. 30×900

12. 80×300

13. 20×5000

14. 40×2000

15. 50×6000

16. 70×4000

17. $500 + 800$

18. $300 + 400$

19. $700 + 700$

20. $200 + 900$

SET 12.2, USE WITH PAGES 372–373.

Estimate. Use any method you wish.

1. 73
   × 21

2. 88
   × 32

3. 47
   × 48

4. 31
   × 63

5. 29
   × 19

6. 498
   × 9

7. 706
   × 4

8. 382
   × 5

9. 417
   × 3

10. 288
    × 7

11. $1.96
    × 29

12. $3.05
    × 41

13. $8.94
    × 32

14. $2.79
    × 58

15. $4.21
    × 63

SET 12.3, USE WITH PAGES 374–375.

Write the product.

1. 79
   × 50

2. 31
   × 90

3. 13
   × 70

4. 17
   × 90

5. 21
   × 20

6. 191
   × 80

7. 170
   × 80

8. 156
   × 30

9. 841
   × 70

10. 496
    × 10

11. 40 × 30

12. 60 × 78

13. 80 × 851

14. 80 × 804

15. 40 × 142

16. 90 × 225

SET 12.5, USE WITH PAGES 378–379.

Write the product. Use an array diagram to help you multiply.

1. 87
   × 93

2. 85
   × 74

3. 64
   × 77

4. 22
   × 41

5. 94
   × 99

6. 32
   × 64

7. 63 × 68

8. 36 × 27

9. 66 × 63

10. 17 × 29

11. 68 × 36

12. 37 × 31

13. 52
    × 67

14. 97
    × 85

15. 21
    × 69

16. 45
    × 17

17. 82
    × 18

18. 63
    × 42

SET 12.6, USE WITH PAGES 380–381.

Write the product.

1.   81   2.   35   3.   11 pt   4.   11   5.   94   6.   24 in.
    × 92   × 69   × 53   × 34   × 79   × 52

7. 13 × 79   8. 82 × 45   9. 23 × 81 lb

10. 54 × 47   11. 69 × 77   12. 56 × 11

13.   42 m   14.   89   15.   69   16.   51   17.   87   18.   21
     × 11   × 65   × 35   × 95   × 42   × 76

SET 12.8, USE WITH PAGES 384–385.

Write the product.

1.   144   2.   582   3.   138   4.   954 yd   5.   182
    × 11   × 71   × 59   × 89   × 31

6. 64 × 651 yd   7. 14 × 239   8. 86 × 923 oz

9. 44 × 725   10. 11 × 804   11. 14 × 855

12.   387 c   13.   383   14.   805   15.   362   16.   415
     × 38   × 64   × 36   × 97   × 11

SET 12.9, USE WITH PAGES 386–387.

Write the product.

1. $0.11   2. $0.81   3. $0.16   4. $0.42   5. $0.98
    ×   53   ×   95   ×   44   ×   44   ×   43

6. 67 × $0.89   7. 66 × $0.55   8. 29 × $0.44

9. 79 × $6.24   10. 25 × $1.51   11. 69 × $5.51

12. $1.81   13. $8.57   14. $7.96   15. $6.97   16. $9.71
     ×   38   ×   75   ×   41   ×   68   ×   44

SET 12.10, USE WITH PAGES 388–389.

Write the product.

1. $87 \times 3 \times 89$ 2. $5 \times 85 \times 29$ 3. $81 \times 12 \times 7$

4. $42 \times 37 \times 2$ 5. $49 \times 8 \times 78$ 6. $6 \times 22 \times 67$

7. $2 \times 38 \times 22$ 8. $83 \times 45 \times 3$ 9. $14 \times 8 \times 88$

10. $6 \times 41 \times 17$ 11. $27 \times 7 \times 95$ 12. $74 \times 1 \times 44$

13. $28 \times 59 \times 5$ 14. $6 \times 91 \times 38$ 15. $38 \times 36 \times 3$

16. $92 \times 7 \times 26$ 17. $79 \times 28 \times 6$ 18. $6 \times 84 \times 14$

19. $68 \times 8 \times 17$ 20. $67 \times 6 \times 11$ 21. $7 \times 25 \times 32$

SET 13.1, USE WITH PAGES 398–399.

Write the letter of the correct quotient.

1. $400 \div 80$
   a. 5
   b. 50
   c. 500

2. $1600 \div 4$
   a. 4
   b. 40
   c. 400

3. $3600 \div 90$
   a. 4
   b. 40
   c. 400

4. $6400 \div 80$
   a. 8
   b. 80
   c. 800

Write the quotient. Use mental math.

5. $800 \div 40$ 6. $280 \div 70$ 7. $200 \div 50$

8. $360 \div 4$ 9. $1800 \div 3$ 10. $7200 \div 80$

11. $2500 \div 50$ 12. $5400 \div 60$ 13. $6300 \div 700$

14. $2400 \div 4$ 15. $8100 \div 9$ 16. $4900 \div 700$

17. $3600 \div 600$ 18. $3000 \div 5$ 19. $4200 \div 60$

Write the missing factor. Use mental math.

20. $30 \times \blacksquare = 210$ 21. $\blacksquare \times 60 = 2400$ 22. $500 \times \blacksquare = 1500$

23. $\blacksquare \times 40 = 2000$ 24. $60 \times \blacksquare = 1200$ 25. $900 \times \blacksquare = 2700$

26. $30 \times \blacksquare = 2100$ 27. $\blacksquare \times 5 = 500$ 28. $\blacksquare \times 3 = 900$

SET 13.2, USE WITH PAGES 400–401.

Estimate the quotient. Write the two multiples of 10 the estimate is between.

1. $32\overline{)1682}$ 2. $38\overline{)792}$ 3. $67\overline{)4934}$ 4. $44\overline{)600}$

5. $790 \div 22$ 6. $5243 \div 66$ 7. $2043 \div 25$ 8. $2578 \div 42$

9. $23\overline{)790}$ 10. $19\overline{)534}$ 11. $21\overline{)930}$ 12. $63\overline{)3276}$

SET 13.4, USE WITH PAGES 404–405.

Divide.

1. $51\overline{)98}$ 2. $15\overline{)80}$ 3. $17\overline{)42}$ 4. $27\overline{)45}$ 5. $14\overline{)52}$

6. $65 \div 13$ 7. $81 \div 11$ 8. $66 \div 32$

9. $78\overline{)488}$ 10. $14\overline{)126}$ 11. $98\overline{)686}$ 12. $93\overline{)129}$ 13. $53\overline{)109}$

SET 13.5, USE WITH PAGES 406–407.

Divide.

1. $47\overline{)517}$ 2. $11\overline{)808}$ 3. $49\overline{)751}$ 4. $49\overline{)659}$ 5. $14\overline{)266}$

6. $45\overline{)718}$ 7. $22\overline{)601}$ 8. $49\overline{)703}$ 9. $16\overline{)730}$ 10. $72\overline{)792}$

11. $753 \div 24$ 12. $292 \div 16$ 13. $396 \div 12$

14. $778 \div 62$ 15. $763 \div 22$ 16. $990 \div 45$

SET 13.7, USE WITH PAGES 410–411.

Divide.

1. $26\overline{)66}$ 2. $27\overline{)80}$ 3. $25\overline{)75}$ 4. $15\overline{)51}$

5. $83 \div 59$ 6. $84 \div 21$ 7. $70 \div 11$

8. $37\overline{)255}$ 9. $85\overline{)425}$ 10. $77\overline{)154}$ 11. $93\overline{)129}$

HANDBOOK

DATA BOOK 464

ALMANAC. 464
Highest Waterfalls in the World 464
Rainfall. 464
Animals' Fastest Speeds. 465
Tall Trees in the U.S.A.. 465
NBA Lifetime Scoring Leaders. 466

ATLAS 467
Average Temperatures of Florida Cities . .467
Mileage Map in Southeast U.S.A.. 468
Flight Distances in U.S.A.. 469

GENERAL INFORMATION 470
Airport Flight Guide. 470
Floor Plan. .470
Lunch Room Takeout Menu 471
Pumpkin Muffin Recipe 471
Bean Stem Growth 472
Variety Video Sale 472
Garden Center Price List 472
Table of Measures 473

INDEPENDENT STUDY. 474

Tips for Problem Solving 474
Tips for Doing Mental Math. 476
Tips for Estimating 478
Study Tips .480
Using Your Textbook 482
Tips for Working Together 484
Learning to Use a Calculator 486

REFERENCE SECTION 488

Glossary. 488
Index 499

DATA BOOK

SOME OF THE HIGHEST WATERFALLS IN THE WORLD

Waterfall	Location	Height (in feet)
Gersoppa	India	829
Vettisfoss	Norway	1200
Angel	Venezuela	3281
Staubbach	Switzerland	984
Upper Yosemite	California	1430
Multnomah	Oregon	620
Feather	California	640
Tugela	Africa	3000
Lower Yellowstone	Wyoming	310
Lower Yosemite	California	320

Tropical Forest in Brazil (in centimeters)

Jan.	24.9
Feb.	21.1
Mar.	21.1
April	10.2
May	5.3
June	0.8
July	0.5
Aug.	2.8
Sept.	5.1
Oct.	11.4
Nov.	15.0
Dec.	20.6

Desert in California (in centimeters)

Jan.	8.9
Feb.	7.6
Mar.	7.4
April	1.3
May	1.3
June	0.0
July	0.0
Aug.	0.0
Sept.	0.3
Oct.	1.5
Nov.	3.6
Dec.	5.8

AVERAGE RAINFALL

ANIMALS' FASTEST SPEEDS

Cheetahs can run **75** miles per hour.

Giraffes can run **32** miles per hour.

Gazelles can run **50** miles per hour.

Rabbits can run **35** miles per hour.

Reindeer can run **32** miles per hour.

Zebras can run **40** miles per hour.

TALL TREES IN THE U.S.

Tree	Height (in feet)	Tree	Height (in feet)
Beech	124	Magnolia	79
Bigleaf Maple	106	Mountain Ash	58
Cedar	209	Redwood	362
Elm	125	Sourwood	114
Larch	115	White Oak	107

DATA BOOK

NATIONAL BASKETBALL ASSOCIATION LIFETIME SCORING LEADERS (through 1990–1991)				
Player	Years	Field Goals	Free Throws	Total Points
Kareem Abdul Jabbar	20	15,837	6,712	38,387
Wilt Chamberlain	14	12,681	5,356	31,419
* Julius Erving	16	11,818	6,256	30,026
* Moses Malone	15	9,709	8,486	27,908
* Dan Issel	15	10,421	6,591	27,482
Elvin Hayes	16	10,976	5,356	27,313
Oscar Robertson	14	9,508	7,694	26,710
* George Gervin	14	11,362	2,737	26,595

* Includes statistics during play in the American Basketball Association

AVERAGE HIGH TEMPERATURES OF FLORIDA CITIES (°F) From the records of the National Weather Service											
	Jan.	Feb.	Mar.	Apr.	May	June	July	Aug.	Sept.	Oct.	Nov.	Dec.
Apalachicola	61	63	68	75	82	86	87	88	85	78	69	63
Daytona Beach	69	70	74	80	85	88	90	89	87	81	75	70
Fort Myers	75	76	80	85	89	90	91	91	90	85	80	76
Jacksonville	65	67	72	79	85	88	90	90	86	79	71	66
Key West	76	77	79	82	85	88	89	89	88	84	80	76
Lakeland	70	72	76	82	87	90	90	90	88	82	76	71
Miami	76	77	79	83	85	88	89	90	88	85	80	77
Orlando	70	72	76	81	87	89	90	90	88	82	76	71
Pensacola	61	64	69	77	84	89	90	90	86	80	70	63
Tallahassee	64	66	72	80	87	90	91	90	87	81	71	65
Tampa	71	72	76	82	87	90	90	90	89	84	77	72
West Palm Beach	75	76	79	83	86	88	90	90	88	84	79	76

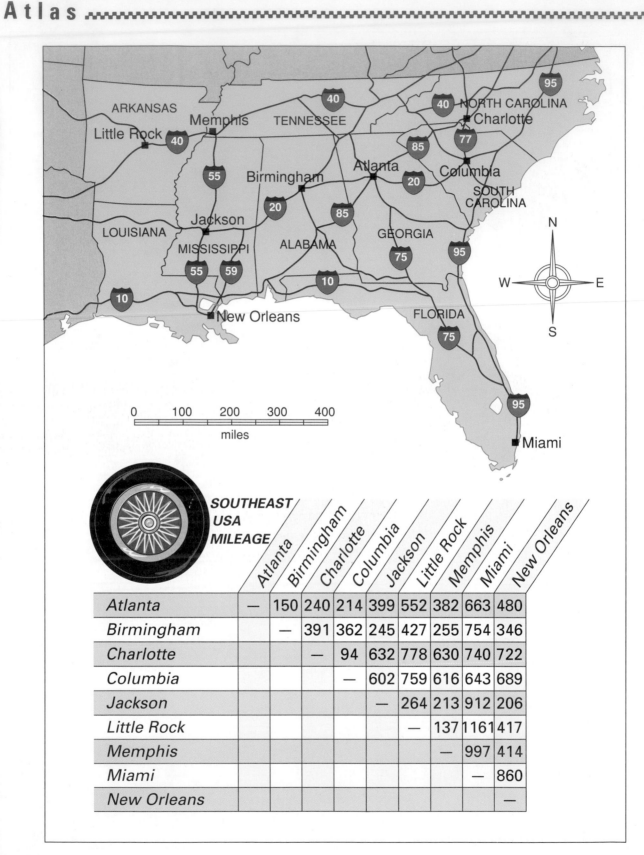

SOUTHEAST USA MILEAGE	Atlanta	Birmingham	Charlotte	Columbia	Jackson	Little Rock	Memphis	Miami	New Orleans
Atlanta	—	150	240	214	399	552	382	663	480
Birmingham		—	391	362	245	427	255	754	346
Charlotte			—	94	632	778	630	740	722
Columbia				—	602	759	616	643	689
Jackson					—	264	213	912	206
Little Rock						—	137	1161	417
Memphis							—	997	414
Miami								—	860
New Orleans									—

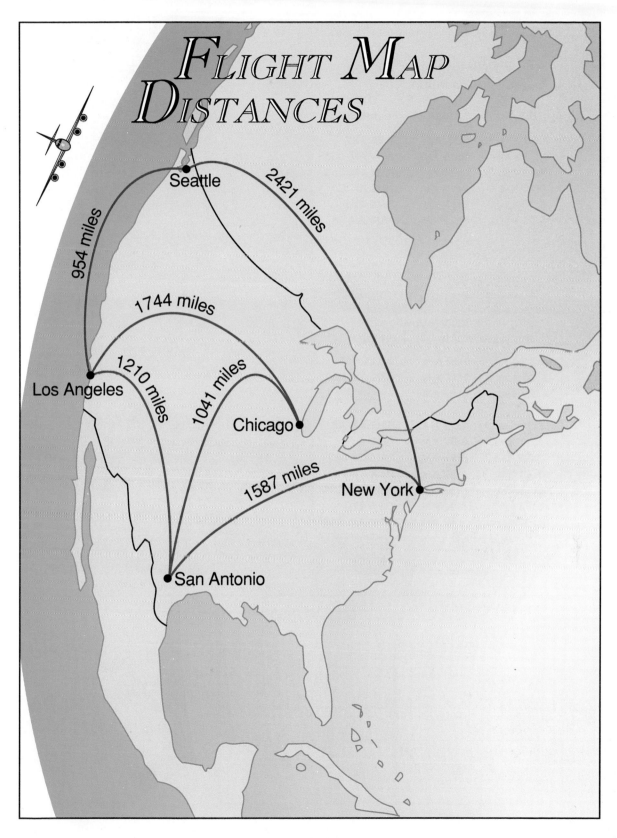

Flight Map Distances

Seattle

954 miles

2421 miles

1744 miles

1210 miles

1041 miles

Los Angeles

Chicago

1587 miles

New York

San Antonio

DATA BOOK

FROM NEW YORK (JFK AIRPORT) TO MIAMI

LEAVE	ARRIVE	FLIGHT AIRLINE
8:00 A.M.	10:55 A.M.	TWA 187
9:00 A.M.	12:06 P.M.	PAN AM 403
12:15 P.M.	3:21 P.M.	PAN AM 363
4:20 P.M.	7:26 P.M.	PAN AM 77
4:30 P.M.	7:37 P.M.	TWA 471
6:15 P.M.	9:21 P.M.	PAN AM 45

AIRPORT FLIGHT GUIDE

FROM MIAMI TO NEW YORK (JFK AIRPORT)

6:35 A.M.	10:52 A.M.	DELTA 460
8:00 A.M.	10:37 A.M.	PAN AM 360
11:29 A.M.	3:54 P.M.	AMERICAN 542
1:30 P.M.	4:22 P.M.	PAN AM 48
1:50 P.M.	4:37 P.M.	TWA 4
3:35 P.M.	6:27 P.M.	PANAM 362
3:40 P.M.	6:27 P.M.	TWA 186
6:15 P.M.	8:57 P.M.	PAN AM 364
8:22 P.M.	11:06 P.M.	TWA 470
9:00 P.M.	11:42 P.M.	PAN AM 368

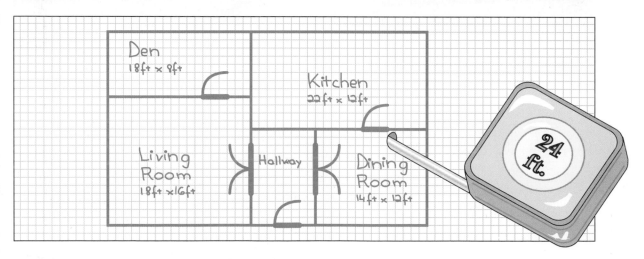

Den 18ft × 9ft

Kitchen 22ft × 12ft

Living Room 18ft × 16ft

Hallway

Dining Room 14ft × 12ft

24 ft.

Takeout Menu

The Lunch Room

HOT SANDWICHES

Turkey Club—Turkey, Bacon
 Lettuce & Tomato $4.35
BLT with mayonnaise $2.75
Reuben with Swiss, Kraut,
 and Russian Dressing $3.95
Frankfurter (topping extra) .. $1.25
Prime Rib Plate $5.45
Cheeseburger $2.50

SALADS

Chef's Salad $3.25
Tossed Salad $2.25
 Dressings: Italian, Russian
 or Creamy Blue Cheese
Salad Plate—Your choice of
 Tuna, Chicken, or Egg
 Salad on a bed of fresh
 lettuce $4.35
Citrus Fruit Salad and
 Cottage Cheese $3.95
Vegetable Platter $3.50

EXTRAS

Tomato or Lettuce $0.15
Cole Slaw $0.25
Onion $0.10
Cheese $0.25
French Fries $0.95
Onion Rings $1.25

DELI SANDWICHES

Roast Beef $2.95
Turkey Breast $2.95
Boiled Ham $2.75
Bologna $2.45
Domestic Cheese $2.45
Imported Cheese $2.45
Combination (Ham, Bologna,
 Salami and Domestic
 Cheese) $2.95
Italian Combination $3.25
Tuna Salad $2.75
Chicken Salad $2.55
Egg Salad $1.65
Seafood Salad $3.35

All served on fresh
Bakery roll: rye,
whole wheat or white

BEVERAGES

Soda or Iced Tea $0.60
Lowfat Milk $0.40
Fresh Juice $0.65
Coffee or Tea $0.55

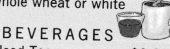

PUMPKIN MUFFINS

makes 1¼ dozen

¾ cup brown sugar
¼ cup molasses
½ cup soft butter
1 beaten egg
¼ cup pecans

1 cup cooked
 mashed pumpkin
1 tsp baking soda
¼ tsp salt
1¾ cups flour

Preheat the oven to 375°. Grease ½-cup
muffin pans or use muffin liners.
Use an electric mixer to blend sugar,
molasses and butter. Add egg and pumpkin
and mix well. Mix the flour with the
baking soda and salt. Add to the pumpkin
batter and blend well. Stir in pecans.
Fill muffin pans half-full with batter.

Bake at 375° for 20 minutes.

Record of Height of Bean Stem Growth

Number of days after stem appears	Stem height in inches				
	1	2	3	4	5
plant 1	$\frac{1}{2}$"	$\frac{3}{4}$"	2"	$2\frac{1}{2}$"	$3\frac{1}{4}$"
plant 2	$\frac{1}{4}$"	$\frac{1}{2}$"	$1\frac{1}{2}$"	2"	$2\frac{3}{4}$"
plant 3	$\frac{1}{2}$"	$\frac{3}{4}$"	$1\frac{3}{4}$"	$2\frac{1}{4}$"	3"

Variety Video Spring Sale

Item	Price
Compact Disc Player	$219.95
AM/FM Cassette Disc Player	299.95
Combination VCR/13" Color TV	549.95
AM/FM Clock Radio	19.95
Stereo Amplifier	229.95
Belt-drive turntable	99.95
Stereo Speaker System	199.95/pair
Blank Audio Cassettes	6.95/pack of 5
Remote VHS Video Recorder	229.95
VHS Autofocus Camrecorder	1099.95
Compact Disc Lens Cleaner	19.95
Auto Reverse Double Cassette Deck	179.95

GARDEN CENTER PRICE LIST

CLAY POTS		COUNTRY VASES	
4 inch	$0.49	10 inch	$7.49
5 inch	$0.79	12 inch	$9.98
6 inch	$0.98	14 inch	$14.98
7 inch	$1.98	16 inch	$22.98
8 inch	$2.49	18 inch	$29.98
9 inch	$2.98	20 inch	$39.98
10 inch	$4.98	22 inch	$59.98
12 inch	$6.98	24 inch	$69.98
14 inch	$11.98		

TABLE OF MEASURES

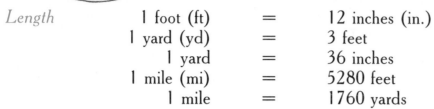

Customary Measures

Length	1 foot (ft)	=	12 inches (in.)
	1 yard (yd)	=	3 feet
	1 yard	=	36 inches
	1 mile (mi)	=	5280 feet
	1 mile	=	1760 yards
Liquid	1 cup (c)	=	8 fluid ounces (fl oz)
	1 pint (pt)	=	2 cups
	1 quart (qt)	=	2 pints
	1 gallon (gal)	=	4 quarts
Weight	1 pound (lb)	=	16 ounces (oz)
	1 ton (t)	=	2000 pounds

Metric Measures

Length	1 centimeter (cm)	=	10 millimeters (mm)
	1 decimeter (dm)	=	10 centimeters
	1 meter (m)	=	10 decimeters
	1 meter	=	100 centimeters
	1 kilometer (km)	=	1000 meters
Liquid	1 liter (L)	=	1000 milliliters (mL)
Mass	1 kilogram (kg)	=	1000 grams (g)

Time

1 minute (min)	=	60 seconds (s)
1 hour (h)	=	60 minutes
1 day	=	24 hours
1 week	=	7 days
1 year	=	12 months
1 year	=	52 weeks

TIPS FOR PROBLEM SOLVING

1. If you are stuck on a problem, that's all right. Problems are not supposed to be easy, otherwise they would not be problems.

2. There are no magic rules to take the place of thinking. These tips can only help you get in the right frame of mind. They cannot solve the problem for you.

3. Remember the Problem Solver's Guide.

- **Understand** Make sure you know what is happening in the problem and what the problem is asking for.

- **Try** Do not give up. Keep trying different things. If one idea does not work, try another.

- **Look Back** Check over what you have done to see that it makes sense.

4. If you do *not* understand the problem, try these ideas:

- Read the problem again slowly.

- Picture in your mind what is happening in the problem.

- Make notes or draw pictures.

- Look up or ask about words you do not know.

- Cooperate with a friend or a group of friends.

474

5. If you understand the problem, but do not know what to try, you might try one or more of these strategies:

Make a Table	See pages 28–29.
Make a Diagram	See pages 48–49.
Make a List	See pages 80–81.
Make a Plan	See pages 126–127.
Make a Model	See pages 158–159.
Guess and Check	See pages 196–197.
Make Notes	See pages 222–223 and 232–233.
Use Simpler Numbers	See pages 290–291 and 292–293.

6. Take chances. Do not be afraid to explore. Have lots of scrap paper handy.

7. When you look back, ask yourself these questions:

• Does my answer make sense?

• Does it fit what the problem is asking for?

• Are my computations correct?

TIPS FOR DOING MENTAL MATH

$$30 + 50 + 70 + 40 + 60$$

$$100 \quad + \quad 50 \quad + \quad 100$$

$$250$$

Mental math is often faster and easier than using either a calculator or paper and pencil. When doing mental math, remember the following tips:

- Using paper and pencil methods in your head is not always very efficient. There are special mental math strategies that work better.

- There are usually several good ways to do each problem.

- Be flexible; learn to see numbers as close to others. For example, 39 is 1 less than 40.

The mental math strategies shown on these pages will give you some ideas. Do not be afraid to invent methods of your own!

OPERATING WITH MULTIPLES OF 10, 100, AND 1000

Use basic facts to help you add, subtract, multiply, and divide multiples of 10, 100, and 1000.

8	80	800	8,000	$30 \times 5 = 150$
+4	+40	+400	+4,000	$30 \times 50 = 1500$
12	120	1200	12,000	$30 \times 500 = 15,000$

15	150	1500	15,000	$8 \div 2 = 4$
− 7	− 70	− 700	− 7,000	$80 \div 2 = 40$
8	80	800	8,000	$800 \div 2 = 400$

BREAKING NUMBERS APART

How much do both items cost together?

Replace numbers with other numbers that are easier to work with mentally.

$49¢ + 29¢ = $ ■

49¢ is 50¢ − 1¢
29¢ is 30¢ − 1¢

$$50¢ + 30¢ = 80¢$$
$$80¢ − 2¢ = 78¢$$

The answer is 78¢.

$350 + 150 = $ ■

Break 350 into 300 + 50.
Break 150 into 100 + 50.

$$300 + 50 + 100 + 50$$
$$400 + 100$$
$$500$$

The answer is 500.

ADDING ON

Add on in steps from the smaller number.

$40 − 19 = $ ■

$$19 + \boxed{1} = 20$$
$$20 + \boxed{20} = 40$$
$$\text{So, } 19 + \boxed{21} = 40.$$

The answer is 21.

Remember: Be Flexible!

$25 + 29 = $ ■

I know that 25 + 25 = 50 because two quarters equal 50¢. Now 29 is 4 more than 25; so I'll add 4 to the total.
$$50 + 4 = 54.$$
So, 25 + 29 = 54.

I think of 29 as 30 − 1. First, I add 30 to 25.
$$25 + 30 = 55$$
I've added 1 too many. So I'll subtract 1.
$$55 − 1 = 54$$
So, 25 + 29 = 54

Both methods are good mental math strategies!

TIPS FOR ESTIMATING

You can estimate when:

- you want to save time and work.

- an exact answer is not needed.

- you do not have paper and pencil or a calculator with you.

- you want to see if a calculation is reasonable or if you pushed a wrong button on your calculator.

> I wonder if $5 is enough to buy both items.

$2.56

NOTEBOOK

$1.95

The idea behind all estimation strategies is to use numbers close to the original numbers that **you** can work with mentally.

The estimation shown on these pages will give you some ideas. Do not be afraid to invent methods of your own!

Estimate:
$2.56 is less than $3
$1.95 is less than $2.
So, $2.56 + $1.95 is less than $5.
I do have enough money!

FRONT-END ESTIMATION

Addition

First: Add the front digits.

$$\begin{array}{r} 256 \\ 159 \\ 382 \\ +119 \\ \hline \end{array}$$

Rough estimate: **700**

Then: Adjust by looking for groups of 100.

$$\left.\begin{array}{r} 256 \\ 159 \end{array}\right\} \longleftarrow \text{about 100}$$
$$\left.\begin{array}{r} 382 \\ +119 \end{array}\right\} \longleftarrow \text{about 100}$$

Adjusted estimate: 700 + 100 + 100 = 900

Subtraction

Subtract the front digits.

$$\begin{array}{r} 7821 \\ -5369 \\ \hline \end{array}$$

Estimate: **2000**

OR

$$\begin{array}{r} 7821 \\ -5369 \\ \hline \end{array}$$

Closer Estimate: **2500**

INDEPENDENT STUDY

478

ROUNDING

Susan and her family drove 387 miles to the Grand Canyon.

When someone asked Susan how far they drove, she said, "about 400 miles."

Susan estimated the number of miles by rounding 387 to 400.

Here are some examples of how to use rounding to estimate.

$$\begin{array}{r} \$5.69 \longrightarrow \$6 \\ +\$2.85 \longrightarrow \$3 \\ \hline \text{Estimate: } \$9 \end{array}$$

$$\begin{array}{r} 829 \longrightarrow 800 \\ -486 \longrightarrow -500 \\ \hline \text{Estimate: } 300 \end{array}$$

$$\begin{array}{r} 47 \longrightarrow 50 \\ \times\ 5 \longrightarrow \times\ 5 \\ \hline \text{Estimate: } 250 \end{array}$$

Remember: Be Flexible!

I can round both numbers and then subtract.
$$500 - 300 = 200$$

I can also use front-end estimation.
$$500 - 200 = 300$$

Here are three good ways to estimate.
$$545 - 297$$

I can round just one number for a closer estimate.
$$545 - 300 = 245$$

All three estimates are reasonable: 200, 245, and 300

S TUDY TIPS

What Did You Learn Today?

We remember better if we review what we learn in math class each day. At the end of the class, you should answer these questions. Write the answers on a piece of paper because it will help you think more clearly.

Today I learned

Today I reviewed

I want to learn

I have this question

Share this information with some of the students in your class.

Try answering these questions each day for the next two weeks. You should find that this short review will help you remember the new ideas that you are learning in math.

FINDING INFORMATION

Do you know what the word **polygon** means? If so, write the meaning in your own words.

If you are not sure of the meaning there are places to go for help. Your math book has a glossary and an index. Find **polygon** in the glossary at the back of your book. Copy the meaning on a piece of paper.

Find **polygon** in the index. Turn to the page which is listed and copy that meaning onto your paper.

A dictionary can also give you information. Find the meaning of **polygon** there and copy it onto the same paper. You do not have to copy all of the meanings from the dictionary, just the ones that have to do with mathematics.

Which meaning do you like best?

Now, write the meaning of *polygon* in your own words. You might also give an example and label it.

Find the meanings of the following math words: *rectangular array, perimeter.*

Whether you are working on math in school or at home there are many places to go for help.

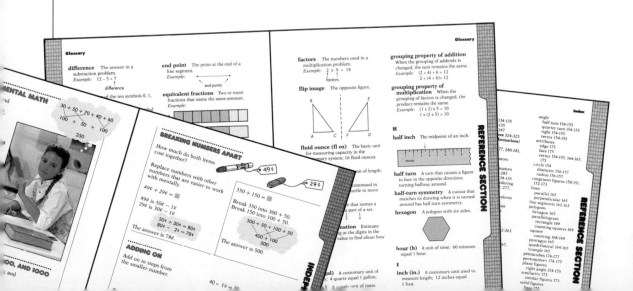

Using Your Textbook

Math can be a lot of fun, and your new book will help make it that way this year. In this book, you will find projects to do at home or in school, exercises to practice what you have learned, and challenging questions that ask you to think in new and different ways about things you already know.

Some lessons use calculators or computers. You will work with partners to make mathematical discoveries and to complete projects. You will be exploring many new ideas about math this year.

Knowing about your new book and how to best use it can help you. To get you started, here is a description of some features you'll find:

The **Connections** page of every chapter tells a story about mathematics that is related to the chapter's topic and to science, history, art, language, or another subject. The story will help you understand how mathematics connects to the world and why the lessons in the chapter are important for you to learn. (See page 213.)

In the lessons, you will learn about new topics by doing activities and thinking, writing, and talking about what you are learning.

"Think" questions are a part of many lessons. These are questions you will discuss in class with the help of your teacher. "Think" questions help you make sure you understand the lesson. (See page 86.)

For the **Math Log,** you use your own words or pictures to describe what you have learned. (See page 53.)

CHAPTER 3

Connections

Think

INDEPENDENT STUDY

482

In many lessons in your book, you will be able to teach yourself something new about math based on what you already know. This is fun because you can be both the teacher and the student. You and your classmates will explore and make discoveries about mathematics by drawing diagrams, studying patterns, cutting out shapes, and measuring objects. A lesson of this type is on page 254.

Math is an important part of your life. You are often "doing" math and you may not even know it! Many lessons in your book show you how to use the math you have learned in a situation that you might find in your life today or in the future. You can find a lesson like this on page 328.

Many lessons contain activities for you. One of the activities is **Project.** Projects are math games for you to make and play, patterns for you to design and draw, objects for you to build, and other interesting things. Projects are a good way to practice and have some fun with the lesson. (See page 347.)

This Handbook section contains many helpful pages. The **Tips for Problem Solving** guide will help you solve word problems. Refer to it whenever you get stuck on a problem. (See pages 474–475.)

The **Data Book** contains information on many topics, including sports, weather, maps, and plants. You will use the Data Book to answer questions, draw graphs, and make predictions. (See page 463.)

You will find extra practice problems (called **More Practice,** pages 420–462), a section on important **Mental Math** and **Estimation** skills (pages 476–479), and a **Glossary** (page 488) to use when you don't know or remember the meaning of a word.

CHALLENGE

COOPERATIVE • LEARNING

UNDERSTAND TRY THINK LOOK BACK

INDEPENDENT STUDY

9123456
1234567
2345678
3456789
4567891
5678912
66789123
8912345
39123456
71234567
12345678
3456789
44567891
5678912
66789123
7891234
8912345
39123456
71234567
12345678
2345678
34567
5678
67891
8912
39123
71234
12345
23456
34567
5678
66789
67891
78912
39123
71234
12345
23456
34567
5678
66789
67891
78912
39123
71234
12345
23456
34567
5678
66789
67891
78912
91234
12345
23456
34567
5678
66789
67891
78912
91234
12345
1234567
23456789
44567891
5678912
66789123
7891234
78912345
39123456
71234567
23456789
44567891
5678912
66789123
7891234
78912345
39123456
71234567
12345678
44567891

TIPS FOR WORKING TOGETHER

Cooperative learning helps you and your group develop important life skills. Here are some skills to work on:

MAKING CHOICES Decide who, when, what, where, and how to do the project.

COOPERATING Everyone in the group takes part in the project and works together. No one is left out.

BEING RESPONSIBLE Everyone is responsible for their part of the project and for seeing that the whole group finishes the project.

INDEPENDENT STUDY

LISTENING Let others talk about their ideas. Have them explain how they got an answer. Have them tell what they do or do not understand.

USING WORDS Help your groupmates. Praise a good suggestion or a job well done. Ask questions when you are having difficulties. Talk about your ideas.

THINKING Be creative. Apply what you already know to learn new concepts. Look for patterns, rules, or strategies. Explore and make sense of new ideas.

BEING INDEPENDENT Take charge of your learning. Use your teacher as a helper.

LEARNING TO USE A CALCULATOR

A calculator can be a very useful tool when you are doing mathematics. You will not need all the keys just to get started.

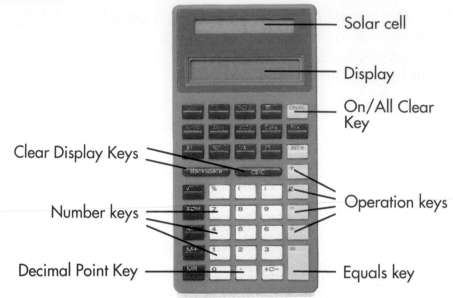

Solar cell

Display

On/All Clear Key

Clear Display Keys

Operation keys

Number keys

Decimal Point Key

Equals key

Entering Numbers

Try putting your telephone number into the calculator. To enter each digit, press a number key. The number should appear in the display.

How many digits does the display hold?

Press the numbers in order, starting with 1.

What did you see?

Clearing The Display

If you make a mistake in entering a number, you can press the CE/C key to clear the display. The calculator display will show 0, and you can start entering the number again.

If your calculator has a Backspace key, you can use it to clear only part of a calculator display.

Press: 9 3 4 Backspace Backspace What happened? You should notice that the calculator display shows 9. Only the 3 and 4 were cleared.

4567891
5678912
6789123
7891234
8912345
9123456
1234578
3456789
4567891
5678912
6789123
7891234
8912345
9123456
1234567
2345678
3456789
4567891
5678912
6789123
7891234
2345
3456
5678
6789
7891
8912
9123
1234
2345
3456
4567
5678
7891
8912
9123
1234
2345
3456
4567
5678
6789
8912
9123
1234
2345
3456
4567
5678
6789
7891
8912
9123
1234
2345
3456
4567
5678
6789
7891
8912
789123
7891234
8912345
9123456
1234567
2345678
3456789
4567891
5678912
7891234
8912345
9123456
1234567
2345678
3456789
4567891
5678912
6789123
8912345
9123456

Practice entering and clearing. Enter each number below. Remember to press the decimal point. Press ON/AC after each to clear the calculator.

419   10.5   912.5   5897.6

Using the Operation and Equals Keys

The +, −, ×, and ÷ signs are used just as they are with paper and pencil.

Press: 6 2 + 5 1.

What do you think the sum is? Check by pressing =. The answer will show in the display.

What happens if you press = again? You should see 164 in the display. Why?

When you press = again, the calculator adds 51 to 113. Each time you press =, the calculator will add 51 to the last sum. This is the way to make the calculator count by 51's.

To make the calculator count by 0.1's, press

0 + . 1 = = = = = =. Try it!

What did you see? You should see 0.1, 0.2, 0.3, 0.4, 0.5, 0.6.

Can you make the calculator count backward by 0.1's starting from 10? Press 1 0 − . 1 = = = = =.

Your calculator may not be like the one shown on page 486. It may have different labels on the keys. It may have different features. Draw a picture of your calculator and label the keys. As you try the activities, make notes to yourself about what your calculator can do and what it cannot do.

INDEPENDENT STUDY

Glossary

A

addend   A number added.
Example: 5 + 9 = 14
                    ↑   ↑
                  addends

A.M.   The hours from 12:00 midnight to 12:00 noon.

angle   A figure that can be used to show a turn.

area   A measure of how much surface is covered by a figure.

array   An arrangement of objects in equal rows.

array diagram   A simpler way to show an array.

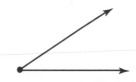

B

BACK (BK)   A command in Logo that directs the turtle to move backwards.

bar graph   A graph using bars of different lengths to show and compare information.

bug   An error within a computer program.

C

capacity   The maximum ability of a container to hold liquids or solids.

centimeter (cm)   A metric unit of length; 100 centimeters equals 1 meter.

centimeter ruler   A ruler marked in centimeters.

circle   A closed plane curve with every point the same distance from the center.

circle graph   A graph that shows a total amount divided into parts.

command   In Logo, a direction to do something.

common factor   A number that is a factor of two or more numbers.
Example: common factors of 18 and
                  24 : 1, 2, 3, 6

common multiple   A number that is a multiple of two or more numbers.
Example: common multiples of
                  2 and 3 : 6, 12, 24, 30

488

computer program   A set of commands that tells a computer what to do.

cone   A solid that has a circular base and comes to a point.

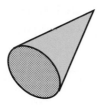

congruent figures   Figures that are the same size and shape.

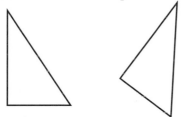

cube   A space figure having six square faces the same size.

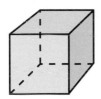

cup (c)   A customary unit of capacity; 2 cups equal 1 pint.

customary system   The measurement system that uses foot, quart, pound, and degree Fahrenheit.

cylinder   A solid that has parallel, congruent circular bases.

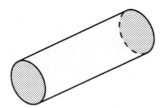

D

data   Facts.

day (d)   A 24-hour period.

decimal   A number with one or more digits to the right of a decimal point.
Example: 1.4   2.03   0.569

decimal point (.)   A symbol used to separate dollars and cents in money amounts; a symbol used to separate ones and tenths in decimals.
Example: $1.50   3.2
decimal points

decimeter (dm)   A metric unit of length; 10 centimeters equals 1 decimeter.

degree (angle)   A unit for measuring angles.

degree (temperature)   A unit for measuring temperature.

degree Celsius (°C)   The metric unit for measuring temperature.

degree Fahrenheit (°F)   The customary unit for measuring temperature.

denominator   The number written below the bar in a fraction .
Example: $\frac{1}{4}$ ← denominator

diameter   A line of symmetry of a circle.

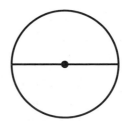

REFERENCE SECTION

difference   The answer in a subtraction problem.
Example: 12 – 5 = 7
↑
difference

digit   Any one of the ten symbols 0, 1, 2, 3, 4, 5, 6, 7, 8, or 9.

dividend   The number that is divided in a division problem.
Example: 36 ÷ 9 = 4
↑
dividend

divisor   The number by which the dividend is divided in a division problem.
Example: 36 ÷ 9 = 4
↑
divisor

divisible   When a number is capable of being divided into equal parts without a remainder.

dollar sign ($)   A symbol written before a number to show dollars in money amounts.

Example: $1.50
↑
dollar sign

E

edge   The segment where two faces of a solid figure meet.

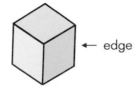
← edge

elapsed time   Time that has gone by.

END   A command in logo that completes a procedure.

end point   The point at the end of a line segment.
Example:

endpoints

equivalent fractions   Two or more fractions that name the same amount.
Example:

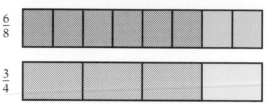

$\frac{6}{8}$

$\frac{3}{4}$

equivalent measures   Measures that have the same amount.
Example:
42 inches = 3 feet 6 inches = $3\frac{1}{2}$ feet

estimate   A number close to an exact amount. An estimate tells *about* how much.

even number   A whole number ending in 0, 2, 4, 6, or 8.
Example: 56   48

expanded form   A number written as the sum of the values of the digits.
Example: The number 2469 can be written as 2000 + 400 + 60 + 9 (number form), or 2 thousands + 4 hundreds + 6 tens + 9 ones (short word form).

F

face   A flat surface of a solid.

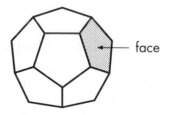
— face

490

factors The numbers used in a multiplication problem.
Example:

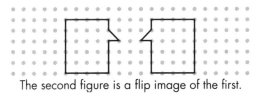

2 x 9 = 18
factors

flip A move that makes a figure face in the opposite direction..

The second figure is a flip image of the first.

fluid ounce (fl oz) The basic unit for measuring capacity in the customary system; 16 fluid ounces equal 1 pint.

foot (ft) A customary unit of length; 12 inches equal 1 foot.

FORWARD (FD) A command in Logo that directs the turtle to move forward.

fraction A number that names a part of a whole or a part of a set.
Example: $\frac{1}{2}$ $\frac{1}{3}$ $\frac{3}{4}$

front-end estimation Estimate made by looking at the digits in the greatest place value to find *about* how much.

G

gallon (gal) A customary unit of capacity; 4 quarts equals 1 gallon.

gram (g) A metric unit of mass (weight).

grouping property of addition When the grouping of addends is changed, the sum remains the same.
Example: (2 + 4) + 6 = 12
2 + (4 + 6) = 12

grouping property of multiplication When the grouping of factors is changed, the product remains the same.
Example: (1 x 2) x 5 = 10
1 x (2 x 5) = 10

H

half inch The midpoint of an inch.

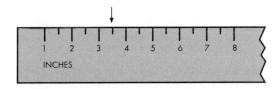

half turn A turn that causes a figure to point in a different direction.

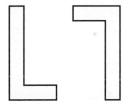

half-turn symmetry A figure that matches its tracing when it is turned halfway around has half-turn symmetry.

hexagon A polygon with six sides.

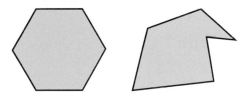

hour (h) A unit of time; 60 minutes equal 1 hour.

I

inch (in.) A customary unit used to measure length; 12 inches equal 1 foot.

REFERENCE SECTION

491

REFERENCE SECTION

inch ruler A straightedge marked in inches used for customary measurement.

is divisible by When a number can be divided exactly by another number, that number is said to be divisible by the other number.
Example: 27 ÷ 3 = 9
The number 27 is divisible by 3.

K

kilogram (kg) A metric unit of mass (weight); 1000 grams equal 1 kilogram .

kilometer (km) A metric unit of length; 1000 meters equal 1 kilometer.

L

LEFT (LT) A command in Logo that directs the turtle to move left.

line A straight, endless path.

line graph A graph that shows change over a period of time.

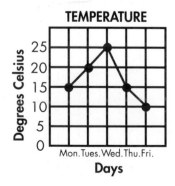

line of symmetry A line along which you could fold a figure so that both sides match.

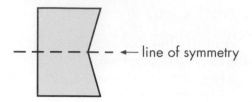
line of symmetry

line plot A diagram showing data on a number line.

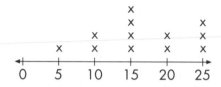

line segment Part of a line having two endpoints.

A●————————————————●Z

liter (L) The metric unit of capacity; 1000 milliliters equal 1 liter.

LOGO A computer language that uses a turtle to draw pictures.

M

mass The amount of matter in an object.

mean The average of a set of numbers, found by adding the numbers in the set and dividing by the number of addends.

median The number that falls exactly in the middle when a set of numbers is arranged in order from least to greatest.

meter (m) A metric unit of length; 100 centimeters equal 1 meter.

metric system The measurement systems that uses meter, liter, gram, and degree Celsius .

mile (mi) A customary unit of length; 5280 feet equal 1 mile.

milliliter (mL) A metric unit of capacity; 1000 milliliters equal 1 liter.

millimeter (mm) A metric unit of length; 10 millimeters equal 1 centimeter.

million 1000 thousands or 10 hundred thousands; the number after 999, 999 is one million (1,000,000).

minute (min) A unit of time; 60 seconds equal 1 minute.

missing factor In a multiplication sentence, when one factor and the product are given.
Example: 5 x ■ = 45
⟍ missing factor

mixed number A number that has a whole number part and a fraction part.
Example: $2\frac{1}{6}$

mode The number that occurs most often in a set of numbers.

multiple A product of two whole numbers.
Example: 4 x 2 = 8.
The number 8 is a multiple of 4 and of 2.

multiplication property of one If any factor is multiplied by one, the product is the same as that factor.
Example: 4 x 1 = 4   1 x 51 = 51

multiplication property of zero If any factor is multiplied by zero, the product is zero.
Example: 7 x 0 = 0   0 x 238 = 0

N

net A flat pattern that folds into a solid.

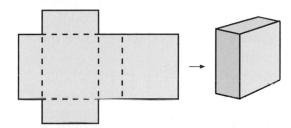

numerator The number written above the bar in a fraction.
Example: $\frac{1}{6}$ ← numerator

O

odd number A whole number ending in 1, 3, 5, 7, or 9.
Example: 67   493

one hundredth One of 100 equal parts; $\frac{1}{100}$ or 0.01.

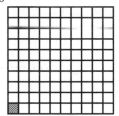

one tenth One of 10 equal parts; $\frac{1}{10}$ or 0.10.

ordered pair   A pair of numbers that names a point on a grid.

order property of addition
When the order of two addends is changed, the sum remains the same.
Examples: $4 + 1 = 5 \mid 62 + 34 = 96$
$1 + 4 = 5 \mid 34 + 62 = 96$

order property of multiplication
When the order of the factors is changed, the product remains the same.
Examples: $3 \times 5 = 15 \mid 2 \times 117 = 234$
$5 \times 3 = 15 \mid 117 \times 2 = 234$

ordinal numbers   Numbers used to show order. *Examples:*   first, second, third.

ounce (oz)   A customary measure of weight; 16 ounces equal 1 pound.

P

palindrome   A number whose digits are the same from left to right and from right to left.
Example: 22   636   1551

parallel lines   Lines that are always the same distance apart.

pentacube   A solid figure made up of five congruent cubes, with each cube having at least one face connecting with another cube.

pentagon   A polygon with five sides.

Examples:
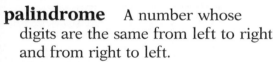

pentomino   A plane figure made up of five congruent squares connected to each other along whole sides.

perimeter   The distance around a figure. The perimeter of this rectangle is 12 cm.

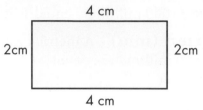

4 cm + 2 cm + 4 cm + 2 cm = 12 cm

perpendicular   Two lines or line segments that cross to form right angles.

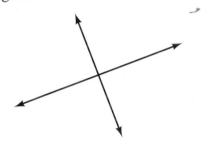

pictograph   A graph that uses pictures to stand for data.

pint (pt)   A customary unit of capacity; 2 pints equal 1 quart.

place value   The value of a position in a number.
Example: In 7943, the digit 7 is in the thousands place.

Thousands	Hundreds	Tens	Ones
7	9	4	3

P.M.   The hours from 12:00 noon to 12:00 midnight.

point   An exact place or position in space, represented by a dot.

polygon   A figure made up of line segments with three or more sides.

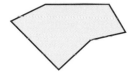

pound (lb)   A customary unit of weight; 16 ounces equal 1 pound.

prediction   Something that is guessed in advance, based on previous experience.

prime number   A number with only two factors, itself and 1.
Examples: 2   3   7   11   17

prism   A solid that has two congruent parallel bases joined by faces that are parallelograms.

probability   The chance that an event will occur.

procedure   In Logo, a list of commands that tells the turtle what to draw.

product   The answer in a multiplication problem.
Example: 5 x 3 = 15
          ↑
        product

pyramid   A solid having a polygon for a base with all other faces triangular and sharing a common vertex.

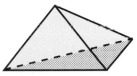

Q

quadrilateral   A four-sided figure.

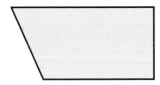

quart (qt)   A customary unit of capacity; 4 quarts equal 1 gallon.

quarter   Name for 25¢, one fourth, or $\frac{1}{4}$.

quarter inch   One fourth of an inch.

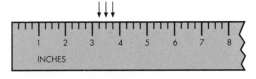

quotient   The answer in a division problem.
Example: 36 ÷ 9 = 4
              ↑
           quotient

REFERENCE SECTION

R

radius   The distance from the center of a circle to any point on a circle.

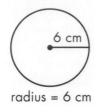

radius = 6 cm

rectangle   A polygon having four sides and four right angles. A square is a kind of rectangle.

rectangular array   An arrangement of objects in equal rows.

Example: 3 × 14

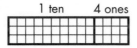

1 ten   4 ones

rectangular prism   A prism having 6 rectangular faces.

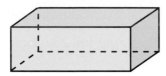

remainder   The number left over in a division problem when the dividend is not divisible by the divisor.
Example:

$$9\overline{)38} \quad 4\ R2$$

REPEAT   A command in logo that directs the turtle to perform a command more than once.

rhombus   A four sided polygon with all four sides equal.

RIGHT (RT)   A command in logo that directs the turtle to move right.

right angle   A quarter turn; an angle with a measurement of 90°.

90°

rounded number   a number expressed to the nearest ten, hundred, thousand and so on. 436 rounded to the nearest ten is 440.

S

second (s)   A unit of time; 60 seconds equal 1 minute.

side   A line segment forming part of a figure.

similar figures   Figures that have the same shape, but are not necessarily the same size.

simplest form   A fraction whose numerator and denominator have no common factor greater than 1.
Example: $\frac{2}{3}$ is the simplest form of $\frac{8}{12}$

slide   A motion in which every point of a figure moves the same distance in the same direction.

slide arrow   An arrow that shows the distance and direction to slide a figure.

sphere   A solid having the shape of a ball.

square   A polygon with four right angles and four equal sides.

square centimeter (sq cm)   A metric unit used to measure area.

square inch (sq in.)   A customary unit used to measure area.

square number   A product that can be shown by a square array.

standard form   The usual, or common, way of writing a number, using digits.
Example: The standard form of twenty-seven is 27.

sum   The answer in an addition problem.
Example: 5 + 4 = 9
                                ↑
                               sum

survey   A way to collect data by asking questions of many people.

T

temperature   A measure of how hot or cold something is.

thermometer   An instrument that measures temperature.

ton (t)   A customary unit of mass (weight); 2000 pounds equals 1 ton.

triangle   A polygon with three sides and three vertices.

turn center   A point around which a figure is turned.

turn image   The position of a figure after a turn.

U

unit price   The cost of one item.

V

value   In 324, the 2 is in the tens place. Its value is 20.

vertex (vertices)   The corner point of an angle, a closed plane figure, or a solid.

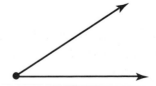

REFERENCE SECTION

volume   The number of cubic units that could fit inside a container, such as a prism or a cone.

W

whole number   Any of the numbers 0, 1, 2, 3, 4, 5, and so on.

Y

yard (yd)   A customary unit of length; 3 feet equal one yard.

yardstick   A ruler marked in inches and feet, that is one yard long.

Z

zero property of addition   The sum of zero and one addend is the addend.
Examples: $4.9 + 0 = 4.9$
$0 + 6.7 = 6.7$

REFERENCE SECTION

Index

A

Addition. *See also* Estimation, Mental math, Properties, Rounding.

annexing zeros, 354-355

basic facts, 25, 42-43

decimals, 354-355, 358-359, 381

denominate numbers, 52-53, 55, 66-67

fractions, 276-277, 280-281, 284-285, 321

mixed numbers, 288, 321

regrouping

  ones as tens, 52-53, 54-55, 66-67

  tens as hundreds, 52-53, 54-55, 66-67

related to multiplication, 108-109

three or more addends, 54

whole numbers, 52-53, 54-55, 66-67, 85, 129, 191, 215, 235, 238-239, 407

Algebra. *See also* Properties.

equations

  missing factors, 116, 399

  missing symbols, 25, 61, 65, 122-123, 229, 237, 381

  missing terms, 42-43, 116-117, 131, 253, 257

  number sentences, 109, 113

expressions

  comparing, 381

functions, 366-367

graphs

  ordered pairs, 162-163

inequalities, 24-25, 256-257, 344-345

Angles. *See* Geometry.

Area. *See* Measurement.

Array diagram, 190-191, 192, 378-379, 380, 384

Assessment

Chapter Test, 36, 70, 102, 144, 182, 208, 242, 270, 296, 332, 364, 392, 416

Cumulative Review, 37, 71, 103, 145, 183, 209, 243, 271, 297, 333, 365, 393, 417

Section Review, 17, 35, 57, 69, 91, 101, 121, 143, 167, 181, 199, 207, 227, 241, 259, 269, 283, 295, 315, 331, 351, 363, 383, 391, 409, 415

Average. *See* Statistics.

B

Balance. *See* Manipulatives, Measurement.

Bar Graph. *See* Graphs.

Basic Fact Strategy. *See* Addition, Subtraction, Mental Math.

C

Calculator, 67, 72-73, 136-137, 202-203, 204-205, 298-299, 343, 350-351, 358-359, 386-387, 394-395, 413, 418-419, 486-487

Calendar, 328 329

Capacity. *See* Measurement.

Celsius, degree, 324-325

Challenge

elapsed time, 327

logical reasoning, 77, 201, 225

measurement, 385

mixed numbers, 289

number sense, 61

patterns, 43, 123, 253, 343

probability, 95

problem formulation, 163

problem solving, 239, 261, 389

rounding, 33

visualization, 165

Chapter Opener

connections

  art, 41

  critical thinking, 275

  estimation, 107, 337

  language arts, 247

  money sense, 1

  science, 149, 213, 301, 369

  social studies, 187, 397

  statistics, 75

Chapter Test. *See* Assessment.

Choose a Computation Method, 282

calculator or mental math, 350, 358-359

exact or estimate, 198

mental math or paper and pencil, 120

Circle graph. *See* Graph.

Circles. *See* Geometry.

Comparing and ordering

capacity, 312-313, 320-321

decimals, 344-347, 375

expressions, 381

fractions, 254-255, 256-257, 277, 285, 303

length, 304-305, 318-319

weight, 314

whole numbers, 24-25, 65

Computer, 210-211, 244-245, 272-273

Congruent figures. *See* Geometry.

Connecting Cubes. *See* Manipulatives.

Consumer math

better buy, 334-335, 402-403, 410-411, 418-419

checking accounts, 72-73

comparing prices, 334-335

estimating costs, 204-205

making change, 30-33

order form, 386-387

total cost, 204-205, 334-335, 386-387, 402-403

unit price, 418-419

Cooperative learning, 5, 7, 9, 11, 15, 19, 20-21, 29, 45, 47, 49, 63, 81, 83, 85, 92-93, 96-97, 98-99, 113, 118-119, 127, 132-133, 134-135, 137, 138-139, 141, 152-153, 159, 169, 174-175, 176-177, 178-179, 197, 202-203, 205,

223, 230-231, 233, 250-251, 254-255, 260-261, 264-265, 278-279, 280-281, 307, 308-309, 310-311, 313, 314, 322, 325, 328-329, 338-339, 347, 348-349, 359, 387, 402-403

Counters. *See* Manipulatives.
Critical thinking, 3, 14-15, 21, 23, 25, 50-51, 52-53, 59, 61, 64-65, 76-77, 82-83, 86-87, 88-89, 93, 94-95, 99, 105, 108-109, 110-111, 114, 116, 119, 125, 129, 133, 135, 137, 140, 147, 151, 153, 163, 168-169, 170-171, 173, 179, 188-189, 191, 193 194-195, 200, 204-205, 216-217, 219, 221, 224, 228, 231, 237, 238-239, 251, 255, 263, 275, 281, 284, 287, 299, 302-303, 306-307, 308-309, 313, 318, 322, 324, 326, 344-345, 346-347, 349, 353, 355, 356-357, 359, 370-371, 372-373, 378-379, 380-381, 384, 388-389, 398-399, 404, 410-411
Cultural Diversity, 72-73, 298-299, 334-335, 366-367, 394-395, 418-419
Cumulative Review. *See* Assessment, Maintain.
Customary system. *See also* Measurement.
capacity, 312-313
length, 302-303, 304-305, 308-309
weight, 314
Cylinder. *See* Geometry.

D

Data. *See* Statistics.
Data Book, 464-473
using, 25, 65, 77, 85, 171, 201, 235, 257, 327, 358, 389, 413
Decimal Squares. *See* Manipulatives.

Decimals. *See also* Estimation, Mental math.
addition, 354-355, 358-359, 381
comparing and ordering, 344-345, 346-347, 375
equivalent decimals, 344-345, 354-355, 356-357
and fractions, 342-343
hundredths, 338-339, 340-341, 342-343
and mixed numbers, 342-343
number sense, 342-343
place value, 340-341
reading, 342-343
rounding, 352-353, 359
subtraction, 356-357, 358-359, 381
tenths, 338-339, 340-341, 342-343
writing, 340-341, 342-343
Decision making, 205, 334-335
Degree. *See also* Measurement.
angle measure, 154
temperature, 324-325
Diameter. *See* Geometry.
Divisibility. *See* Division.
Division. *See also* Estimation, Mental math.
basic facts, 112-113, 114-115, 116-117, 124-125, 128-129, 130-131, 140-141, 161, 169
checking quotients, 214-215, 220-221, 404-405, 406-407
dividends, 114-115
divisibility, 230-231
divisors, 114-115
fact families, 130-131
meaning of, 112-113
money, 234-235, 410-411
patterns, 124-125, 128-129, 130, 140-141
quotients, 114-115
with zeros, 228-229

related to multiplication, 112-113, 114-115, 128-129, 130-131, 214-215, 218-219, 220-221, 224-225, 228-229, 398-399, 400-401, 404-405, 406-407
related to subtraction, 112
remainders, 214-215
interpreting, 216-217
rules, 116-117
whole numbers, 112-113, 114-115, 116-117, 124-125, 128-129, 130-131, 140-141, 161, 169
one-digit divisors, 214-215, 216-217, 220-221, 224-225, 228-229, 230-231, 236-237, 238-239, 249, 267, 355
two-digit divisors, 404-405, 406-407, 410-411, 412-413

E

Elapsed time. *See* Measurement.
Equations. *See* Algebra.
Estimation
differences, 58-59, 352-353, 358-359
front end, 50-51, 58-59, 188-189, 362, 372-373
adjusted estimate, 50-51, 362
rough estimate, 50-51, 362
gross estimation, 2-3, 4-5, 278
halfway point, 12-13
measures
capacity, 313, 320-321
length, 305, 309, 319
mass, 322
perimeter, 307
temperature, 324-325
time, 326-327
weight, 314
products, 188-189, 194, 200-201, 204-205, 372-373, 374-375, 384-385

quotients, 218-219, 220-221, 224-225, 228-229, 235, 236-237, 400-401, 404-405, 406-407
rounding to estimate, 58-59, 73, 188-189, 352-353, 372
sum, 50-51, 55, 56, 352-353, 358-359, 362
using number lines, 352-353
Estimation Tips, 478-479
Events. *See* Probability.
Excursion
math to math, 38-39, 104-105, 146-147, 184-185, 210-211, 244-245, 272-273, 298-299, 366-367, 394-395
math to the real world, 72-73, 334-335, 418-419
Expanded form. *See* Place value.
Expressions. *See* Algebra.

F

Factor tree, 146-147
Factors, 110-111, 134-135
common, 134-135
Fahrenheit, degree, 324-325
Flips. *See* Transformations.
Fraction Bars. *See* Manipulatives.
Fractions
addition, 276-277, 280-281, 284-285, 321
like denominators, 276-277
unlike denominators, 280-281, 284-285
comparing and ordering, 254-257, 277, 285, 303
and decimal equivalents, 342-343
denominator, 248-249
equal parts, 248-249
equivalent, 250-253
fractional parts,
of a set, 260-261, 262-263
of a whole, 265

meaning, 248-249
mixed numbers, 266-267, 288-289
numerator, 248-249
simplest form, 252-253
subtraction, 276-277, 280-281, 286-287, 321
like denominators, 276-277
unlike denominators, 280-281, 286-287
writing, 248-249
Frequency table, 2, 76-77, 78-79, 92-93
Functions. *See* Algebra.

G

Games 7, 11, 45, 47, 141, 255
Geoboard. *See* Manipulatives.
Geometry. *See also* Measurement, Transformations.
angle
half turn, 154-155
quarter turn, 154-155
right, 154-155
vertex, 154-155
attributes
edge, 175
face, 175
vertex, 154-155, 165, 175
circle, 155
diameter, 156-157
radius, 156-157
congruent figures, 150-151, 172-173
lines
parallel, 165
perpendicular, 165
line segment, 162-165
pentacubes, 177
pentominoes, 176-177
polygons
hexagon, 164-165
parallelogram, 164
pentagon, 164-165
quadrilateral, 164-165
rectangle, 169
quadrilateral, 164-165
triangle, 164-165

similar figures, 173
solid figures
base, 175
cone, 174-175
cube, 174-175
cylinder, 174-175
edge, 175
face, 175
prism
pentagonal, 175
rectangular, 175
triangular, 175
pyramid, 174-175
sphere, 174
vertex
angle, 154-155
polygon, 164-165
solid, 175
visualization, 165, 176-177
Glossary, 488-498
Graph. *See also* Algebra.
bar
making, 78-79, 95, 105
reading, 3, 78-79, 88, 117, 412-413
using, 3, 78-79, 88, 117, 412-413
circle
reading, 86-87, 89
using, 86-87, 89
line
making, 84-85, 325, 359
reading, 84-85, 89
using, 84-85, 89
line plots
making, 142
reading, 142
using, 142
ordered pairs, 162-163
pictograph
making, 83
reading, 82-83, 115
using, 82-83, 115

H

Handbook, 463-498
Data Book, 464-473
Independent Study, 474-487
Reference Section, 488-498

Index

I

Inequalities. *See* Algebra.

L

Line graph. *See* Graphs.
Line plot. *See* Graphs.
Line segments. *See*
    Geometry.
Lines. *See* Geometry.
LOGO, 210-211, 244-245,
    272-273

M

Maintain
    addition and subtraction
        facts, 25
    area, 195
    comparing decimals, 375
    comparing fractions, 277
    comparing numbers, 65
    elapsed time, 345
    mixed practice, 85, 129,
        161, 191, 215, 235,
        249, 267, 321, 355,
        381, 407
    multiplication, 405
    ordering fractions, 285,
        303
    place value, 55, 99
    using graphs, 117
Manipulatives
    Balance, 314, 322
    Connecting Cubes, 176-177
    Counters, 33, 112-113, 230-
        231, 238
    Decimal Squares, 338-339,
        340-345, 347
    Fraction Bars, 250-251,
        252-257, 276-277, 280-
        281, 284-285, 286-287
    Geoboard, 164-165
    Number Cubes, 10, 105,
        299
    Place-Value Blocks, 10-11
    Play Money, 30
Maps, 9, 12-13, 60, 68, 81,
    166, 294
Math Log, 16, 53, 87, 93,
    111, 171, 193, 231, 263,
    287, 313, 357, 379, 401,
    414

Mean. *See* Statistics.
Measurement. *See also*
    Customary system,
    Estimation, Geometry,
    Metric system.
    area, 170-171, 195, 385
        finding length and width,
        394-395
    area readiness, 169
    calendar
        reading, 328-329
        using, 328-329
    capacity
        customary units
            cup, 312-313
            fluid ounce, 312-313
            gallon, 312-313
            pint, 312-313
            quart, 312-313
        metric units
            liter, 320-321
            milliliter, 320-321
    choosing appropriate tools,
        308-309
    choosing appropriate units,
        305, 320-321
    choosing better estimate,
        305, 319, 322, 324-325,
        326-327
    comparisons
        capacity, 312-313, 320-
            321
        length, 304-305, 318-319
        weight, 314
    diameter, 156-157
    equivalent measures, 304-
        305, 312-313, 314, 316-
        317, 318-319, 320-321,
        322, 326-327
    length
        customary units
            foot, 304-305
            half inch, 302-303
            inch, 302-303
            mile, 302-303
            yard, 304-305
        metric units
            centimeter, 316-317
            decimeter, 318-319
            kilometer, 318-319
            meter, 318-319
            millimeter, 316-317

    mass
        gram, 322
        kilogram, 322
    measurement lab, 308-309,
        313
    perimeter, 306-307, 317
    temperature
        below zero, 324-325
        degrees Celsius, 324-325
        degrees Fahrenheit, 324-
            325
        writing, 324-325
    time
        day, 326-327
        elapsed, 326-327, 345
        hour, 326-327
        minute, 326-327
        second, 326-327
    tools
        balance, 314, 322
        clock
            analog, 326-327
            digital, 326-327
        ruler, 302-303, 306-307,
            308-309, 316-317
        thermometer, 324-325
        yardstick, 308-309
    volume
        cube, 178-179
        rectangular prism, 178-
            179
    weight
        ounce, 314
        pound, 314
        ton, 314
Median. *See* Statistics.
Mental math
    addition, 6-7, 44-45, 46-47,
        100, 370-371
    basic facts, 6-7
    division, 140-141, 224-225,
        228-229, 398-399
    multiplication, 136-137,
        193, 201, 370-371
    patterns, 136-137, 140-141,
        370-371, 398-399
    subtraction, 6-7, 44-45,
        100, 357
Mental Math Tips, 476-477

REFERENCE SECTION

502

Metric system. *See also*
Measurement.
capacity, 320-321
length, 316-317, 318-319
mass, 322
Mixed numbers
addition, 288-289, 321
concept of, 266-267
and decimals, 342-343
subtraction, 288-289, 321
writing, 266-267
Mode. *See* Statistics.
Money. *See also* Estimation,
Problem solving.
addition, 52-53, 54-55
combinations, 26-27, 30-
31, 32-33
counting, 26-27, 30-31
division, 234-235, 410-411
identifying, 26-27
making change, 30
multiplication, 204-205,
386-387
rounding, 15, 33
subtraction, 61, 64-65, 66-
67, 381
writing, 26-27
Money sense, 23, 32-33
More Practice, 420-462
Multiples. *See* Numeration
and number theory.
Multiplication. *See also*
Estimation, Mental
math, Properties,
Rounding.
array diagrams, 190-191,
378-379
basic facts, 108-109, 110-
111, 116-117, 118-119,
122-123, 128-129, 130-
131, 136-137, 161, 169
denominate numbers, 374-
375, 380-381, 384-385
doubles, 122-123, 128-129,
131
fact families, 130-131
factor, 110-111
meaning of, 108-109
money, 204-205, 386-387
multiples, 132-133
product, 110-111

regrouping
with, 192-193, 194-195,
200-201, 378-379,
380-381, 384-385
without, 192-193, 194-
195, 200-201, 378-
379, 380-381, 384
related to addition, 108-109
related to division, 112-
113, 130-131, 214-215,
218-219, 224-225, 228-
229, 400-401, 404-405,
406-407
tables, 110, 118-119, 122-
123, 128, 130
three factors, 116-117, 388
whole numbers, 108-109,
110-111, 116-117, 118-
119, 122-123, 128-129,
130-131, 136-137, 161,
169, 388-389
one-digit multipliers,
190-191, 192-193,
194-195, 200-201,
215, 235, 249, 267,
355
two-digit multipliers,
374-375, 378-381,
384-385, 404

N

Number Cubes. *See*
Manipulatives.
Number line
decimals, 342-343, 352-353
halfway points, 12-13, 14
using number lines, 12-13,
14-15, 22-23, 342-343,
352-353
whole numbers, 12-13, 14-
15, 22-23
Number sense. *See*
Decimals, Estimation,
Mixed numbers, Whole
numbers.
**Numeration and number
theory.** *See also*
Decimals, Estimation,
Fractions, Mixed
numbers, Place value,
Whole numbers.

common factor, 134-135
common multiple, 132-133
divisibility, 230-231
prime numbers, 146-147
Roman numerals, 38-39
square numbers, 184-185

O

Ordered pairs, 162-163
Ordering. *See* Comparing
and ordering.
Outcomes. *See* Probability.

P

Parallel lines. *See* Geometry.
Pattern Blocks. *See*
Manipulatives.
Patterns
finding, 119, 130, 132-133,
136-137, 140-141, 230-
231, 370-371, 398-399
geometric, 43, 175
numerical, 27, 110, 119,
122-123, 124-125, 128-
129, 130, 132-133, 136-
137, 140-141, 230-231,
253, 343, 370-371, 398-
399
Pentagon. *See* Geometry.
Perimeter. *See* Estimation,
Measurement.
Permutations, 96-97
Pictograph. *See* Graph.
Place-value Blocks. *See*
Manipulatives.
Place value. *See also*
Manipulatives,
Numeration, and
number theory.
chart, 10-11, 340-341
decimals, 342-343
expanded form, 10-11, 18-
19
short word form, 10-11,
342-343
standard form, 10-11, 18-19
whole numbers, 10-11, 18-
19, 55
word form, 342-343

Index

Play money. *See* Manipulatives.

Polygon. *See* Geometry.

Prime factorization, 146-147

Prime number, 146-147

Prism. *See* Geometry, Measurement.

Probability
as a ratio, 94-95
comparing
probable outcomes, 94-95
results of experiments, 92-93, 98-99, 299
results of predictions, 92-93, 97, 98-99, 299
events
dependent, 104-105
independent, 104-105
experiments, 92-93, 95, 98-99, 105, 299
outcomes, 94-95
least likely, 94-95
most likely, 94-95
permutations, 96-97
predictions, 92-93, 97, 98-99, 299
recording results, 92-93, 95, 97, 98-99, 105, 299

Problem formulation, 33, 63, 65, 86, 113, 115, 163, 195, 279, 359, 413

Problem Solving
applications 16, 25, 33, 41, 43, 51, 55, 56, 59, 61, 65, 67, 68, 73, 79, 100, 109, 111, 113, 115, 117, 120, 123, 125, 129, 131, 135, 138-139, 163, 166, 171, 180, 193, 195, 201, 202-203, 206, 215, 217, 219, 221, 226, 229, 235, 237, 239, 249, 257, 263, 264-265, 267, 268, 277, 278-279, 285, 289, 310-311, 314, 319, 323, 327, 328-329, 330, 345, 348-349, 350, 353, 355, 357, 358-359, 371, 373, 375, 376-377, 379, 381, 385, 389, 399, 402-403, 404, 407, 408, 414
Problem Solver's Guide, 8-9
Problem Solving Tips, 474-475
skills
does the answer fit the problem? 90
finding needed information, 25, 65, 76-77, 85, 171, 201, 235, 257, 327, 358-359, 389, 413
logical reasoning, 77, 201, 225, 261, 382, 387, 389
not enough information, 34, 123
using data, 2-3, 24-25, 30-31, 43, 46, 50-51, 52-53, 54-55, 59, 61, 65, 66-67, 68, 72-73, 76-77, 78-79, 82-83, 84-85, 86-87, 88-89, 94-95, 100, 110-111, 115, 117, 122-123, 124-125, 127, 128, 131, 135, 137, 142, 162-163, 166, 169, 171, 177, 178-179, 192-193, 195, 200-201, 205, 210-211, 235, 237, 240, 257, 262-263, 267, 278-279, 298-299, 327, 328-329, 330, 346, 348-349, 353, 355, 356-357, 358-359, 360-361, 371, 373, 376-377, 381, 386-387, 389, 390, 407, 410-411, 412-413, 414
using math sense, 62-63, 240, 258, 360-361, 390
strategies
Guess and Check, 196-197
Make a Diagram, 48-49
Make a List, 80-81
Make a Model, 158-159
Make a Plan, 126-127
Make a Table, 28-29
Make Notes, 222-223, 232-233
Use Simpler Numbers, 290-291, 292-293

Project
circles, 155
decision making, 205
estimating weight, 314
estimation, 3, 5, 169, 307, 322
game, 7, 11, 45, 47, 141, 255
graph, 359
making models, 177
mental math, 137
multiples, 133
number sense, 15, 21, 23
numeration, 19
ordering decimals, 347
patterns, 175
prisms, 179
problem solving, 135, 279, 387
similarity, 173
statistics, 83, 349
temperature change, 325
using fractions, 265
using measurement, 309

Properties and Rules
addition
grouping, 42-43
order, 42-43
zero, 42-43
division, 116-117
multiplication
grouping, 116-117, 388-389
order, 116-117
property of one, 116-117
zero, 116-117
subtraction, 42-43

Pyramid. *See* Geometry.

R

Radius. *See* Measurement.

Rectangle. *See* Geometry, Measurement.

Rectangular array, 112-113, 134-135, 184-185, 190-191, 378-381, 384-385

REFERENCE SECTION

Regrouping. *See also*
Addition, Multiplication,
Subtraction.
hundreds as tens, 60-61,
64-65, 66-67
ones as tens, 52-53, 54-55,
66-67, 192-193, 194-
195, 200-201, 380-381,
384-385
tens as hundreds, 52-53,
54-55, 66-67, 192-193,
194-195, 200-201, 380-
381, 384-385
tens as ones, 60-61, 64-65,
66-67
thousands, 54-55, 60-61,
64-65, 66-67, 194-195,
200-201, 384-385
Remainders. *See* Division.
Roman numerals, 38-39
Rounding. *See also*
Estimation.
decimals, 352-353, 359
to estimate
differences, 58-59, 352-
353
money, 15, 33, 352-353
products, 188-189, 372-
373
sums, 56, 352-353
using a number line, 14-15,
22-23, 352-353
whole numbers, 14-15, 16,
22-23, 99

S

Section Review. *See*
Assessment.
Similarity, 173
Skip-counting, 5, 27, 82-83,
132-133, 326-327
Slides. *See* Transformations.
Solid figure. *See* Geometry.
Square. *See* Geometry,
Measurement.
Square number, 184-185
Standard form. *See* Place
value.
Statistics. *See also* Graphs.
average, 238-239, 406-407,
412-413

data
collecting, 3, 15, 21, 76-
77, 78-79, 85, 92-93,
95, 308-309, 313,
325, 349
organizing, 3, 78-79, 93,
95, 105, 325, 349
recording, 2-3, 21, 76-77,
78-79, 93, 95, 105,
118-119, 132-133,
151, 153, 308-309,
313, 325, 349
measures
mean, 298-299
median, 298-299
mode, 298-299
surveys, 76-77, 83, 349
tally, 2, 76-77, 92-93
Strategies
basic facts
doubles, 110-111, 122-
123, 128-129
fact families, 130-131
skip-counting, 82-83,
132-133
estimation
front end, 50-51, 58-59,
188-189, 362, 372-
373, 478-479
rounding, 56, 58-59, 188-
189, 352-353, 372-373
mental math
adding on, 100
breaking numbers apart,
44-47
multiples of 10, 100,
1000, 6-7, 136-137,
140-141, 201, 224-
225, 228-229, 370-
371, 398-399
problem solving
strategy development
Make Notes, 232-234
Use Simpler Numbers,
292-293
strategy introduction
Make Notes, 222-223
Use Simpler Numbers,
290-291

strategy review
Guess and Check, 196-
197
Make a Diagram, 48-49
Make a List, 80-81
Make a Model, 158-159
Make a Plan, 126-127
Make a Table, 28-29
Study Tips, 480-481
Subject integration
art, 40-41, 264-265, 278-
279
language arts, 16, 33, 64,
65, 85, 87, 113, 115,
163, 195, 247, 279,
325, 359
science, 59, 65, 76-77, 108,
149, 213, 301, 325
social studies, 12-13, 24-25,
38-39, 85, 89, 201, 358-
359, 397
Subtraction. *See also*
Estimation, Mental
math.
across zeros, 64-65
annexing zeros, 356-357
basic facts, 25, 42-43
checking differences, 60-
61, 64-65, 356-357
decimals, 356-357, 358-
359, 381
denominate numbers, 60-
61, 64-65
fractions, 276-277, 280-
281, 286-287, 321
large numbers, 60-61, 64-
65
mixed numbers, 288-289,
321
money, 60-61, 64-65, 66,
381
regrouping
with, 60-61, 64-65, 66-67
without, 60-61, 64-65,
66-67
related to division, 112-113
whole numbers, 60-61,
64-65, 66-67, 85,
129, 191, 215, 235,
407

Index

Symmetry. *See*
Transformations.

T

Technology. *See* Calculator,
Computer.
Temperature. *See*
Measurement.
Time. *See* Measurement.
Time zone, 294
Transformations
  flips (reflections)
    flip image, 150-151
    mirror image, 150-151
  slides (translations)
    slide arrow, 160-161
    slide symmetry, 160-161
  symmetry
    half turn, 156-157
    line of, 156-157
    slide, 160-161
  turns (rotations)
    half turns, 154-155
    quarter turns, 154-155
    related to angles, 154-
      155
    turn center, 152-153
    turn image, 152-153
Triangles. *See* Geometry.
Turns. *See* Transformations.

U

Using Your Textbook, 482-
  483

V

Vertex. *See* Geometry.
Visualization
  with pentacubes, 177
  with pentominoes, 176-177
Volume. *See* Measurement.

W

Weight. *See* Measurement.
Whole numbers. *See also*
  Estimation, Mental
  math, Place value,
  Rounding.
  addition, 25, 52-53, 54-55,
    66-67, 85, 129, 191,
    215, 235, 238-239, 407

comparing and ordering,
  24-25, 65
division, 41, 112-113, 116-
  117, 124-125, 128-129,
  130-131, 140, 161, 214-
  215, 216-217, 220-221,
  224-225. 228-229, 230-
  231, 236-237, 238-239,
  249, 267, 355, 404-405,
  406-407, 410-411
finding a fraction, of 265
multiplication, 108-109,
  110-111, 116-117, 118-
  119, 122-123, 128-129,
  130-131, 136-137, 161,
  190-191, 192-193, 194-
  195, 200-201, 215, 235,
  249, 267, 355, 374-375,
  378-379, 380-381, 384-
  385, 388-389, 404-405
number sense, 15, 20-21,
  23, 61
numeration, 19
place value, 10-11, 18-19,
  55
reading, 14-15, 16, 22-23,
  99
rounding, 22-23, 99
subtraction, 25, 60-61, 64-
  65, 66-67, 85, 129, 191,
  215, 235, 407
writing, 10-11, 18-19
Working Together Tips,
  484-485

Z

Zeros
  in addition, 42-43
  in division, 116-117, 228-
    229
  in multiplication, 116-117
  in subtraction, 42-43, 64-65

REFERENCE SECTION

CREDITS

The Fraction Bars illustrated and used in this book were created by Professor Albert B. Bennett, Jr., of the University of New Hampshire and Dr. Patricia S. Davidson of the University of Massachusetts, Boston. Decimal Squares were created by Professor Bennett.

The publisher would also like to thank Stride Rite Children's Group, Inc., Boston, MA; Pearle Vision Center, Burlington, MA; Belmont Medical Supply, Belmont, MA; Professional Hearing Center, Brookline, MA; Bread and Circus, Wellesley, MA; Bridge School and Clarke Middle School, Lexington, MA; and Melrose Middle School, Melrose, MA.

"Tuesday I was Ten" from DON'T EVER CROSS A CROCODILE copyright © 1963 by Kaye Starbird, J.B. Lippincott Company, is reprinted by permission of Marian Reiner for the Author.

Revision Designer • Ruth Lacey
Revision Photo Research • Nina Whitney

Illustration Credits

Ernest Albanese: 137 Meg K. Aubrey: 60, 61, 88, 126, 166, 173, 184, 218, 219, 252, 286, 310, 311, 337, 353, 362. Fanny Mellett Berry: 96, 97, 142, 143, 372, 390. Andy Christie: 15, 22, 264 (l), 265 (r), 333, 365, 408, 411, 414 (c, b). Cynthia W. Clark: 82, 276, 288, 289. Jim Deigan: 16, 30, 43, 54, 55, 110, 114, 115, 188, 206, 256, 262, 263, 407, 410. Len Ebert: 8, 9, 23, 32, 66, 67, 158, 159, 192, 193, 226, 227, 354, 360, 361. Meryl Henderson: 28, 29, 46, 90, 104, 258, 259, 266, 278, 279, 304, 314, 315, 317. Bob Lange: 39, 49, 111, 124, 127, 234, 235, 240. Heidi Lutts: 154 (tl, tr). Robert Mansfield: 138, 140, 294, 329, 334, 335, 346, 347, 376, 428. Laurie Marks: 98, 223, 232, 265 (l). Mas Miyamoto: 362. Ann Neumann: 51, 76, 195, 359, 386, 387, 403, 414 (t), 415. Michael O'Reilly: 34, 45, 62, 63, 80, 81, 204. Julie Pace: 135. Tom Powers: 50, 194, 200. Carol Schwartz: 10, 228, 229, 236, 237. Susan Spellman: 6. Gary Torrisi: 68, 69, 73, 118, 132, 133, 166, 230, 231, 244, 245, 302, 303, 312, 313, 344. Cathy Trachok: 78, 117, 131, 134, 198, 199, 203. Joe Veno: 12, 13, 125, 378, 384, 418, 419. Lane Yerkes: 20, 21, 196, 197, 268, 269, 285, 292, 293, 308, 309, 328, 329.

Photo Credits

iii,iv,vii,vii,ix,xi,xii, © Nancy Sheehan. 1, 2, 3, 4, 5: John Lei (Omni-Photo Communications, Inc.) 7: Richard Haynes. 11: John Lei (Omni-Photo Communications, Inc.). 14: Ann & Myron Sutton (FPG). 17: G. Colliva (The Image Bank). 18: E. Nagele (FPG). 24: Kjell B. Sandved (Photo Researchers). 26: John Lei (Omni-Photo Communications, Inc.). 27: R. Kord (H. Armstrong Roberts). 30, 31, 33: John Lei (Omni-Photo Communications, Inc.). 38: Sebastiao Barbosa (The Image Bank). 40, 41: John Lei (Omni-Photo Communications, Inc.). 42: Nancy Sheehan. 44: (The Picture Cube). 48: David Madison (Bruce Coleman). 52: George & Judy Manna (Photo Researchers). 53: Paul Steel (The Stock Market). 56: Felicia Martinez (Photo Edit). 57: John Lei (Omni-Photo Communications, Inc.). 58: Wolfgang Bayer (Bruce Coleman). 59: A. Schmidecker (FPG). 64: Ernie Sparks (The Stock Market). 65: Michele Sassi (The Stock Market). 74: Jerry Sarapochiello (Bruce Coleman). 75: John Lei (Omni-Photo Communications, Inc.). 77: Larry Grant (FPG). 80: Ron Grishaber (Photo Edit). 84: John Lei (Omni-Photo Communications, Inc.). 85: Dennis Hallinan (FPG). 86: Gary D. McMichael (Photo Researchers). 87: David Weintraub (Photo Researchers). 92: Ken O'Donoghue. 93: Richard Haynes. 94, 95: Ken O'Donoghue. 96, 97: Michal Heron. 105: Walter Bibikow (The Image Bank). 107: John Lei (Omni-Photo Communications, Inc.). 108: l Runk/Schoenberger (Grant Heilman Photography); r Roy Morsch (The Stock Market). 119: Richard Haynes. 120: Dick Lauria (FPG). 121: Tony Freeman (Photo Edit). 123: John Lei (Omni-Photo Communications, Inc.). 129: Bob Daemmrich. 136: H. Wendler (The Image Bank). 139: Richard Hutchings (Info Edit). 141: John Lei (Omni-Photo Communications, Inc.). 142: Michael Rothwell (FPG). 146: J. Myers (FPG). 147: Elise Lewin (The Image Bank). 148: John Shaw (Tom Stack). 149, 151, 157: John Lei (Omni-Photo Communications, Inc.). 152: l, Frank Pedrick (The Image Works); m, John Eastcott/Yva Montuik (The Image Works); r, Camermann Int'l. 154: t Renata Hiller (Monkmeyer); b Ken O'Donoghue. 164: Ken O'Donoghue. 168: Richard Haynes. 172, 176: John Lei (Omni-Photo Communications, Inc.). 177: Ken O'Donoghue. 179: Richard Haynes. 180: John Lei (Omni-Photo Communications, Inc.). 184-5: Richard Haynes. 186: Larry Lefever (Grant Heilman Photography). 187: l Frank Cezus (FPG); r C. L. Chryslin (The Image Bank). 188: Laurie Platt Winfrey. 191: Jennifer Goerk Lyden (Carousel). 198: Bruce Byers (FPG). 202: l John Neubauer (FPG); r Santi Visalli (The Image Bank). 206: Mike Valeri (FPG). 210: Bill Losh (FPG). 212: John Lei (Omni-Photo Communications, Inc.). 213: l George D. Dodge (Bruce Coleman); r John Lei (Omni-Photo Communications, Inc.). 214: Richard Haynes. 215: Robert Fried. 217: Susan McCartney (Photo Researchers). 220, 221: John Lei (Omni-Photo Communications, Inc.). 222: l Maria Taglienti (The Image Bank); c Marc Romanelli (The Image Bank); r Maria Taglienti (The Image Bank). 224: Lawrence Migdale (Photo Researchers). 232: Gabe Palmer (The Stock Market). 233: David R. Frazier (Photo Researchers). 236, 238: John Lei (Omni-Photo Communications, Inc.). 239: (Focus on Sports). 246: Dick Lauria (FPG). 247: t Tony Freeman (Photo Edit); bl Frank Siteman (The Picture Cube). 250: Michal Heron. 251, 254: John Lei (Omni-Photo Communications, Inc.). 255: Michal Heron. 256: Mary Kate Denny (Photo Edit). 257: W. Hill (The Image Works). 258: l Jeff Dunn (The Picture Cube); c Vandystadt (Photo Researchers); r Jeff Dunn (The Picture Cube). 260: Michal Heron. 264: John Lei (Omni-Photo Communications, Inc.). 268: Richard Mackson (FPG). 274: Lawrence Migdale. 275: John Lei (Omni-Photo Communications, Inc.). 280: l Michal Heron; r John Lei (Omni-Photo Communications, Inc.). 281: John Lei (Omni-Photo Communications, Inc.). 282: R. Rowan (Photo Researchers). 290: l Richard Hutchings (Photo Researchers); r Sal Maimone (FPG). 291: Stanley Rowin (The Picture Cube). 295: Robert Brenner (Photo Edit). 299: John Lei (Omni-Photo Communications, Inc.). 300: James M. Majuto (FPG). 301: l Kenneth Garrett (FPG); r John Lei (Omni-Photo Communications, Inc.). 304, 306: Michal Heron. 318: l John Lei (Omni-Photo Communications, Inc.); c Laurie Platt Winfrey; r David Young-Wolff (Photo Edit). 319: Janert Ltd. (The Image Bank). 320: John Lei (Omni-Photo Communications, Inc.). 321: l and r John Lei (Omni-Photo Communications, Inc.); c Harry Hartman (FPG). 322: John Lei (Omni-Photo Communications, Inc.). 323: t R. Rowan (FPG); b John Lei (Omni-Photo Communications, Inc.). 325: John Lei (Omni-Photo Communications, Inc.). 326: Ed Wheeler (The Stock Market). 330: Stephen J. Krasemann (Photo Researchers). 336: Bill Bachman (Photo Researchers). 338, 339, 340: Richard Haynes. 342: Gary Faber (The Image Bank). 348: Bob Daemmrich (The Image Works). 349: Leo Mason (The Image Bank). 350: Barbara Van Cleve (Tony Stone Worldwide); r Ken O'Donoghue. 352: Doug Plummer (Photo Researchers). 356: Bob Daemmrich (Stock Boston). 358: T. Alvez (FPG). 359: Richard Weymouth Brooks (Photo Researchers). 363: Frank Cezus (FPG). 366: Bob Woodward (The Stock Market). 368: Don Mason (The Stock Market). 369: Michal Heron. 370: David H. Wells (The Image Works). 374: t (White House Historical Association); b (National Gallery of Art). 375: Bob Daemmrich. 376: Ken O'Donoghue. 377: Susan Van Etten (The Picture Cube). 380: George Mars Cassidy (The Picture Cube). 388: t Marty Heitner (The Picture Cube); b R. P. Kingston (The Picture Cube). 389: James H. Simon (The Picture Cube). 395: Michal Heron. 396: Nicholas De Scoise (Photo Researchers). 397: John Lei (Omni-Photo Communications, Inc.). 398, 400: Michal Heron. 402: tl David Ball (The Picture Cube); c James Marshall (The Stock Market). 404: Charles Krebs (The Stock Market). 406: Tim Childs (Sports Chrome). 412: A. T. Willet (The Image Bank). 413: David C. Bitters (The Picture Cube). 428: t Al Tielemans (Duomo); b (Duomo).

Handbook Credits:

Maps by General Cartography. Charts by J.A.K. Graphics. Art on pages 471,473 by Len Epstein. Art on pages 474-5, 477, 478, 480, 484-85, 487 by Lorreta Lustig.
Photo credits:
464: Sjostrept (FPG). 466: J. Zimmerman (FPG). 470: David Noble (FPG); D. Hallihan (FPG). 476: Bill Losh (FPG). 477: Doug David. 479: Fujisaki (FPG). 482,486: Ken O'Donoghue.